LIBERTY'S MARTYR
The Story of
Dr. Joseph Warren

LIBERTY'S MARTYR
The Story of Dr. Joseph Warren

A Novel

Janet Uhlar

Published by Dog Ear Publishing
4010 W. 86th Street, Ste H
Indianapolis, IN 46268
www.dogearpublishing.net

ISBN: 978-160844-012-2
Library of Congress Control Number: Applied for

His death served to adorn the cause for which he contended, excited emulation,

and gave a pledge of perseverance and ultimate success. In the grand sacrifice,

of which a new nation was that day to celebrate in the face of the world,

to prove their sincerity to Heaven, whose Providence they had invoked,

the noblest victim was the most suitable offering.

William Tudor, 1823 (Historian)

· 1 ·

A Dream Fulfilled

WAS IT ENGLISH? He stood still for a moment, one ear cocked toward the door, straining to hear it again. Then, above the boisterous laughter, bits and pieces of a muffled conversation drifted down the hall through his closed chamber door. Yes, it was English. There could be no doubt.

"They are getting bold tonight!" eighteen-year-old Joseph Warren muttered to himself. Within the perimeter of the Harvard College campus, the scholars were allowed to speak only in the Latin tongue—unless they were merely muttering to themselves.

He looked about the small, sparsely furnished room, and spotted his quill, penknife, and ink well. The young man gathered them together and gently placed them in his writing box, then bent over a battered trunk and positioned the box carefully in it along with the few other items that belonged to him. He had accumulated very little over the past four years in the way of personal possessions. He would be returning home taller in stature—he now was a slender six feet. He definitely had increase his knowledge, and a formidable stack of worn textbooks sitting on the table attested to this. He hoped he had increased in wisdom as well.

A loud rap on the door interrupted his thoughts, but there was no time to respond to the knock before the door flung open.

"Warren, what are you doing in here?" exclaimed Edmund Dana. "Everyone is waiting. You are packing? Surely that can wait until later!"

"You had better watch yourself!" Joseph warned his classmate in perfect Latin.

"Oh, Warren!" Edmund cried, his dark eyes reflecting the mischievousness within. "We are free tomorrow! No longer bound by rules and regulations! No longer plagued by semistarvation and exhaustion!"

"Ever so dramatic, Dana!" Joseph interrupted with amusement—and in English.

"You had better watch yourself!" Edmund whispered back in Latin. "The walls have ears!"

Joseph responded with a wry smile.

"Ah, Joseph! Maybe you are not such a stick in the mud after all!" Edmund chuckled as he plopped on the bed and began to rummage through the items in the trunk.

"What are you talking about?" Joseph asked, nervously looking toward the door as if one of the tutors would appear. He would not put it past Edmund Dana's clever sense of humor to taunt him into speaking English to make sure that he—and he alone—was caught.

"Relax, Warren! There is no one in this dorm but those of us who can fully appreciate our pending liberty!" He shouted, flinging his arms in the air. "You have been a stick in the mud! Studious, attentive, industrious, obedient."

"I have had my share of close calls with the faculty!" Insulted, Joseph tried to convince Edmund that he had not been so virtuous after all.

"Close calls! Name one!"

"I—I was fined for being absent without permission—four times!" Joseph replied with confidence.

"Ha! Absent without permission?" Edmund could barely speak through his laughter. "You were helping your mother with the crops. I hardly call that being absent without permission!"

"Well, I was fined!" Joseph defended himself.

Edmund continued to laugh.

"All right," Joseph began again with an air of determination. "What about the time I climbed through the window of your chamber—three stories up! Do you remember that?"

"Of course I do! We locked you out," Edmund replied, wiping tears of laughter from his eyes. "We locked you out because you insisted on keeping us from making plans for a food fight in the Commons—" Edmund paused for a moment. Then suddenly, quite serious, he continued, "You risked breaking your own neck to keep us from going through with that foolhardy plan. I cannot look out that window without remembering it. No sooner had you landed your feet safely on the floor when that old drain spout you had climbed up gave way and crashed to the ground."

Joseph went over to the table as Edmund spoke and busied himself with his papers and books.

"That drain spout falling scared us half to death. You could have been killed, but it did not even phase you! What was it you said? 'It served my purpose.'"

"I feel bad about that drain spout," Joseph said, an uneasiness suddenly rising up within him.

"Forget about it, Warren!" Edmund cried, the impish smile once again upon his face. "That spout was in dire need of replacement. It probably was as old as Harvard Yard!"

"Probably," Joseph muttered, no longer interested in defending himself against being labeled virtuous. His Puritan upbringing had taught him to strive for such qualities. His personal conviction drove him to repent for yielding so easily to pressure from his classmate.

"You still are an old stick in the mud, Warren," Edmund assured him as he stood to leave. "That incident can hardly be counted as sowing wild oats. On the contrary, you probably saved us from being expelled!" He walked to the door and then turned. "We are gathering in Elbridge Gerry's chamber. They refuse to start without you."

"What are they planning?" Joseph asked, expecting Edmund's ridicule for being so cautious.

Edmund let out a quick laugh that sounded more like a grunt. "Are you afraid we might do something naughty?" he teased. Then with a look that betrayed his affection, he added, "We are intending to reflect on our years at Harvard. Will you join us, Master Warren? I will make sure they do not dwell on that broken drain spout!"

"I will be there," Joseph agreed and smiled.

Though Edward had closed the door behind himself, Joseph's eyes remained fixed as if he were still there. Both of them had entered Harvard with the hopes of making medicine their chosen profession. Now, due to financial problems at home, Joseph would have to support his family. He had accepted the position of schoolmaster at the Latin school he had attended before coming to Harvard, and his medical training must therefore be put off indefinitely, while Edmund would walk right into his apprenticeship. For a brief moment Joseph felt a pang of jealousy.

He had dreamed of becoming a physician since childhood, his inspiration coming from his grandfather, Dr. Samuel Stevens, who had diligently cared for Joseph's left hand after it had been severely injured and it seemed that it would have to be amputated. He lifted his left hand and momentarily studied it. In the end, only the tip of the thumb had been removed.

Walking to the window, Joseph observed the workers below who were setting up the staging necessary for the next afternoon's commencement ceremony. The campus yard was bustling with the workers' activity and with the lower classmen passing through the courtyard from building to building. The students' long robes rippled in the breeze, lending them a rather graceful appearance, Joseph thought.

Joseph looked down at his own robe. Tomorrow he would trade it for the robe of a graduate. Then he could shed the entire costume completely and would be able to don the attire of a man.

His attention shifted back to the campus, its grass-covered courtyard enclosed on three sides by the antique, four-story brick buildings that contained the classrooms and housed the students. One spindly elm stood pathetically on the far edge of the courtyard, offering little in the way of shade or beauty. The open end of the rectangular yard was protected from the frequently traveled dirt road by a formidable brick wall.

He contemplated how the town of Cambridge would be packed the next morning with families who had traveled from all parts of New England to honor the graduating class of 1759. After all, commencement was a grand celebration, second only to the annual election.

His mother would certainly be present, along with his three younger brothers. The youngest would need to sit upon her lap if he hoped to see anything at all. Joseph smiled as he imagined this favorite brother scampering upon his mother's knees.

Would his mother cry as he received his diploma? Though she usually maintained her composure, he imagined she would. His education had been so important to her—and such a financial burden. Had his father been alive— Ah, there it was, the very reason for the depression he found himself fighting in the midst of all this excitement: his father's absence.

Hardly a day passed that Joseph did not think of his father. His untimely death, occurring only weeks after Joseph began college, was a shock that no one in the family had truly recovered from, though they had been forced to adapt.

Tears began to pool in his eyes as he felt the sense of loss within. He could not even look at his reflection in a mirror without thinking of his father. The same fair features greeted him when he looked at himself: the deep-blue eyes, the blond hair—even his broad shoulders. To celebrate this milestone in his own life without him—even bearing his father's name—somehow seemed unthinkable at the moment.

Joseph wiped the tears from his eyes, determined to shake off these feelings for his mother's sake. He also had his classmates to think about. Their own joy might be hindered if they suspected how he felt.

To his surprise, he had come to realize that he had the ability to affect his classmates' moods, even to persuade them to see things his way or to take actions he suggested. "The qualities of leadership," one of the tutors had once observed in reference to Joseph's ability.

"Leadership?" Joseph laughed nervously at the thought of it. If what he had experienced with his classmates was leadership, he preferred to not be responsible for it. He found the fact that others were willing to follow his lead a bit unnerving. When he had become conscious that he had this ability, he had tried to set a good example, but had he? What about things like the broken drain spout?

Joseph saw little need for any qualities of leadership in the life he wanted for himself. His desired to settle into his own niche in Puritan society, helping people as his grandfather had done while rearing a family under a wise and loving hand as his father had done.

Tomorrow he would take the first step on his journey to manhood, a journey he hoped would prove as peaceful as his early childhood had been. And why should it not be? Great Britain was well on her way to defeating her long-time enemy, France. This victory would drive the French troops from the American frontier and would bring an end to the present horrors of the French and Indian War.

The future looked very bright indeed, Joseph thought with a smile that was more forced than ready. Despite the fact that his father would not share tomorrow's excitement and that he could not continue his education this year or perhaps even next, he still looked forward to the respectable position of schoolmaster that awaited him. He already knew his students and their families. They were all intelligent, well-behaved boys, one of them being his brother.

Joseph turned from the window and pushed the half-filled trunk under the bed with his foot. The packing could wait. After all, his classmates were waiting.

The repetitive call of a lone whippoorwill signaled the sun's setting. Within a moment's time, the whippoorwill was joined by a multitude of hidden night creatures harmoniously serenading anyone that cared to listen.

Distracted from his work, Joseph stopped to enjoy the familiar summer melody as it played through the open windows of his bedchamber. The temptation to leave the task at hand and walk in the cool of the evening was great. Yet, books and papers lying on the desk before him required immediate attention. The only way to counter the oppressive heat within the house was to simply remove one's frock and waistcoat.

The bedchamber door slowly creaked open behind him, and Joseph turned to see which of his brothers was attempting to enter quietly. Ten-year-old Eben poked in his head full of golden curls.

"Are you very busy, Joseph?" the boy asked softly. "Should I see if Sam could help me, instead?"

Liberty's Martyr

"Help you with what?" Joseph asked as Eben slipped his tall and lanky form through the partially opened door.

"I'm having trouble with one of the problems you assigned," Eben replied rather timidly.

"Which one is it?" Joseph reached out for Eben's slate.

"The division problem," he muttered.

A quick study of his work revealed the trouble. "Eben, recite for me the multiplicands of nine," Joseph instructed as he continued to look over his brother's work. Eban obediently did as he was told, making two errors. Joseph turned to his brother and with a hint of a smile said, "Ebenezer, it would seem that you have not given enough time to the memorization of your multiplication tables."

"I—I suppose I rushed through them some," he responded timidly, eyes cast downward.

"You will find that if you diligently apply yourself step by step in your studies, things will come much easier as you progress."

Without looking up, Eben nodded.

"Now I want you to memorize Colossians chapter three, verse twenty-three, 'And whatsoever ye do, do it heartily, as to the Lord, and not unto men.'" Joseph wrote the verse out for Eben as he quoted it. "Then review your multiplication tables until you have them perfected."

"Yes sir," Eben responded, taking the slate and the written quotation from his brother.

"Eben," Joseph called as the boy pulled the door open to leave. His brother turned to face him, his mopish expression plainly revealing his state of mind. "I had no trouble with the multiplicands of nine, but it took me the longest time to memorize the sixes!" Joseph's confession brought a quick smile to Eben's face and a twinkle to his blue eyes.

No sooner had the sound of Eben's footsteps faded away than he could hear another brother approaching.

"Joseph, can you spare a minute?" seventeen-year-old Sam asked.

With a gesture that indicated that he would be with him in a moment, Joseph continued to write before turning to face Sam. "What is it?"

"I want to take Eben with me next week to deliver a load of apples in Braintree. Mother said I need to clear it with you first."

"He has already fallen behind because of the days he has missed to make such deliveries with you," Joseph replied. He noticed the color drain from his brother's face even as he spoke.

Sam's uneasiness in dealing with the public concerned Joseph. What had appeared to be common bashfulness was developing into a deep fear. But why? Certainly Sam did not lack intelligence—he ran the farm now, a remarkable feat at such a young age. Beyond that, with his tall, muscular form and dark hair and eyes, Sam was an exceptionally attractive young man.

"Who is it that you are making this delivery to?" Joseph quickly inquired.

"A new customer, a merchant named Sawyers. I—I just received his order the other day. We've—we've never met," he stammered.

"I am not sure I like this, Sam."

"The lad wants to be a farmer. What better learning experience can he have than to make occasional trips with me? There'll be plenty of math involved, bookkeeping and the like," Sam was desperately trying to sound convincing.

"Sam, this is to be the last trip for a good while, do you understand? I am only letting him go this time because it's a new customer."

"I know, Joseph. Thank you!"

"You have to promise me one thing. Drill him on his multiplication tables and grammar rules as you ride, would you?"

"Of course, Joseph. No problem! I'll be happy to do it!" And with that, Sam left the room with a definite bounce in his walk.

As he turned back to his work, Joseph heard the small voice of his youngest brother in the hall wishing Sam good night. The door slowly creaked open and shut again, and Joseph pretended to be deep in thought. He listened as the six-year-old tiptoed over to the bed, struggled from the bed stool to pull back the bedding, and finally climbed upon the feather mattress.

The work completed, Joseph closed the books before him. He stood, picked up the burning candle from the desk, and turned toward the bed.

"What have we here?" he asked with pretended surprise at finding Jack in the room. The boy's large, dark eyes peeped out over the muslin sheet, a head full of brown, shoulder-length curls enveloping his small face.

"Mama told me not to disturb you, and I didn't! I washed up in her room."

"A good thing," Joseph said as he set the candle on the nightstand and reached for the book he had placed there earlier. "I bet you were filthy after running about all day."

"Oh, no! I wasn't dirty much at all! I went swimming in the pond today. I wish you would come with me sometime soon. We always have such fun."

"I would like to do that." After removing his shoes, Joseph sat on the bed next to his brother.

"When? When would you like to do that? Tomorrow?"

"Yes, tomorrow it shall be! Right after I get back from school." Jack's small face radiated his delight.

"What's that you're reading?" Jack inquired, watching Joseph prop the book up on his bent knees.

"It's a medical text. I am reading about intestinal obstruction." Joseph was amused by his curiosity.

"Intestinal destruction," the boy echoed the words, as he understood them, causing Joseph to laugh. "Will you read it to me?"

"You would not understand it. It's not even written in English."

"It's not?" Jack strained to get a look at the pages of the book, as if he could distinguish between written English and any other language. "Do you think I'll ever understand it?"

"Yes, you will understand it in time."

"Good thing!" he exclaimed with a sigh. "I can't be a good doctor unless I understand about intestinal destruction!"

"That's right," Joseph agreed. He slid his arm under the small boy's shoulders and pulled his lying form closer to himself.

"Joseph, since I can't understand the words, would you tell me a story instead?"

"What kind of story do you want to hear?"

"One about Papa," he replied, his eyes fixed on his brother's face.

Joseph was taken back by the request, and his surprise was obvious. When Jack was only two years old he had witnessed their father's death, a scene that continued to haunt his young mind through occasional nightmares. Though he listened intently whenever their father was mention, he never initiated the conversation himself.

"What was he like, Joseph? What was he really like?" There was a pleading in Jack's dark eyes.

Joseph lifted the boy so that they were sitting by his side, keeping his arm around his shoulders to hold him close. "There were three things that Papa loved more than anything," Joseph began softly as he looked at his youngest brother.

"What were they?" Jack whispered.

"His God, his family, and his country."

"But how do you know? Did he tell you?" the boy asked with wonder.

"He did not have to tell me. I could see it for myself. Do you remember how he would read to us each evening from the Holy Writ?"

Jack shook his head.

"You don't?"

"No, I can't remember nothin' much about him."

"Well, Papa would often hold you on his lap. The words came alive when he read them, and his excitement for them showed.

"And I suppose he loved us as much as a father could. He provided for us even when it meant going without certain things for himself. He was always there to instruct us, to encourage us," Joseph paused as he tenderly smiled at Jack, "and to discipline us when we needed it.

"He was proud to be an Englishman—prouder still to be an English colonist. He once told me how he believed that the American colonies would one day become a great source of pride and strength to Great Britain."

A chill went up Joseph's spine as he recalled the conversation. With hands placed firmly on Joseph's shoulders and a gaze that seemed to penetrate right into his very soul, his father had admonished him to defend the colonies against all forms of aggression. "I would rather see a son of mine dead than a coward," the elder Warren had said. The words echoed through Joseph's mind.

"Do you believe that, too?" Jack's question interrupted his brother's recollection.

"What? Oh, yes, I believe it," Joseph replied, quickly shaking the ominous feeling that overcame him whenever he recalled that scene.

"Is our name famous?"

"Famous?" Joseph chuckled. "Why do you ask?"

"Because people call our apples Warren russets."

"Well, I suppose that means our apples are famous. They are called Warren russets because Papa worked so long to develop them to what they are now."

"I don't like to go into the orchard," the small boy confessed. "When I get big enough I'll chop down the tree that killed Papa." As he looked up at his brother, Joseph could see tears spilling over.

"A tree is not like a person or an animal. It's not capable of harming anyone. Papa lost his balance while picking apples from that tree. It was an accident, Jack, a horrible accident."

The boy did not respond.

"Did you know that that tree was Papa's favorite?"

"His favorite?" Jack echoed softly.

"It is the biggest and most productive tree in the orchard. I think Papa would be happy if we took good care of it just like he did," Joseph suggested as he tightened his hold on the little boy.

Jack nodded in silent agreement, his eyes still fixed on his brother's.

"And did you know that the orchard was one of Papa's favorite places to be? It seems to me that he would want you to like being in the orchard, too."

"Do you really think so?" Jack asked just above a whisper.

"I do. Maybe after our swim tomorrow, we can walk through the orchard. I will show you the trees I used to climb when I was your age. Do you think you would like to do that?"

"I'm scared!" The little body trembled.

"You do not have to decide tonight. You do not have to go in at all if you do not want to. But if you do, I will be with you."

A cloud of dust formed behind Jack as he ran to meet his brothers. "Ya still gonna swim with me, Joseph? You can come too, Eb!" he called out.

"I don't have any time for swimming, between chores and homework," Eben answered, accompanied by a disgruntled look at his oldest brother.

"You're still coming, aren't you?" Jack asked with alarm, claiming Joseph's free hand.

"I have been looking forward to it all day," he replied with a smile as Jack began to skip by his side.

"Oh, I almost forgot. Mama wants to talk to you first. Something about her trip to Boston today, I think. Ya wanna race home?" the little boy breathlessly asked.

"It's a fair distance from here to the house," Joseph pointed out, peering down the long country road.

"It's not so far! I just ran from there, and I'm not tired at all!"

"Jack, you don't stand a chance against Joseph!" Eben exclaimed, prompting a gesture from Joseph to be quiet.

"I would not be too certain about that," Joseph replied with a wink for Eben as he handed him the books in his arms.

The race proved to be a close one. At least it appeared that way to Jack.

Upon entering the house, Joseph went directly to the kitchen to find his mother. Mary Warren stood before a small fire in the open kitchen hearth peering into a cast iron kettle. With the heavy lid in one hand, she slowly stirred the pot's steaming contents, releasing the aroma of rabbit stew. Locks of dark brown hair cascaded from her cap, forming soft ringlets on her damp forehead.

"Did you manage to accomplish everything you set out to do in Boston today, Mother?" Joseph inquired as he grabbed a plum from the bowl of fruit sitting on the table.

She turned to him with her youthful smile and wiped her beaded brow with the hem of her apron. "Yes," she answered. "Everything went quite well, indeed." With a soft clank, she placed the lid on the kettle and hung the wooden spoon on a hook along the inner wall of the massive fireplace.

"Why don't we go into the parlor where it's cooler," his mother suggested as she walked past him. He discarded what remained of the plum and followed.

"Did you have time to stop at Dr. Lloyd's and withdraw my request?" he asked, seating himself in the worn easy chair facing the faded velvet settee on which his mother sat.

He had submitted a request to begin his two-year apprenticeship in the fall in the hope that he would have money put aside to pay for his education. However, the family's financial needs had taken everything he had earned, and his education would have to wait.

"Yes, and I have wonderful news!" she said. "Dr. Lloyd inquired as to why I was withdrawing your application. He was greatly impressed with your accomplishments at Harvard. When I told him of our financial situation, he suggested that you begin your apprenticeship anyway. We can pay him over the course of the next four years. Sam is managing the farm nicely—we should see a good profit this harvest—so we will not be dependent on the wages you will earn as schoolmaster. But we will have to take some money now and purchase a new suit of clothes—fine wool challis for a physician's apprentice, I should think," she said looking at the rather coarse, heavy fabric of his plain brown knee breeches, waistcoat, and frock coat.

Joseph waited for her to continue, certain that she had more to tell him. When she did not immediately do so, he felt compelled to ask, "Surely, Mother, he wanted something as collateral to secure his investment?" He was apprehensive about her reply.

"Yes, of course he does," she hesitated. Then fixing her determined gaze upon him, she continued, "He will accept a deed to a portion of the farm."

"What? How much of the farm, Mother?" he asked, trying not to let his fear and anxiety show.

"Two-fifths."

"Two-fifths? What two-fifths, Mother?" he asked, concerned as to how she would divide the ninety-acre farm.

"The back pasture and a corner portion of the orchard abutting it—that should roughly amount to thirty-six acres. It's the only way, Joseph. We could never manage to pay the fee all at once or even in a few payments," she reminded him as the color drained from his face.

"And you are to get back to him on this?" Joseph asked insistently.

"Son, he is the finest physician in Boston, having studied in both England and Scotland. How could I turn down this generous offer? I did not need time to think about it. I signed the necessary papers already."

Joseph stood up and walked across the room to the window. He knew that she was waiting for his response.

"Mother!" He uttered the word but said no more. What could he say? Her decision, in his opinion, was rash and out of character, and he wished she had consulted him first.

A few awkward moments of total silence elapsed as he stared blankly through the rippled panes of glass. Then turning to face her, he said, "It will be a great burden for me, Mother. I am concerned for you and the boys."

"Jehovah promises to care for widows and fatherless children. I believe He has made this provision for you, Joseph, and shall provide for our needs as well."

He walked to her side, bent down, and kissed her on the forehead. "I promised Jack I would spend some time with him this afternoon." Joseph was aware that his reaction had both startled and hurt her, but any words spoken now might prove more damaging.

Mary Warren nodded.

Back outside, Joseph attempted to give his full attention to his youngest brother. Hand in hand, they strolled the vast orchard as Joseph explained the sense of pride this land brought, land that had been in the family for three generations. Now it was at risk in order to provide for his education.

The Lloyd household was accustomed to the awkwardness of new apprentices trying to adapt to the family. The incoming apprentices brought with themselves the desire to please and a fear of offending.

Joseph was in awe of the wealth Dr. Lloyd possessed. The magnificent home overflowed with fine European furniture. Its spacious, tall rooms were decorated throughout with beautiful oil paintings and brilliant tapestries. Thick, luxurious draperies adorned the windows, framing the scenes of the colorful English gardens that lay beyond.

Dr. James Lloyd's reputation as the finest teacher of all Boston's physicians was well founded. He truly desired to pass the knowledge he had attained on to the young men in his charge. His apprentices were not banished to the damp, musty cellar to prepare medicinals day in and day out as so many physicians' apprentices were. Dr. Lloyd believed in a more practical approach to teaching his students and frequently had them at his side, whether in his surgery or out making house calls. Before long, Joseph was working alongside his master in the care of patients. By the end of his first year, he was able to tend to minor problems in the doctor's surgery as well as to be sent out alone on some house calls.

One such home was that of Richard Hooton, a prominent merchant who had been stricken with lingering, deadly consumption. Mr. Hooton was unwilling to tie up the doctor's valuable time with routine treatments, and so he requested that an apprentice be sent instead.

"There, is that more comfortable?" Joseph asked as he repositioned the pillows behind his patient's shoulders and gently shifted his frail body into a better position. Richard Hooton's physical appearance had once commanded respect. Now, he was little more than skin and bones, too weak to even stand.

"Thank you, my boy," the elder man whispered. "Sit down. Visit with me for a while. I shan't keep you long," he rasped, pointing an unsteady hand to the overstuffed chair beside the bed.

Joseph sat, as he always did following Mr. Hooton's treatment, ready to relate the news of Boston to this once vigorous businessman. This visit was different than previous ones, however, for Mr. Hooton was not interested in any outside news today.

"Tell me, Mr. Warren, how do the grounds appear? Are the gardens being kept up? Is the house in order?" Mr. Hooton's words were slow and soft. Though not as elegant an estate as that of Dr. Lloyd, the house and gardens were indeed quite impressive.

"Your aunt appears to be doing a fine job of keeping things in order, sir."

"Good, good," the elder man sighed. "I worry about them—my aunt and my daughter, I mean. It won't be easy for two women alone. Elizabeth especially will have a hard time of it without a mother or father."

"There are those who will look out for them, Dr. Lloyd included," Joseph offered.

"Yes, James has been a good friend. Elizabeth has known him from birth. She thinks of him as an uncle."

Joseph was aware of this, having witnessed on numerous occasions the girl's warm greeting for his teacher, even referring to him as Uncle James.

"Elizabeth's future concerns me a great deal," Mr. Hooton confided. "She will soon be of marrying age and will be heiress to a small fortune. There are many who would marry her for such a fortune."

"Have you talked to her about this?"

"I have tried, but the girl refuses to discuss anything related to my passing. We have been very close. She is my only child. Her mother died when she was very young. My aunt loves her dearly, but she's quite old now. The house belongs to my aunt, you know."

Joseph shook his head negatively in response. He had been unaware of this.

"It was built by my uncle. He was the one who founded the business. Of course, Elizabeth will stay here until she weds, longer if she—"

A tap on the door interrupted Richard Hooton's sentence.

"Enter," Joseph called out upon receiving Mr. Hooton's signal to do so.

Elizabeth came into the room carrying a steaming bowl of broth.

"Here you go, Papa." The sixteen-year-old girl went straight to her father's side without acknowledging Joseph's presence. But this was typical behavior from Elizabeth toward him. The most Joseph ever got from her was a cold hello.

"Eat this, and I am certain you will feel much better, Papa." She smiled sweetly at her father as she placed a napkin across his chest.

Joseph watched in silence as the girl spoon-fed her father. She was skinny—too skinny, in his estimation. Her shapeless form, combined with her huge, dark eyes and girlish hairstyle, gave her the appearance of a younger child, rather than one on the brink of womanhood.

Her hair was truly her glory—waist length and as close to true black as he had ever seen on any Englishwoman. Her small, dimpled chin only added to her youth, lending to her the appearance of a pouting child.

At first, Joseph had found it easy to dislike this girl, but he was now having second thoughts about his attitude. When he had first met her, he had assumed her unfriendliness was due to extreme shyness, but the passing of time had proven that assumption false. He had then come to the conclusion that she was spoiled and just plain rude.

It had only recently dawned on him that Elizabeth's coldness toward him might be due to her father's condition. As Richard Hooton had just shared, the girl refused to admit that her father was dying. She was frightened, and it occurred to Joseph that somehow his presence added to her fear.

Her father's rapid deterioration had begun around the time Joseph began making house calls with Dr. Lloyd. Now it was Joseph, not Dr. Lloyd, who administered the uncomfortable and sometimes painful treatments her father required.

A well of compassion sprang up in him as he watched the pitiful girl lift the spoon to her failing father's lips. She coaxed him to eat as a mother would a small child. Silently, Joseph prayed for forgiveness in having misjudged her so.

Elizabeth had been called to her father's bedside to receive his last tender kiss. She now stood trembling in a dark corner, watching helplessly as Dr. Lloyd and Joseph worked.

Richard Hooton had been silent for sometime, then the sound of his labored breathing ceased. A cry of despair came from the corner of the room, prompting Joseph to look in that direction. Elizabeth was in the arms of her elderly aunt, sobbing uncontrollably. Quickly, Dr. Lloyd reached down to feel for a pulse. None was found, and he pulled the sheet up to cover his patient's face.

After collecting the medical supplies, Joseph found Dr. Lloyd in the parlor. He was conversing with family members and friends who had gathered.

Elizabeth had separated herself from the others. Seated alone on the settee, her blank stare was fixed on the portrait of her father that hung above the fireplace. Joseph walked toward her and sat down. The girl did not respond to his presence.

"I am sorry, Miss Hooton. I wish I had the means to ease the pain you feel," he offered softly.

"What do you know of my pain, Mr. Warren?" Elizabeth's words were spoken just above a whisper.

Joseph paused and took a deep breath before replying. Somehow he had to make this girl realize that he was not her enemy.

"I was fourteen when my father died. He was healthy and full of vigor," he said as he studied the portrait of her father along with her.

Elizabeth turned to face him, not with her usual cold stare but with a look of compassion. "What happened?" she whispered as if afraid to ask.

"He broke his neck in a fall and died instantly. I had no opportunity to say good-bye or to express my love for the last time."

"Tell me. How is one able to go on with such pain and grief?" she asked with a sob.

"Time has a way of healing," he offered tenderly. "I know it does not seem possible right now, but you will find that it is true. It does not mean you will not miss him"

Joseph rose to join Dr. Lloyd, who was preparing to leave.

"Will I never see you again, Mr. Warren?" the girl asked with alarm as she unwittingly grabbed hold of his wrist.

"I hope to attend the funeral." He could see by her expression and by the fact that she kept her hold on his wrist that she was not put at ease by his answer. Strange as it seemed, his customary visits, which had been a source of distress to the girl, would now be missed. He understood her pain and how much she now needed his friendship.

"I will try to stop by on occasion, Miss Hooton. I really will," he assured her.

In the weeks that followed, Joseph's visits to the Hooton mansion were irregular. As his apprenticeship advanced and responsibilities increased, the trips became more and more infrequent. But in the time he spent in the company of Elizabeth Hooton, Joseph developed a genuine fondness for the girl. He likened it to what a brother might feel toward a younger sister.

To his surprise, Joseph discovered that she was actually quite sensible. Her interests went beyond the realm of what was commonly considered a woman's world. Richard Hooton had no reason to fear that his daughter would be taken advantage of because of her wealth. When the time came, she would choose her husband wisely. Joseph was confident of this.

The hour was late. The other apprentices had already been sent off to bed, but Joseph was asked to remain.

"Come, Mr.—excuse me—Dr. Warren, and we will toast your future!" Putting his arm about Joseph's shoulders, Dr. Lloyd guided him into the elegant study where numerous sconces hung from the mahogany walls, their flickering light revealing the treasured collection of leather-bound books.

"It feels good to hear the title, does it not?" Dr. Lloyd asked as he handed Joseph a glass of Madeira. "You have worked hard for it." Then, raising his crystal goblet, he toasted, "To Dr. Joseph Warren. May your ability to heal be blessed by heaven itself. May your compassion never interfere with your judgment. And may prosperity be the reward of your desire to help others.

"Sit down, my boy, sit down," Dr. Lloyd instructed after both took a sip of the wine. He directed Joseph to a velvet-upholstered chair, then lowered his thick-girthed frame into another. "You will do well in Boston. I am delighted that you decided to set up your practice here. I suppose I should be a bit apprehensive."

"Apprehensive, sir?" Joseph was confused.

"Joseph, you are the most able and devoted student I have ever taught. I sensed you would be from the very beginning—even when I reviewed your application and college records. You had a strong desire then to study medicine. All the long, exhausting hours, all the gruesome scenes and even foul individuals you have encountered in the past two years have not dissuaded you in the least.

"You have the potential of becoming one of the finest physicians Boston has ever seen, and that—my student, my colleague, my competition—is why I should be apprehensive." The warm, kindly smile Joseph had come to find so comforting and reassuring over the past two years was upon his master's face.

Joseph was taken aback. It was a compliment—a great compliment coming from this beloved teacher. Yet, with it came a most uneasy feeling.

"You will take some of my patients with you. It is to be expected. But I know you well enough, Joseph, not to feel threatened by your rise to, shall we say, medical glory?

"I also know that my practice is large enough to withstand it. And do not be deceived, it will take time for you to establish yourself to the point of being financially comfortable, but you shall. Of that, I have no doubt.

"Some more wine, Doctor?" Dr. Lloyd asked as he held up the crystal decanter, its rich purple content sparkling in the candlelight.

"Thank you, sir, but no."

"You have learned much in the past two years," Dr. Lloyd continued as he carefully placed the decanter back on the table. "Medicine is advancing by leaps and bounds. New procedures and ideas will come out of Europe, or even be developed here. Some may seem questionable at first. Have an open mind, Joseph. Medicine certainly has many advances to make.

"You have already been subject to ridicule because of a few techniques and beliefs I brought home with me from my European studies. My prayer is that you'll not let such close-minded thinking alter what you have been taught here."

Joseph knew full well that he was referring to the controversy among the local physicians about Dr. Lloyd's intervention in complicated cases of childbirth, which was considered to be best left to the midwives. Persecution had also come because of his strict adherence to keeping his hands clean and demanding his apprentices do the same.

If the secret lectures he conducted on human dissection were to become public knowledge, the townspeople themselves would turn on him and very likely drive him out of Boston.

"Sir, though other physicians may hurl their abuses, I have seen the results of such sound teachings and will continue in them."

Dr. Lloyd nodded his head upon hearing Joseph's reply.

"My door is always open to you, Dr. Warren. Should you have a question or need assistance, I am here for you."

"Thank you, sir."

"I trust that you will continue to attend the lectures on anatomy?"

"I will, sir."

"Good," he said, and smiled. "Come the first of the month, you will be your own master and determine your own schedule. Until then, I will continue in that position. You had better get some sleep, for tomorrow promises to be a busy day."

• 2 •

Elizabeth Hooton

NOW BE CAREFUL not to use that arm for two weeks. Come back then, and I will recheck it," Joseph instructed the injured man as he helped him with his winter wrappings.

"Thanks, Doc," his patient replied.

Joseph pulled back the curtain that separated the small examination room from the waiting area. Mr. Gardiner moved slowly past him toward the outside door and took hold of the knob with his good arm.

"I can't pay you, Doc, not in cash," he confessed, still facing the door. Then turning he added, "But I have firewood. Could you use a rick of wood, Doctor?"

"A rick of wood?" Joseph replied thoughtfully. "Yes, Mr. Gardiner, have it delivered and stacked, and I will consider your bill paid in full."

"I'll do that, Doc. I'll have it brought by tomorrow morning," Mr. Gardiner promised as he opened the door and left.

"A rick of wood," Joseph said aloud, though no one remained in the small surgery to hear. "I could certainly use more wood." With a shiver, he turned to the hearth in the waiting room and threw another log on the fire. "A rick of wood is a fair trade, but a little bit of money would also be appreciated every now and then," he admitted while maneuvering the log with a poker.

Daily he fought the temptation to become discouraged. Bills had to be paid, which included the payments to Dr. Lloyd. This bill, in particular, burdened him most. But it would do no good to become anxious and discouraged.

Dr. Lloyd's prediction of his future came to mind. "Medical glory," Joseph mused, finding the words humorous at best. "Ah, but he did warn me that it would not be easy getting started."

Joseph already had quite a few patients, but most were charity cases that he did not have the heart to turn away. Perhaps they could help Sam with the farm work and pay off their debt that way, he reasoned.

He walked to the desk in the corner of the room and sat down. In his daybook he entered Mr. Gardiner's visit. The numerous outstanding accounts seemed to jump out at him from the pages—Mr. Willis, Mrs. Martin, Mr. Hall . . . .

"Lord, if you could see fit to give a wealthy merchant or two enough confidence in my ability, I truly would appreciate it," Joseph prayed aloud with a playful smile. "A successful barrister, perhaps," he continued as he leaned back in the wooden chair and clasped his hands behind his head. "Father, I would even be delighted if you would see fit to send a half dozen sailors with money in their pockets."

As he spoke, the surgery door opened, and a man entered. His hat and coat were dusted with windblown snow. A scarf covered his nose and mouth as protection from the bitter cold. Only his eyes were visible under the brim of his tricorn. His eyes were so dark that Joseph immediately recognized the burly silversmith Paul Revere. It had become a matter of habit that they pay each other a social call whenever one was in the other's neighborhood.

"Paul!" Joseph stood to greet his friend. "What brings you out this way so early in the day?"

Paul pulled the scarf away from his face. "My Deborah is sick," he announced gravely.

Joseph quickly reviewed the names and faces of Paul's three children in his mind. Deborah was his oldest.

"What are her symptoms?" Joseph inquired, reaching for his greatcoat.

"She's been feverish for a few days, complaining of aches and pains. We didn't worry too much about it, but this morning—" Paul stopped as if afraid to continue.

Joseph stood in front of him now. He stopped buttoning his cloak and looked up at his friend questioningly.

"She has a rash, and I've learned that others in the neighborhood have been similarly stricken."

Joseph briefly laid his hand on Paul's shoulder in response to the fear in his piercing black eyes. "Where did the rash first appear?" he asked.

"On her face. It covers her face."

As they walked through the cobblestoned streets of Boston's North Square, Joseph noted the eerie silence. Just one block from the waterfront, this area of Boston was normally bustling with activity. Only the smell of sea air and the cry of the gulls hinted that the wharves were close by. The tidy, small houses and well-maintained artisan shops of the comfortable neighborhood offered no sign of life. Even the town pump stood motionless. Despite the cold temperatures, there should have been some activity. The Revere home was easily spotted down the length of North Street, its three stories towering above the surrounding houses.

Warm air greeted the men as they entered the Revere house, and Paul immediately led Joseph to a small upstairs bedchamber where family members had already crowded. Upon entering the stuffy room, Joseph detected a repulsive odor emitting from the child's diseased body. "Everybody is to leave but Deborah's parents," Joseph immediately ordered. As Paul shooed the others out, Joseph directed Paul's wife, Sara, away from the bed to a nearby chair.

He took note of the disfiguring pustules covering the little girl's face. The redness of the rash was in sharp contrast to the white nightcap upon her head and the pillowcase on which it rested.

"She's so very hot," Sara began, her voice shaking. "She's been sweating all night long, yet she's constantly chilled. I can't seem to make her warm."

Though covered to the chin with a heavy quilt, the small body continued to shiver uncontrollably.

"It is good that she is perspiring," Joseph said, gently forcing the closed eyelids open one at a time. "I want her to be kept warm so she does perspire freely." After a quick look at her tongue, he pulled the quilt back, taking hold of a clammy little arm and feeling for a pulse. Though Deborah whimpered in protest of the cold air, he took his time in studying the rash that covered her entire body. After tenderly palpating her abdomen, he pulled the warm quilt over the shivering form.

There was no doubt in Joseph's mind of the diagnosis. The immediate problem was how to tell his friend that his fears were well founded. Paul and Sara Revere's daughter had contracted the most dreaded disease known throughout the colonies: smallpox.

Paul followed Joseph out of the bedchamber, leaving Sara with the sick child. To Joseph's relief, Paul spoke first.

"It's the pox, isn't it?" It was more of a statement than a question. He kept his voice low, almost in a whisper, so that the others could not hear.

"It is," Joseph replied.

"What do I do now?" Paul asked, aware that strict laws existed to keep such diseases contained.

"The councilmen will strongly advise that you bring Deborah to the pest house."

"Never! I would never send one of my lambs to such a place!" Paul exclaimed.

Joseph placed his hand gently on Paul's arm in an attempt to both comfort and calm him.

"She'll be staying here," Paul stated with stubborn determination.

"In that case, your family will be quarantined for a month. Make whatever arrangements you must quickly. It is an enormous task, I know, but we will have to report my diagnosis as soon as possible. The councilmen will have you display a red flag outside your door as a warning to others to stay away. They may want to post a guard to make certain no one enters this house but me."

Paul's face grew pale as Joseph spoke. "There's so much to be done!"

"The pox may just infect Deborah," Joseph began slowly, trying to prepare Paul. "Or the entire family could be afflicted. There is no way of knowing."

"Inoculation. What about inoculation?"

Joseph hesitated before answering. "Paul, it is still viewed in this colony as a controversial treatment. The Massachusetts General Court has not given its approval."

"What's your opinion of it, Joseph? Does it work?" Paul was growing desperate.

"Yes, I have no doubt of it," Joseph replied quickly.

"How is it done?"

"A small amount of the venom can be taken from a pustule on Deborah. I would then gather as much as possible on the head of a needle and insert it into a vein on your arm. You will develop mild symptoms within a week. They will last for a few days. You are likely to feel weak for about a month."

"Have you been inoculated?" Paul asked.

Joseph was hesitant to answer.

"It's one thing to support a theory and quite another to believe in it to the point of undergoing the procedure yourself. I have no intention of putting my family at risk over a theory," Paul said in response to Joseph's hesitation.

"I have been inoculated." Though Dr. Lloyd thought it best to protect his apprentices from possible exposure, Joseph would not expound any further. Paul understood that participation in the smallpox inoculation was considered a violation of colony law.

"What are the dangers?" There was a note of apprehension in Paul's voice.

"There is a slight chance of a severe reaction—even death. But the chances are much greater if one takes the pox naturally," Joseph explained with confidence. "Who were the women in the room when we arrived? Do they live here?"

"My mother does, but not my sisters. Dear God! My sisters have been exposed!" Running to the head of the stairs, Paul shouted out their names.

"They've gone home. They'll be back later today," Paul's mother called back from the bottom of the stairs.

"Maybe I can catch them before they reach their homes," Paul said to Joseph, poised to race down the stairs.

Joseph reached out and grabbed hold of his arm. "Have they been in and out of the house these past few days?"

Paul nodded.

"Then there is no need. They have already exposed their families. And from what you have told me and from the feel of things out on the streets, many families on this end of town have already been stricken."

Leaving medication and instructions for Deborah's care, Joseph departed. In the morning he would return to check on the child and secretly inoculate the rest of the family.

Within a few weeks' time, smallpox was running rampant throughout Boston. Despite the precautions taken to contain the disease, it quickly reached epidemic proportions.

There was not even time to fire the embers in the hearth against the winter air that had seeped into the kitchen. A single candle offered the only light as Joseph quickly ate a slice of bread and hunk of cheese, washing it down with cold apple cider. As he reached for his greatcoat, which hung by the door, he heard approaching footsteps.

"Joseph, I need to talk to you before you leave," Mary Warren said as she appeared in the kitchen, a candle in her hand and a quilt draped about her delicate shoulders. She turned, softly closing the door behind her. "Joseph, I am fearful for your health."

"Mother, I am fine—a bit tired perhaps."

"Please hear me out." She placed the candle on the long, rectangular table. Then reaching out her hand, she grabbed hold of his arm. "I am aware that inoculation is banned in the colony, but—" she hesitated. "I believe in saving lives, even if it means breaking the law. I know inoculation works. It was proven effective to any not overtaken by superstition during the epidemic of 1721."

"You were a very small child then, Mother. How is it that you have such confidence in it?"

Tears in his mother's eyes glistened against the candle's light. "I was very young, but I do remember. My grandmother died along with my beloved aunt, for whom I was named, and her infant son. The epidemic lasted for nine months. Half of the population in Boston contracted it—one out of six died. The victims the disease did not claim were left blind, deaf, or scarred for life."

She reached up and wiped her tears. "My father was busy with his patients day and night, as you are now. He would come home to steal an hour's sleep long after we had gone to bed and leave before we arose. For months we barely saw him, but there is one particular morning I shall never forget!"

Joseph waited as his mother struggled to relate her memories of this nightmarish time in her young life.

"Rev. Cotton Mather had read of the success of inoculation in the Orient. He brought the information he had gathered to a doctor in Boston by the name of Zabdiel Boylston in hope of convincing him to attempt the procedure. Dr. Boylston agreed, beginning with himself and Rev. Mather. Satisfied with the results, they offered to treat others. A few brave souls came—most panicked at the thought, overcome by a spirit of superstition much as what we still see today. The General Court declared it illegal. Though many ministers supported this life-saving measure, most physicians refused to give it any consideration. Rev. Mather and Dr. Boylston were greatly persecuted."

"And what was grandfather's opinion of inoculation?" Joseph asked.

"Your grandmother awakened my brothers, sisters, and me during the wee hours of the morning. I remember that it was still very dark, and we were all so groggy. Your grandfather was there. It had been weeks since we had seen him. We cried out to him, wanting him to hold us, but there was no time. One by one my mother pulled us close to her body as my father administered the knife and inserted a pin contaminated with the pox into our arms. He said nothing as he proceeded to wrap each of our wounds. Exhausted though he was, he made certain to kiss each head before going out into the night."

Mary Warren reached up to cup her son's face in her hands. "I see that same look of absolute exhaustion in your eyes that I then saw in his."

"I am tired, Mother, but I am young and healthy. I will be fine."

"Please tell me you have been inoculated, Joseph."

"I have."

"Praise be to God," she whispered, placing her hands over her heart. "And tell me that you will inoculate your brothers this morning—before you leave."

"The disease is contained in Boston, Mother. They are not in danger."

"Yet. Not in danger yet. But it will not stay contained in Boston for long. People will panic and begin to flee by the hundreds, just as they did during the last epidemic. Soon the countryside will be exposed. Until the members of the General Court come to their senses, the disease will continue to spread, kill, and maim."

"Believe me, Mother, the physicians and apothecaries have done everything possible to try to convince them not only to legalize inoculation, but to open two smallpox hospitals as well. They seem to turn a deaf ear to us."

"Do you have the venom in your bag?" she asked, fixing her eyes on his.

"Yes."

"Then help me wake your brothers."

Seemingly unafraid of the pain involved, eight-year-old Jack freely offered his arm to his brother. He watched as Joseph carefully made a small gash with his knife and then inserted a pin contaminated with pus from a smallpox victim.

"Feel a bit queasy?" Joseph asked him as Mary Warren wrapped her youngest son's arm.

"No." Jack appeared to be troubled.

"You're sure you're all right?"

The boy nodded.

Joseph went on to inoculate Eben and Sam.

"You know what's expected of you," he said packing his medical bag. "I'll be gone the best part of each day. Don't let me hear of any complaints about the medication. Mother, you will need to start them on the ipecac right away," he announced as he pulled a small bottle from the bag. Joseph fully expected young Jack to protest. Instead, he obediently opened his mouth for his mother and swallowed the ipecac.

"Do you understand the reason for purging your body?" Joseph asked Jack, who was always eager to learn such things. He nodded his head in reply.

"Good." Joseph was concerned by his behavior. Bending down in front of his brother, he lifted Jack's chin with his finger, forcing the boy to look at him. "Most adults are terrified of smallpox. There is no shame in a lad your age feeling a bit frightened of it, too."

Tears welled up in Jack's eyes. "But I want to be a doctor like you. How can I be a doctor if I'm scared of things like smallpox?" the boy asked ashamedly.

"It is natural to feel this way, Jack. Smallpox is a fearful disease. But you will not be contracting smallpox, not really. And once your body has fought the little bit I put into it, you will not be vulnerable to it. It cannot frighten you again."

"If the fever gets real bad, will you—I mean—you have so many patients to take care of now. Will you be able to help me, too?"

"Of course, I will!" Joseph exclaimed as he put his arms around the boy and pulled him close. "Jack Warren, you are the most important patient I have. If the fever is bad, I will be here to see you through it. I will always be here when you need me."

The meeting was adjourned, and the councilmen quickly removed themselves from the room. It appeared that every physician in Boston had turned out. Hopes had been high upon their arrival that the requests made for legalizing inoculation and opening the smallpox hospitals would finally be granted, but the stubbornness of many of the men who sat on the General Court had left the physicians demoralized.

Murmurs of complaints would have been expected upon hearing the decision, but the doctors were too exhausted to complain. A tomblike silence filled the room as each man lifted his weary body to continue his endless rounds of house calls.

Joseph draped his greatcoat about his shoulders and bent down to pick his hat up off the chair.

"Dr. Warren," James Lloyd's familiar voice was heard from behind. "How are you holding up, my boy?" the former teacher asked as Joseph turned to greet him with a handshake.

"I am tired, sir, just like everyone else," Joseph replied with a weary smile.

"They will hear us. Unfortunately, it will probably take a case or two of smallpox in the towns surrounding Boston. Mark my words, as soon as it threatens their hometowns, the entire Court will beg us to inoculate their families and act as though opening these hospitals was their idea!"

"It is a shame, though, that the countryside has to be put at risk before they act," Joseph sighed.

"It is the nature of man, I suppose. It is easy to ignore another's difficulties until it affects one personally. Ah, how rude of me! Dr. Warren, have you met my newest apprentice?" Dr Lloyd asked as he turned to look at the young man standing by his side. "Dr. Joseph Warren, this is Mr. John Jeffries."

"Yes, sir. Mr. Jeffries and I were acquainted in college. How are you, Mr. Jeffries?" Joseph asked the younger man, extending his hand to him.

"Fine, Doctor, thank you."

Joseph detected a mischievous daring in the handsome face of the younger man. "You have a fine teacher here," Joseph commented.

"I am well aware of it, sir," Jeffries replied with a confident smile.

"Dr. Lloyd," Joseph began, again directing his attention to his former master. "I would like to be one of the residents when the hospitals are established. Having no wife or children, or even an established practice other than my smallpox patients, I am better suited to remain at the hospital than those with greater responsibilities."

"It may be a lengthy residency," Dr. Lloyd warned.

"I am sensible to it, sir."

"Then you will certainly be assigned a position once the Court comes to its senses. Now, it is time to get back to work," he said as he buttoned up his coat. "By the way," Dr. Lloyd began again. "Have you been by the Hooton mansion?"

"Not for quite a while—months in fact." Realizing that it had been so long since his last visit, he felt a sense of guilt.

"I am concerned about the Hooton ladies. I have not been able to convince them to take the inoculation. It is the old woman, you know. She can be terribly stubborn. She has actually quarantined the household from the town. I cannot seem to convince her that taking the inoculation is safer than risking infection. I have no patience with the woman, I am afraid, and I am troubled that Elizabeth is at risk. Maybe you could convince her."

"I will certainly make the attempt." Joseph shared Dr. Lloyd's concern.

"I would appreciate it. Funny, the way Elizabeth talked, I was under the impression that you had been by recently," Dr. Lloyd remarked. Then with a definite twinkle in his eye, he added, "It has been a few months since you last paid a visit?"

Joseph nodded his head in reply.

This brought a wide grin to James Lloyd's face. "Ah, you shall be pleasantly surprised at the changes."

"Sir?" The statement confused Joseph.

"Elizabeth—she is not a little girl anymore. I am not sure what it is exactly. She has gained some weight, blossomed out. But it is more than that. Don't you agree, Mr. Jeffries, that Miss Hooton is a lovely young woman?"

"Most definitely, sir!" John Jeffries agreed wholeheartedly.

"I know what it is!" Dr. Lloyd exclaimed. "It was the sparkle in her eyes whenever your name was mentioned, and it seemed to be mentioned a lot! Yes, that was it!" With a wink and a pat on Joseph's back, James Lloyd turned and walked away, followed closely by his apprentice.

No doubt the good doctor is pleased with himself, Joseph thought as he realized how red his face must be.

Even though he was greeted warmly at the Hooton mansion, Joseph felt very uncomfortable. He was not sure if it was due to Dr. Lloyd's comments or because he knew he had neglected to visit the ladies for so long. Despite his uneasiness, Joseph was able to persuade them to take the inoculation.

He was surprised at Elizabeth's willingness to assist him as he preformed the procedure on her aunt and the servants. Then, without so much as a flinch, she received the painful cut on her own arm.

As Joseph wrapped her wound, he found his hands were trembling. Dr. Lloyd was right. Elizabeth was no longer a child, and the change in her had a definite effect on him.

"I will be back to check on you—er, I mean the household. Let's see. Today is Tuesday. I will return on Thursday." Even as he spoke the words, Joseph realized that he was returning sooner than he did for his other patients. The mild fever associated with the inoculation would not even begin for three or four days, but he felt a need to keep an attentive eye on this young woman.

The fortress on Castle Island was an excellent location for a smallpox hospital—except in the dead of winter. Regardless, Fort William was chosen as one of the two hospital sites, and here Joseph Warren, along with one other physician, set up residency.

The fort consisted of forty-eight barracks. Each room could easily sleep ten patients or more, depending upon how many could be squeezed into a bed. The turnover of patients was fast. After being inoculated. They would spend a week under the observant eye of the resident physicians, and then vacate their beds for others.

Then there were those who had already been stricken with the deadly disease when they came. They stayed much longer as their condition warranted more care. All too often in these cases, the disease was too far advanced, and they died.

With so many individuals passing through the hospital, many ailments unassociated with smallpox itself required treatment, too. It was a good opportunity for free medical care, and many took full advantage of it.

Week followed week. Joseph lost track of time as he poured himself into his work. Sleep became a luxury that he could only obtain by stealing an hour here or there. Meals were eaten in haste.

The long, cold winters of Massachusetts, which Joseph had known his entire life, were intensified on this harbor. The frigid gales of early March swept over this small bit of land with no trees to break their force.

Joseph frequently walked along the barren shore to obtain fresh air and escape the putrid stench of the pox. He would stand at the water's edge, enjoying the brief solitude, and longingly gaze across the two-mile expanse between the island and Boston with its church steeples rising above the horizon, their bells echoing across the harbor. The merchant ships glided past the island, their huge sails driven by the piercing wind.

Warm scenes of home filled his mind—so close, yet beyond his reach.

His family wrote him regularly, and his mother's packages of baked goods were greatly welcomed. He looked forward to receiving news from his own family, and Paul Revere had stayed in touch as well, keeping Joseph updated on little Deborah's improvement. To his delight, Elizabeth Hooton had also taken it upon herself to write. Her letters arrived by way of Dr. Lloyd. They were filled with such encouragement that he found in them a source of strength even on his most trying days.

He often wrote his replies in haste, and for this reason he doubted that he was properly communicating his appreciation for her concern and his growing affection toward her. Considering this, Joseph felt an urgent need to return to Boston. Dr. Lloyd's apprentice, John Jeffries, was largely to blame for Joseph's feeling of urgency. Jeffries had been in Elizabeth's company on a number of occasions since Joseph's retreat to the island, and he seemed to take pleasure in relating his encounters with her whenever he came to the hospital with Dr. Lloyd.

Joseph took comfort in knowing that James Lloyd would not tolerate any courting by his apprentices. Thus, Jeffries would not be able to pursue any kind of formal relationship with Elizabeth during Joseph's absence. But in the meantime, Jeffries certainly did have a better opportunity to win her affection just the same.

Coming to his senses, Joseph realized that jealousy and lovesickness were hardly reasons enough to abandon his post. Wrapping his arms tightly across his chest, he attempted to maintain some warmth against the bitter cold. With a deep sigh, he considered his plight.

"Elizabeth is fond of me," he said aloud with a definite air of confidence. "Therefore, my commitment to the hospital should only increase her affection— should it not?"

A gust of wind hit him full in the face, momentarily taking his breath away. He turned his back to the wind and looked upon the treeless island.

With bold determination, he decided to communicate his feelings to Elizabeth clearly. True, he could not court her while he was on the island, but there was no reason why his intentions could not be made known.

Residency on the island suddenly had greater purpose for Joseph. The hospital offered to him the opportunity to win the confidence and friendship of the townspeople who had no commitment to any one physician. They would be the foundation of his practice, one that would grow large enough to support a family of his own.

Roxbury, 6 June 1764

My Dearest Elizabeth,

It is over, and all of Massachusetts Bay has reason to rejoice. Never have so many survived such an epidemic.

I was rowed to Long's Wharf this morning and from there escorted to Roxbury. Had I my own carriage, I would have been tempted to stop by to pay you a short visit.

'Tis best I did not. Your dear aunt would certainly have been taken aback by my rough appearance and forbidden such a vagabond from keeping company with her most gracious niece.

I am in dire need of rest. Monday, I shall promptly return to my surgery. It is my hope to call on you that evening. If this is convenient—please let me know.

I am, my dear girl, your most humble and devoted servant,
Joseph

Elizabeth gently ran her fingers over the gracefully written words of the letter as it lay on the dressing table. Each one had been memorized. This very evening he would call.

She picked up the hairbrush lying beside the letter and began to pull it through her long, thick hair over and over again. Quickly weaving the dark strands into a braid, she gathered it softly on the top of her head with hairpins. Then, gazing at her reflection in the dressing glass, she studied her appearance. This was the hairstyle Joseph had once commented on, but somehow it did not seem just right.

There was a knock on the door. "Come in," Elizabeth called.

"Are you ready, child? Dr. Warren should be here shortly," Elizabeth's aunt reminded her.

"Oh, Auntie, I cannot seem to get my hair to do what I want. And what do you think of this gown? Perhaps the blue one would look better?" Elizabeth studied her reflection from all sides. The pale yellow silk gown was adorned with a pink rose-trellis pattern and was bordered on the skirt and sleeves with white lace trim.

"That particular gown is lovely on you, child, quite complementary with your dark hair," she replied with an affectionate smile. Her rich, blue eyes hinted at the beauty she once possessed.

"I am hardly a child anymore! Oh, please, Auntie! I will be embarrassed to tears if you talk to me like that in front of Dr. Warren!" Elizabeth exclaimed.

"He has heard me refer to you as child in the past. It has not seemed to dissuade him thus far," her aunt assured her. The passage of time had afforded the elderly woman an air of stable maturity, which remained undaunted by her niece's excitement. She bent her slight form and smoothed the lace about the hem of Elizabeth's gown. "Now sit down, and I will see what I can do about your hair."

When Elizabeth was seated in the chair, the older woman released, then loosened, the braid and expertly began to reweave it. "I know you have been receiving letters on a regular basis from Dr. Warren," her aunt began. "I would never pry as to their content, but I feel certain, given the fact that he is making this social call so quickly after returning from his duties at the hospital, that he feels a great deal of affection toward you. It is time for the good doctor to settle into marriage, and I think it is safe to assume that he hopes to do so with you."

"He has not said as much in the letters," Elizabeth softly replied.

"Being a gentleman, I would not expect that he would, for there must be an official courtship first. That is what he is intending to begin this evening—am I right?"

"Yes," Elizabeth replied timidly.

Her aunt became silent as she neatly fashioned the braid into a bun on Elizabeth's head. "Go and look. Tell me if it is what you had in mind."

Elizabeth walked to the dressing glass as instructed.

"Well?"

"Yes, Auntie, it is exactly how I wanted it. Thank you!"

"You are welcome, dear," the older woman said, stepping behind her niece and placing her hands upon her shoulders. "You look quite beautiful, Elizabeth," she commented, gazing at the girl in the dressing glass. The youthful head of hair reflected as pure a black as the elderly head reflected white.

"Tell me, child, do you feel the same affection toward the doctor as he feels toward you?"

"Yes, Auntie, I do."

"Promise me one thing, Elizabeth," her aunt said, gently turning the girl around to face her. "Be absolutely honest with yourself throughout this courtship. Do not hesitate to seek the counsel of others, and especially that of the Lord in private prayer. Marriage is a most serious commitment, and to spend a lifetime with the wrong person can seem an eternity."

"But, Auntie, you know Dr. Warren. He is a very good man!"

"Indeed he is!" her aunt agreed. "But this does not necessarily mean that he is the best choice for you. John Jeffries has a definite interest in you as well."

"Mr. Jeffries? Oh, Auntie, please!"

"It is something to consider, child. Many girls simply jump at the first offer of marriage."

"I am not doing that. There is just no comparison between the two. Certainly you can see that!"

"No, I am not sure I do. Both are compassionate, dedicated young men. Both are well educated and should be able to provide nicely for a family. In fact, John Jeffries would appear better situated in this regard, as he is not responsible for a widowed mother and younger siblings. They are both rather handsome—"

"There is simply no comparison!" Elizabeth protested.

"Come now, dear. John Jeffries is an attractive man.

"That is not what I mean, Auntie!" Elizabeth exclaimed, moving away from the older woman, a bit red in the face.

"Then tell me what you do mean, child."

"It is hard to put into words. Mr. Jeffries is a kind man. I am not denying that. He is attractive. I would have to be blind not to notice," she admitted with a playful grin. "And, he comes from wealth, therefore is already financially secure. This is a known fact. The difference is their character. There is an inner strength in Joseph Warren. A spiritual side to him that Mr. Jeffries lacks. There is an openness about him, an honesty that makes him vulnerable to others. But instead of making him appear weak, it adds to his strength."

"Your father would be proud at your level of maturity, Elizabeth. Indeed, he would be very proud!"

Circular ripples disrupted the still water of the pond as the stone sank to the bottom. Joseph watched Elizabeth search the ground for another stone. Picking one up, she gracefully tossed it into the water, unaware that her enthusiasm over such a simple activity amused him.

"It must have been wonderful growing up here," she commented, noting the grin on Joseph's face.

"A farm is a fine place to grow up, but there's also a lot of work involved."

"I'm sure there must be, but—" She looked toward the orchard. "Did you get to climb the trees?"

"I most certainly did."

"And did you swim here?"

Joseph laughed at her childlike curiosity. "I still do!"

"Really? I never could, you know." Elizabeth said softly. "Auntie insisted that it wasn't ladylike to run or jump. If I were ever to have climbed a tree, she would have died! Whenever you bring me to visit your family, I try to imagine what it must have been like to grow up here. If you had had a sister, your mother would have taken her swimming, don't you think?" Elizabeth eagerly awaited his answer.

"I have never given it any thought," he said with a laugh.

"Oh, I think she would!"

"Have you ever skipped a rock on the water?" he asked.

Elizabeth's eyes widened in response to his question. "No. Whatever do you mean?"

"We need a flat stone." Quickly finding the right shape of stone, he shot it across the water's surface.

"Five skips!" Elizabeth exclaimed. "I counted five skips!"

"You try it," Joseph suggested, explaining how she would have to use her wrist to throw it properly. He then moved out of her way, finding a nearby maple tree from which to watch her progress.

After a few failed attempts, she finally succeeded. Excited by her simple accomplishment, she turned to Joseph expecting a similar reaction. Though he was staring straight at her, his expression was not what she had anticipated. He appeared deep in thought and seemed to look right through her.

Elizabeth rubbed her hands together to wipe off the dirt.

"Your brother Sam seemed more relaxed at dinner this evening, don't you think?" she asked, attempting to draw him out.

"I did not notice," Joseph replied.

"Really? Well, I did. On the other hand, Jack seemed disturbed by my presence," she added.

"Why do you say that?"

"I suspect he does not like sharing your attention with me."

Joseph raised an eyebrow in response to her statement, but he did not say a word. It was true. Elizabeth Hooton occupied his time and attention. This beautiful young woman had captivated his heart, and he was perfectly content to let it remain hers.

He wanted her for his wife. But that decision brought him an awful turmoil. Perhaps he had overstepped his bounds. After all, she was the daughter of a wealthy man, and he was only a struggling physician with debts hanging over his head.

There would be those who would claim he married her for her inheritance. The motives of a wealthy man would never be questioned, and her comfort in life would be secure.

What of John Jeffries? He came from wealth and would immediately call on her if Joseph were to cease courting her.

And then there was John Hancock, perhaps the wealthiest man in the colonies. He was a good bit older than Elizabeth, it was true, but he was a kind and attractive man who obviously was interested in her! He had seen the way Hancock was drawn to her at every social event they attended.

But Joseph did not wish to be free of her. He needed her by his side for life and tormented himself by questioning whether this need was out of pure selfishness.

"Is something troubling you, Joseph?" Elizabeth finally asked. Completely engrossed in his thoughts, he did not fully comprehend her words.

Focusing on her, he was again stunned by her beauty as the sunlight played upon her black hair, lending to it am almost purple hue. The gaze of her huge, dark eyes was fixed upon his fair ones. The sense of wonder he had seen in them only moments earlier was no longer there. What were they reflecting? Concern? Fear?

"I wish you would tell me what is on your mind," she said.

"I have decided to rent a house in Boston," he began hesitantly. Pulling a leaf off the tree he was leaning on, he riveted his attention upon it rather than meet her eyes. "I could tell you that it is because I need to be closer to my patients, but the truth is I want to be closer to you." He dropped the leaf and looked at her. "In fact, what I truly want is for you to live there with me as my wife, Elizabeth."

As she moved toward him, Joseph placed one hand on her shoulder to prevent her from holding him. With the other, he gently laid his fingers upon her lips to keep her from speaking.

"Elizabeth, please hear me out before you say a thing. I probably have no business even asking, and if your father were alive, he would have decided from the start whether or not I was right for you.

"You know I have certain financial responsibilities. I have to help my mother out, and I have my tuition to pay off. With a home of my own, I will only be able to make ends meet at present." He felt her lips move under the gentle pressure of his fingers as she tried to speak.

"Shh—please let me finish. I know what you are going to say, and I will not touch your inheritance. If you are to become my wife, that money will be invested as a security for your future in case something should happen to me.

"You will have to give serious consideration to this fact, Elizabeth. It means we may struggle at first. You are accustomed to living comfortably. John Jeffries or John Hancock could treat you like a queen from the start, but with me—"

Elizabeth pulled his hand from her lips. "I would prefer to live in a wilderness shack with you rather than in a mansion with either of them!" she exclaimed.

"Love can wear thin when faced with many financial obstacles," he interjected.

"And the fact that they possess great wealth does not guarantee that love will endure," she returned. "To begin with, I feel no such affection toward them. And as for my father's approval," she began, placing both her hands on his upper arms, "he thought very highly of you. On many occasions he told me that I would do well to marry a man who possessed such qualities as those you displayed."

"Really?" Joseph replied.

"Really."

"Was he aware that you detested me at the time?" he inquired with a grin.

Elizabeth smiled back. "Everyone was aware that I detested you. I was so blind."

Joseph pulled her into his arms, resting his head against hers. "I just want you to be happy. Heaven knows, I now have more love for you than I ever thought my heart could hold!"

"Then let me share your life. Surely the greatest wealth we can possibly possess in this world already exists between us!"

Joseph lifted his head and looked down at her. Her eyes met his.

"I love you," she whispered, her dark eyes moist with tears.

His lips met hers in a kiss that assured commitment—a kiss that promised fulfillment. And so, on the evening of September 6, 1764, twenty-three-year-old Joseph Warren took seventeen-year-old Elizabeth Hooton to be his wife.

• 3 •

Samuel Adams

IT WAS AN opportunity Joseph had been hoping for. The host had given the reason for his invitation as wanting to get better acquainted with Joseph and his new bride, but Joseph suspected that there was more to the story.

Sam Adams, an influential member of the Massachusetts General Court, had been studying Joseph for some time, although he did not know why. As Elizabeth and he rode in his chaise along the icy streets of Boston, Joseph recalled overhearing a conversation after meeting on Sunday. Sam had approached the aged Lydia Hancock, "Mrs. Hancock, it is wonderful to see you up and about. Last I heard, you were feeling quite poorly. I understand you have taken on a new physician."

"Yes, Mr. Adams. My nephew suggested we engage the services of young Dr. Warren. He is physician to the lieutenant governor's family. My John is of the opinion that if Dr. Warren has proven his ability to the lieutenant governor, then we should have him caring for our family."

"By the look of you, Mrs. Hancock, Dr. Warren's reputation is deserved."

Joseph found it curious that Sam Adams was so interested in him, and he had asked a few questions of his own. Whenever Joseph brought up Sam Adams's name, it seemed that whomever he spoke to considered him a friend, yet no one knew very much about Sam's personal affairs.

The chaise glided to a stop in front of an old house on Purchase Street.

"Certainly this could not be it," Elizabeth stated.

"I followed the directions. Look at the step." Joseph pointed with his gloved hand to the granite step, which had engraved in it the initials *S. A.* As he examined the house from the chaise, he noted with wry amusement that Samuel Adams cared about his property no more than he cared about his own personal appearance. Though always clean, his clothing was tattered with wear and showed signs of being moth eaten. His wavy, gray hair hung loosely about his shoulders, with as little care given to dressing it as possible. The house was in obvious need of fresh paint. The roof desperately needed new shingles and a few panes of glass in the windows as well. As Joseph escorted Elizabeth up the icy, granite stairs leading to the front door, he spotted wood rot on the doorframe, and as they waited for a response to their rapping, he noticed that the brass knocker was tarnished from years of neglect.

"Good afternoon, my friends!" Sam's greeting was as warm as the air that escaped through the open door. "Please, come in! Let me take your winter wraps," he offered, quickly closing the door behind them. The aroma of roasted meat and freshly baked bread and pies was inviting. "Mrs. Adams, the Warrens have arrived!" Sam called out while helping Elizabeth remove her bulky, hooded cloak.

"Dinner is ready. I hope you brought a healthy appetite!" their rather unkempt host remarked, his brows hanging thickly over dark blue eyes. His complexion was florid and his expression careworn, though the lines throughout his face indicated a ready smile.

There was an air of dignity in his countenance. He seemed almost majestic, Joseph noted with a sense of awe.

Sam led them through the foyer into the dining room where Betsy Adams busied herself with last minute preparations. She appeared to be a good bit younger than her husband. Joseph guessed that she was about half Sam's age. Sam had been a widower for a number of years, his first wife having died after giving birth to a stillborn son, and he had remarried only recently.

One would not necessarily consider Betsy Adams homely, but neither was she pretty. Her eyes were warm and friendly—nearly the exact shade of her light brown hair. Unlike her husband, Betsy was rather petite and appeared well groomed in her simple, green-striped, cotton dress and white cap.

"I am so happy you could join us. I understand that social functions are not always convenient for a physician," she said with a smile. Then, scanning her preparations one last time, she removed her white apron, obviously pleased with what she had seen. The colorfully decorated table with its delicate china and polished silver seemed in sharp contrast to the plain furnishings and peeling silk wallpaper. The table was over laden with turkey, ham, rice, bread, and corn. Pudding and fruit pies completed the feast.

"Please be seated," she said, indicating which chairs the Warrens should occupy.

Joseph and Elizabeth comfortably sat themselves at the table, and Sam led everyone in a blessing over the food.

"Will your children be joining us, Mr. Adams?" Elizabeth asked, placing the linen napkin on her lap.

"They are presently visiting with their grandparents, Mrs. Warren. But speaking of the children, young Samuel has a desire to study medicine at Harvard." Sam directed his attention to Joseph. "Perhaps one day you will take on apprentices. You have made quite a reputation for yourself already, Doctor. Your praises are sung from the splendor of the Hancock mansion to the mud and mire of the ropewalk. It is my understanding that even Lieutenant Governor Hutchinson has taken you on as his family physician. That is quite an honor for one so young as yourself."

"Indeed it is, Mr. Adams, and I am extremely grateful for the lieutenant governor's confidence in my ability."

"I have heard some remarkable stories about your medical skill, Doctor. Is it true that you can reduce dislocations without the use of pulleys?"

"In some cases."

"Then the stories are accurate. It is my understanding that such a feat would take a fair amount of physical strength!" He turned to the women and added, "It was only last week that Micah Long from Newbury Street told me how his brother's shoulder was set by the good doctor. Using only his bare hands, he slipped the bone back into the joint."

Joseph ate his meal in silence as Sam went on to regale them with story after story. He wondered where Sam was leading.

"Come, Dr. Warren," Sam said as they finished the meal, "let us retire to the study. I believe Mrs. Adams would enjoy the opportunity to converse with Mrs. Warren, but she has no hope of doing so with me here." Sam looked at his wife and smiled. "Am I right, Mrs. Adams?" he asked.

"Yes, Mr. Adams, you are!" Betsy replied playfully.

Joseph followed his host into the study, illuminated only by the fire in the hearth. Sam moved to the center of the room, where two well-worn leather chairs stood facing one another, and extended the wick in the oil lamps that were set on the small end tables alongside each chair. The light instantly revealed the treasure of this frequented room. Bookshelves lined one entire wall, their contents spilling over and piled on the shelves and scattered throughout the room. A few books sat open on the rolltop desk in a darkened corner, along with two ledgers. Some were piled on the end tables alongside the twin leather chairs. A few books had even been carefully placed on the chairs themselves.

"Your patients are not only commenting on the skill you exhibit, but also on the freedom and eloquence with which you communicate your disappointment over the late acts of Parliament. Your remarks have caused many men in this town to become concerned with what is going on in England with regard to the colonies." Sam gestured for Joseph to sit in the chair facing his, reverently removing the open books that occupied it. He placed his hand on a rack of pipes on the end table, taking hold of two and offering one to Joseph. The younger man declined. "Have you met James Otis?" Sam asked, filling the pipe from a pouch of tobacco.

"No sir, but I have a great appreciation for his writings—and his arguments before the court."

"Then you have read his work?"

"What man in Boston has not? I was introduced to his works shortly after the completion of my studies at Harvard. I have found myself in full agreement with his arguments during the past four years but have not been in a position to act upon it."

"Act upon it?" Sam asked, lighting his pipe, his brow raised.

"Yes, Mr. Adams. Now that my practice is established—now that I have the responsibility of a family, I feel the need to not only be informed of the political concerns of this colony but to form an opinion and express it."

"To your patients?"

"To my patients, at the town meetings—"

"In the newspaper, perhaps?"

The question took Joseph by surprise. "I have never given it any thought."

"You should. One can influence a great many individuals through the written word." He made a sweeping gesture with his arm at the books in the room, authors with whom Joseph was familiar: Locke, Blackstone, Montague, the poetry of John Milton, the plays of William Shakespeare, Calvin's Commentaries, and the writings of Samuel Rutherford as well.

"Consider the effect James Otis's writings have had thus far. Did you say you have read his work on the Sugar Act?"

"Yes, sir, as well as his writings on the Navigation Act, the Writs of Assistance, and the Proclamation Act. I am in agreement with Mr. Otis. They claim the taxes being laid upon us are protective taxes—to pay our share of the cost of maintaining the army during the French and Indian War. Yet, we freely taxed ourselves to this end and volunteered the service of our ablest men.

Sam puffed thoughtfully on the pipe and listened as Joseph continued. "Besides the fact that Parliament is issuing these taxes from a distance of 3,000 miles with no form of true representation for the colonies.

"As Mr. Otis stated so truthfully, sir: taxation without representation is tyranny. I am appalled by the seeming ignorance of certain members of Parliament toward the colonies. The mother country shall certainly reap the reward of our prosperity if we are allowed to develop industry and trade to its full potential. We can, and should, mature in the protective shadow of her greatness—intertwined with her as the oak and the ivy."

Joseph sighed. "But, how can we do this when they forbid us from settling on the frontier, thus limiting our resources for furs and timber? How can we do this when they decide to put such a high tax on molasses as to completely deprive the rum distilleries of any profit? How can any merchant make an honest living when such limitations on trade with other countries are forced upon him?"

Sam studied the younger man for a moment. "As a responsible member of this community and as a Christian, do you condone the smuggling activity of many of these merchants?"

Joseph smiled knowingly. "That is a very dangerous question, Mr. Adams."

"Only the answer can prove damaging, and only then if spoken to the wrong person," Sam coyly responded.

"And how do I know for certain whether or not you are the right person?"

"You do not. But my political opinions are fairly well known, and I am aware that you have been inquiring of me in response to my queries of you!" he said with a chuckle. "Those you have spoken to who have vouched for my character are honest and trustworthy men: Parson Cooper, William Cooper, and John Adams, my cousin."

"I do believe they are honest and trustworthy,"

"Then will you answer the question?" Sam challenged Joseph with a steely eye.

Joseph watched the smoke curl up from Sam's pipe for a few seconds before responding. "As a responsible member of the community and as a Christian, I do condone the smuggling activity forced upon the merchants of these colonies."

"And, Dr. Warren, could you please explain to me how, as a Christian, you can condone this?"

"I certainly can, Mr. Adams, with chapter and verse to support the conviction I have formed, but I will not—at least not until you first express to me how it is that you have come to this same conviction."

Sam's laughter was deep and infectious. "I do like you, Dr. Warren! Indeed I do! Of course, I will tell you. The strict limitations on trade and the severe taxation being imposed will bring to ruin many businesses. As you well know, it is not only the merchants who are threatened, but every soul in these colonies, from the clerks, dock workers, and sailors to the farmers, attorneys, and physicians," he said pointing to Joseph.

Joseph raised his hand and pointed back at Sam. "And eventually, members of the General Court."

"Indeed. We will all be affected by and by. And being a port town and therefore totally dependent on sea trade, Boston will experience the outcome sooner than most. The merchants cannot possibly make a profit, nor even pay those in their hire, if they adhere to the restrictions and taxation presently imposed. Only through smuggling can they hope to continue on. Only then can they feed their own families and pay their help that they might feed theirs. Only in their making a profit and paying their help do you get paid, Doctor. For in a port town, if the ports are closed, few have money to spend, even on medical needs. So how can I condone from a scriptural standpoint what appears to be an illegal, rebellious act in response to the limitations Parliament is imposing? Chapter and verse?" Sam asked playfully.

Joseph smiled as he nodded his head.

Sam put down his pipe. Then standing, he walked across the room to the rolltop desk in the darkened corner, gingerly retrieving an old, oversized Bible.

"I think you will agree that the overall principle of scripture in this regard is that we have been created in the image of God, and because of this we have dignity and worth. We are to reflect God's image in our own creativity and diligence. Many verses in the Psalms and Proverbs speak of God's abundant blessing on the fruit of one's labor. I suppose we can begin here." Sam opened the King James Version to a particular passage. "'But if any provide not for his own, and specially for those of his own house, he hath denied faith, and is worse than an infidel.' This, of course, is from the first book of Timothy, the fifth chapter, and the eighth verse. And would you care to add one of your own?" Sam asked, carefully handing Joseph the Bible.

Joseph received the book with both hands. The tenderness with which Sam handled it revealed its value to him. The binding itself was impressive. The leather cover was adorned with massive brass mountings and clasps. As he opened the cover, he noted that the first inscription in the family record was made back in 1713 by a Mr. Samuel Adams.

"Did this belong to your father?" Joseph asked.

"Yes, it did."

"It is quite beautiful," he commented as he turned to the sought-after passage.

"The book of Judges, chapter six, verses eleven and twelve," Joseph announced. Sam seemed perplexed.

"'Gideon threshed wheat by the winepress, to hide it from the Midianites. And the Angel of the Lord appeared unto him, and said unto him, The Lord is with thee, thou mighty man of valor!'"

Comfortably leaning back in his chair, Sam placed his arms behind his head and grinned. "'To hide it from the Midianites,'" he repeated cheerfully. "I never saw that before. How delightful! And let's not forget the story of Rehoboam!"

"Certainly not," Joseph agreed. "But let's pray that it doesn't get to that point. Perhaps our friends in Parliament will soon convince it of the damage it is inflicting on the colonies."

"We have very few friends in Parliament," Sam's forlorn response came as he lowered his arms. "And King George III, like King Rehoboam, is young, inexperienced, and apparently takes counsel from the wrong source. We received word only yesterday that yet another form of taxation is to be imposed on the colonies. They are referring to it as the Stamp Act. I fear it will prove more oppressive than any thus far."

"How so?"

"They propose to tax the internal dealings of the colonists: newspapers, business documents, legal documents, and even diplomas."

A sick feeling gripped the younger man upon hearing this report. "It cannot be so."

"It can, and I fear it will be."

"You said, 'We received word.' Of whom are you speaking?" Joseph asked.

"James Otis, Parson Cooper, myself, Edes and Gill, and even a few others. We meet once a week to discuss these topics, and—" He stopped as if uncertain as to whether he should finish the sentence. "We call it the Long Room Club. Might you be interested in joining us?"

"Yes, sir. I would."

"Very good. Be here at seven on Monday. I'll lead you to our meeting place."

The open chaise offered little protection against the biting wind. Beneath the thick wool blanket, Elizabeth snuggled close to her husband, her face buried against his shoulder, prompting him to coax the mare from a walk to a slow trot. Only one unfamiliar with the winding and often narrow streets of Boston would dare go any faster, especially on runners. Just a few, like themselves, were still traveling, eager to reach their homes after the evening's activities.

All of the businesses they passed on Court Street and Franklin were closed, and many houses already stood in darkness. The oil lamps lining the street burned clear and bright, illuminating the way. From this light Joseph could make out the signs over artisans' shops as they swung back and forth, creaking ominously in the wind.

The sign above the office of the *Boston Gazette* caught Joseph's attention, but not because of the wind. To the contrary, this sign remained absolutely still despite the forceful gusts. Curious, Joseph slowed his horse and stared at the unyielding banner, a brightly painted wooden sentinel who kept a faithful vigil over Court and Franklin Streets. It must be firmly anchored, he thought. Sam had mentioned the names of Edes and Gill, the publishers of the newspaper, as being members of the Long Room Club. He wondered if they were as firmly anchored in the political ideas Sam and he had been discussing.

Aware that Elizabeth was cold and tired, he urged the horse on toward home. Upon their arrival, Joseph's first concern was to stoke the fires and tend to the horse. When he finally completed his tasks, he sought out his wife, finding her in the bedchamber. She was laying out a fresh suit of clothes for him should he need to make a house call during the night.

"You were rather quiet on the ride home from the Adamses," Joseph remarked, taking off his frock coat.

"As were you." Elizabeth responded with a smile.

"Hmm— I suppose I was," he said pensively, draping his coat across an easy chair positioned close to the blazing hearth. He began to unbutton his waistcoat. "Did you enjoy yourself?"

"Yes, Mrs. Adams is a kindly woman—very easy to converse with."

"And what is your summation of Mr. Adams?"

"The truth?" she asked, pulling the quilt back under the canopy of their bed.

He looked up from the buttons and smiled. "Of course!"

"He seems to be a good man—extremely proper. I know he's well thought of by many. However—"

"However?" Elizabeth had his full attention.

"I acquired the sense that he has examined us and knows everything there is to know. It was almost as though he could see into our very souls!" she exclaimed, causing him to laugh. "I am quite serious, Joseph! How is it that when I shared with Mrs. Adams that we were expecting the arrival of a baby this summer, she responded by saying that Mr. Adams had already informed her! Certainly you did not tell him!"

Joseph shook his head in response.

"Except for my aunt and your mother I have told no one. So how is it that Mr. Adams would know?"

"He can see it upon your face—that glow women in your condition exhibit," Joseph answered as he moved toward her, taking her into his strong arms.

"Come now, Doctor. If there is a glow, rest assured that it is the result of perspiration on this poor creature's forehead as she fights back the constant sensation that she will momentarily be sick to her stomach!"

Joseph laughed.

"I could not help but overhear some of your conversation with Mr. Adams. Are you planning to attend that meeting?"

"Yes, I think so. Why?"

"I am a bit frightened at the thought of it. What might they do there?"

"They discuss what is happening. Mr. Adams spoke of writing letters to the newspaper. Parson Cooper attends. Certainly the fact that the parson is there should set your mind at rest."

"To be sure, but then some of the parson's sermons on the divine institution of civil government and its responsibilities to serve the people sound like Mr. Adams wrote them!" she teased with a weak smile.

Joseph kissed her on the forehead and pulled away, walking toward the wash-basin. "A lot of anger and bitterness is building because of Great Britain's actions. Maybe the men who form this club will find a way to channel it into something constructive."

He fixed his eyes on hers. "In this colony we have had the freedom to govern ourselves. Yet our rights are slowly being stripped from us—rights ordained by God. In letting them go, we will be submitting to that yoke. Would to God that the king intercedes for us, but what if he fails to do so? I cannot accept the shackles without a fight, Elizabeth. I will not watch in idleness as you and our children are enslaved. To do this is to deny my duty to God and my manhood itself! Do you understand?"

Although Joseph's words were spoken softly, there was an authority in his voice that she had never heard. His convictions in this matter were firmly established, and he would not be compromised. As frightened as Elizabeth still felt for the safety of her husband, she loved him all the more for it.

The weak rays of the February sun filtered through the parlor windows, and a blazing fire in the hearth provided the warmth the sun lacked. From the aroma emanating from the kitchen, Joseph was certain that breakfast was about ready. Carefully placing his antique Bible on the table, he relaxed in the winged-back chair—eyes closed—awaiting Elizabeth's call.

A loud rap on the front door startled him. Entering the foyer, he heard Elizabeth coming from the kitchen.

"I will get it," he called to her as he reached to open the door, bracing himself for a cold gust of winter air. On the doorstep stood a young man whom Joseph did not recognize.

"Dr. Warren?" he asked. Without waiting for a response, he continued. "His Honor, Lieutenant Governor Hutchinson, wishes to extend to you an invitation to dine with him this noon at the British Coffee House. Your reply, sir?"

Joseph was surprised by the unexpected invitation. "Tell the Lieutenant Governor that I will be honored to dine with him," he quickly replied.

"Yes, sir. Your servant, Dr. Warren," the messenger said and went on his way.

As Joseph entered the kitchen, he found Elizabeth placing two steaming bowls of porridge on the plain, rectangular table.

"Another house call to make this morning?" she asked, turning to grab a small clay container full of raisins.

"No, an invitation to dine with one of my patients at noon," Joseph replied, still uncertain of what to make of it all.

"Who?" she asked as she carefully removed the teakettle from the crane in the hearth and poured the hot water into two waiting mugs.

"Thomas Hutchinson."

Elizabeth's expression plainly revealed her apprehension. "The lieutenant governor? You are to dine with the lieutenant governor?"

"He is my patient."

"Is he ill?" she asked, returning the kettle to the fire and sitting down at the table.

"No, not that I know of."

"Perhaps he desires to speak with you about your involvement with these different groups or the meetings you have been attending with Mr. Adams and Mr. Otis. Maybe he has read your letters in the newspapers," she replied with a slight tremble in her voice.

Joseph reached out and placed his hand on top of hers. "My name does not appear on the letters."

"Oh, but Joseph, he must be aware that you are involved with men who openly oppose Parliament!"

"We do not oppose Parliament, Elizabeth. We oppose the Stamp Act and the other atrocities which that body has forced upon the colonies."

"But the lieutenant governor does not agree with your stand. Do you think he will try to persuade you to leave these groups or else risk losing him as a patient?"

"Perhaps. And if that is his intention, I shall have one less patient by day's end."

The watchful vigil of the wooden sentinel continued day and night—rain, shine, or even snow. Joseph smiled at the brightly painted, carved figure as he passed below it into the office of the *Boston Gazette*. The club Sam Adams had invited him to attend met in the *Gazette* office. Its very name was derived from the long room directly above the print shop in which the members met.

"Good evening, Dr. Warren," the printer's apprentice greeted him from behind the press. "Mr. Edes is expecting you, sir. He and the others are already upstairs."

"Thank you, lad." Joseph needed no help in finding his way, for he had attended the meeting several times already.

The nineteen members of the Long Room Club were assembled at the large table board, which rested upon four trestles situated in the center of the room.

"We were hoping you would not be detained too long, Doctor," James Otis said, standing at the head of the table. He was a great leviathan of a man whose large, neckless form commanded respect. He pointed to an empty wooden chair that Joseph was to occupy between Sam Adams and Benjamin Edes.

"I am sorry to interrupt, gentlemen," Joseph offered. He had a quick smile for Paul Revere, who had also recently become a member.

"We were just getting started," James Otis replied.

"This room is unbearably hot!" the wealthy merchant John Hancock blurted as he pulled at his cravat. Removing a clean, embroidered handkerchief from beneath his ruffled shirtsleeve, he began to pat his brow. "Just because the hearth is oversized does not mean you have to put a full rick of wood in it, John!" He directed his sarcasm to his childhood friend, John Adams.

"I had nothing to do with the fire tonight, Jay," Adams stated. The delicate features of his plump face showed no sign of distress over Hancock's verbal lashing.

"Well, who did?" Hancock demanded.

Joseph noted the sudden smirk on John Adams' face as a chuckle came forth from his cousin, Sam. "Parson Cooper, was it not you that I saw stoking the fire when I arrived?" John Adams asked, his eyes fixed on Hancock.

"Indeed, it was me!" the parson quipped with a definite twinkle in his friendly eyes. Many of the men assembled around the table were members of his flock, including John Hancock. None would challenge him.

Hancock appeared momentarily flustered. "Oh—well—then, perhaps, if the parson agrees to it, we could open a window or two?"

"If you are warm, Mr. Hancock, then feel free to open the windows a crack, with your permission, Parson," Sam said, impatient to get started.

"By all means, Mr. Hancock," the parson answered. The wide grin on his face clearly indicated his delight in John Hancock's response.

"Dr. Warren, I understand you had dinner with the lieutenant governor this afternoon," Sam Adams began as John Hancock busied himself with the windows.

"Does anything escape your notice, Mr. Adams?" Joseph asked. His smile revealed the affection he already felt toward the older man. "Yes, we did dine together, and I suppose you probably know what we discussed, too."

"As a matter of fact, I do!" Sam returned the smile. "Hutchinson has appointed you the administrator in the Wheelright bankruptcy case."

"What?" shouted John Adams from across the table. "A physician to handle such a complicated case! This is absurd! Can you believe such a thing?" he asked, looking at fellow attorneys James Otis and Samuel Quincy. Their response obviously supported his opinion.

Nathanael Wheelright had been one of the wealthiest men in the colonies. With the instability of the paper currency, intensified by a depression following the war with France, Wheelright's empire had collapsed. The news of this collapse caused grave concern among other merchants.

Joseph was troubled by John Adams's outburst. John was always upfront with his thoughts and feelings. Joseph had come to admire this quality in him. Now, considering John's knowledge of the complexities of such a bankruptcy case, Joseph wondered why the lieutenant governor had chosen him to perform this duty.

"One would think that Mr. Hutchinson would certainly have appointed an attorney to such a complicated case as this," James Otis began, staring at Joseph. "This leads me to believe that he chose you with an ulterior motive."

"I agree with you, James," Sam added. "Perhaps the lieutenant governor wishes to buy our young friend's support for British policy with this appointment. You are bound to make yourself a handsome amount for your trouble, Joseph."

"Or perhaps he hopes to tie him up with this," Samuel Quincy commented. "You will deserve a substantial fee by the time this case is settled. The case has the potential of dragging on for years. You will be expected to appear in court often and to be responsible for a great deal of paperwork." As perhaps the brightest, young attorney in Boston, Samuel Quincy had extensive knowledge of such cases.

"I suspect, Doctor, that Mr. Hutchinson is concerned about your growing popularity. Not only with those who tend to agree with you and are easily excited by your comments, but especially by your ability to gain support, even from those who have stood loyal to Parliament. If he can find ways to keep you occupied, you will have less time to converse with your patients or to meet with us!" James Otis thoughtfully observed.

"Whatever Hutchinson's intentions are," Sam Adams said, putting a comforting hand on Joseph's shoulder, "we will be sure to see that they are not carried out. You are administrator of the Wheelright estate. That is a fact, and within this room we have enough attorneys to be of assistance to you."

"I will be happy to assist you in any way I can, Joseph," Samuel Quincy offered. His relaxed manner and friendly smile had a calming effect upon the whole room. "I do not intend to let Hutchinson have you that easily!"

The fears of the merchants were well founded, for following the Wheelright crash, many others had fallen into bankruptcy. The effects of Wheelright's failure reached beyond those involved in trade, dragging down many of various means. Joseph, too, began to feel the effects of the crisis. Before long, even Mary Warren was having difficulties meeting her bills and looked to Joseph for help.

His anxiety increased when he was unable to make a payment on her debts for two months in a row. As the end of the third month approached, he sat at the secretary in the corner of the parlor scratching numbers out on paper.

Elizabeth sat on the worn settee in silence and watched. Her embroidery work lay upon her lap, a threaded needle in her hand, but her thoughts were on her husband.

She had the answer to his dilemma, an answer he had vehemently rejected time and time again. Though she was apprehensive about upsetting him further by again suggesting that her inheritance be used toward the mounting debts, she saw no way around it. Silently, she prayed for wisdom for how to approach him.

The scratching stopped. Joseph placed the quill pen into its holder and sat completely still for a moment, staring at the figures before him.

"There is not enough money again this month. We cannot cut back any more than we already have." He turned to face his wife and added, "Dr. Lloyd has agreed to wait, but Mother is in such debt. Her creditors will not be put off any longer."

Elizabeth's heart sank upon seeing him so disturbed. She set her embroidery down, and with great effort due to her advanced pregnancy, she arose from the settee and waddled over to the secretary. She positioned herself behind him, placing her hands on his shoulders.

"You can't just turn it over to them," she remarked softly as she bent down to kiss his cheek. She could feel the tightness in his shoulders as she began to massage them. "Remember, you told me that I should invest my father's money in property?"

There was no response.

"Well, I have found just the piece. It meets all the qualifications you insisted upon. It is in a good location. It promises to be profitable—a secure investment for our future."

"Elizabeth, we shan't get into this again," his stern response came.

"Yes, I think we shall!" Her pert reply surprised him.

He was taken back by her words.

Elizabeth moved to his side and leaned against the secretary, facing him. She could not clearly read his expression. Was it anger or mere astonishment? No doubt a mixture of both, she thought. She was exploring uncharted waters. She had never before willfully confronted him in such a manner. Outwardly, she appeared confident and relaxed. Inwardly, she was afraid of what his reaction might be.

"I possess a large sum of money. It is mine, not yours—or so you keep telling me! If it is mine, then I have the right to do with it as I please! I resent that, being my lawful husband, you refuse to use the money as your own. And then you have the nerve to keep me from touching it! Decide now, sir, if you have ownership of it or not. If you do, then use it to free your family's property. If not, then do not expect to control what I do with it!"

"Elizabeth! That is quite enough!" he said with a controlled, but strained, tone.

"I am not finished, yet," she firmly replied. Her eyes were fixed on his with bold determination. She walked away from the secretary, stopping in front of the settee.

Joseph stood and faced her.

"Are you concerned about how people will talk if my inheritance is used to pay your family's debt? Is that what keeps you from doing the logical thing?"

"I am illogical, am I?" He was angry now.

"Not usually, but in this case you certainly seem to be. Were he still alive, my father would insist you use his money. Joseph, you are carrying a great load financially. Few in this town are under the strain you are, trying to support two households with the economy as it is.

"If the gossips in this town want to talk, let them! Your family became mine when I took your name. If they need financial help, I am obligated to give it to them. Or do they not consider me part of the family?" she asked.

"Of course, they do," he answered.

"Then, please let me help them by taking the money," she pleaded softly. Tears began to run down her cheeks as she slowly lowered herself onto the settee.

There was a brief moment of uncomfortable silence.

"Please forgive me, Elizabeth," Joseph said. "You are right about using the money. But believe me, I am not concerned about what people will think. I had honestly hoped that it could be kept as a security for you."

"Why do you worry so about the future?"

"I have seen too many woman left widowed and forced to struggle day in and day out to support themselves and their children, my mother included." He walked over and sat beside her. "I would feel better if I knew you were financially secure should anything happen to me."

"Paying the debts will not use up all of the money. We can invest what is left," she answered as she wiped the tears from her cheeks. Then, looking up at him, she slipped her hand into his and softly said, "I appreciate your concern for me. I really do."

Joseph looked upon her tear-stained face and sighed. "How concerned can I really be when I get you this upset with our baby due any day. I am sorry," he said, putting his arm behind her shoulders and gently pulling her close to him.

JOSEPH WARREN

ELIZABETH WARREN

JOHN WARREN

58

Photograph © 2009 Museum of Fine Arts, Boston.

JOSIAH QUINCY JR.

Photograph © 2009 Museum of Fine Arts, Boston.

SAMUEL ADAMS

Photograph © 2009 Museum of Fine Arts, Boston.

PAUL REVERE

The Putnam Foundation, Timken Museum of Art, San Diego, CA

MRS. THOMAS GAGE

• 4 •

Sons of Liberty

A FAINT, SALTY sea breeze finally began to stir, bringing the crisp scent of the ocean and a hint of cool air that had been longed for during the daytime.

Elizabeth attempted to secure the heavy, floor-length draperies back from the open bedchamber windows to allow more of the precious air to enter the room. The task complete, she sat on the window bench, her legs comfortably extended on the maroon, velvet cushions. As the gentle breeze brushed against her cotton night-gown, her body began to respond to its cooling effect.

From the window Elizabeth could see the glow of lanterns and torches in the distance. She had expected the demonstration to end hours earlier. Yet, as darkness set in, the gathering seemed to grow with a new fervor, and the crowd grew louder as the summer night wore on. Elizabeth's concern for her husband intensified with each passing minute.

Joseph had left early that morning to participate in what was to be a peaceful demonstration against the detested Stamp Act. What little she could see and hear from the second-story windows during the day seemed to indicate that it was so. But the mood had definitely changed, and the crowd was beginning to sound more like a mob.

The oppressive heat had caused their newborn to be restless throughout the day. From the light of the single candle positioned on the dressing table behind the hooded cradle, Elizabeth was relieved to see that Betsey was sound asleep. The young mother smiled as she gazed at her baby. Dressed in a muslin gown, Betsey looked comfortable, with her little legs tucked under her diapered bottom and only her tiny pink toes exposed. Concerned that the baby might get a chill from the changing night air, Elizabeth gently felt the little blonde head, then reached for a thin blanket at the base of the cradle and pulled it over the sleeping child.

A sudden crash from the street below quickly brought Elizabeth back to the window. She watched as the shadowed figures of two boys ran down the cobble-stoned road, toppling empty milk jugs and pounding on the doors as they passed.

"Did I bolt the front door?" she whispered to herself. Uncertain of what the answer was, she picked up the candleholder from the dressing table and prepared to go downstairs to check.

A creaking sound from below caused her to stop at the top of the staircase. The sudden flickering of the candle in her hand indicated that the door in the foyer had opened. Quickly blowing out the flame and as quietly and quietly as she could manage, Elizabeth slipped back into the bedchamber.

Her heart was pounding as she moved toward the cradle. Perhaps it is Joseph, she thought. All I need do is call out his name, and my fears would vanish upon hearing his reply. But what if it is not Joseph? Then whoever it is will know I am alone!

She gasped as she heard the door close downstairs. "Dear Lord," she whispered, "Please let it be Joseph."

Those are not his footsteps, she thought as she crouched beside the cradle. The intruder moved slowly up the stairs with heavy steps.

She could hear her own heart pounding as he approached the bedchamber. A man's form appeared and remained motionless at the threshold. The dim light from outside gave little illumination, but Elizabeth knew he was staring at her. She searched the darkened form for a familiarity that would reveal it to be her husband.

"Is all the noise keeping the baby awake?" Joseph's tired voice broke the terrifying silence.

Elizabeth placed her hand over her heart and took a deep breath. She stood and replied, "No, it does not seem to bother her."

Joseph walked into the room. Finding a candle, he proceeded to light it.

"You should have bolted the front door," he casually commented, then kissed her lightly on the lips. "You are trembling! Are you ill?" he asked with concern.

"No, I am fine, though I was concerned about you," she said, hoping to avoid telling him how frightened she had been only a few moments before and receiving a scolding for not locking the door.

"Look at your face!" she exclaimed, seeing in the brighter light how burned it had become from standing in the hot sun all day. "Does it hurt?" she asked, gently pressing her finger against his cheek.

"Not unless you touch it!" he protested with a smile as he took hold of her delicate hand.

"I am surprised Betsey can sleep through all the noise." He went to the cradle and lovingly stroked the sleeping infant's cheek. "I wish she would wake up. I have not had the opportunity to hold her all day."

"Bite your tongue, Joseph Warren. And I would thank you to back away from that cradle! She has been fussing all day from the heat, and you want to wake her now!" Elizabeth scolded with a smile as she returned to her seat before the open window.

"What is happening out there?"

Joseph walked over to take a look for himself. "I do not know," he said somberly, then walked away. "I was called to treat a patient in Milton, a woman whose skirt caught on fire while she was preparing dinner." He was clearly upset by it. "Elizabeth, be careful around the kitchen fire, especially when you have little ones about competing for your attention," he cautioned as he gestured to their sleeping daughter. It was a warning he gave her often, as such a gruesome scene was all too common.

"As I was preparing to leave, Sam Adams, Mr. Otis, and Samuel Quincy said they were planning to head home shortly themselves." He stopped speaking as he poured water into a basin and rinsed his hands and face. "Oh, before I forget, Samuel Quincy invited us to dine at his home after meeting Sunday morning." He said, grabbing the towel, which lay folded beside the washbasin. "When I left Boston, everything was peaceful. I suspect it is the rabble from the south end of town acting up, as they tend to do in such gatherings. There are a lot of angry men out there. Some have no work because of this recession. Even those who do are struggling to provide for their families. This Stamp Act," he spoke the words with contempt, "will greatly increase their hardship. They are trying to find a way to vent their anger."

"Then did any good come of this demonstration?" Elizabeth asked as she walked to the canopied bed and pulled back the bedding.

"I hope so," he said with a sigh, gazing out the window as he dried his hands. "Thousands of people were there, Elizabeth. We gathered by the huge, old elm tree on Essex Street. We've named it the Liberty Tree. Do you know which one I mean?" he asked as he changed into his nightclothes.

"I know the one."

"There were two effigies hanging from the tree. One was of Boston's stamp master, Andrew Oliver. The other was of Lord Butte."

Elizabeth was aware that Lord Butte was the British minister who was viewed as responsible for encouraging the hated Stamp Act.

"The discovery of the effigies caused such excitement that most merchants closed their shops. Businesses throughout Boston were shut down. Lieutenant Governor Hutchinson ordered the sheriff to remove the effigies from the tree. But the sheriff was fearful of upsetting the massive crowd and refused to comply with the order."

Joseph blew out the candle and climbed into bed next to his wife. "I believe that Sam Adams can harness and direct the anger in the men of this colony. Today he challenged them to work together in an attempt to secure their rights. He suggested that they refer to themselves as the Sons of Liberty. But we can talk more about this in the morning. I think it would be wise for you to take advantage of Betsey's peaceful slumber and try to get some yourself," he said leaning over to kiss his wife good night.

As he rolled over, his sunburned cheek brushed against the pillow. The slight discomfort he felt reminded him of the poor woman in Milton. He dozed off while praying for her, hoping that the opium he had left would be enough to deaden her pain until he returned in the morning.

With the morning light came news of the mob's attack on the stamp master's house.

Two weeks later the mob gathered again. Its destructive acts were rampant on this sultry summer night, ending at the home of Lieutenant Governor Hutchinson.

News of these senseless, destructive acts brought much grief to the members of the Long Room Club. "Thank God no harm came to the lieutenant governor or the stamp master," Samuel Quincy said to those gathered, "but the wanton destruction of their property is inexcusable. We will be viewed as a bunch of violent mobsters, gentlemen. Word will quickly spread that this group you are trying to form, Sam, these Sons of Liberty, were behind this whole outrage!"

"Mackintosh is in jail." John Adams replied. "He's known by all to be the leader of that mob! Soon enough people will realize that he, and he alone, led them."

Joseph glanced across the table at Sam Adams, who was carefully studying every man at the table. He appeared to be aware of every word spoken, and sometimes it seemed even of every thought.

"There is no one in this room, I'm sure, who can blame the men of Boston for being angry," Sam began. "They are hard workers who see little return for their efforts. They lash out in the dark simply because they do not know what else to do. They destroy because they lack proper leadership. We need to educate them about what is occurring in Parliament and the short- and long-range effects on these colonies. We need to teach them how to defend the rights that are being stripped from us all. That mob, gentlemen, shall be tamed," he paused, "and it shall not go into the streets of Boston again without a man from this table at its head."

Just as Joseph had anticipated, Sam Adams would harness the energy of the Boston mob, thus creating a force that would be difficult to ignore.

The day the colonists had dreaded for more than a year finally arrived, and on November 1, 1765, the Stamp Act officially went into effect. Massachusetts Bay was prepared. Sam Adams had presented his fourteen resolves before the Massachusetts General Court, clearly stating the rights of the people. They were unanimously adopted.

Groups calling themselves the Sons of Liberty began to form in many of the colonies. Nine colonies had even elected delegates to meet in New York in October to attend a Stamp Act Congress. This level of unity seemed nearly miraculous. The colonies had stood together in declaring their loyalty to King George III, but they also demanded their rights of no taxation without representation and of trial by jury.

Business came to a standstill throughout the colonies as businessmen refused the stamps. The courts were forced to close when the attorneys refused the stamps. Yet, the most harmful effect felt by Great Britain was the refusal of the colonists to buy British goods. This boycott, it was hoped, would send a resounding message back to Parliament.

A burst of winter air flooded into the farmhouse through the open door. Mary Warren secured the blanket around Betsey's chubby little legs, which had worked their way out of the cozy covering.

"Elizabeth, you must be half frozen!" Mary exclaimed from the rocking chair by the hearth as her daughter-in-law hastened to close the door.

"It is cold out there. I'm certain my feet have turned to blocks of ice." Elizabeth pulled off her woolen gloves and proceeded to remove her hooded cape, which was spattered with snow. She hung the cape on a hook near the door.

"Come, put your shoes and stockings near the fire to dry. Take that blanket and wrap it around your bare feet, and pull that chair over here where it is warm," Mary instructed, first pointing to a blanket draped neatly over the arm of the settee and then to an easy chair close by. "Is Joseph still doctoring that cow?"

"No, he is finished."

"I intend to speak to him about keeping you out there in the cold. Certainly one of the boys could have assisted him. Sam should have."

"He did not keep me out there, Mother. All the boys helped." Elizabeth replied as she pulled the easy chair next to the rocker as instructed. She sat down and, bending forward, gingerly wrapped her tingling feet with the blanket. "Joseph suggested I come in a few times, but I wanted to stay. I do not see much of him these days—" Her voice drifted off sadly.

Then, with a sudden change of mood, she added, "While they were tending to the cow, they all decided to build a snow fort. Of course, even before the building was completed, they started hurling snowballs at one another."

Mary looked back toward the hooded cape on the hook. Traces of snow were still upon it. "Did my sons throw snowballs at you?" she asked incredulously.

Elizabeth shrugged, and with a sheepish grin, she nodded. "It was me, Joseph, and Jack against Sam and Eben. We had the fort, but Sam and Eben's strategy was to aim everything my way and keep Joseph and Jack so busy shielding me that they had no time to put up a good defense. Joseph and Jack were getting slaughtered, and I was getting cold!" she said with a laugh. Her mother-in-law shook her head in amused disbelief.

"Did Betsey behave herself?" Elizabeth asked, peeking at the sleeping baby.

"She was an absolute angel!" Mary momentarily dropped her gaze to the child in her arms. Then looking back at Elizabeth, she said, "What did you mean by the statement that you do not see much of Joseph these days? I was aware that this Stamp Act boycott had interfered with his practice. Have things improved? Is he seeing more patients?"

"The boycott has not actually interfered with how many patients he sees, only with getting paid for seeing them. People still call on him for help. He would never turn them down," Elizabeth said with a smile that indicated that she was in agreement with his decision. "It is not really his patients that have him so busy, not in the evenings, anyway. It is the boycott itself and the meetings he attends as a result."

"Meetings?"

"As I understand it, most of them have to do with the boycott. One evening they meet in North Square with a group of artisans. Another evening the Sons of Liberty meets. Then there is the one with Mr. Adams, Mr. Otis, and Parson Cooper. Then there are the town meetings. Now he is talking about making a serious attempt to regularly attend the meetings at St. Andrew's."

"The Masonic lodge? I thought he lost interest in that long ago," Mary commented.

"He did—at least he has not attended or made mention of it since he was still an apprentice."

"I understand his involvement in these other groups you have mentioned. I fully agree with and support what they are attempting to do through this boycott. But why would he feel a need to become active in the lodge with so many other things occupying his time?"

Elizabeth appeared more than a little uncomfortable. "I accidentally overheard a conversation when Sam Adams and Paul Revere came by the house a few days ago. They asked Joseph if he would consider becoming active at the lodge again. From what I could gather, the most respectable men of Boston attend. I heard Mr. Revere say that the men converse freely after the lodge meetings about anything that might be of mutual interest to them, including politics. Mr. Adams feels that because Joseph already has the respect of many of these men, both Whig and Tory alike, he might be able to convince the lodge members who have not yet taken a stand for liberty to do so. And he might win some of the others over as well."

The baby squirmed, and Mary lifted Betsey over her shoulder and began to pat her back. "Out here on the farm, I don't always stay in touch with what is going on in Boston. In the past I depended on Joseph's father, and then Joseph, to keep me abreast. Since Joseph left home, Sam is my link, but his interest is minimal. I know that Joseph's medical skill has attracted some influential patients, but how is it that he has become so influential with Whig and Tory alike?" Behind the genuine curiosity Elizabeth detected a deep sense of pride in her mother-in-law's dark eyes.

"Mainly through his patients and through his work at the smallpox hospital—and even back to his apprenticeship. Uncle James frequently entertains. And though he is not in full agreement with the restrictions and taxes that Parliament has put on us, Uncle James firmly believes we should submit to its authority just the same. Being a Tory himself, those he is closely associated with are Tories, and Joseph mingled with them often."

Betsey began to cry, prompting Elizabeth to take the blanket from around her feet and drape it over her shoulders so she might discreetly nurse the baby. Mary stood and placed the fussing infant into Elizabeth's arms.

"This involvement in the lodge that Mr. Adams and Mr. Revere have proposed frightens me," Elizabeth confessed, nervously looking toward the door as though expecting someone to enter.

"What do you mean, Elizabeth? How does it frighten you?"

"It is not only that they want him to attempt to influence the political views of some members. It appears to be more involved than that. From what I can gather, there is a type of hierarchy in the lodge. Those men in the higher positions command the respect of the others. I do not fully understand it, so therefore I cannot properly relate it." She looked again toward the door and continued just above a whisper. "It is as though it is an army with a chain of command. They are asking him to make a long-term commitment. It is very well planned, but to what end, I do not know."

"Have you discussed it with Joseph?" Mary asked with growing concern.

"He said it is nothing to be concerned about and that the outcome of this boycott will probably determine how involved he gets with it, whatever that means."

The sound of boisterous conversation outside the door indicated that the Warren brothers were about to disrupt the ladies' time alone. Again the cold air flooded in as the door flew open.

"Where is Jack?" Mary asked.

"He said he isn't ready to come in yet," Sam replied as the three older brothers struggled to get out of their wet, winter wraps.

"You are all soaked to the skin. Certainly Jack must be as well! All of you get upstairs and put some dry clothes on." The three of them obediently moved toward the staircase.

Joseph returned Elizabeth's smiling gaze as he ascended the stairs. "Have you warmed up?" he asked.

"Yes. Who won?"

"Jack and I held the fort!" he announced with a proud smile and a shiver, then disappeared with the others to the upper level.

"You would think Joseph had more sense than to leave Jack out there to catch a chill," Mary complained as she walked toward the door. Suddenly the door swung open, exposing the red-cheeked twelve-year-old.

"You should see the snow fort we built, Mother! There was no way Sam and Eben could conquer it! What a battle we had!"

"You can tell me all about it after you have changed," his mother stated, closing the door behind him and helping him hang up his soaking wet wraps. After shooing Jack toward the staircase, Mary Warren went into the kitchen to prepare a pot of hot tea.

By the time she returned, her three older sons were comfortably seated by the freshly stoked hearth. Joseph, dressed in one of Sam's frocks, was holding Betsey.

"Mother, it is time to make some serious plans for Jack's education. He will be ready for Harvard in two years," Joseph announced as Elizabeth helped his mother pour the tea.

"Two years?" Sam exclaimed. "The lad won't be ready in two years! He's not as bright as you were. Have you forgotten that he couldn't even read until he was nearly ten?"

"Only because no one had time to sit down and work with him when he was younger. He caught on quickly. Not only did he learn to read and write at an astonishing rate, but his schoolmaster says he is already ahead of his classmates in his Latin skills. The truth is, Jack is extremely bright!"

Turning to his mother, he added, "Elizabeth and I have decided to help with his college tuition. The heiress here insists on it," he said with a wink for Elizabeth as she placed a steaming cup of tea on the small table at the end of the settee. "After he graduates, he can apprentice under me."

Sam and Eben began to laugh.

"I will be ready to take on apprentices in a few years," Joseph pointed out to his brothers, unsure of what they found so amusing.

"May I suggest that you take no other apprentices when Jack serves his time?" Eben said with a grin.

"Why not?" Joseph asked.

"You overindulge the boy," Sam replied before Eben could.

"Any other apprentices would be severely neglected, and left to learn on their own!" Eben added with a teasing grin.

"I do not overindulge him," Joseph insisted with a smile. "Elizabeth, Mother— do I overindulge Jack?"

The women replied by joining in the laughter of Sam and Eben.

"Well, maybe I do, but only a little!" he murmured.

• 5 •

Josiah

THE WELCOME NEWS came on a Friday in the spring of 1766 when the ship docked at Boston's port: the Stamp Acts had been repealed. Celebrations erupted throughout the colonies, and Boston' was not outdone anywhere. Festivities began early the following Monday with church bells ringing. Cannons boomed from Castle Island and were echoed by the ships in the harbor. The Liberty Tree was decorated with flags and streamers, and musicians paraded the streets with violins, flutes, and drums. As evening fell, homes in Boston remained well lit. John Hancock provided refreshments on the Boston Common, along with a magnificent fireworks display that would be remembered for many years.

"Premature celebration, gentlemen!" James Otis raved. "That's all it was, a premature celebration! Nothing has really changed at all!" His large form paced the floor of the long room. He stopped only long enough to toss a copy of the Declaratory Act on the table.

Every man in the room had experienced intense frustration when news of this latest act reached the American shores, but James Otis seemed almost out of control of his emotions and his ability to reason. Tonight he was in a rage over the injustices of Parliament. Tomorrow he might very well condone them and publicly declare his belief in the all-encompassing authority of Parliament over the colonies.

Sam Adams and the others studied their confused friend for a moment, throwing worried glances at one another. The change in James Otis's personality had become a matter of great concern to them. His mood swings were occurring more frequently, and he was becoming even more unpredictable.

"Sammy, they refuse to free us from this bondage," James Otis lamented, his narrow eyes fixed on Sam Adams. Then, dropping down into a chair, he rested his head upon his folded arms on the table as if exhausted by his outburst.

"How can we say we haven't gained a victory, gentlemen?" merchant William Molineux began cautiously, which was quite unusual for the ill-tempered Irishman. With a look of apprehension, he glanced at the weary James Otis as he spoke. "The Stamp Act was far more grievous than this new act!"

It was true that the Declaratory Act enforced no specific tax upon the colonists, only a declaration that Parliament had the authority to lay a tax upon them whenever that body felt it was appropriate.

"Of course it was!" John Hancock agreed wholeheartedly, a bright smile upon his handsome, rather gaunt face. "And relations with the mother country will now improve dramatically as trade is restored to normal—" He stopped speaking when he caught a glimpse of Sam Adams, who as always was seated at the head of the long, narrow table.

Sam had a wry smile for his wealthy friend, a smile that obviously made John Hancock quite uneasy. "Come now, Mr. Hancock," he said, "you certainly know that Mr. Otis is right!"

Characteristically a nervous man, John began to fidget as Sam spoke. The smile remained upon Sam's lips.

"As much as you and Mr. Molineux would like to again fill your pockets with the profits you earn from trade with Great Britain, you both can be sure that this lull will not last."

Sam stood and, bending over, rested the palms of his hands firmly on the table before him. His countenance became deadly serious as his eyes took in each man seated about him. "All Parliament has given us is time to prepare for their next move. They have clearly stated that we are subject to their arbitrary control. Whatever their next oppressive act may be, you can be certain of this, gentlemen. They will be better prepared to face any resistance we may show."

The conversation stopped when the door to the *Gazette* printing shop opened.

"I was not aware that we would be hearing from your flaming pen this week, but it is always a welcome event, Doctor," Sam Adams greeted Joseph. Quite at home in the printing office, Sam leaned leisurely against Benjamin Edes's desk, his arms folded casually across his chest.

"Thank you for the compliment, Sam, but my visit today is of a professional nature," Joseph replied with a friendly smile.

"Did you make the necessary arrangements, Doctor?" Benjamin Edes asked from his seat at the desk.

"Yes, Dr. Jeffries has agreed to take care of my patients. I plan to leave in about a week."

Sam had a perplexed expression on his face, and then with a smile he asked, "Could there actually be something happening in Boston that I am unaware of?"

Benjamin Edes began to laugh as he reached for the letter Joseph held out to him. "Will wonders never cease? Joseph, you have managed to accomplish something that few can attest to. Quite a feat, Doctor! Quite a feat, indeed!"

Joseph smiled in response. "I'm taking a trip over to Stafford, Connecticut. I want to check out the mineral springs there. They are rumored to have miraculous healing properties."

"I never thought of you as one who believed it that sort of thing," Sam Adams remarked lightly.

"Miracles of God, I do believe in. Miracle cures—well, I will readily admit to being a skeptic. But I cannot deny that such phenomena occur and are even being reported in the latest medical reports out of Europe. My patients are asking me questions about these reported cures from the Stafford waters. So, I believe I owe it to them to check it out."

"How long will you be gone?" asked Edes.

"No longer than a week, Lord willing. I will have a report ready to be printed in the *Gazette* upon my return."

"If you find that the waters do have healing properties, the demand for the Stafford water will be so great here, it will be difficult to keep up the supply," Benjamin exclaimed as he walked toward the press.

"If the reports are true," Joseph began hesitantly, "then I am seriously considering a move for my family to Stafford."

Sam's expression revealed his great alarm at the announcement. "But, Joseph, your services are needed here," he said, standing erect. "Not only as a physician, but also as a leading voice in the cause of liberty. Great Britain is not done with us yet, my friend!"

"Sam, the decision will not be an easy one by any means, and first I must witness these miracle cures for myself. But if it is as rumored, physicians will be needed in Stafford for the throng of people who will flock there for treatment. There will be much to be learned about that water and its effect upon the health of the human body.

"I am still struggling to stay ahead here, Sam," Joseph continued, trying to ease his own feeling of guilt. "As busy as I am, I cannot meet my bills. Many of my patients are unable to pay me, and I cannot live on promissory notes or expect others to live on mine. And, Sam, voices in the cause of liberty are also needed in Connecticut."

"That may be true, Joseph. That may be true. And there are a dozen or more I would gladly send if need be. But you, sir, are not one of them!"

Sam's fears were unfounded. Joseph's trip to Stafford exposed how many desperate people were being deceived. Peddlers sold bottles of the so-called miracle waters at a high price, but Joseph discovered that they were filled with ordinary well water. Had they been filled with the mineral water from the Stafford springs, Joseph concluded that the results would have been no better. After much observation and questioning, he believed there was not enough evidence to substantiate the cures that had been claimed.

Before submitting his report to the newspaper, Joseph called on James Lloyd. After hearing Joseph's findings, the older physician came to the same conclusion.

"I am disappointed," Lloyd said. "I had hoped—against my better judgment—that the stories were true. I have a few patients who are in need of a miracle cure. By the way, have you had a chance to read today's *Gazette?*"

"No. I have not seen it, sir," Joseph replied.

"I usually do not read it anymore—tends to get my blood boiling. Dr. Jeffries subscribes to it and brings one by on occasion."

"John Jeffries's political views are almost identical to yours. Why would he subscribe to the *Gazette?*" Joseph asked.

"It has become somewhat of a hobby for him to try to identify the letters you have written."

Joseph laughed. "Really? Then that means he has to read through every letter printed?"

"It would seem so," Dr. Lloyd replied with a grin. "John is a rather unique fellow."

"That he is."

"The reason he brought the paper by was to show me a letter written about Dr. Young—Thomas Young, that is. Do you know him? He recently moved here from New York."

Joseph nodded his head in acknowledgment. "Yes, sir, I know of him."

"He has been accused of gross negligence by another physician, who used an alias name, of course. According to the letter in the paper, Dr. Young bled to excess a female patient. Her death followed shortly thereafter. Dr. Young's response, if he dares to give one, should be most interesting!"

Thomas Young did respond to the accusation in the days that followed, and he claimed that his patient's death was not related to bloodletting. A war of words between the two doctors ensued, causing the physicians of Boston to take sides in the argument. From the contents of the letters, Joseph decided that Young's defense was weak and his knowledge and ability to practice medicine questionable.

As Joseph's opinions of the controversy began to appear in the *Gazette* under the name Philo Physic, Young's attention turned from his original accuser to this new one. For every defense that Young put forth, Joseph had a refutation. Joseph's attacks became more direct, his accusations bolder. His attempts to expose errors in the medical field were no less charged with fervor than were his attempts to expose the errors of Parliament.

He accused Young of neglecting to continue his medical studies once his formal education was completed and of having little knowledge in the procedure of blood-letting. Joseph emphasized that the procedure should be done only when necessary, and then only in moderate amounts. Philo Physic's position was that Dr. Young was incompetent and had, in fact, bled his patient to death.

Dr. Young was infuriated by the remarks, especially as he began to lose patients. When he discovered that Philo Physic was Joseph Warren, he threatened legal action. Young made it clear that he intended to sue Joseph for ruining his reputation as a physician in Boston.

The citizens of Boston awaited Joseph's response to the threat of a lawsuit. Outwardly, he showed no sign of concern. He had written what he believed to be the truth and saw no reason to fear punishment for it.

The grand finale to the Young–Warren controversy occurred with Philo Physic's letter in response to the threatened lawsuit. Dr. Young's threats to sue Joseph for damaging his reputation simply brought his challenge to Dr. Thomas Young. "Prove you had a reputation to damage." No charges were ever filed, and Dr. Young kept his distance from Joseph, who was content to let the relationship continue at that level.

"Come in, Joseph. Make yourself comfortable. I will be with you in a minute," Samuel Quincy said, standing before his law desk. He gestured to an easy chair positioned alongside the Chippendale secretary on the opposite end of the room.

Joseph smiled at the young boy at Samuel's side. Probably no more than ten years old, the skinny, ragged child eagerly anticipated the minuscule fee he would receive for delivering the attorney's message.

"Take this to the Province House. The governor is awaiting it. See that you hand it to the governor's secretary. Do you understand?"

"Yes sir." The child took the sealed letter and the payment for his service. "Thank you, sir!"

"Joseph, have you spoken to any member of the Long Room Club this morning?" There was an air of confidence in Samuel's manner. His large, warm eyes and handsome, well-defined features complemented his magnetic personality. He walked toward Joseph and seated himself at the secretary. He held a document in his hand.

"No. I spent the night treating a patient in Dedham. I feared I would miss this appointment, Samuel."

"We will get to the Wheelright matter," Samuel said, laying his hand on the pile of neatly stacked papers on the desk. "But first I think you might want to take a look at this." He handed Joseph the paper in his hand.

Occasional involuntary sighs were Joseph's response as he read through the document. "When did this arrive?" he asked, passing the paper back to Samuel with a trembling hand.

"The ship docked at first light. Sam Adams has called for a meeting at the long room tonight."

Joseph's glassy eyes looked straight ahead as the shock of the news sank in.

Samuel looked down at the paper. "Well, at least Lord Townshend had enough of a backbone to identify himself as the creator of this latest atrocity! Sam Adams warned us that additional violations would come. I had begun to believe it was over."

"That is because they've given us more than a year's reprieve since the Stamp Act's repeal," Joseph began. The glassiness of his eyes began to fade, and he reached for the paper on Samuel's lap. "The taxes herein are grievous—but we can simply boycott the items listed—glass, lead, paper, paint, tea. They know we are capable of enduring the inconvenience. They know that a boycott is probable."

Joseph fixed his eyes on his friend's. "Samuel, it is not the tax they are after. What they are attempting to do by demanding that our appointed officials be paid by the Crown, rather than by the people they serve, is quite obvious. If a dog will not bite the hand that feeds it, then, given the nature of man, he will want to please the source of his support, be it the people or the Crown. And so, any governor, judge, or sheriff who has convictions and does not support British policy will be quickly replaced by one who does. This situation is terrifying!"

"You are right. It is. We must pray for men who will not be compromised to fill these positions. One already has."

"What position? By whom?" Joseph asked.

"I have been offered the position of solicitor general," Samuel replied. He stood and walked back to the law desk where he retrieved another paper and handed it over to Joseph.

The expression on Joseph's face was obviously not what Samuel Quincy had anticipated.

"Joseph, it is a vital position. I can oversee the rights of the individual in the court system."

"What of your law practice?" Joseph asked.

"I will have to give it up."

Joseph stood and moved behind the chair. His knuckles turned white as he grabbed hold of the wooden back. "Then your sole support will come from the Crown?"

Samuel did not respond.

"Do you not see what they are doing, Samuel? Remember when Hutchinson appointed me administrator of the Wheelright case?" He gestured to the pile of papers on Samuel's desk. "Your response then was that you would not let Hutchinson have me that easily."

"I will still offer you counsel in regard to the Wheelright case. I have already discussed it with my brother Josiah. You know Josiah. He is willing to help with this case. He promises to be a brilliant attorney."

"It is not the Wheelright case that I am concerned about, Samuel! I know I can get help with that. I am concerned about you! If there is a risk that Hutchinson can influence me by that appointment, how much greater is the risk of influencing you with such an illustrious position from the Crown?

"Joseph, it was obvious what I should do. I have already made my decision," his obstinate reply came.

"The boy?" Joseph exclaimed, looking toward the door.

"Yes. By now the governor has my reply. And Joseph, I have no doubt but that it was the right thing to do!"

Joseph watched the interaction of the Quincy brothers as they discussed the legal papers before them. The love they shared toward each other was evident, as well as Josiah's admiration for Sam. Beyond the similar features and fair coloring, which hinted at their relationship, the differences between the brothers were vast.

Samuel's build was as sturdy as Josiah's was frail. Sam's ruddy complexion made his younger brother's to appear paler still. Even with the disparity of ten years, Josiah's chronic ill health caused him to look much older than his twenty-two years. And, as Samuel's love of liberty began to wane, Josiah's only intensified.

"Josiah will submit the papers to the court tomorrow" Samuel said as he stood from the seat by the desk. "You will be expected to be present, but that will be the extent of it." He walked toward the door where vacant side chairs lined the wall waiting to seat the next day's patients. From one of the chairs he picked up his greatcoat, tricorn, and cane.

"Certainly this will not be the end of the bankruptcy case, but I am sure John Adams will be of assistance. I doubt Otis can be depended on anymore," he commented in reference to James Otis's mounting mental instability. "With the load of my current duties, I will not be able to offer you any more time."

"I did not expect you would be able to, Samuel," Joseph replied, getting up from his seat behind his desk and walking toward him. "And I want you to know how much I appreciate your help thus far. Thank you." He extended his hand, his eyes fixed on those of his friend.

"You are welcome, Doctor." Samuel returned the handshake.

"I have missed seeing you at the meetings. Will you be able to attend next week?"

Samuel turned away, reaching for the door. "I will try, Doctor. I will try. I will see you at service on Sunday." And with that he left.

Josiah appeared uncomfortable. "I should be on my way and let you get home to your family."

"My dear wife is accustomed to having me out anymore," Joseph mumbled, pulling a gold pocket watch from his waistcoat to check the time. "It is still early. We really have not had time to sit and get acquainted. Are you married, Mr. Quincy?"

"No sir. I am not."

"Are you living at your father's estate in Braintree now that your apprenticeship is complete?" Joseph asked, having already observed that Josiah's left eye did not seem to move. The physician part of him wondered if his vision was impaired.

"Yes, sir. I am. It is a fair commute from Boston to Braintree, but I'm sure you are quite familiar with it," Josiah commented, aware that Joseph had a number of patients in Braintree, including his father and stepmother.

"I heard you ask my brother to attend the next meeting. I assume you mean the Long Room Club?"

Joseph did not respond, though his countenance revealed his surprise.

"Samuel told me about it. He has told others as well. He will not be back. He warned me not to get involved should I ever be invited to attend."

Still Joseph did not respond.

Josiah appeared more than uncomfortable. His one good eye focused aimlessly on different objects in the surgery as he fumbled for something to say to break the awkward silence.

"It seems that the atmosphere in the Province House is extremely tense now that Governor Bernard has nullified the recent vote of the seven men elected to the General Court," he finally offered.

"All seven are members of the Sons of Liberty," Joseph quickly pointed out.

"As am I," Josiah stated.

Joseph nodded in silent acknowledgement.

"I fear the governor has gone beyond his authority in nullifying these appointments. The people are right to voice their protests. It seems that Governor Bernard is trying to determine who he can trust in his administration. Solicitor General Samuel Quincy longs for the approval of the governor, and therefore has come to believe that we, being subjects of the Crown, must submit to its every decree. He is no longer one of you—"

Joseph detected a tear in the young attorney's weak eye.

"And I pray that his betrayal shall not reflect on the patriotism of my dear father or myself, Dr. Warren."

"I tell you, I don't know who left that letter here," Benjamin Edes repeated for the third time. "I found it on my desk, read it, and printed it!"

The mystery author who signed himself Hyperion did much to stir the people of Boston against the Townshend Act. Yet, every member of the Long Room Club, the primary writers of such stirring material, denied being the author. Certainly the style of this author was different from any of the members of the group. This mystery writer's work was not so wordy as that of John Adams, nor as dramatic as John Hancock's, nor was it as straightforward as that of Joseph Warren's. But with a soothing manner, he captured his audience.

"Joseph, leave your letter on my desk. I'll take care of it in the morning," Benjamin instructed.

Joseph nodded without looking up from his work.

"Sam, I'm going home. When you and the doctor are finished, will you please lock up?"

"Of course, Benjamin. And you are certain you have no idea who left that letter?"

"Oh, Sam—" Benjamin moaned as he left the room.

"Finished," Joseph announced. "How shall I sign myself this time?" he asked, not really expecting any reply from Sam. Then deciding on an assumed name, he sealed the letter.

"I am totally baffled. No one knows who this Hyperion is. How could such a talent escape my notice?" Sam said as he shook his head in disbelief while straightening out the pile of papers before him.

"Listen to this," Sam said as he began to read a portion of the mystery letter. "'When they endeavor to make us perceive our inability to oppose our mother country, let us boldly answer; "In defense of our civil and religious right, we dare oppose the world; with the God of armies on our side, even the God who fought our fathers' battles, we fear not the hour of trial, though the hosts of our enemies should cover the field like locust." If this be enthusiasm, we will live and die enthusiasts.'"

Sam gently placed the paper down on the table. Then, looking up at Joseph, he exclaimed, "We must find this man!"

Joseph fixed his gaze upon his friend, and with a teasing smile he rhythmically tapped his own letter against the table. "I know who he is, Sam. I have been waiting for the others to leave so that we might discuss the matter in private."

"Is this your work?" Sam appeared surprised at the thought.

"No. I wish I had such ability. The credit belongs to Josiah Quincy."

"Any relation to our illustrious solicitor general?" Sam asked sarcastically.

"His younger brother."

"Ah—" Sam was thoughtful. "Can he be trusted?" he asked with squinted eyes.

"He is Hyperion. You read what he believes," Joseph replied, pointing to the letter Sam had been so inspired by.

"His brother once claimed to hold similar beliefs."

"Let us not judge Josiah by his brother's lack of convictions. Both Josiah and his father are committed to the cause of liberty," Joseph insisted. "He took it upon himself to assist me in the Wheelright bankruptcy when Samuel bailed out."

"Josiah Quincy—was he the young man who gave that stirring oration on patriotism at the Harvard commencement recently?"

"Recently?" Joseph asked with a laugh. "Sam, that was two years ago. Yes, that was him."

"I have been so busy that I had forgotten about that promising lad. A Boston Cicero!" Sam exclaimed, annoyed at himself for his oversight. "I have never heard a man speak as he did that day. His voice was so commanding, so loud, and yet, not at all strained. No, I take that back," Sam said with a far-off expression upon his face. "I have heard one other with such ability to project his voice: George Whitefield."

This name was quite familiar to Joseph. The story of this remarkable minister and the effect of his preaching on the inhabitants of Boston during the Great

Awakening was well known. His own parents, newlyweds at the time, had been among the 15,000 that had flocked to the Boston Common to hear him.

"Ah, but that was before your time, my boy. We will have to talk at length one day about the Reverend Whitefield. I understand he resides in New Hampshire now. Bring the young Mr. Quincy to our next meeting, will you?"

Elizabeth moved as quickly as her advanced stage of pregnancy would allow, opening the front door before the second knock.

"Mrs. Warren, good day to you," Sam Adams greeted her with a warm smile as he and Josiah Quincy tipped their hats. "May we speak to your husband, Madam?"

"Could you possibly discuss your business with him this evening, gentlemen? He is resting now," she replied, determined to protect Joseph from any unnecessary interruptions.

"Mrs. Warren," Josiah began in his soft, gentle manner. "It is important that we speak to him now."

"I hesitate to disturb him," she replied apologetically. "He was out all night attending a birth and all morning on house calls. He is quite exhausted," Elizabeth paused, but the two showed no sign of leaving. "How important is it?" she asked.

"Extremely important," Josiah assured her.

Elizabeth looked back toward the staircase and sighed. "Come in out of the cold, gentlemen, and I will awaken him. Please make yourselves comfortable," she said as she left the men in the parlor and went to get Joseph.

Sam and Josiah took off their winter wraps, draping them neatly over an easy chair near the entrance of the parlor. Josiah sat down on the settee, seemingly weakened by periodic bouts of coughing, while Sam wandered toward the open secretary across the room, drawn by a book that lay on top.

"Dr. Warren will be down in a few minutes, Elizabeth asked upon her return. "May I get you some tea?" Both men thanked for her hospitality.

Soon Joseph entered the parlor fumbling with the buttons on his shirtsleeves. His frock coat lay draped over one arm. Josiah and Sam were both surprised by how much younger he seemed when his natural blond hair was exposed, not being powdered or styled in his usual manner.

"Good afternoon, gentlemen," he greeted his unexpected guests with a tired smile as he put on his frock coat. Josiah began to cough. "Be certain not to leave until I give you something for that."

Sam walked to the settee and sat down next to Josiah as Joseph seated himself in the easy chair facing them.

"We are sorry to disturb your sleep, but—" Sam began, stopping when Elizabeth entered the room.

She carefully placed a steaming pot of tea on the side table as Sam went on to comment about the book he had just browsed. After pouring tea for each of them, Elizabeth left, softly closing the parlor door behind her. Only then did Sam return to the explanation of why they were there.

"Have you heard about the possible lawsuit being brought against the *Gazette?*"

Still groggy from lack of sleep, Joseph was sipping from the steaming cup of tea in an attempt to become more alert. Between sips, he shook his head in the negative.

"All of Boston is talking about it," Sam paused as if unsure whether Joseph was alert enough to comprehend what was being said.

"Governor Bernard is distraught over a letter that he claims was an attack against him. He is determined to have the author of this letter, alias True Patriot, exposed to the public by the owners of the *Gazette.*"

Joseph glanced at the parlor door to make certain it was closed tightly. Placing the cup and saucer on a small table next to the chair, he waited for Sam to continue.

"Your name is being linked to the letter. Who revealed your identity, I don't know!"

Then, in a reassuring tone, Josiah spoke. "Mr. Edes and Mr. Gill came to my office as soon as they were officially notified. They said they would not admit to your being the author, even if brought before the General Court."

"Your advice on how to proceed, gentlemen," Joseph calmly responded.

"If Edes and Gill hold out, as I am certain they will, then there is no problem. Bernard cannot sue you because you are the rumored author. Beside that, nowhere in the letter is either Bernard's name or office mentioned. This may become a fierce battle of words and threats, but keep calm, my friend, and it will pass," Josiah advised.

"Another thing," Sam added. "The closing remark in the letter has been grotesquely misunderstood by many of its readers. There is great agitation over your concluding rhyming couplet: 'If such men are by God appointed, the devil may be the Lord's anointed.' Relating our governor to Satan is being viewed as profanity. You may want to clarify this in another letter to the *Gazette.*"

"Has Parson Cooper been made aware of this?" Joseph asked, curious about the parson's reaction.

"Yes, we discussed it this morning. He is not surprised by Bernard's reaction any more than I am. Even though you exercised wise caution in not referring to the governor by name or position, one would have to be a fool not to know that the letter was about him. No one has dared to publicly rebuke his misdealing so forcefully as you did, and Bernard is in a rage. But you apparently anticipated such a reaction," Sam stated, noting how relaxed Joseph appeared as he spoke.

"Bernard's threats do not bother me. I did not say anything that was not true, and Bernard knows it to be so. So does every man in this colony. What troubles me is the accusation of profanity on my part. Gentlemen, I never intended to be profane. How did the parson react to this?" Joseph's countenance changed even as he spoke, revealing his deep concern over the accusation.

"He fully understood your meaning and gave the couplet a hearty 'Amen!'" Sam replied with a comforting smile. "A second letter to clarify the questionable point will serve a good purpose."

"I will seek Parson Cooper's advice on how to best clarify my meaning. True Patriot's next letter will be at the *Gazette* office as soon as possible," Joseph assured them as they stood to leave. He turned to Josiah, who was coughing again, and said, "You have had that cough for quite a while now, Josiah. Let me examine you."

"No, no—do not waste your time! It is only a cold," Josiah assured him.

Joseph got up and went into the foyer. He quickly returned with his medical bag and pulled out a bottle of elixir and handed it to Josiah. "Take a tablespoonful every six hours or so. It should help that cough."

"Thank you. And what do I owe you for it?" Josiah asked.

"Nothing. Gentlemen, thank you for bringing this matter to my attention," Joseph said politely as he walked his friends to the door. Turning toward the kitchen, he quickly reviewed in his mind how he would break the news to Elizabeth before she heard it from someone else.

In his anger over the letter, Governor Bernard immediately sent messages to both chambers of the General Court: the House of Representatives and the Governor's Council. Bernard stated to them that the article by the True Patriot was libelous, and he demanded that measures be taken against the author.

While the town officials busied themselves on determining what to do with the True Patriot case, Joseph had another letter published in the *Gazette*. In addressing the charge of profanity, he stated: "My design was to compare wicked men, and especially wicked magistrates, to those enemies of mankind, the devils; and to intimate that the devils themselves might boast of divine authority to seduce and ruin mankind, with as much reason and justice as wicked rulers can pretend to derive from God or from His Word a right to oppress, harass, and enslave their fellow creatures. The beneficent Lord of the universe delights in viewing the happiness of all men. And so far as civil government is of divine institution, it was calculated for the greatest good of the whole community; and whenever it ceases to be of general advantage, it ceases to be of divine appointment, and the magistrates in such a community have no claim to that honor which the Divine Legislator has assigned to magistrates of His election."

Urging the town officials to judge the case before them righteously, he ended his appeal with these words: "I shall, at all times, write my sentiments with freedom, and with decency, too—the rules of which I am not altogether unacquainted with. While the press is open, I shall publish whatever I think conducive to general emolument; when it is suppressed, I shall look upon my country as lost and with a steady fortitude, expect to feel the general shock. —A True Patriot."

In spite of Joseph's appeal, the Governor's Council pronounced the first letter to be insulting and profane. They felt that the author deserved punishment.

The House of Representatives disagreed with this decision. They declared that the liberty of the press was a great bulwark of the liberty of the people. When the case was introduced to the grand jury, they refused to indict the True Patriot.

• 6 •

British Occupation

A SOFT KNOCK on the bedchamber door roused Joseph from his sleep, and he threw on his robe before going out into the hallway to speak with his apprentice. Elizabeth stirred when he returned. Quietly he began to dress by the dim light of a single candle.

"What time is it?" Elizabeth whispered drowsily.

"Eleven o'clock," he whispered back, trying not to disturb the sleeping children.

"Oh, Joseph," she moaned, "here you have a free night to get to bed early and you are called out. Who needs you tonight?"

He hesitated before answering. Her concern for his need to rest was greatly appreciated. She would not be at all pleased to learn that this house call was not of a medical nature.

"I am going over to the Hancock mansion," he answered, lowering his voice as little Josey stirred.

"Is Miss Lydia ill?" Elizabeth inquired.

"No. No one is ill. John and Sam have been discussing the seizure of Hancock's sloop, Liberty. It would seem that John has changed his mind on how he wants to handle the situation."

"In the middle of the night?" Elizabeth exclaimed, causing the baby to awaken. "Surely they can wait until the morning to discuss this with you!"

"The night is still young as far as John and Sam are concerned. And apparently they cannot wait until morning," Joseph reached into the cradle and gently lifted his crying son. "Shh, before you awaken your sister," he whispered to little Josey as he handed the hungry baby to his mother. "You cannot blame me for awakening him tonight," he said with a smile.

"You are not at all disturbed about being summoned from a sound sleep to hear Mr. Hancock's and Mr. Adam's latest ideas. In fact, you enjoy it, don't you?"

As Joseph buttoned up his waistcoat, he pretended not to hear her, but his grin revealed the truth.

"Did John Hancock smuggle cargo into Boston aboard that sloop?" Elizabeth asked bluntly.

"Rumor has it that he did," Joseph replied with a wink.

"How in the world did he get it past the tax collectors?" she asked.

"The captain of the *Liberty* had the tax collector locked in one of the cabins while the smuggled cargo was unloaded. The fact that Hancock smuggles cargo to avoid the tax is not at issue here. We are aware that he smuggled it. This is his only means of avoiding a tax that he believes to be unjust and unlawful. It would be far easier for a man like him to pay the tax and be done with it than to run the risk of being caught."

Joseph went to the dressing table and lit the candles on either side. Then picking up the brush, he began to pull back his loose hair into his typical neat queue as he continued to speak. "He does it because he stands on the principle that he is an Englishman with the rights of an Englishman. He will not willingly submit to their arbitrary controls, no matter how much easier that would be. The issue here is the seizure of the Liberty. They have no proof that John smuggled in cargo, and yet they seized the sloop. The manner in which it was seized was in violation of law. This is the issue we hope to proceed with in court—that is, if John agrees to go forward with it."

"If he agrees?" Elizabeth asked.

"Yes," Joseph answered, grabbing his frock coat from the chair. "As of this afternoon, he planned to pay the fee and have the sloop released. To have her out of commission will cut heavily into his profits. As a business decision, freeing the sloop would be a wise move."

"But you do not agree with that decision?" Elizabeth asked.

"It really is of no matter whether or not I agree. It is John's business and John's neck in the noose."

Elizabeth was obviously startled by his choice of words. "Joseph!" she gasped.

"A poor choice of words. I am sorry," he replied.

"And what of the rumored arrest warrants for Mr. Adams and Mr. Hancock?"

"They are no more than rumors. I do not want you to worry about them," he offered, attempting to calm her. "This summons to the Hancock mansion leads me to believe that Sam was able to convince John to let the British keep the sloop and go to court over it. Elizabeth, we could not have planned it better ourselves. The people are becoming more infuriated every time they pass by the harbor and view the Hancock sloop. There—plain to the view of all—is the mighty British man-of-war Romney, sent to seize and chain the small, defenseless sloop *Liberty* beneath her guns. The scene in the harbor symbolizes our present struggle: Great Britain has us bound in chains."

"I still do not understand why you have to go over there tonight!" Elizabeth protested.

"To be the mediator. I told the tax commissioner that John would be paying the fine tomorrow. Since the plans have apparently changed, he will need to be informed."

"He will be quite upset at being disturbed from a sound sleep," she said.

"Ah—" Joseph began with a chuckle. "I am sure he does not sleep too soundly. I do not believe there is a British-appointed tax collector throughout the American colonies who sleeps soundly. Their consciences will not allow it." Little Betsey sat up in the trundle bed on the floor, blond curls flowing from her nightcap.

"Papa, is it morning time?" the two-year-old girl asked, rubbing her eyes.

"No, Angel, it is not morning yet," he tenderly replied as he lifted the little girl from her bed. "Elizabeth, do you have room for one more?" he asked, tucking Betsey in beside her brother. Kissing all three, he said, "Sleep well. I will see you in the morning." He extinguished the candles on the dressing table. Then taking the single candle from the nightstand in one hand and his shoes in the other, he left his family in the darkness to resume their peaceful slumber.

As he walked across the Common, Joseph reflected on the incident that had occurred there only a few nights earlier. Upon hearing that the *Liberty* had been seized, the Sons of Liberty had become enraged. They were driven by riotous anger as they had been two years earlier when the homes of the revenue officer and Lieutenant Governor Thomas Hutchinson were attacked.

The patriot leaders had heard that a riot was threatening, and they quickly moved into action in an attempt to restrain the violent mob. Joseph, Sam Adams, Parson Cooper, and some others had arrived where the crowd had gathered on the Common and quickly evaluated the situation.

The mob had pulled a pleasure boat belonging to one of the tax commissioners onto the Common. They formed a circle about the boat and proceeded to set it on fire, shouting with excitement as it became engulfed in flames.

When Sam Adams began to speak, the mob became silent. "We will defend our liberties and property by the strength of our arm and the help of our God. Now you should go to your homes!" With these words, the crowd dispersed.

Rumor had it that Governor Bernard and many prominent Tories were requesting military protection from Great Britain. It was said that they feared more rioting, and their only protection would be the king's troops in Boston.

But Joseph did not believe the rumors. The incident a few nights earlier was minor, having been quickly brought under control. Certainly it did not warrant such an outrageous request for military protection.

The first rays of the autumn sun peeked over the eastern horizon. Boston's harbor always appeared peaceful at this early hour, and the blazing beauty of the rising sun enflamed the still ocean water.

Joseph stood on Long Wharf, his gaze fixed upon the harbor, yet its brilliance went unnoticed. Overcome with a sense of horror and anger, he viewed the newly anchored British warships.

The arrival of the eleven men-of-war had occurred the previous afternoon. He had been on a house call until after dark, and in the early morning light he witnessed the fearful sight for himself.

These mighty warships of the most powerful navy on earth had been sent to Boston, not to defend the colonies of the mother country but to police her harbors. Officers and enlisted men of the king's army had been unloaded from six ships. They came ashore to enact their orders as a police force on the streets of the "rebellious" port town.

"There are many in Boston and throughout the colonies who would blame us for this atrocity," declared a voice from behind Joseph.

Startled, he turned to find Josiah Quincy.

"I tossed and turned the entire night wondering whether they could be right," Josiah added.

Joseph knew the "us" Josiah spoke of were the more outspoken and active patriot leaders of Boston.

"They claim that we went too far in our opposition to the Townshend Act," Josiah continued. "We did not gain much popularity over the pathetic picture painted by the tax collectors and their families—even when Governor Bernard fled to Castle Island in fear of the 'Sons of Perdition,' as they enjoy calling us. Their plea to Great Britain for military protection because of the *Liberty* incident was quite dramatic."

"Grotesquely exaggerated, I will grant you that," returned Joseph, disgusted at the thought of it. "The Sons were angry over the sloop's seizure and by the fact that many of us were threatened with being arrested for our so-called sedition. But their anger was quickly brought under control."

"Sedition," Josiah repeated with a tone of disbelief. "We are accused of high treason for demanding our birthright. Again they violate the rights of Englishmen by sending a standing army in a time of peace, yet we are accused of sedition for speaking against such violations! Joseph, how do we make them understand? How do we get them to listen to us?"

"What was your conclusion this morning, Josiah, after tossing all night?"

Joseph asked, not really expecting an answer. "Are we to blame?" At the moment he, too, was uncertain.

"How long ago did your family settled here?" Josiah asked. Though the question confused him, Joseph answered without hesitation.

"More than a century ago."

"Mine, too. They did not find a thriving port town but were faced with hostilities and hardships to which we are totally unaccustomed. They did not even have the support of Great Britain. She scorned them, but by the grace of God, they managed to establish this colony. They longed for the blessing and affection of the mother country, which only came, so it seemed, when it discovered there was a potential for profit. Now that is not even enough, and Great Britain intends to bleed us dry." Josiah gazed out at the warships. "We are the sons of Great Britain, not her bastards, and certainly not her slaves!"

Sharing Josiah's grief, Joseph fixed his gaze on the warships. "We will not concede to a position less than that of a true son, nor willingly submit to shackles, not as long as the Puritan blood of our ancestors and their love for liberty still flows through our veins! Would to God this problem could be solved peacefully and quickly!"

Life in Boston changed dramatically. The townspeople watched helplessly as British soldiers encamped on the Boston Common, a favorite leisure area for the town. Winter quarters were established in Faneuil Hall, the public meeting place, as well as in several merchant warehouses.

The main guard was posted just outside the Province House. Two cannons were positioned, ready at all times to fire upon the colony's seat of government if necessary. This constant threat caused great anxiety for the members of the General Court.

The youngsters of Boston watched the soldiers with wide-eyed excitement, easily impressed in their innocence by the colorful uniforms, military expertise, and first-class weaponry. Lifestyles and habits that had been previously viewed as unacceptable to the Puritan community were now blatantly displayed by the troops, enticing their young admirers to imitate their behavior.

Street brawls became commonplace as soldiers and citizens clashed. Both married and unmarried women found it unsafe to walk the streets alone. Passes were required for those who went out of Boston, and curfews were put into effect. Anyone caught out on the streets after hours was harassed by the soldiers.

Day after day the Sons of Liberty faced this occupation. Unable to rectify it, they patiently waited, continuing to submit their pleas for justice to Great Britain. The secret meetings of the Long Room Club continued, and the newspapers continued to print articles defending liberty, freedom, and the rights of Englishmen. And some merchants even continued to smuggle in goods.

Joseph's newborn daughter squalled as he wrapped a blanket securely around her tiny body. When he lifted her, the crying ceased. Suddenly he realized that his hands were trembling as he held his daughter close to his chest.

Just a few moments earlier he had been working against time trying to get her to take her first breath. The listless, white body he had held in his hands only a few moments ago was now lively and pink.

Feeling the stillness in the room, he took a moment to offer a silent prayer of thanks. Though his back was to Elizabeth and his mother, he could sense their apprehensive gaze. They waited, too frightened to speak.

What am I to tell Elizabeth, Joseph wondered? Should I pretend that all is well, sparing her further concern over the baby? Or should I be honest with her from the start?

The child was weak due to her premature birth. Such small, fragile babies seldom survived infancy, but this little one was a fighter. He had already witnessed that.

Joseph turned to face his wife. Walking to the bed, he gently placed the baby beside her. "She is every bit as beautiful as her mother," he said with a tired, weak smile.

Elizabeth stared intently at the little bundle in her arms, her first look at the child she had just given birth to. She then turned her gaze on Joseph. He could see the longing in her eyes for him to reassure her that all was well. Try as he might, he could not hide the anguish he felt.

"She is so tiny," Elizabeth said softly, finally breaking the silence.

Joseph stroked a dark curl on the nursing baby's head. "Her lungs are strong. Often such small ones have great difficulty because their lungs are underdeveloped. But little Mary has a good, strong cry. We must be sure to keep her warm," he continued. "In the midst of winter in this drafty house, it will not be easy. She is to be bundled with a cap on her head at all times." He looked up at his mother who stood at the bottom of the bed. She immediately picked up a small woolen cap from the dressing table and handed it to her son. Gently, Joseph slipped it over the baby's head.

"Keep her cradle close to the hearth. Always change her there." Then grasping Elizabeth's hand he added, "We will keep her warm while you fatten her up, and all of us will pray, my darling."

With the arrival of spring, hope for Mary's survival was renewed within the Warren home. As blossoms burst forth in radiant color and trees once again draped themselves in delicate green, the cold dead of winter was quickly replaced with warmth and life.

But the change in the weather had no positive affect on little Mary Warren. She gained weight slowly, her small body still weak and frail.

On many occasions Joseph would awaken during the night to discover that Elizabeth was not beside him. In the darkness he would see the silhouette of her figure against the moonlit sky, kneeling beside the cradle. Gently the grieving mother would caress her sleeping child.

He longed to go to Elizabeth, to hold her in his arms and promise her that Mary would be well. He wanted to take the child, whom he so loved, and somehow transfer some of his strength into her weakened body. But he could do neither.

In the stillness he watched helplessly as his beloved wife stole a quiet moment to be alone with the child who she knew would soon be gone from her. In a torment that only a parent could fathom, he pleaded with heaven for the wisdom needed to save Mary's life.

Such wisdom was not granted, and it was with heavy hearts that Joseph and Elizabeth Warren laid their infant daughter to her eternal rest.

Governor Francis Bernard hastily left Boston in the summer of 1769, having been summoned to appear before King George III. There and before the members of Parliament, he would give his biased view of the situation in Boston. The names and activities of leaders such as Otis, Adams, Warren, and Hancock would be blamed.

It was not long before rumors began to circulate that the leaders of the Sons of Liberty would soon be arrested. James Otis's name headed the list of offenders who were to be shipped to Great Britain for trial.

The strain of this, coupled with the harassment by British officers and Tory newspapers, was more than poor Otis could endure. Already showing signs of distress, he became an even greater object of his friends' concern as his symptoms intensified.

"Elizabeth, we are home!" Joseph called up the stairs as Lemuel and he placed their hats and medical bags on the foyer table. Entering the kitchen, they began to serve themselves from the pots Elizabeth kept warm above the fire.

"Have you seen Sam Adams?" Elizabeth asked breathlessly on entering the kitchen.

"No, what has happened?" he asked, noting the fear in her eyes.

"It is James Otis. It seems he went to the Royal Coffeehouse earlier this evening. He was rambling on when he got there, demanding an apology from a Tory by the name of Robinson for accusing him of being disloyal to the king!"

Joseph sighed deeply. James's lapses from reality were becoming more frequent. No Son of Liberty in his right mind would enter the Royal Coffee House, for the more distinguished Tories and British officers gathered there in their leisure time.

"In a rage, Robinson attacked Mr. Otis. Some of the officers joined in. The tables were knocked over and the candles with them." Joseph reached out a comforting hand to his wife as her voice began to tremble and tears began to fall.

"A gentleman passing by, one of the Sons, entered the darkened tavern when he heard the sounds of furniture breaking. He found Robinson and the others beating poor Mr. Otis with their canes. Somehow he managed to pull him out, but not before having his own wrist broken. Two gentlemen came by looking for you to tend to Mr. Otis. I'm sorry, I do not know who they were."

"What time did this happen?" he asked, struggling to restrain his anger.

"Around eight o'clock."

"Do you know the extent of James's injuries?"

"They said his skull was laid open."

"I am going over there to check on him. Do not wait up for me, Elizabeth. I may spend the night." Turning to his apprentice, he said, "Mr. Haywood, finish eating and get some sleep. If I'm needed, you know where to find me."

He returned his hat to his head and took hold of his medical bag. Catching a glimpse of his own walking cane propped against the wall, Joseph grabbed it and went out into the darkened streets.

The head injuries that James Otis received from the attack pushed him even further from reality. If during the attack the candles had not been knocked over and the room darkened, Joseph believed that more accurate blows would have killed him.

James was now lost in a world of his own, coming back to reality only for brief periods. To make matters worse, he now reacted violently in his confusion.

Joseph had always suspected that James's wife was partly to blame for his distress. She was a Tory, and she made sure everyone knew that her political opinions differed from those of her husband. Now she was making plans to have her seriously ill and injured husband moved to the country. With him out of the way, she could proceed with the plans she had threatened for so long: marrying off their daughters to Tory gentlemen.

"Dr. Warren!" John Adams called to him from across the street where Josiah Quincy, John Hancock, and he stood.

"Good afternoon, Doctor," the short, stout John Adams addressed Joseph as he approached them. "Will you join us for dinner? Josiah and I have to discuss with you some details concerning your next court appearance in the Wheelright case. And, as for Jay," he said, grinning at John Hancock, "he can just endure the conversation for a while and then pick up the tab."

"Indeed, Doctor, do join us!" John Hancock jovially said, always eager to entertain his friends.

"Thank you, John. Tell me, how did things go today, gentlemen?" Joseph asked, aware that the three of them had appeared in court that morning in regard to the seizure of the *Liberty*.

"About as we expected," John Adams replied. "This is going to take time to straighten out. Much time, I'm afraid. And I'm not sure that Jay here can take the pressure," he said, smiling at his childhood friend.

"Come, gentlemen, let's eat," John Hancock insisted, ignoring the last remark.

As the men were about to enter the Bunch of Grapes Tavern, Joseph hesitated, reaching out and placing his hand on Josiah's arm.

"Josiah, is that Robinson across the street?" he asked, peering in the direction he had indicated.

"Yes, that's him," Josiah answered bitterly.

"Excuse me for a minute, gentlemen," Joseph said as he left his friends where they stood.

With long and purposeful strides he crossed the cobblestoned street, dodging the traffic. Before his friends had the opportunity to respond, Joseph was alongside the infamous tax collector. Quite unexpectedly, he grabbed Robinson by the arm and pulled him into a nearby alley, pinning him up against the brick wall.

"So I finally get the opportunity to confront the scoundrel who delights in beating invalids when the odds are so much in his favor. Your courage overwhelms me, Mr. Robinson!" Joseph's fierce anger was evident in his voice. "How about if we even the odds a bit, eh, Robinson?" he exclaimed as people began to gather around them. "You and me. Your choice of weapons—bare fists if you prefer! Oh, but your skill is best noted in your use of a cane, isn't it?" Joseph shouted, yanking the cane from Robinson's hand and snapping it in two over his knee. He tossed the pieces to the ground.

"Dr. Warren! Let go of him!" Josiah urged as he pushed through the crowd with Hancock and Adams close behind.

"Joseph!" came the soothing voice again. "This is not the way to settle it. When Mr. Otis is recovered, we'll take Robinson and the others to court," Josiah assured him, laying his hand on his friend's arm.

"He will never recover—never!" Joseph said in despair. The mind which Joseph and the others had so admired was now gone forever.

"Whether or not Mr. Otis recovers, we will settle this matter in court," John Adams promised, trying to reassure and dissuade him at the same time. Joseph loosened his hold on Robinson's shoulders but kept a tight grasp on the frightened man's coat sleeve.

"My offer still holds, Robinson—you and me," he snarled through clenched teeth.

Robinson managed to pull his coat free of Joseph's grasp and quickly disappeared into the crowd, leaving the pieces of his cane scattered on the ground.

Making his way through the throng of people that had gathered, Joseph and his friends headed back toward the tavern.

James Otis's case did go to court. The circumstances of the attack were such that the court quickly ruled in his favor. The judge ruled that the offenders were to pay a large sum of money in retribution for the injuries suffered, but to the bewilderment of all, James vehemently insisted that all he would take was enough to pay his friends for their medical and legal assistance.

· 7 ·

The Massacre

WITH A GOOD bit of maneuvering, Jack managed to place his chin firmly on the formidable pile of books he was carrying and also shift the worn and overstuffed carpetbag from one hand to the other. With an arm free, now he could easily grab hold of the doorknob.

To his delight and surprise, the waiting area was vacant. With a thud, he dropped the heavy load onto one of the empty side chairs lining the wall.

Joseph and his apprentice, Lemuel Haywood, quickly appeared at the threshold of the examination room. There they found the sixteen-year-old, adorned in his college gown, gathering the books that had spilled onto the floor.

"Jack, what are you doing out of school?" Joseph asked with concern. Then spotting the carpetbag, he added, "Have you gotten into trouble?"

The boy turned to face the men. "It depends on how you look at it," he said, toying with his brother's mounting concern. "Cambridge is not enjoying such good health." Jack made a gesture toward the empty waiting room. "Professor Hamilton became ill this morning, so the president decided to let those in his charge off for the afternoon."

"And what of tomorrow?" Joseph asked. It was only Friday, and there still should be classes scheduled for Saturday morning.

"My class tomorrow is with him. They will not have a replacement for him until Monday, and he will not be up and about for a spell." There was a hint of a smile on Jack's face as he considered this prospect. "But we have been assured that it is not serious," he added, feeling a twinge of guilt for having found pleasure in the former thought.

"Of course, it is not serious!" Lemuel interjected with a smile. "That man will outlive us all!" Few living people could remember attending Harvard College without Professor Hamilton being there.

"Get the liniment if you would, Mr. Haywood." Joseph said to the apprentice as he walked toward his desk and seated himself behind it.

Jack occupied the chair in front of the desk, slumping down until he appeared quite comfortable. "The very thought of the professor outliving us frightens me!"

he responded, his dark eyes displaying a similar emotion. "That man will live to teach our sons—our sons' sons—just out of pure spite!"

Joseph began to laugh.

"Forgive me, Joseph," Jack continued with all seriousness. "But love for my sons will force me to defect. My boys will attend Yale!"

"He is really a personable fellow," Joseph offered, still grinning. "In time you will come to appreciate his firmness."

"Ah, yes, much like one comes to appreciate the pox or Black Death after they have lived through it!"

"I am sorry, Doctor," Lemuel began with a grin as he came out of the examination room. "I know you wish to encourage the lad, but I find the analogy to be quite fitting. I still tremble whenever I meet the professor on the street."

Joseph also experienced the same sensation, but he thought it best to keep it to himself. "Well," he began, in the hopes of redirecting the conversation, "no doubt you are wanting to go home to spend your holiday. I will take you out to the farm after dinner."

"Holiday?" Jack exclaimed. "Professor Hamilton made certain we had work enough to keep us busy." He glanced at the books on the chair. "We will be fortunate if we finish the assignment by Monday. I am afraid the only hope I have of finishing it is by working through tonight and Sunday night as well. Thank God for the Sabbath," he mumbled. "Not even Professor Hamilton can force his students to work on the Sabbath."

"So you are not going home?" Joseph was confused.

"I cannot—well, I could, but Mother would never stand for me to be up all night. I could have stayed at the college. Most of the others did. Maybe I should have, but I thought—" Jack stumbled over his words as Joseph waited. "I was hoping you could help me, not with the actual work, but I need further instruction in some areas, encouragement in most— I could have stayed at school," he repeated in his distress, "but the others don't understand it any more than I do. By the time I left, many of them already were beginning to talk to themselves!"

Joseph had a sympathetic smile for his brother. "We'll just have to get Elizabeth to brew us up a pot of coffee tonight!" he said. Before his eyes, Jack's entire countenance changed as though a heavy burden had been lifted.

"Are you ready, Doctor?" Lemuel's question drew Jack's attention.

Joseph removed his cravat and tucked it away as the apprentice dabbed a bit of the liniment onto his fingers. The aroma of wintergreen suddenly filled the room. Bending his head downward, Joseph rested his forehead on one hand while he held his queue out of the way with the other.

Jack watched as Lemuel began to vigorously massage the back of his brother's neck. "What is the problem?" he asked with concern.

"I must have pulled a muscle. It has been annoying me all day," Joseph replied. His eyes were closed, and his body slowly relaxed as the oil and Lemuel's gifted touch began to work their magic. "This place has been bustling all day. It has not been as quiet as it now appears."

"A sore neck, eh?" Jack returned with a chuckle.

Joseph opened his eyes and saw his brother's broad smile. "And what do you find so amusing?" he asked, thinking Jack's reaction was rather odd.

Suddenly Jack became very serious. "I am sorry, Joseph. What has gotten into me? It must be the pressure of school. A stiff neck could be a symptom of a serious disorder." He straightened up in the chair and placed his fist against his chin, studying his brother in a feigned, but thoughtful, silence.

"Taking your age into account, I am sure we have nothing to worry about," he began, sounding very mature. "Mr. Haywood, do continue to massage the good doctor's neck, for all we can do is treat the symptoms and try to make his aging body more comfortable!" His grin returned.

"Well, well, aren't you the kidder, Jack?" Joseph smiled back at him as he gestured for Lemuel to stop.

"Mr. Haywood, do you know what day this is?" Jack asked, his eyebrows cocked in anticipation of Lemuel's reply.

"The eleventh of June," the apprentice stated.

"Ah, but do you understand the significance of this date?" Though speaking to Lemuel, Jack had his eyes fixed on his brother, who was busy fastening his cravat. "Today, my friend, is the anniversary of Dr. Warren's birth. Next year he will turn thirty!" Jack whispered the last sentence as if trying to spare Joseph, but he whispered it just loud enough for Joseph to hear.

Jack stood and walked to his brother's side. He placed his hand upon Joseph's shoulder and gravely said, "It is all downhill from here. Your stiff neck attests to the fact that the years are catching up with you, my dear brother!"

Joseph laughed at his exaggerated look of sympathy. "So, do you think you might finally be a match for me? Do you?" Joseph was referring to their wrestling and racing one another when Jack was younger.

"A match? No sir! I have no doubt that I would leave you in the dust!"

It was a challenge—offered in jest, but a challenge just the same. The brothers silently contemplated the challenge without shifting their gaze.

The sound of the surgery door opening put an end to the jesting. Paul Revere entered, a broad smile upon his rugged face. He removed his tricorn and congenially greeted each one by name.

"Do you have a moment to talk?" he asked Joseph.

"Yes, come sit down."

Jack and Lemuel prepared to leave.

"Why don't you two stay," Paul addressed the younger men while still smiling as he pulled a letter from his frock coat and handed it to Joseph. "The news I bring will soon be all over Boston! It's from the Grand Lodge of Scotland! Open it! Open it!" he instructed Joseph, who was not moving fast enough to suit Paul's enthusiasm. Not able to wait, Paul blurted the message out himself.

"They have appointed you provincial grand master! You have been given jurisdiction over all of North America!"

Joseph was stunned by his words. "All of North America?" he repeated in disbelief. He looked down at the letter to see if perhaps Paul had read it wrong.

"Never in my wildest dreams did I imagine you could go so far! You're the first to be appointed this title. Are you even thirty yet?" Paul asked breathlessly.

"Twenty-nine today, as a matter of fact!" Jack was quick to offer.

"Today's your birthday? What better day to receive such news?" Paul exclaimed.

Joseph did not seem to hear them. He walked back to his seat, his eyes glued to the words on the page before him.

"This title will command the respect of every man who is a member of the craft throughout the colonies—Whig and Tory alike!" Paul verbalized Joseph's very thoughts. "And there are many who are still unsure of where their loyalties will lie. This appointment can be a means of persuading them.

"Consider the difference in the attitudes of the king's troops! Those of the craft among them will be required to respect your position of authority. This includes most of the officers!"

Joseph quietly pondered this statement for a moment. Then he carefully folded the letter and placed it in his pocket. "Get the word out that there will be a special meeting tonight to inform all lodge members," Joseph instructed Paul as he stood up. He looked at Jack and added, "I will have time to get you started before I leave tonight."

Jack was stunned and amazed. The news of this appointment was important, so important one would hardly have expected Joseph to remember any tedious, prior commitment such as playing tutor for a younger brother.

"Congratulations, sir," Lemuel said as he offered Joseph his hand.

Joseph seemed taken aback by the apprentice's gesture. Then a slow, vibrant smile came over his face as he extended his own hand to receive Lemuel's. "Thank you," he replied joyously, as if the realization of the message had just hit him.

Paul Revere's boisterous laughter came from behind, and with a single stride he stood beside Joseph giving him a hearty slap on his back. This was the reaction he had been waiting for.

Jack's proud smile spoke for itself.

"I will take you to the house. I want to tell Elizabeth about this before it goes any further," Joseph said to his brother, walking to the chair piled with books. He handed some to Jack along with the carpetbag, keeping possession of a fair size pile himself.

Jack led the way to the door, respectfully holding it open for his brother and Paul Revere.

"Have you seen Sam Adams about?" Joseph asked Paul before stepped outside.

"No."

"I will try to locate him myself. If you should run into him before I do, tell him we need to talk." As he passed through the open door, Joseph acknowledged his brother's good manners. This brought to mind the conversation in which they had been engaged prior to Paul's arrival. He stopped just outside the doorway and turned to face Paul. "Can you meet me at the clearing by the Mill Pond in the morning—say, seven o'clock?" His laughing eyes caught hold of Jack's. "After studying all night, we'll be in need of some fresh air by then." Then turning back to Paul, he awaited his reply.

"I—well, I guess so." Though agreeable, Paul's bewilderment was evident.

"My brother has stated that I am no longer a match for him athletically. What do you think about that?"

Being six years older than Joseph, Paul threw a playful glare in Jack's direction.

"I want you and Mr. Haywood to witness the outcome of a race between us." Joseph's attention shifted back to his brother. "Do you consider 200 yards to be a fair contest?"

"Two hundred yards? Is that all? I should think half that distance would be enough. I certainly do not want you to overdo!" Jack's eyes sparkled mischievously.

Joseph replied with confidence, "It will be 200 yards, and we will see who leaves whom in the dust!"

Quietly Elizabeth entered the small, dimly lit parlor where she found Joseph relaxing on the settee. His mind was far away as he stared at the dancing flames in the fireplace, the warm glow reflecting off the ceramic tiles lining the hearth's open-ing. As she sat down next to him, Elizabeth suddenly realized how weary she was. With the day's chores completed and the children tucked into their beds, she final-ly had a moment to relax. She tossed her satin slippers off and, lifting her legs, tucked her feet under her body and snuggled close to Joseph's side.

"Did you see Jack this afternoon?" she asked, remembering that he had asked her to pack some baked goods and cheese earlier to deliver to his brother.

Joseph placed his arm around his wife's shoulders. "I saw him briefly. He sends his love and thanks. I checked on his academic performance. He continues to do well, quite well." Joseph's pride in his brother was evident.

"My main reason for stopping by the college was to evaluate the standings on the young men who applied for apprenticeship. I have decided to take two from the next graduating class."

"Two?" Elizabeth repeated, not sure she had heard him correctly.

"Yes," he answered, sensing she was disturbed by his announcement.

"Sam Adams wants me to take on his son, which I had pretty much decided to do as a favor to Sam. I tell you, Elizabeth, Samuel Jr. is a bright one. I expect he will make a fine physician. The other young man is equally bright. David Townsend is his name. With these two, I believe I have the best Harvard has to offer in the med-ical field for 1770."

He looked at her and paused, then added with a smile, "My dear girl, you are wondering how we will fit more than one apprentice into this tiny house."

"We simply cannot," she stated matter-of-factly.

"Our finances are steadily improving, and I think it is time to move to a larger house, darling."

"Move?" Elizabeth asked, showing no excitement over the prospect. With the birth of another child expected soon and feeling as weary as she did at the moment, Elizabeth dreaded the thought of a move. "When?"

"The house I have in mind will be available in early spring, well before the baby is due. I will make it as easy as possible for you. I promise."

"And just where is this mystery house that you have already picked out without my knowledge?" She found it hard to be upset with him, for his excitement was apparent.

"It is the old Greenfield house. It will be perfect for us. Plenty of room for our growing brood, more apprentices, and even my surgery!"

Elizabeth's face brightened with the thought of Joseph's surgery being right in the house. "Which Greenfield house is it, Joseph?" she asked, thinking of the three houses the Greenfields rented out.

He turned his gaze away and answered her so softly she could barely make out his words. "On Hanover Street."

Elizabeth laughed. "Did you say Hanover Street? I know just the house you are talking about. Yes, it certainly is big enough for us. But the best thing about that house, I am sure, is that it is so conveniently located right next door to the Green Dragon! I will never see you once we move there. You will spend all your free time at the Green Dragon!" she accused him with a smile.

The Masonic Lodge had recently purchased the Green Dragon Tavern. Lodge meetings were held only once a month, so this left the tavern open for other uses throughout the remainder of the month. The Green Dragon had quickly become the favorite meeting place for the Sons of Liberty.

"Every time one of the Sons has a question, idea, or problem, he will come knocking at our door. You will call a meeting and gather with them all at the Green Dragon!" Elizabeth teased.

"I will not!" Joseph countered, amused by her teasing accusations. "I shall spend no more time there than I do now. And if we live that close, I will not have to deal with the constant interrogation of the soldiers in the streets at night."

Elizabeth became alarmed. She had heard the men complain occasionally of this infringement on their freedom to come and go as they pleased at night, but she had not realized that it happened so frequently.

"I am fortunate enough to be able to hide behind my medical bag."

"What do you mean?"

"When a soldier demands to know where I am going, I simply hold up the bag for him to see. Without saying a word, I am allowed to pass by," Joseph said. "I hardly think they would approve of my passing if I told them what I was really up to. 'Ah, Mr. Soldier, I am off to meet with my fellow rebel Bostonians to plot our seditious acts against the Crown!'"

"Joseph!" Elizabeth scolded sharply, sitting up straight.

"That is what they consider us, Elizabeth: rebels. They do not understand how we can attempt to regain our liberty and still be loyal to the Crown. If we do not humbly bow and submit, they see us as seditious plotters!" As he turned his attention back to the flames in the hearth, Elizabeth noticed that his mood had become somber.

"We received a letter from one of our friends in London today that related an incident in Parliament. It seems those members who have been sympathetic to our situation made an attempt to have the Townshend Act repealed. Lord North disagreed—" Joseph's words drifted off as he seemed to become engrossed by the flames. Elizabeth knew better. Lord North had proved to be one of the greatest hindrances to hearing the appeals of the colonies, and Joseph was having emotional difficulty in dealing with the day's news.

"Lord North said—" His voice shook, and his attention remained fixed on the flames. "He said that America must fear the mother country before she can love her. He expressed his desire that Parliament never think of a repeal until they see America prostrate at their feet."

Elizabeth slipped her hand in his, again leaning her head against his shoulder. No words would help right now. The flames remained the center of their attention, and silence filled the room.

"Josiah, were you going to have any material printed in this week's *Gazette*?" Sam cheerfully called out as the younger man prepared to leave the newspaper's office.

"Yes sir," Josiah replied, pulling an unsealed letter from his frock coat. "Look it over, gentlemen. You may want to make some changes." He handed the letter to Joseph, who was at his side.

"Shall we sit down and look at it together?" Sam asked. He was always eager to read Josiah's work.

"I cannot," Josiah said with an apologetic determination. "I promised Abigail I would be home early tonight. She gets lonely sitting in the house by herself."

"She ought to go sit with my wife. Then she won't be lonely!" Paul Revere interjected. With six children and the seventh on its way, there was always plenty of activity at the Revere home.

Joseph chuckled at Paul's remark, then smiled at his newlywed friend. "I suspect Josiah misses Abigail as much as she misses him! Go on home. We can take care of this."

"I am sure you can," Josiah said with a smile of gratitude for Joseph. "Well, good night then, gentlemen!" He quickly disappeared out the door before Sam had the opportunity to object.

"I have come into contact with a gentleman living in Boston who is eager to join us," Sam suddenly announced. "He possesses many qualities that would prove valuable."

"Did you invite him to meet with us?" Paul asked.

"I did, but he is hesitant. He is not sure that he will be welcome here," Sam replied, looking at Joseph as he spoke.

Joseph's attention was divided between Josiah's letter and the conversation.

"Sam, you have pretty much handpicked this group yourself. If you think he belongs here, who would argue with you?" he remarked without looking up.

"A good point, Doctor. And seeing that you feel that way, a written invitation from you will provide the reassurance this gentleman needs in order to join us!" Sam replied with a mischievous grin, which Joseph failed to see.

"Certainly, if you think it will help. I will be certain to see to it tomorrow. Who is he?" Joseph asked as he lifted the mug on the table before him and took a drink.

"Thomas Young!" Sam quickly replied.

Joseph turned his full attention to Sam, his eyes wide with disbelief as he began choking on the punch.

"Young? Dr. Thomas Young?" he cried after regaining his power of speech. "You do not seriously expect me to coax him into coming!"

"He will not come unless the invitation is from you," Sam responded. His merry blue eyes twinkled at the amusement he found in his friend's reaction.

"What? Are we dealing with a child here?" Joseph blurted.

"Perhaps two," Sam observed with a playful smile, which only proved to increase Joseph's perturbation.

Joseph waited a moment before replying as he tried to regain his composure. "Sam, I have never disagreed with your judgment before—but I do here. This man, in my opinion, is not responsible! He is an avowed atheist. You know that! No doubt that accounts for his irresponsibility. Why an atheist would want to settle in a Puritan colony to begin with is beyond me! What of your incessant prayer that Boston become a Christian Sparta? How do you hope to accomplish this with the likes of Thomas Young in a position of leadership?" Joseph rambled on.

"Joseph, I do not dispute your professional opinion of the man. I trust your judgment here, or I would not be placing my son under your tutelage. But I do not want Dr. Young to meet our medical or spiritual needs. I want him here because he holds firmly to our desire to regain our liberty, our freedom."

"But what does he base this on, Sam?" Paul asked, coming to Joseph's aid. "We claim that our rights are ordained by God. Our strength is found in this truth. Obviously, Dr. Young cannot share this belief."

"Obviously," Sam agreed looking from Paul to Joseph. "But he has a talent for speaking and writing. That we need. We cannot continue to rely on the same writers in the *Gazette*. Even under assumed names," he emphasized pointing to Josiah's letter on the table. "The readers will soon figure out who the authors are. We need fresh voices, fresh ideas!

"I'm sure you don't realize it, but Dr. Young has a great deal of respect for you."

"Respect?" Paul chortled, "I wonder if he threatens to sue everyone he respects!"

Joseph slowly turned his gaze from Sam to Paul and back to Sam, appearing to be stunned by the entire conversation.

"He does respect you," Sam continued, ignoring Paul's remark, "and he is eager to befriend you. I am afraid a personal invitation from you is the only means of bringing him to us."

"I do not know, Sam. I do not believe I can bring myself to do it," Joseph protested as he suddenly sat erect, straightening the pages of Josiah's letter.

"Now this beats all!" Sam exclaimed with a chuckle.

Joseph looked at him, void of expression.

"Who would believe it, Paul?" Sam addressed the silversmith though his gaze was intent upon the physician. "When one of the members of the Long Room Club deals rudely with our Tory friends in a moment of heated fervor, who goes out of his way to make amends for our rude behavior?"

"Dr. Warren," Paul replied without hesitation.

"And, Paul—" Sam began again.

Joseph turned to the face the burly Frenchman as Sam addressed him. The stern expression that met his gaze warned Paul not to play into Sam's attempt to prevail upon Joseph to take the role of peacemaker in the uncomfortable situation.

"You would think a man who is so concerned with the feelings of a Tory would be at least equally concerned with the insecurity of a fellow Son of Liberty?" Sam continued to hold Joseph under his gaze, reasonably certain that he had accomplished his purpose.

"I would not attempt to presume upon the man," Paul's unwavering sense of loyalty to the young physician shone through in his sure smile.

A quick laugh was Sam's response to Paul's reply, a reply Sam hardly expected, though he should have. But the deed was already done, despite Paul's noble attempt to spare his friend.

"Sam, I am not sure we need the likes of Thomas Young in the Long Room Club," Joseph reluctantly began, "but if you insist, I will send a letter of encouragement to him immediately on the morrow."

A slow smile came over Sam's face. "Good! Look at it this way, Doctor. Perhaps you and Benjamin Church will have a positive influence on Young's medical ability." He was referring to Dr. Church, a fellow member of the Long Room Club.

A deep sigh was all Joseph could manage in the way of a response. Sam watched as Joseph and Paul exchanged a curious glance.

"Is there something wrong, gentlemen?" Sam inquired.

Again Joseph sighed, uncertain of how to answer. "I have been meaning to talk to you about Church," he began hesitantly, choosing his words carefully. "I am not sure what it is, Sam, but there is something about that man that makes me uneasy. Maybe we should not be so open in his presence."

"What do you mean?" Sam asked with concern. "Is it a professional problem?"

"No, nothing like that. Church is a good physician. I do not know what it is about him. I just know I cannot seem to shake my sense of unease."

"Do you feel the same way, Paul?" Sam asked.

"I do, sir," Paul quickly agreed.

"Well, gentlemen, if you could give me something to base this on, I might consider it. But to distrust the man simply because you both may have a personal dislike for him—please, gentlemen, we need to pull together, not apart!"

A demonstration planned to protest the Townshend Act by the Sons of Liberty began as scheduled, despite the frigid February temperature. Joseph's intentions to participate were thwarted by a steady influx of patients through his surgery that afternoon. The strained atmosphere in the surgery was intensified when two men burst into the room.

"Dr. Warren! There has been a shooting down on the waterfront! Your services are required immediately!"

"Mr. Haywood, see to the needs of these patients!" Joseph ordered as he grabbed his medical bag and raced out the door.

While running to the waterfront, the men informed Joseph that shots had been fired into the crowd of demonstrators, injuring two boys.

By the time Joseph arrived at the scene, eleven-year-old Christopher Snyder was dead. Christopher's young friend lay in a nearby house with a musket ball in his leg and a finger severely mutilated. Joseph quickly proceeded to remove the musket ball, but with no hope of repairing the finger, Joseph was forced to amputate it.

The man responsible was taken into custody. Yet the people of Boston could not help but wonder whether justice would be served. This Tory would likely be pardoned despite the fact that he killed one boy and injured another, simply because he was loyal to Parliament.

"Another cup of tea, Joseph?" Elizabeth asked as he paced back and forth across the parlor floor.

"What? Oh, yes, I suppose—On second thought, no, no thank you," he replied.

"This green tea from Holland is just not quite the same." Lemuel Haywood complained, declining a second cup himself.

"Perhaps the boycott will end soon," Elizabeth commented, looking to Joseph for a response. She saw that his thoughts were elsewhere as he continued to pace nervously.

"Joseph, I thought you told me you had a meeting to attend this evening?" she inquired, finally drawing his attention.

"Yes, but I was detained too long on my last call. I am sure they are ready to adjourn by now."

"It is a miserable night to be out anyway—bitter cold." Lemuel remarked.

"There is trouble in the air tonight," Joseph said, revealing his anxiety. "Groups of angry men are wandering about the streets aimlessly. Trouble is bound to break out."

"When curfew is sounded, they will quickly return to their homes," Elizabeth offered.

"I hope so—oh, I do hope so!" As Joseph spoke, the grandfather clock in the parlor struck nine. Almost as if the clock's chimes were a cue, church bells began to peal an alarm from the direction of the Brattle Street Meeting House. Other bells from quickly joined them across town. This was a signal that usually indicated a fire!

Startled, Joseph and Lemuel sprang to their feet and ran toward the door. The summons would bring the majority of men into the streets, for even a small fire posed a threat to the entire town that had so many wooden buildings.

"Elizabeth, bolt the door behind us!" Joseph ordered as he shoved his arms through the sleeves of his greatcoat and put on his hat and gloves. "Do not let anyone in until they identify themselves and their business, and then only if you know them to be a friend."

Elizabeth stared at him with a puzzled expression, uncertain of why he would give her such instructions.

"I am not at all certain this is a summons to a fire," he said as he grabbed his medical bag.

Lemuel took down the fire bucket that hung near the door. As they stepped out onto the doorstep, Joseph heard Elizabeth drop the bolt behind them.

An eerie darkness penetrated the town as bewildered men poured into the snow-covered streets. The cloud-filled sky veiled all available light from the heavens. Their threat of snow seemed just that, for the temperatures were much too cold to permit a storm.

Though no one was certain as to what the emergency was, all were rushing toward King Street in the direction of the Province House. A large crowd had gathered already by the time Joseph and Lemuel arrived, and they pushed their way through the throng as they worked their way up front where groups of men hovered over still, apparently lifeless forms lying in the snow.

"Dr. Warren, is that you?" the familiar voice of Dr. Lloyd called out as his slave held a torch in Joseph's direction to better illuminate his face.

"What has happened here?" Joseph asked, distraught by the scene before him.

"Just what has been expected for weeks. Some of the men and boys began throwing ice and rocks at a lone sentry. He called for help. The added strength of guards didn't stop the mob, though. Shots were fired, and you can see the result!" Dr, Lloyd stopped and gestured to the fallen figures. "Four men are thought to be dead. Dr. Church and I are examining them now. A few have been wounded. Over there," Dr. Lloyd said as he pointed to a huddled group of men. "They say that he is dead. I have not checked yet."

"I will do it," Joseph offered.

The men moved out of Joseph's way as he approached.

"Be careful, Doc! His brains are splattered all over the snow around his head!" a voice called out as Joseph crouched beside the body.

Horrified, Joseph saw that a bayonet had been plunged through the skull of the man before him. Carefully opening the dead man's blood-soaked coat and shirt, he found a musket ball lodged in his chest. "Does anyone know the identity of this man?" he asked.

"That's Sam Gray," someone called back in a trembling voice. "You might be interested to know, Doc, that he got into a fight the other night with Private Kilroy. Kilroy is one of the soldiers who fired on the crowd tonight—." Convulsive sobs momentarily prevented him from speaking. "I saw that son of Satan thrust poor Sam with his bayonet after he shot him. I saw him do it! God help us all, I saw him do it!" The man sat down in the snow, burying his head in his hands, and wept unashamedly.

"Can we take Sam home now, Doc?" another voice called out.

"No, not yet. The sheriff will have to examine the body first. Stay here with him if you would. Do not let anyone touch him until the sheriff gives orders to have him moved. Do you understand?"

Obviously in a state of shock himself, the man nodded as he peered at the mutilated body of his friend.

The crowd became more agitated as news of the shootings spread. Joseph scanned the faces around him, searching for Sam Adams or someone from the

Long Room Club who could attempt to bring control to the mounting chaos.

Directed to the side of a wounded man, Joseph gave up the search. He knelt in the snow, and with only the light of hand-held torches, he began to work. With the bleeding finally under control and a temporary bandage applied to his wound, Joseph called out, "Get this man out of the cold!"

Turning to Lemuel, he gave quick instructions. "You go with him. Clean the wound and bandage it properly. Do you have laudanum in your bag?"

"Yes, sir, I do."

"Good. Give him two drams. Come back here when you are done and find me!" he shouted above the rising clamor.

The front of Joseph's breeches was drenched, causing his body to shiver as he moved to the next victim. His gloveless, blood-covered hands were growing numb. As he worked on the man before him, he experienced the sick sensation of relief as the warm, fresh blood came in contact with his frostbitten fingers.

"Dr. Warren, can I be of assistance?" a familiar voice called out from beside him. There on his knees in the snow was Dr. Thomas Young.

Joseph hesitated only a moment. "Yes, take over here."

As Joseph turned away, he heard John Jeffries calling out to him. The injured man lying before John was screaming in pain. Joseph rushed toward John and knelt at his side, momentarily distracted by John's apprentice who was on his hands and knees behind him, vomiting violently.

The light of a torch revealed to Joseph that John was pale and shaky. And though the night air was frigid, perspiration was beaded on the younger physician's face. John's hands were covered with blood and his open medical bag was toppled over next to him. Immediately John locked his eyes on Joseph's.

The injured man was lying on his side with his back toward the physicians. Gently and without taking his eyes off Joseph's, John lifted the man's tattered and blood-soaked coat, exposing the injury. A portion of the man's spine was gone. Fragmented vertebrae and torn spinal cord protruded from the gaping wound.

"What do we do?" John asked.

Joseph shared a bewildered glance with his colleague, shaking his head as he absentmindedly ran a bloodied hand through his hair.

"I have no opium left—ran out of bandages already—" John added.

Joseph pushed his own medical bag toward him. "There's opium in there."

John grabbed the medical bag and quickly removed a small glass vial. Pulling the cork out with his teeth, he quickly took hold of the injured man's head and turned his face upward as he poured a large portion of the vial's contents down the man's throat. The man choked on the bitter fluid.

At the same time, Joseph quickly removed his greatcoat and frock together. Then he yanked off the cuff links around his wrists and grabbed the sleeves of his shirt to tear them off. He stuffed the sleeves into the gaping wound.

A group of men gathered around, preparing to carry the injured man to his home. John Jeffries gave them instructions as they gently placed him on a blanket, and then lifted him by its edges. Joseph watched the men carry the injured man away, with John and his visibly shaken apprentice following close behind.

Joseph was startled as someone placed his greatcoat back over his shoulders and bare arms. He turned and looked up at Paul Revere, who offered his hand to help his friend to his feet.

"I'm searching for Sam or Josiah," Paul yelled above the noise of the mob. "One of them needs to calm this crowd, or we'll have a bloody massacre on our hands!"

As though in a trance, Joseph turned away from the morbid scene of the screaming man being carried off and looked down at his blood-drenched hands. Slowly he lifted them, never taking his eyes from them.

Paul's attention was drawn to his friend's hands.

"A massacre?" Joseph uttered, his voice shaking. "Paul, there's already been a massacre."

Even as Joseph spoke, the doors to the balcony of the Province House flew open, and the light from within illuminated the gruesome scene below.

With a clear view of the balcony, Joseph saw Thomas Hutchinson, the acting governor, emerge. The sheriff and various members of the General Court were assembled about him. Sam Adams was at his side.

"Gentlemen, please! Please, give me your attention!" the governor shouted, his arms extended above his head. A sudden hush fell over the crowd.

"We are all shocked by this tragic occurrence. The soldiers responsible have been taken into custody. The entire incident will be thoroughly investigated, I promise you."

A murmuring arose from the crowd, accompanied with shouts of, "How can we trust you, Governor?" And "You're one of them, Hutchinson!"

"Please, gentlemen! I am as shocked as any by this inexcusable act of violence. Justice will be served! Please, you must return to your homes. Nothing can be accomplished until the sheriff has a chance to properly investigate the scene. That cannot be done until the sheriff is certain that a riot will not break out. This means that you must return home. A town meeting has been called for eight o'clock tomorrow morning at Faneuil Hall. Please, go home to your families until then."

Slowly—miraculously—the mob began to disperse. However, Bostonians did not rest that night, and with the dawn's first rays, more than one thousand men were gathered at Faneuil Hall, the town's public meetinghouse.

A vote was taken and a committee elected, led by Sam Adams, to go to the governor and demand that the troops be removed from Boston.

Aware that the townsmen might take matters into their own hands if he did not respond, Hutchinson agreed to have the troops moved to Castle Island, and the town was immediately evacuated of the British troops.

"Dr. Warren, do you have a moment to talk?" Josiah Quincy asked upon entering Joseph's new surgery.

"Yes. Things are quiet here. Mr. Haywood, take charge please," Joseph directed. He then led his friend into the main house. Working their way around wooden crates, they came into the parlor.

"Please excuse the disorder. Being so close to delivery, Mrs. Warren is not to bother herself with much of this unpacking. With me and my apprentice—well, it just may take some time," Joseph apologized, removing some loose items from the two easy chairs. "Please have a seat."

Josiah smiled in reply and sat down.

Joseph could see that he was troubled. "What is wrong, Josiah?"

He hesitated for a moment. "A man named Forester came to see me this morning. He is a friend of Captain Preston."

"Preston? The officer in charge of the guard who was responsible for the massacre?" Joseph asked. The colonists were already referring to the shooting as the "Boston Massacre."

"Yes, the same man," Josiah answered, appearing restless as he spoke. "Mr. Forester has been trying to retain an attorney for Preston and his men. It seems that the attorneys who are Tories have refused the case. They are afraid of what the Sons might do to them. Preston sent Forester to me."

"To you?" Joseph began to laugh but abruptly stopped, seeing that Josiah remained serious. "Surely you are not considering taking on this case?" he asked in astonishment.

"I do not honestly see how I can refuse it and live with that decision," he replied as he rose from the chair and began pacing the floor. "Can I hold liberty so dear, and then deny another his right to counsel? As he fails to obtain such counsel, day after day, for reasons of fear on the part of the attorneys in this town or simple prejudice, his trial—their trial—is jeopardized. Joseph, is that not one of the basic rights we cry out for—the right to a fair trial?"

Joseph made no response. He felt ashamed of himself as Josiah spoke. This friend was a man of principle and honor.

"I am quite certain that I shall risk losing some friends over this, Joseph," Josiah added, wondering how Joseph viewed him now.

"Then they were never true friends to start with, sir," Joseph replied with a smile.

"John Adams has agreed to assist me if I decide to defend them."

Joseph nodded, not at all surprised that John would make a decision in favor of justice.

"Tell me, is Preston's story convincing? Do you doubt that the shooting was a willful, ordered act?" Joseph asked.

"Yes, I believe there is strong evidence to prove it was not."

"You are aware that I am on the committee to collect depositions from the eye-witnesses. The stories are pretty horrifying. I saw the mutilated bodies myself. It will be difficult to disprove," Joseph said.

"I have no intention of attempting to disprove the truth. If these men are guilty, I wish to see them properly punished. If innocent, then free. I only want to be certain of the truth."

"Who could believe this turn of events possible?" Joseph asked.

Josiah stopped pacing, listening as Joseph spoke.

"Josiah Quincy, so distrusted by the Massachusetts Bar because of your zeal for the liberty of Americans that they refuse you the customary, respected robe of a barrister. And you have agreed to defend the king's soldiers accused of murdering colonists because no one else will. And who is to prosecute these men but your staunch Tory brother. The reversal of roles is ironic! If it were not so serious, it might be humorous."

The meeting of the Long Room Club adjourned. One by one the members departed. Only Joseph, Josiah, Sam Adams, and his cousin John remained.

"We are ready for this trial and quite confident of our stand," John Adams announced to Sam and Joseph. Josiah quietly reviewed paperwork for the trial, which John had brought, as the others talked.

"Confident of what, Cousin John?" asked Sam in an annoyed tone. "That those soldiers are innocent? Those muskets did not fire by themselves! And we have five graves to prove the soldiers who pulled the triggers are murderers!"

"That mob forced the soldiers to defend themselves," John protested.

"They could have fired above the crowd," Joseph offered. "I am sure that would have been enough to disperse them."

"Would it have been?" John asked. "That mob was agitated and expected trouble. Some say they even planned for such trouble all day."

"The mob!" Sam exclaimed. "It was the soldiers who posted announcements all over town stating their intention to confront any inhabitants who dared taunt them that evening!"

"Tell me this, Cousin Sam. Who was the man seen urging the mob on right before the shooting? Some say it was you!" John accused.

"That is absolutely ridiculous, John! Reports are that this mysterious man in the red coat was a tall man. This alone hardly fits my description. Do you actually believe me to be some sort of maniac, deranged enough to promote such a tragedy?"

"Your plans to further your demands for our rights through the deaths of these men are public knowledge."

"My demands for our rights?" Sam bellowed. "Are you now to be counted among those bowing before the mighty Great Britain as her humble slave?"

"I simply want to enjoy this peace we have finally attained. My desire is to remove my family to our country farm and enjoy life," John answered in a calmer tone.

"No one can blame you for that, John," Joseph began. "We all want to live in peace. But we do not have that yet! True, most of the Townshend duties were repealed, and how strange that it occurred on the same day as the Massacre. But, as usual, Parliament still maintains their unquestionable authority over us by maintaining the tax on tea."

"My family will not drink the blasted tea! But beyond that, gentlemen, I do need to think of my family. Because I have taken on this case, I am jeered at and shunned by those who I once considered friends. Josiah will report the same treatment. Even our wives are subject to such persecution."

"It is as John says," Josiah agreed. "But I expected as much."

"Tell me, gentlemen," Sam began, regaining his composure. "How do you expect to deny the fact that two of the bodies were actually mutilated by the soldiers?"

"We do not expect to deny it, Sam," Josiah responded calmly. "The truth of what occurred that night has been covered up and exaggerated by most of those who witnessed the events. I will give the witnesses the benefit of the doubt and say that the horror of what they saw caused this.

"That some of the soldiers acted willfully—it is probable. That all did—it is simply not so. Witnesses, including the bookseller, Henry Knox, a high Son of Liberty, heard Captain Preston order his men not to fire. They then watched as he risked his own life trying to bring order back to his guard.

"Even our main witness has stated that the soldiers acted in self-defense. Patrick Carr—"

"Patrick Carr?" Sam interrupted. "Patrick Carr is dead!"

"Yes, but his testimony will be read in court. Who more than Carr had reason to accuse the soldiers of willfully firing on the crowd? While on his deathbed after being shot by those very same soldiers, he stated that he believed they fired in self-defense. Who can argue with such a statement?"

"That statement was given to John Jeffries, a known Tory!" Sam directed his attention to Joseph, knowing he and Jeffries were friends. "Can we believe that Jeffries did not alter the statement to his own liking?"

"Not a chance," Joseph replied firmly. "Oh, there is no doubt that Jeffries is a devout Tory, but he is also an honest man. He is as appalled by what happened that night as we are. He watched Patrick Carr suffer a long and agonizing death. Jeffries was deeply troubled at having witnessed it. He actually was more determined to see the soldiers punished after that ordeal than we were."

A knock on the door startled the men.

"Who could that be?" John Adams whispered.

Sam went to the door, opening it only a crack to protect the identity of those assembled in the long room.

"Please excuse the interruption, sir. I am looking for Dr. Warren," Joseph immediately recognized his apprentice's voice. He stepped out of the room, closing the door behind himself.

"My wife has gone into labor," Joseph announced to his friends upon his return. She is frightened about the health of this baby."

"Has she reason to be?" Josiah asked with concern; as his wife was due to give birth any day.

"No, I have every reason to expect this baby to be healthy and strong."

"Mrs. Adams experienced this same fear after we lost our little girl," Sam confessed. "To be truthful, so did I."

Sam seemed concerned as he handed Joseph his hat, but he did not say a word.

When little Mary was ill, Sam's interest in the infant's well being greatly touched Joseph. When she died, Sam was there to offer comfort. He had mourned the death of four of his own children. He fully understood such grief.

"Gentlemen, this is a happy occasion!" Joseph reminded his friends whose expressions were better suited for a death rather than a birth. "Everything is fine."

The men responded to his words with a smile.

As Mary Warren left the bedchamber to announce the birth of another brother to the children, Joseph pulled a chair over to the bed to be closer to Elizabeth and their infant son.

"All of them certainly do resemble their papa," Elizabeth said as she looked intently at the small bundle in her arms.

"Is that a complaint?" he asked with a smile.

"No, not at all. They are all beautiful!" she answered without looking away from the baby she cradled in her arms.

"Were you hoping for a daughter?" he asked softly as he gently pushed her long dark braid behind her shoulder.

"I suppose I was. Somehow I imagined another daughter would fill the void left by Mary. But I am truly delighted with him. He is precious." She hesitated for a moment, then fixed her gaze on Joseph, her eyes filling with tears. Her voice began to shake as she asked, "Is he healthy, Joseph? Will he survive?"

"Dear Elizabeth, he is as healthy as any infant I have seen." His throat ached as he fought back his own tears. Tenderly lifting her hand, he kissed it. "Shall we call him Richard, after your father?"

"I would like Richard to be his Christian name, but do you mind if we call him Dick instead?"

"Dick?" Joseph was surprised by her request.

"Richard seems like such a big name for such a little boy. I can only picture my father when I hear it. I know it must sound silly," she said as Joseph smiled affectionately at her as he held on to her hand.

"I do not think it is silly," he assured her. "Anyway, the others have never been referred to by their Christian names. So why should little Richard be? Are you ready to have Betsey and Josey come in to meet their brother?"

Colonel Quincy heard a rider approaching and placed the hoe he was using against the rail fence. Taking off his hat, he wiped the perspiration from his brow with his shirtsleeve, then returned the hat to his head and peered down the dirt road in an attempt to identify the visitor. As the sleek, black mare came into better view, the colonel instantly recognized its owner.

"Dr. Warren! What a pleasant surprise! Are you making a house call in Braintree?" the colonel asked as Joseph reined the horse in beside the fence and spryly dismounted.

"I just finished with a patient and decided to stop and see how you are doing, sir," he answered, reaching out to shake the colonel's hand. "How are you and your lady?"

"Just fine, Doctor."

"Putting some vegetables in?" Joseph asked.

"A few. You know how much I enjoy staying busy in the garden, be it vegetables or flowers." The colonel stated looking over the hoed rows that were neatly taking shape. The commanding physical appearance of this elderly man never failed to impress Joseph.

"Mrs. Quincy will be delighted to have you out here on a social call for a change. Please, won't you come inside for some refreshment?"

Joseph turned his gaze on the colonel's house, which was originally built as his country estate. The architectural details were elegant, with its classic portico and Chinese fretwork balustrade. "As much as I would like to, I am forced to decline. If only there were more hours in a day, perhaps then I could find time to socialize more. I am afraid soon my patients will only associate my presence with pain and will avoid my company altogether!" Joseph said with a chuckle.

"I do not think you have to worry about that, Doctor," the colonel stated matter-of-factly. "I am not aware of anyone who does not welcome your company."

"Ah, Colonel, you are not speaking the truth! I happen to know that your son, Samuel, is not a great admirer of mine!" Joseph responded with a forced smile.

"Nor of mine, or young Josiah's when it comes to our views on politics. The debates that occur when the three of us are together are—well…. Mrs. Quincy and the daughters-in-law quickly make their way out of the room! I especially feel sorry for Samuel's wife. Hannah's convictions are with us. The changes in Samuel since his appointment as Solicitor General have been a cause of great distress. I am afraid their marriage is suffering."

"Mrs. Warren and I have been concerned about Hannah and the children. We have had no contact at all now that Samuel has removed their membership from the Brattle Street congregation."

"When did he do this?" the colonel asked. With the question came the depth of agony he suffered, reflected in his clear, blue eyes.

"Before the massacre—. I am sorry, Colonel. I assumed you knew."

"No need to apologize, Doctor. I am only surprised that Josiah did not tell me."

"I imagine he only feared the pain it would cause you, sir," Joseph offered in defense of his friend.

The colonel wiped a tear from his eye. "Is he attending King's Chapel?" he asked, aware that many of Tory persuasion worshipped there.

"Yes sir, he is."

"I wondered how long it would take. I do not imagine it was easy for him to sit under Parson Cooper's preaching, given his change of heart—rather, his hardness of heart. I love him dearly and will continue to pray until my dying breath that he turn back from the direction he is headed. Is Josiah back on his feet yet?" the colonel asked. The question took Joseph by surprise.

"Josiah? I do not know what you mean, Colonel." Joseph answered, suddenly aware that he had not seen his friend since the birth of Josiah's son the previous week. "He has not been to any meetings lately. I assumed it was because he was staying with Abigail during her recovery."

"When Mrs. Quincy and I went by to see the baby, Josiah was sick in bed. I urged him the have you come by. He assured me that it was only a cold. Would you do me a favor, Joseph?" the colonel asked, obviously worried about his son. "Would you check on my boy for me?"

"I will be at his door first thing in the morning," Joseph assured him.

Abigail Quincy promptly answered Joseph's knock. She was surprised to see him standing on the doorstep with his medical bag in hand.

"Good morning, Doctor," she greeted him. "Please come in." Her face was pale. She appeared not only to be tired, but anxious as well.

"Good morning, Madam," he greeted her. As he stepped into the foyer, he removed his hat. "I am surprised to find you up and about so early in the morning, Mrs. Quincy," he stated cautiously, noting not only the pallor of her cheeks but also the dark circles below her bloodshot eyes. "Newborns have a way of depriving their mothers of vital rest. Is no one here to help you out?"

"My sister was here. She has returned home now. I do expect one of my father's servants to come by today."

Joseph nodded his approval. "When she arrives, be sure to give her full charge of the household chores. You take the baby and get some rest. That means back to bed!" he scolded with a kind smile. "I am wise to how new mothers feel pressured to return to their daily routine. Do not give in to the temptation!"

Abigail nodded shyly.

"And how is Master Josiah III?" he asked referring to the new baby.

"Just fine," she said through a tired smile.

"Good! Tell me, is your husband about?"

Abigail's countenance brightened. "He is upstairs getting dressed. I will tell him that you are here," she replied as she reached out and briefly touched Joseph's arm as though offering her appreciation.

When Abigail returned, she informed Joseph that her husband requested that he come upstairs. Upon entering the bedchamber, Joseph found his friend in a weakened state and struggling to dress.

"Make yourself comfortable, Joseph," Josiah said, pointing to a chair. A violent coughing spell suddenly overcame him.

Abigail watched helplessly from the door. There was a silent pleading in her expression as she looked from her husband to Joseph.

"Is the baby sleeping?" Joseph asked Josiah's frightened wife.

"Yes," she replied, tears threatening to spill over.

He moved toward her and laid a comforting hand upon her upper arm. "I want you to go lie down while I examine your husband, all right?"

Her gaze drifted back to Josiah as he continued to be racked by the coughing. Unable to speak, she slowly nodded her head and left the room. Joseph closed the door behind her and went to his friend's side. He supported Josiah's weight with his own strong arms until the coughing ceased.

"Is something wrong, Joseph?" Josiah asked, as though nothing out of the ordinary had just occurred.

"Yes, something is wrong! Something is obviously wrong! Your father asked me to come by. He is worried about you! It would appear that you've been avoiding me!"

"I am not avoiding you—"

"Then why have you not sent word that you were ill?"

"Because, Doctor, there is no need for you to waste your valuable time examining me." He stopped abruptly, coughing violently once more.

Joseph held on to him.

"Tell me, Dr. Quincy, where did you study medicine? I was under the impression that you studied law at Harvard?" Joseph said when the coughing ceased.

"I have seen these symptoms. I watched my eldest brother waste away from them: diminished appetite, upset stomach, severe coughing, night sweats. No spitting up of blood yet, but it will come soon enough."

Joseph remained silent, again supporting the convulsing body of his friend as he had another attack.

"I have consumption, Joseph, and there's nothing you can pull from your bag or mix in your surgery that will cure it. Nothing!"

You do not know for certain that it is consumption, Josiah."

"It is most definitely consumption, and I have known for months."

"Why, Josiah? Why would you not tell anyone?"

"At first it was because I did not want to accept it myself. A cold—I told myself, it was simply a cold—" And the coughing started again.

"Then," he began after the attack ended. "After I accepted my fate, I saw no point in saying anything at the time. There was nothing you could do to cure it, and the symptoms were not severe enough to treat. I had hoped Abigail and I could rejoice at the birth of our son without this pending darkness robbing her of her joy." With no strength left in his frail body, Josiah fell into his friend's arms as the coughing returned.

Feelings of sorrow and grief overwhelmed Joseph as he was forced to agree with Josiah's diagnosis. As he held his friend's weak body against his own, Joseph realized that this young, vibrant, and loyal friend would soon be claimed by an early grave. The realization caused him to hold onto Josiah tighter still.

"I have neglected my work for so long. I must give some attention to the cases pending," Josiah protested as Joseph moved toward the bed with him.

"You are in no condition to do that, Josiah." Joseph said, seating Josiah on the edge of the feather mattress.

"People are depending on me, Doctor. And in a very real sense their lives, liberty, and property hang in the balance. I cannot neglect them any longer."

"You have no choice!" Joseph stated as he took a spoon and a small dark bottle from his bag. "I will contact John Adams and see if he is able to help."

"Do not tell him of my illness. Not yet."

"Josiah, you cannot keep this from your family."

"I do not intend to." He began to cough again. "I—I want to break it to Abigail and my father first. Please, Joseph!"

"I will not tell him the diagnosis—just that you are quite ill and in need of assistance," Joseph said as he pulled the cork from the bottle and poured the syrupy medicinal into the spoon and gave it to his patient.

Josiah reached up and grabbed Joseph's arm in a vehement grasp. "Get me back on my feet, Joseph. As I see it, I may have a few years left, Lord willing. There is so much to do and no time for self-pity. Please promise me that you will help me avoid it," Josiah pleaded, searching Joseph's face for an answer.

Joseph saw strength and courage in Josiah's eyes he had not seen before. "I will be here for you," he promised.

"If you follow the instructions I gave, you should see a dramatic improvement in the lad," Joseph said to Abigail Adams as he followed her down the narrow, winding staircase to the lower level of the small house. Five-year-old John Quincy waited quietly for them at the base of the stairs. The smudges of dirt on his tan breeches and sagging stockings showed that he had been playing outside.

"But I am afraid that confining little Thomas to bed will prove to be a difficult task," he added with a smile. Then, laying a hand on the boy's head, he added, "I am certain that John Quincy will be happy to help by keeping Thomas company. Do you think you can sit with your brother and tell him a story?"

"Yes sir," the small boy replied with a smile that indicated his eagerness to be with Thomas. John Quincy's soft, brown hair flowed loosely, reaching halfway down his back as the boy tilted his head to look up at the doctor.

"Good lad! Now let me see—." Joseph began to search the pockets of his frock coat and waistcoat. "She has never failed me yet—but where could they be? Ah, ha! Here they are!"

To John Quincy's delight, Joseph pulled a small package from his pocket. When he opened the brown wrapping, the young boy's eager, brown eyes widened as he saw the candy drops inside.

"Mrs. Warren always makes certain that I have a supply of these. One for Thomas and one for you," Joseph said, handing the boy two candy drops.

"May Nabby have one, too, sir?" the small boy asked, concerned that his sister would miss out on this extraordinary treat.

"Of course, she may," Joseph answered, handing John Quincy another drop. "Where is Nabby?"

"With the new kitties in the barn," John Quincy replied, revealing the origin of the dirt on his breeches and stockings. His face glowed when he viewed the three candy drops.

"You be sure to save Nabby's for her. Go now and give Thomas his, and then sit with him and tell him a long story."

"Tell Tommy a story 'bout what, Dr. Warren?" the little boy asked.

"Tell him about the trip we made to Boston last week," John Adams suggested from the open door to his office. "I think he would like to hear all about our trip."

With a beaming smile, the little boy flew up the staircase.

"Dr. Warren, can you spare a few minutes to visit?" John asked with a smile.

Joseph offered John his hand. "It has been a while, John. I had hoped to see you here today!"

"How is my little one?" John asked.

"Thomas will be fine."

"That is very good to hear. Mrs. Adams gets worried at the first sniffle," he replied, his affectionate gaze fixed on his wife.

"Indeed, Mrs. Adams does become uncharacteristically quiet when one of her brood is ill," Joseph said with a warm smile for Abigail. A very intelligent and well-versed woman, Abigail was not one to hesitate in sharing her thoughts on any given subject—and her husband respected her input.

Abigail's soft smile illuminated her rather plain face. "Being the wife of a barrister-farmer, my thoughts are presently preoccupied with putting up vegetables. I would welcome you both into the kitchen, and we can discuss whatever topic is of interest to you as we prepare the peas."

"Neither of us is dressed for the occasion, I am afraid, my dear," John said playfully as he looked from his fine wool frock coat, knee breeches, and ruffled cotton shirt to Joseph's. Being more suitably attired in a drab blue, cotton dress and white apron, Abigail's smile was reflected in her large, dark eyes.

"Perhaps the doctor would appreciate a hot cup of tea before going back out into the cold. The tea is from Holland," John assured him.

"I can take only a few minutes to visit, John, but not long enough for tea. Thank you for the kind offer." He smiled at Abigail before stepping into the rather large room that served as John's law office.

"Your presence has been sorely missed in Boston, John," Joseph said, seating himself in one of the vacant side chairs near the standing desk situated before a blazing hearth.

John closed the door and moved to the unoccupied chair. "I am in Boston often enough for court appearances."

"I am referring to your presence at meetings. The Long Room Club in particular."

"Ah, the Long Room Club! You still meet, do you?" he asked with a raised brow, pretending to be surprised.

"Yes. There are still a few of us."

"Very few, I suspect. I spoke to Jay the other day. He is not attending, either, eh?" John said, referring to John Hancock. "What do you hope to accomplish? The taxed tea is boycotted. And even after eight of the soldiers were acquitted of manslaughter, the troops were withdrawn from Boston. I see this as an act of mercy from God Himself. The results of that trial proved the aggression of the mob that night. The king may have been very well justified in sending more troops instead of removing those that were here."

"To withdraw the troops was the only sane option to the Crown. You and Josiah provided a masterful defense for the eight who were acquitted, but do not lose sight of the fact that the other two were convicted of manslaughter. We have five fresh graves in the Granary Cemetery, graves that still would be empty if the troops had not been sent," Joseph pointed out.

"But what more can be done, Joseph? Tell me, what more can be done?"

"Somehow we must stop the Crown's appointments to governing positions!" Joseph answered, desperately wanting to convince John of the grave dangers he still anticipated.

"How can we stop it?"

"I do not know, but if we all work together, perhaps we can find a way!" He paused briefly, attempting to control his excitement before he continued. "Hutchinson has been appointed Governor, and who has he appointed under him? Members of his own family—all approved by the Crown. This colony is to be controlled by one family. The lot of them are Tories. We will soon have an aristocracy in Massachusetts Bay!"

"I do not like it any more than you. But again, what can we do to prevent it? I do not want the troops returned to our town and more blood shed as a result!"

"Neither do I, John. Neither do I, but—"

"How is Josiah feeling?" John interrupted, eager to change the subject.

"He is still in remission."

"Good! And tell me, how is James Otis these days?"

"He is living in the country. On Cape Cod with his sister and her family. He is doing better—less violent," Joseph answered.

"I fear for your sanity, my friend. If you and the other members of the Long Room Club do not accept that which cannot be changed, you will become like poor Otis! Take time to enjoy life," John said with concern.

"It is because I enjoy life so that I take all of this so seriously," Joseph replied, disheartened by John's words.

"I am afraid that madness lies in that path," John responded.

Joseph had a weak smile for him. "Then pray for me, John, for I am unable to resist taking it."

Troubled thoughts prevented Joseph from noticing the chill in the crisp, autumn air as he rode back toward Boston. What would it take to revive men like John Adams and John Hancock? The cry now is, "Peace, peace!" Yet, there is no real peace, the honorable peace that my fellow colonists and I desire. Fear of more bloodshed compromises them to be content with any kind of peace. I, too, desire to be content, but at what cost? No, no—after a brief moment's hesitation—I simply cannot do this and be at peace with myself. Silently, he prayed for the wisdom and the strength to stay the course.

· 8 ·

Father and Physician

WITH INTENSE CONCENTRATION, Jack held the vial at eye level and poured a minute amount of grain alcohol into it. With a gentle twist of his wrist, he then swished the liquid in the vial, set it in the rack upon the table, and corked the top. A quick review of the list of medicinals in need of restocking, which lay on the table next to the rack of vials, assured Jack that his task was complete.

Satisfied, he untied the apron from around his waist and turned toward the door. There stood little Betsey, her bonneted head tilted back as she watched him work.

"You are so quiet, my little mouse," Jack said to her with a soft smile. "How long have you been watching?"

"Not too long," the six-year-old replied. "Mama said not to interrupt if you were very busy, so I just waited."

"Good girl!"

"I wish you could take me for a walk, Uncle Jack. It sure would be fun to go to the Common and play tag or something. Josey and Dick would like it, too," the little girl said with a longing in her bright blue eyes. Her blonde curls spilled out of her bonnet, enveloping her small, round face, and then fell softly about her shoulders.

Jack squatted down in front of her. "I wish I could, sweetheart, but I have tasks to attend to."

"When you used to come over before you lived here, you played with us. Now you're here all the time, and you hardly ever do!" she pouted.

"You are right, but it is not because I do not want to," Jack replied, cupping her cheek in his hand. "I am studying to be a doctor now—just like the other apprentices who have come to learn from your papa. And just like them, I have to do the things he tells me."

"I wish Papa didn't tell you to do so much!" she complained, throwing her arms around his neck.

"Maybe your papa will have time to go for a walk after dinner. You should ask him," Jack suggested after returning her hug.

"I don't suppose he will. He's already very late for dinner. Mama says we should go ahead without him."

"Is dinner on the table?" Jack asked. "Did your mama send you in to tell me that, Betsey?"

"Uh-huh."

"Then we better get out there before your brothers and your mama eat it all!"

"They won't eat it all!" Betsey replied with a giggle.

"I am not sure about that!" Jack exclaimed as he turned around and motioned for Betsey to climb upon his back. "Your mama sure looks like she is eating a lot to me. Have you noticed how fat she is getting?"

Betsey giggled. "She's not fat. She has a baby in there!"

"A baby? Well, what do you know about that!" he remarked with pretended surprise as he galloped out of the surgery and into the main house with Betsey on his back.

Already seated, Elizabeth held two-year-old Dick upon her lap, coaxing him to eat, while his older brother complained from the opposite side of the table about how hungry he was. Though she was surrounded by her three children and prepared to welcome the fourth, Jack sensed the loneliness in his sister-in-law as she greeted him. A kind smile formed on her lips, yet her dark eyes reflected the sadness in the endless task of managing a large household alone. Many young mothers had their own mother and sisters to depend on for encouragement, support, and company. But Elizabeth's mother was dead, and there never were any sisters, sisters-in-law, or cousins to fill this void. Her elderly aunt, now quite feeble herself, could offer little by way of encouragement to her niece.

As usual, the oval dinner table was neatly set for eight, a tasty, time-consuming meal laid out. And as usual, due to Joseph's heavy patient load, three seats remained vacant.

"I am sorry to have kept you waiting, Elizabeth," Jack offered. "Josey, we need to say a blessing over the food, and then I will help you get your dinner," Jack said to his four-year-old nephew as he seated himself in the chair next to the boy.

Jack offered the blessing, then prepared the plates for Betsey and Josey as Elizabeth continued to feed little Dick.

"Delicious as usual, Elizabeth," Jack commented after finishing his dinner. "Can I help you with the dishes?"

Elizabeth looked at her brother-in-law with wide-eyed wonder. "You are actually offering to wash the dishes?" she asked.

Jack shrugged his shoulders as he nodded his head. "I must admit that I have washed an innumerable number of dishes at home."

"Yes, but I do not ever remember you volunteering for the task. This can only mean one of two things. Either you are extremely diligent and have completed every assignment Joseph left for you, or you are hoping to postpone a portion of your work."

"Well, I have finished the tasks assigned. The surgery is fully stocked, and all records are up to date. I do have a bit of light reading yet to do—" his voice trailed off.

"Light reading?" Elizabeth asked, noting the sarcasm in his voice.

"Ah, yes. To begin with, there is a thesis paper entitled, 'Is All Disease the Result of Intestinal Obstruction?'"

"I am familiar with that particular work," Elizabeth said with a smile.

"Are you aware that at the time the author was considered to be somewhat radical in his approach and conclusion?" Jack asked, his eyebrows cocked.

"It did not hinder me from marrying him!"

Jack chuckled. "Actually, he draws a fascinating conclusion. It's just—I know the first few weeks of medical apprenticeship do not involve much contact with patients, but I am accustomed to being with people. I spend my mornings alone in the surgery while Joseph and my fellow apprentices make house calls, and then most afternoons alone studying. I cannot tell you how grateful I am for your company during dinner. I suspect it gets pretty lonely for you here throughout the day—and then frequently at night as well," Jack offered.

She looked at him. A hint of a tear began to form in the corner of her eye. "I do not mind being alone during the day. There is always so much to accomplish. But once the children are bedded down for the night—" As little Dick began to squirm, finally finished with his meal, she set him down, free at last to eat what remained in the bowl before her.

"I sometimes wish that Joseph were not pulled in so many directions. I sometimes find myself praying that he become less involved—" Elizabeth stopped speaking when she heard the front door open, and Joseph and the other apprentices came in. "Thank you for the offer to help with the dishes, but you should avail yourself of your chance to study. Doing the dishes will give me something to occupy my thoughts tonight."

Jack made himself as comfortable as possible at his brother's desk and began to read. His concentration was interrupted when a man came bounding into the surgery with news of an accident.

"Joseph, there has been an accident at the home of Caleb Hale!" Jack shouted as he ran toward the dining room.

Immediately jumping from their chairs, Joseph and the apprentices headed for the surgery.

"The Hale boy has been run over by a wagon! His leg is injured—sounds like a compound fracture!"

Joseph quickly placed extra supplies into his bag as Jack spoke. Then he turned to apprentice David Townsend to instruct him to grab the proper amputation knife. There was no need. David already had it.

"Jack, I may need you," Joseph ordered as he rushed to the door. "Come with us!"

Familiar with the location of the Hale home, Joseph raced down the crooked streets and alleys with his three apprentices following close behind. A woman waited on the Hale's doorstep in anticipation of their arrival. She offered no greeting but opened the door for them, and with a trembling hand she pointed in the direction of the stairs.

The agonizing cry of Jacob Hale directed them to the bedchamber. Fourteen-year-old Jacob lay on the bed writhing in pain. His frantic mother and father helplessly sought to bring comfort.

Joseph wasted no time throwing the blanket back, and he began to unravel the blood-soaked strips of ripped bed linen, which had been used to bandage the leg. "What happened, Caleb?" he calmly asked the boy's father without looking up.

"He slipped and got caught under the wagon wheel. I didn't know until I heard him scream out!"

With the bandage removed, the boy's injury was clearly visible. His bone had been broken, the jagged edge protruding through the skin.

Joseph took a deep breath, then turned to his apprentice. "Mr. Adams, stay with the lad." Taking a firm hold of Caleb Hale's arm, Joseph led him into the hallway. Jack and David were motioned to follow.

"The leg must be amputated," Joseph said softly. "If it is not, the lad will die. There is no way I can repair that break." He paused briefly, then added, "Caleb, he may die even if I amputate."

The distraught father could only offer a blank stare.

"The lad has lost much of his blood, and he will lose more when I take the leg. Between the pain and blood loss, he may go into shock.

"But he is a strong boy, Caleb. He has a chance if you let me take the leg. He will surely die if you do not."

Unable to bring himself to verbally agree to this gruesome, though lifesaving, act, the grief-stricken father slowly nodded to indicate his permission.

"Mr. Townsend, clear off the kitchen table," Joseph ordered. "Caleb, help us carry the lad down."

The men gently placed the injured boy on the table. The apprentices began forcing rum into him as Joseph prepared the instruments. Mrs. Hale watched the scene, sobbing uncontrollably.

"Take her into the other room." Joseph said to the woman who had held the door for them upon their arrival. Joseph sympathized with Mrs. Hale's fear, but he could not chance any hysteria on her part during the operation.

After removing his frock coat, Joseph quickly rolled up his shirtsleeves and held his hands over a basin as the young Samuel Adams poured clean water over them.

"Hold him down," Joseph instructed David, Jack, and Caleb Hale as he stepped alongside the table, drying his hands on a clean towel.

The boy screamed louder as the men held his body down with the weight of their own. As Samuel applied the tourniquet, Joseph took a firm hold of the amputation knife. He made a quick, circular incision, cutting through the skin, muscles, and arteries, until the bone was exposed. He paused only briefly as Samuel wiped the blood that had spurted across his face. A visual examination of the bone assured Joseph that he was well above the break, and therefore able to proceed to saw through it.

His apprentices watched in earnest as he carefully tied off the arteries, explaining the procedure to them as he worked. Few physicians took the time to suture arteries. Most preferred the quicker method of cauterizing with hot oil.

The entire operation lasted only a few minutes. The boy's pathetic cries had ceased, and he lay still, too exhausted to move.

While the apprentices took care of bandaging the stump and medicating the boy, Joseph took time to comfort his parents.

"I must go home to get a fresh suit of clothing," he informed them, as his hair, waistcoat, shirt, and breeches were spattered with blood. "One of my apprentices will remain until I return. Mrs. Hale, if you could have a bed made for me on the floor in your son's room, I would appreciate it. I will be spending the night."

Slowly Joseph, Jack, and David walked back to the surgery. "How are you faring?" Joseph asked his brother, who appeared shaken.

Jack was embarrassed by his own reaction. "I have seen you do an autopsy, and I have done numerous animal dissections myself in college. They never bothered me—"

"Dead men do not scream or struggle, nor does the blood pump through their arteries when an incision is made," Joseph responded. "If you were not troubled by what you just witnessed, I would be concerned. Perhaps the most important quality a physician can possess is compassion, but his compassion must never interfere with his ability to reason and act accordingly."

After walking in silence for a few minutes, Joseph continued, "Sleep will not come easy tonight." He knew the younger men assumed he said this because he would be caring for the Hale boy. "Sleep will not come, for as I lie there in the darkness I will again envision the horrified expressions on the faces of that lad's mother and father. In my mind I will hear the boy's screams and see him fighting to be free of my knife. And as I listen to him groaning in his drugged sleep and consider the life now before him, I will be sickened by what I had to do."

The men continued in silence.

"Are you still writing? My goodness, Joseph, what time is it?" Elizabeth asked rather drowsily.

"Three o'clock," he replied, having just heard the clock downstairs announce the hour. "I just finished it. I am sorry that I woke you," he apologized as he rose from the chair and stretched.

"You are not to blame. I simply cannot get comfortable," she complained rubbing her extended abdomen.

"Contractions?"

Elizabeth shook her head in reply to his question.

"Well, it will not last too much longer. That little one will be making his appearance any day now." In a state of exhaustion, Joseph removed his robe and extinguished the candle's flame before he climbed into bed.

"How is it? The oration, I mean?" Elizabeth asked from the darkness.

"Hmmm?" he murmured, already half asleep. "You can read it for yourself in the morning. Good or bad, it will have to do."

"I do not want to read it."

"What?" he asked, surprised at her words. "Why not?"

"Because I have this urge to keep you from giving it," she timidly confessed. "Is it really necessary to continue commemorating the massacre? It has been two years since the soldiers fired on that crowd—almost two years since the trial and removal of the troops. Why must we continue to relive it?" she asked.

"Out of veneration for those killed and hopefully as a means of rekindling the flame of liberty in the hearts of those whose flames have dimmed."

"That is exactly what has me troubled, Joseph! I have heard that the governor himself plans to attend and other Tories along with him. The governor may report any questionable words of disloyalty to the king. Obviously John Adams was not willing to take such a risk," Elizabeth stated, aware that John Adams had declined to give the oration when asked.

"It is true. The governor will be attending, as well as many Tories. But they will be attending mainly because a sense of grief still prevails in regard to the deaths of the five men. I cannot say why John Adams declined to give the oration. But you can rest assured that although I clearly blame Parliament for the transgressions of our rights, I am careful to show only respect to King George III and his authority."

Placing his arm under her shoulders, Joseph eased her body toward his.

"I do not want you worrying needlessly about this. Would you feel better if I had Josiah read it?" he asked.

"It would help." She tried to sound convincing.

"Good. I will bring it by his office in the morning," he assured her with a yawn.

In the brief silence, Joseph began to lapse again into sleep.

"We are going to have a daughter!" Elizabeth softly exclaimed.

"What—" the drowsy response came.

"A daughter! This baby is a girl!" she replied with confidence.

"There is no way of knowing such a thing, Elizabeth. You know that."

"I know of no such thing!" she replied.

"Mrs. Marshall insisted she was to have a son—she had twin daughters. When you were expecting Betsey, you told me she was a boy," he reminded her.

"I simply did not know any better then."

Joseph laughed at her response. "Son or daughter, I love it. And since you obviously feel such a close bond to this baby would you do me a favor?"

"What is that?" Elizabeth asked, sensing his grin in the darkness.

"Make her understand that I will not be free to deliver her until tomorrow evening. I have a full schedule in the morning and anticipate taking a much-needed nap in the afternoon. Seven o'clock tomorrow evening would be fine," his words drifted off as he fell asleep.

"Polly," Elizabeth whispered as she patted her baby within. "You heard your papa, young lady."

With great effort Elizabeth raised her upper body and kissed her husband's cheek. Then with equal effort she moved away from his sleeping form, trying in vain to position herself comfortably.

She felt the fire's warmth as the logs crackled in the hearth. With a sense of contentment, she listened to her husband's deep, rhythmic breathing. Suddenly, she remembered the oration, and a shiver ran through her body. She wished that he had not agreed to make the speech.

The bitter cold weather on March 5 did not hinder the crowd from attending the commemoration. Joseph rose to the podium, which was draped in black, before an audience of 4,000. Without the slightest sign of apprehension, he boldly delivered his oration, saying what he felt had to be said, yet with wise restraint.

With a plea for Great Britain to again allow her colonies to voluntarily provide her with riches, he finished with these words:

"If you with united zeal and fortitude oppose the torrent of oppression; if you feel the true fire of patriotism burning in your breasts; if you from your souls despise the most gaudy dress that slavery can wear; if you really prefer the lonely cottage, whilst blest with liberty, to gilded palaces surrounded with the ensigns of slavery; you may have the fullest assurance that tyranny with her whole accursed train will hide their hideous hands in confusion, shame, and despair. If you perform your part, you must have the strongest confidence that the same Almighty Being who protected your pious and venerable forefathers, who enabled them to turn a barren wilderness into a fruitful field, who so often made bare His arm for their salvation, will still be mindful of you, their offspring.

"May this Almighty Being graciously preside in all our councils. May He direct us to such measures as He Himself shall approve and be pleased to bless. May we ever be a land of Liberty, the seat of virtue, the asylum of the oppressed, a name and a praise in the whole earth, until the last shock of time shall bury the empires of the world in one common undistinguished reign!"

Elizabeth quietly slipped into Joseph's surgery with a tray of food, cups, saucers, and a pot of green tea she had prepared. Josiah Quincy and he sat silently at the desk, so intense in their work that they did not seem to notice her. Gently she placed the tray on the corner of the desk and began to walk back toward the door.

"Thank you," Joseph said without looking up.

"You are welcome!"

"Oh, Elizabeth," he called as she headed back through the surgery door, "I forgot to tell you at dinner—Mr. Copley will be coming by next week to begin a portrait of you."

Surprised by the announcement, Elizabeth did not respond right away. "I would much rather have your portrait done," she finally said.

"I have made arrangements to have mine done after yours," he replied, all the while studying the papers before him.

Again she paused. "It will be difficult with the children, especially with Polly being only a few months old. I really cannot sit for a portrait and leave them unattended."

"I have spoken to Paul Revere about having one of his daughters watch the children during your sittings."

"I am not at all certain that I have a gown that's suitable to wear for a portrait. Perhaps you could postpone it until—"

"Mrs. Warren!" Joseph exclaimed, finally turning to face her. "You certainly have plenty of lovely gowns to chose from. Now, have you any more objections?"

"No," she said softly, glancing at Josiah, who was pretending to ignore the entire conversation. She stood by the door in silence for a moment. "Doctor, will you stay during the sittings?"

"If I am able. Why?" he asked, confused by her behavior.

"It is my understanding that Mr. Copley enjoys nothing more than arguing politics with those who differ with his opinion. No doubt he will do so with you!"

"And why should that bother you so? Heaven knows you have sat through many a healthy debate in this house with guests like John Jeffries, James Lloyd, and other notable Tories!"

"Yes, but none of them were painting my portrait at the time!" Elizabeth protested. "John Singleton Copley is renowned for capturing every detail and expression on canvas. I am not at all certain that I can relax while you and Mr. Copley debate."

"I will try to behave myself," Joseph assured her with a contrite smile.

"I believe you will try, Dr. Warren. Oh, yes, you will try. But if I know you, and I do, dear, and if Mr. Copley persists, you will not be able to remain silent!" She snuck in her final protest as she slipped through the doorway.

"What is it that you find so amusing?" Joseph asked the grinning Josiah. He was delighted with his healthy appearance.

"You will never be able to remain passive with Copley badgering you!"

"I said I would try, and I shall."

"You are aware that when he painted Hancock and Sam Adams, he wasted no time in engaging them in a debate. My father also." Then he added, still grinning widely, "You will not be able to resist any more than I could!"

Distracted from her sewing, Elizabeth studied the portraits hanging above the parlor hearth. Copley had done a magnificent job, as usual. Joseph appeared so lifelike. His warmth, charm, and confidence were fully captured on the canvas.

On the other hand, her own portrait plainly revealed her uneasiness, exaggerated all the more, so it seemed, by the light of the flickering candles and oil lamps. If only Mr. Copley would have concentrated solely on the work before him rather than discussing politics with his subjects' husbands, Elizabeth thought with annoyance. Her only consolation at the moment was that the rich blues used in her portrait and the soft shades of wine in Joseph's blended nicely with the colors of the parlor, including the printed silk wallpaper that formed the background to the life-size portraits. Elizabeth ran her fingers over the dark blue velvet of the settee. Glancing at the shades of ivory and pale blue in the silk upholstery of the easy chairs, she again found herself delighted with these new purchases.

She glanced over at the grandfather clock and noted the time. Dinner had been served, the dishes were done, and the children were bedded down for the night, yet there was still no sign of Jack or the new apprentice, William Eustis. It was not unusual that they would be out this late. Joseph often sent them to check on patients or to run errands. Tonight seemed different somehow, and Elizabeth felt uneasy about their absence.

Unable to concentrate on the detailed work before her, Elizabeth found herself making mistake after mistake, which put her even more on edge. She laid the heap of fabric, which was beginning to take the form of a child's dress, on her lap and glanced across the room at Joseph. He appeared quite relaxed in the easy chair, preoccupied with the book before him. He is unusually quiet on this rare evening at home, she thought. She could not help but wonder if he was feeling poorly. It was not likely, though, for he always had the good sense to retire early when he felt out of sorts.

Elizabeth suddenly realized that it was his odd behavior that caused her to be anxious over the absent apprentices. When she had questioned Joseph at dinner about their whereabouts, his answer had been vague, with an air of secrecy about it.

Being a leading Son of Liberty required a great deal of secrecy on his part. She always knew when she had tread into areas that he decided would put her at risk. Her questions would be checked with the raising of his eyebrows and a teasing smile.

In making light of her question, he intended to put her at ease. She knew the information he held back from her could possibly be deemed seditious or even treasonous, but his eyes gave him away every time. Though his face seemed aglow with the jest, his eyes would plead with her to respect the boundary he set. Such information would most likely bring her distress and might even jeopardize her safety. So he remained silent.

But tonight he not only avoided her questions about the missing apprentices. He avoided her eyes as well.

Joseph slowly lifted his head from the book before him, and Elizabeth assumed that he had felt her steady gaze. She smiled softly in his direction, but he did not see her smile. He was not even aware of her attention. He looked right past her to the grandfather clock. After checking the time, he turned his head in the direction of the French doors that led to the foyer and finally returned to the book.

No sooner had he resumed his reading than they could hear the apprentices enter the kitchen through the back door. Upon entering the parlor, Jack and William awkwardly greeted Elizabeth as if they were surprised to find her there.

She was visibly taken aback at the sight of them. Their clothing was mussed and smudged with dirt, and their hands obviously needed washing. Alarmed, Elizabeth wondered if they had been in an accident or a scuffle.

"It has been taken care of, Joseph," Jack casually addressed his brother before Elizabeth was able to respond to their greeting or their disheveled appearance.

"The others have been informed," William added. Normally reserved and relaxed in his mannerisms, the young apprentice now appeared restless. His large, brown eyes were alive with excitement.

Elizabeth turned her attention from the young men to Joseph. She watched a slow smile come across his face as he received their mysterious report, and she could not help but feel that her presence hindered their communication. Yet Joseph made no attempt to excuse himself to confer with them.

"Did you encounter any trouble?" he asked with a quick shift of his eyes in Elizabeth's direction, indicating to his apprentices that a simple yes or no would suffice.

"No," Jack replied with a smile, which communicated to his brother that there was more to tell—later.

"Good. Get yourselves cleaned up. We will leave shortly," he instructed.

Elizabeth watched as the young men left the room. She was perplexed. They obviously had encountered some sort of trouble for them to appear as they did, yet Jack denied it. However, she found Joseph's obvious acceptance, without question, of his brother's denial the most confusing aspect of all. She turned to Joseph, expecting some sort of explanation of what had just transpired. He had already resumed his reading, unaware of her anxious state.

"What do you suppose happened to them?" she asked with concern.

He raised his eyes to look at her. "Oh, any number of things—boys will be boys…" His words drifted off as his attention returned to the pages before him.

How odd, Elizabeth thought. Joseph was known for his scrupulously clean appearance and for demanding such habits of cleanliness from his apprentices. After waiting in silence for a minute or two, Elizabeth commented, "It is a strange hour for a meeting."

Joseph looked up, hesitating momentarily as he redirected his thoughts to her question. "It was called together at the last minute." He went back to reading.

"What sort of meeting is it?" she asked almost timidly, due to his strange behavior.

"A medical lecture," he replied, not even bothering to look up this time.

"Really?" she was delighted. Joseph has often shared his desire to work with the physicians of Boston to offer such lectures. This late hour is to be expected, considering the busy schedules they all keep throughout the day. Things are finally beginning to make sense, she thought as she relaxed a bit. No doubt his mind is preoccupied with attending this lecture.

"Who will be speaking?" she queried further.

"I will."

His response set her back again. If he knew that he was planning for a lecture, then why did he not at least mention such plans to me? This is not like him.

"What do you intend to lecture on?" she asked with a puzzled expression.

"Anatomy."

"Anatomy?" Her tone plainly revealed her growing frustration. Anatomy is such a basic subject, mastered by every young man who graduates from Harvard seeking a medical career. It seems an unlikely subject for such a lecture.

Joseph noted the change in her voice. He laid the book on the small table beside his chair and looked up at her. "Yes, anatomy," he repeated with a weak smile and in such a way that Elizabeth knew he intended that the discussion, if it could be called a discussion, should end there. "I must get ready," he added as he turned down the wick in the oil lamp, then rose to his feet and proceeded to leave the room.

Elizabeth could no longer contain her frustration. She draped the dress over the arm of the settee and called after him as she stood. "What are spunkers?"

Joseph stopped abruptly. Slowly turning, his expression revealed his surprise. She finally had his full attention.

"I heard Jack and Mr. Eustis talking about spunkers this morning. They stopped as soon as they realized I was there."

He did not respond.

"Is it part of a Masonic ritual?"

"No." he said without hesitation.

"Does it have something to do with the Sons of Liberty?"

"Nooo—" he lingered on the word as if he knew where she intended to go from there and wanted to stall it.

Silence filled the room as Elizabeth waited for an explanation. He knew a simple yes to either of the questions would have put an end to the conversation, but he could not bring himself to lie to her. Now his mind worked quickly to find an answer that would satisfy her curiosity but still be obscure enough to avoid alarm.

"The Spunkers are a group of physicians' apprentices who formed for the purpose of studying together." He sounded very relaxed.

Medical apprentices had precious little free time. Elizabeth was only too familiar with this fact. They would hardly spend it in further studies. "When do they find time? What exactly do they study?" she asked, almost defiantly.

There was no way out of it now. If he ignored her questions, she would be confused and frightened. Yet his answer was sure to accomplish the same end. "They study anatomy."

"Anatomy? By what means?" Her words were spoken just above a whisper as if she dreaded to even utter them for fear of what the answer might be.

He looked her straight in the eye and, with as calm a tone as he could manage and knowing full well that his answer would evoke an emotional outburst, he replied, "Dissection, Elizabeth."

"Merciful heaven!" she gasped as she placed her hands over her heart. "You sent your own brother out to rob a grave!"

It was reported that many European physicians paid good money to have bodies exhumed for the purpose of dissection. Though this practice was illegal, it did not seem to hinder the physicians of Europe. Could such a hideous practice actually be occurring in the colonies—and her own husband be involved?

"Elizabeth, it is not what you think." His voice was soothing, as if he were speaking to a frightened child. He turned and closed the French doors behind him in an attempt to gain privacy.

"Uncle James would never believe it of you!" she exclaimed, staring at him as though he were a stranger.

Joseph was hurt by her words and especially by her look of repugnance. "Dr. Lloyd knows."

Her eyes widened with horror. "What?" she gasped.

"It was by his hand that I witnessed my first dissection. He will be present tonight." Even as he spoke, he wished he could take the words back and somehow find a better way to handle the entire situation.

As the color began to drain from Elizabeth's cheeks, Joseph quickly moved to her side, guiding her back to the settee for fear that she might faint. Then, squatting in front of her, he waited as she quietly wept.

"Did my—my—father's body end up on Uncle—Uncle James' dissecting table?" she struggled with each word. Her eyes were fixed upon her hands, which lay limp upon her lap.

Joseph rested his forehead in his hand and took a deep breath. The scene she was torturing herself with troubled him, and he took her cold, limp hands into his own and looked up at her. "Elizabeth, Dr. Lloyd never even considered such a thing. You must believe that." His words were tender.

"Who then?" she sobbed, lifting her eyes to meet his.

"Prisoners with no family. The General Court agreed that we could have their remains. Yet, when one does pass away, they seem to forget our agreement. The apprentices—the Spunkers—go out to retrieve the bodies, before burial if possible."

She trembled, envisioning them as group of buzzards waiting impatiently, wasting no time to move in on their prey when the final breath was expired.

The fact that he was involved in this wicked activity was enough to frighten her, but more shocking was the realization that he had been able to keep it from her throughout their marriage. She felt betrayed.

How many times had he instructed his apprentices to do what Jack and William Eustis had done tonight? How often did he give such lectures—never letting on to her? Her mind was on the verge of panic as she studied him in silence.

The tears stopped, and though her display of tears during any disagreement between them always made him uneasy, Joseph preferred the tears to the cold, unfamiliar gaze she held on him now. He could feel her hands trembling within his.

"If the General Court has given its approval," Elizabeth began indignantly, "then why do they keep the bodies from you?"

Her tone made him feel like a child being reproved by his mother. Letting go of her hands, he stood up. He intended to answer the question, but not like a cowering boy.

"I never said the court approved of our lectures on anatomy. I said they agreed to give us the bodies." He walked over to the easy chair he had occupied earlier and picked up the book from the table. He remained silent for a moment, staring blankly at the object in his hands. Then, turning his head to face her, he said, "They, like you, and almost everyone else in this colony, consider our need to learn in this manner as a sacrilege."

"And are you so certain that it is not?" Her eyes were fixed on his. The words, though spoken sharply, contained a sincere concern for his soul.

He took a deep, shaky breath before replying. "God has not only given me the ability to heal those diseases that I have a good understanding of, but He has also given me the desire to know more about those I am virtually helpless to fight.

"Elizabeth, you have been with me for nine years. Have I played the part so well that I have fooled even you?" he asked as his own eyes became moist with tears. He turned his face away from her and continued, "Day after day I am faced with death. Would that it came quickly and painlessly, but it seldom does. Old men, young men, women, children, even babies—babies like our Mary." His voice grew faint as he looked over at her again. "I do what I can. I treat their symptoms, take the edge off their pain, but they are still dying, and there is nothing I can do to stop it because I cannot see what is happening. I do not fully understand what effect the disease has.

"A man could go mad being faced with such grief continuously. We are taught, as we teach our apprentices, to put it out of our minds. I have found I can only pretend to." He turned his face from her as if ashamed to make the confession.

Elizabeth's heart ached for him. She had always been aware of the concern he felt for his patients. His compassion made him answer a call for help on the coldest and darkest of nights without so much as a weary sigh. A more compassionate man she had never met. But even this understanding of him could not fully relieve her shock at the discovery she had made.

"How long before the bodies of prisoners are not enough to satisfy this quest for knowledge?" she asked him. The harsh tone had vanished. As he met her gaze, he was relieved to find the warmth to which he was accustomed.

"It will not become like Europe," he promised.

"How can you be certain? What is to prevent it from happening here?" She wanted desperately for his words to be true.

"The moral laws of our society—surely you do not doubt that I respect them?"

She may have doubted it a few minutes earlier, and others might very likely doubt it if they learned of the lectures he conducted, but she knew within herself that it was not so.

"I do not doubt it." Her words were sure.

He walked back to her, holding out his hands to receive hers. Gently slipping them into his, she stood up before him. Joseph pulled her close, holding her tightly within his arms while her thick, dark, perfumed hair brushed softly against his cheek.

"I am sorry I have upset you so," he whispered, tightening his hold on her. "I never wanted to hurt you." As he spoke, he could hear Jack and William coming down the stairs. "I have to go now," he said apologetically.

She buried her face against his chest and tightened her own hold slightly. "I wish—" she began timidly, "I wish that you would not go." Her words were muffled.

Joseph was touched by this last tender attempt to make him reconsider. "I wish there was no need to," he replied softly. As she looked up at him, he greeted her tear-stained face with a loving, sympathetic smile. He bent his head so that his lips might meet hers and placed a gentle kiss upon them.

"I will be late tonight." The words were familiar enough, but the usual ending of, "So do not wait up," did not follow. He knew she would not be able to sleep until he returned.

After walking to the door, Joseph turned to face her, his hand resting on the knob. "We will conduct our study with decency, Elizabeth. The body will be buried before dawn with a sense of respect I am sure he did not receive when buried earlier. When we witness the handiwork of God, we cannot help but be in awe of His workmanship. I thought you might feel better knowing this." He joined his apprentices in the hallway and quickly disappeared from her view.

Elizabeth sat alone in the parlor, listening as the door closed behind them and their footsteps disappeared into the night. He would return in the wee hours of the morning as though nothing out of the ordinary had occurred. But for him it was not out of the ordinary. He had participated before. How many times, she could only wonder.

Frightened for him and confused by her own Puritan beliefs, she wept as she prayed for his enlightenment and her own, not understanding where the problem lay. This discovery was a shock, a shock that still threatened to cloud her respect for him. She refused to let this happen.

Though she might flinch under his touch tonight, knowing that the same hands that caressed and held her had been covered with the blood of a corpse only hours earlier, she would somehow come to accept this part of him. But she did not believe that she could ever be at peace with it.

A Time to Mourn

UNCERTAIN AS TO the exact reason behind Sam Adams and Joseph Warren's visit, Josiah Quincy assumed it had to do with Governor Hutchinson's recent outrage.

"Can I have Mrs. Quincy prepare you both some refreshment?" Josiah asked as his guests followed him into his office. "Perhaps a cup of tea?" he added, noting that Sam, chilled by the brisk November winds, immediately went to the fireplace to warm himself.

"No. No need for refreshment yet. Perhaps later," Sam answered for both of them.

Josiah turned the side chair away from the secretary, which was against the wall, that he might have a better view of the vacant chairs his guests would occupy. Joseph removed his winter wrappings, hanging them neatly on the rack provided, then took Sam's from him and did the same.

"I have been curious since I received the message that you would be dropping by," Josiah commented as the others seated themselves.

"No doubt you heard that yesterday the governor attempted to persuade the General Court to submit to parliamentary authority," Sam began.

"I heard, and you will be interested to know that it was John Adams that brought me the news. He is quite upset about it, gentlemen," Josiah said, looking from one man to the other. "And my understanding is that John Hancock is a bit agitated as well."

"Do you think they might consider joining us once more?" Joseph asked.

"Yes. I asked John directly. He assured me that both he and Hancock would be at the next meeting of the Long Room Club."

"Praise be to God!" Sam uttered with a sigh.

"Indeed, it is not difficult to see the hand of Providence in the unfolding of this situation," Joseph began. "Hutchinson's blunder alone before the Court would not have stirred such contempt. There is not a soul in this colony that would have expected him to say otherwise—for it is his sincere belief."

"That is so," Sam agreed, nodding thoughtfully. "It was the discovery of the letters that incited the people. To attempt such an argument before the Court in the wake of the publication of those letters indicates extreme confusion on the part of the governor—or very poor counsel."

"Confusion on his part for taking such poor counsel!" Josiah interjected. "How could he expect any other reaction from the General Court than what he received? The blatant statements in those letters that English liberties in the colonies should be abridged could only fuel the fire of our passion for liberty." Josiah's enthusiasm triggered a bout of coughing.

Joseph watched with concern as the choking cough consumed his friend. The chill of autumn had brought an abrupt end to Josiah's remission, and the disease was again beginning to take its toll.

"We must try to keep him from getting overly excited," Joseph instructed Sam. The coughing finally stopped after a copious amount of the blood-tinged sputum, so typical of the deadly consumption, was choked out of its victim into a waiting bowl on the secretary.

"I am so sorry, gentlemen," Josiah offered, taking a clean handkerchief from the inner pocket of his frock coat and wiping the beaded perspiration off his forehead.

"Dr. Warren has shared with me his concern for your health," Sam began, his eyes fixed on Josiah's. "I understand that he has counseled you to make a trip southward, where the warmer climate may prove beneficial."

Josiah nodded.

"And is there a possibility that you might follow through with his counsel?"

Josiah looked at Joseph then back to Sam. "No. I intend to remain with my family," he stated.

In frustration Joseph drew a deep breath. He had already explained to Josiah that if he remained, the damp, cold New England winter would very likely bring about his death. His only hope for remission was to spend the winter months in the warmer climate of the southern colonies.

Sam reached out and briefly placed his hand on Josiah's arm. "I have a proposition for you, my friend, which hopefully will entice you to make this trip."

Josiah attempted to speak.

Sam raised his hand in protest. "Hear me out. We know that there are many throughout the colonies who share our concerns and beliefs that the God-given rights of an individual cannot—must not—be usurped by any. There are many, from the northernmost territories of this colony to the plantations of Georgia, who believe with all their heart that resistance to such acts of tyranny becomes the Christian duty of man—for resistance to tyranny is obedience to God."

"And what would my traveling southward have to do with this?"

"Groups of patriots, many referring to themselves as the Sons of Liberty, have formed in each of the colonies."

"I am aware of this, Sam!" Josiah replied impatiently.

Sam had a comforting smile for his friend. "Our hope is to organize the leaders of these groups into committees that will commit to corresponding with other such committees in each of the colonies. As it now stands, we are fragmented. We hold the same beliefs but have no means of encouraging or informing one another of the activities within our own communities. These committees of correspondence, which have worked so effectively between the various towns in Massachusetts Bay, can be used to unite the thirteen colonies as well."

Josiah held a blank stare on Sam.

"According to Dr. Warren, it is vital to your health that you make this trip southward. When you are adequately recuperated, we would ask you to return home by land, making the necessary stopovers in each of the southern colonies to promote such committees of correspondence."

"You are asking me to forfeit the remaining time I have with my wife and son in this scheme, Sam." Though Josiah's tone was restrained, the rage on his face was apparent.

Sam's comforting smile remained. "I would never ask you to do such a thing, my friend, except that your physician is of the opinion that such a trip will save and extend your life, thus granting you more time with your family. The Sons of Liberty will see to the financial needs of your wife and son in your absence, Josiah. I promise you."

"My physician cannot guarantee such a prognosis—can he?" Josiah's biting words were directed toward Joseph.

Impatient with Josiah's defensive posture, Joseph stood and walked behind the side chair, grabbing tightly to the back. He studied his friend for a moment. Josiah's uncharacteristic response was an attempt to mask his fear. This was certainly understandable, but it also revealed his self-pity, which Josiah had made Joseph promise to help him avoid.

"No. I am not God! I cannot guarantee your prognosis should you make this trip. But I can guarantee, without a doubt, that at the rate the disease is coming back upon you, if you stay here, you will not be alive come spring! Another remission can extend your life until next winter and give you that much more time with Abigail and your son."

Josiah did not respond.

"Do you remember that promise I made to you? Do you remember?" Joseph shouted as Josiah averted his gaze. "I must be faithful to that promise!"

As Josiah began to sob, the tormenting cough gripped him once more. Joseph went to him, holding the bowl filled with foul sputum and wiping his friend's brow with his own handkerchief.

When the coughing ceased, the tears continued to pour out. "I do not want to die, yet—" The young man sobbed unashamedly as Joseph squatted before his seated form holding him tightly in his arms.

"I do not want you to die, either. None of us do. But if you stay here, you will do just that. Remember, Josiah. Remember what it was you said to me that day I discovered you had consumption." He looked up at Josiah through tear-stained eyes, fixing a firm, but gentle, gaze upon his friend.

"You said, 'There is so much to do and no time for self-pity.' No one would deny that you have cause for self-pity. But Josiah. There is no time! Will you help yourself by making this trip and help your fellow colonists—help your children and mine—by attempting this mission?"

Josiah nodded in agreement.

Josiah's departure to the South was not a moment too soon, for had he remained even a few days longer, he would have been exposed to Boston's latest epidemic of influenza. Joseph was certain that in such a weakened state, his friend never would have survived.

As the epidemic swept through the town, Joseph toiled through endless hours of house calls. The death toll mounted as weaker patients succumbed to the disease. Few escaped the fever, and Joseph and his apprentices were forced to their own sickbeds. Ever aware of the urgent needs of their patients, they allowed only minimal time for recovery.

Back on his feet again, Joseph helped Elizabeth care for their children as each one came down with the fever. Finally, Elizabeth, too, was stricken.

By the time the fever came upon her, Elizabeth was already in a weakened state, having nursed many others through their illness. Troubled by her slow recovery, Joseph convinced himself that she simply required more rest.

As the days continued to pass, her symptoms began to worsen instead of improving. A rapid, steep rise in temperature caused her body to shake violently, and the chest pain she complained of worsened as the cough intensified. Her breathing became shallow and labored, relieved only by the occasional choking up of a thick, suffocating, rust-colored sputum.

Seeing little relief, Joseph intensified his treatments. He knew the symptoms all too well, but he refused to admit to himself what was happening.

In desperation, Joseph called in Drs. Lloyd and Jeffries for consultation, hoping they could provide the answers that would restore his wife's health.

Lloyd and Jeffries could not help. Joseph had done everything possible, but Elizabeth had developed the dreaded complication of influenza: pneumonia. Little could be done now. She was dying.

Guilt began to haunt him as he blamed himself for bringing the disease home. Often he had worried about such a tragedy developing from his going from house to house treating patients, and he had thought of quarantining himself. But he always had returned home to his own family. This was expected of him and of every physician. Their job was to bring relief to the ill and injured, to risk their own health and that of their families for the good of the community.

Bitterness overcame him as he considered the loss he was about to suffer for this job that demanded so much and offered so little in return, with its long exhausting hours and no dependable schedule as his merchant and barrister friends enjoyed. He had been called out at all hours of the day and night, regardless of the weather or family commitments. He continuously studied to learn more about the diseases he had to treat, and he experienced constant emotional torment from the pain and suffering he witnessed every day. Now his reward for his service was a beloved wife who lay dying and four young children who were about to be deprived of their mother's love.

"What is wrong with the baby?" Joseph asked his brother after watching him jostle her around for a few minutes in a vain attempt to calm her. Normally a very content child, little Polly refused to be consoled. "She sounds as though she is in pain. Is she ill?" He was terrified at the thought of it.

"It is the cow's milk. It does not seem to agree with her," Mary Warren quietly commented as she poured a ladleful of chicken stew into a bowl. After placing the bowl on the table before her eldest son, she took the fretful infant from her youngest.

"Have you examined her?" Joseph asked Jack with concern, ignoring the food before him.

Jack's heart sank as he looked upon his brother's face. Dark circles hung below his bloodshot eyes, which seemed more exaggerated by his cheeks' near colorless pallor. His brother was a man under great stress, tormented and confused.

"She has developed colic," he said reluctantly. "I am afraid she needs a wet nurse." Jack glanced at his mother. Both felt anxious about adding to Joseph's strain. "Isaac Stiles and his wife have already offered to take Polly in if you need help. Mr. Stiles feels that having a baby in the house will be good for his wife after losing their own."

"I will go and speak to them about it," Joseph answered, pushing his chair from the table and slowly rising to his feet.

Jack placed his hand on his brother's shoulder and gently pushed him back into the chair. "I will go. How long shall I tell them that the baby will need to stay, Joseph?"

Joseph buried his face in his hands. Emotionally drained, he found it difficult to think beyond the moment at hand.

Jack's hand remained on his brother's shoulder. He squeezed it gently as he waited patiently for his reply.

"I cannot say—six months—maybe a year." His words were muffled.

"Why, Papa? Why will Polly go for so long?" Betsey's timid little voice was heard from the doorway. "Why would you send Polly away for so long? Mama will be able to take care of her soon, won't she, Papa?"

Slowly lifting his head, Joseph turned to face his daughter. "Come here, Betsey," he called, extending his arm toward her. He sat the little girl on his lap. "Angel, I am not sure that your mama will be able to take care of Polly. Even if she does get well, she will be too weak to nurse your sister."

"Of course, Mama will get well!" Betsey sobbed as tears began to run down her cheeks. "Papa, you're the best doctor in the whole world! You helped us get better. You can help Mama, too! You must help Mama!"

"I wish I could, Angel. I wish I could," Joseph said in despair, his voice shaking. "Your Mama is in the hands of God, and He will do what He thinks best. We must try not to question His will."

The sobbing child clung tightly to her father and he to her.

Rarely leaving home now, Joseph entrusted his patients to the capable care of his brother and William Eustis. Day and night he kept his vigil at Elizabeth's side, occasionally supported by Parson Cooper's presence.

As her condition deteriorated, Elizabeth drifted in and out of consciousness, which had been partly drug induced to lessen her intense pain and partly as a response to her weakness.

While conscious, she would struggle to speak through her dry, blistered lips. Aware of her condition, she assured her husband and her parson that she was prepared to die. Her few, labored words were of her love and concern for Joseph and the children. Her final requests were that her wedding band be given to Betsey and that she be buried alongside little Mary.

Whether she was conscious or not, Joseph would continue to talk as though she were awake. Frequently, he talked about the children or reminisced about their years together. Often he read aloud to her.

Quietly, Joseph placed the Bible on the nightstand and gazed at his wife. Void of color, Elizabeth's face blended with the white muslin pillowcase below her head and the cotton nightcap upon it. Her black hair and blue lips, discolored from lack of oxygen, exaggerated her ghostlike appearance. With constant dread, he watched as she struggled for her every breath, fearing all the while that the next might be her last. In such a state he, too, lapsed into sleep.

A loud crash from outside caused him to startle. He jumped from the chair and quickly went to the window to discover the cause.

A wagonload of split logs had been dumped into the street when the wagon's wheel had come loose. With great commotion, men were attempting to clear the street, as sundown was fast approaching.

When he turned from the window to relate the incident to Elizabeth, Joseph realized that she had managed to sleep through it. Slowly he walked toward their bed.

"Elizabeth?" he called out softly as he made his approach, praying that the shadows of sunset were the cause of the dusky pallor that covered her face. His heart began to pound violently as he moved closer. She lay motionless, with an expression of peace upon her face.

Apart from the violent pounding of his heart and the trembling of his body, Joseph felt numb all over. He could not move. He tried, but he could not.

Seemingly paralyzed, he looked upon his beloved's peaceful form as his emotions flooded over him. He was relieved that her agony had ended, grieved at the loss of her companionship, frightened to face the future without her, angry that she had left him, and ashamed of himself for feeling this anger.

"Elizabeth," he whispered in a pathetic attempt to somehow call her back. But that was all he could do. He remained motionless, paralyzed in his grief.

His eyes slowly scanned her body as he desperately searched for a sign that would indicate she was still with him. "Elizabeth," he whispered again, waiting for her to gasp for breath, open her eyes, lift her hand—anything!

His eyes remained fixed on her hands. They lay softly against the white muslin sheet that covered her body. How small and helpless they always felt when he held him.

The thin, gold band upon her left hand caught his eye. She had never removed this outward symbol of their union, and the thought of removing it, as she had requested, brought to Joseph the realization that she was gone from him—forever.

As his mind yielded to this realization, his body was finally released from its paralytic state. Dropping onto the bed beside her, Joseph gathered up Elizabeth's frail, lifeless form into his strong arms and rocked her gently as he whispered her name again and again.

Outside, the men continued clearing the street, their voices audible through the bedchamber window. Downstairs, the excited cries of the children echoed through the hallway as they welcomed their uncle home. And upstairs, Joseph wept alone. He wept for his children and for the part of him that had died with his dear Elizabeth.

A gentle, steady rain began to fall. Joseph stopped writing and listened as it softly beat against the rooftop, splattering onto the ground below.

He placed his pen in its holder and lifted the paper to review his words. It was a poem—writing about her was a small comfort. He pored over the words he had written:

> *Ethereal spirits see the system's right,*
> *But mortal minds demand a clearer sight.*
> *In spite of reason's philosophic art,*
> *A tear must fall to indicate the heart.*
>
> *Could reason's force disarm the tyrant foe,*
> *Or calm the mind that feels the fatal blow.*
> *No clouded thought had discomposed the mind,*
> *Of him whom Heaven ordained her dearest friend.*

He laid the paper down, stood, and walked to the open window, peering out into the darkness. A gentle breeze caressed his face, bringing with it the fresh scent of the spring rain. It did not seem right to him that the earth was replenishing itself when he felt so empty.

Elizabeth was out there—in the cold, in the dark, beyond his protection—he lamented. Then he quickly recovered, reminding himself of the Bible's teachings on life after death. His inner struggle over his fundamental beliefs had become as agonizing as the loss of Elizabeth itself. Yet he had determined that even in this darkest hour, he would cling to his faith.

He thought he heard one of the children crying. His mother's footsteps went past his door, and soon the crying stopped. All became still as the night dragged on.

Joseph turned from the window with a vacant expression. Slowly he looked about the room, the furnishings neatly arranged to Elizabeth's desires.

The canopy bed was on the wall closest to the hearth, with the cradle usually at its footboard. Elizabeth's dresser was centered between the windows, and a highboy stood on the adjacent wall with a small tea table and side chairs nearby.

In the past this room had enveloped those within its walls with happiness and warmth, even witnessing the first breath of life in the birth of some of his children. But it was no longer a familiar place, Joseph thought, as the shadows in the room added to the gloomy atmosphere. Even Polly's cradle was gone.

This brought to mind the awful realization that he would soon be forced to live apart from all the children, not just Polly. The others would be moving to Roxbury to live with their grandmother.

The breeze rustled the draperies as it continued to blow through the open window. Joseph's attention was drawn to the fabric—fabric chosen by Elizabeth after careful thought and hours spent sifting through bolts of material smuggled from France. Finally settling on a royal blue and ivory urchin print for the drapes and coverlet and matching yardage of ivory lace for the canopy, she had eagerly gone to work on her project.

The decision had been difficult for her to make, Joseph remembered with a smile, and the price had been considerable. But he had been happy to meet the price, for Elizabeth took such pleasure in working with the luxurious fabric after struggling so long with homespun cloth due to the boycott, and it kept her occupied in the evening.

His smile waned as he found himself desperately seeking to escape these thoughts. He walked to the dresser and picked up Elizabeth's brush. Long strands of her black hair were tangled in the bristles. The fragrance of roses from her perfume remained.

Try as he might to escape his thoughts, they haunted him, pulling his eyes back to the coverlet and then the drapes. He realized he had been happy in meeting the price because it alleviated his guilt. Aware of Elizabeth's loneliness due to his frequent absences, he had sought to find ways to occupy her mind, rather than give her his attention.

Somehow he had convinced himself that he must be present at every meeting, respond to every summons, and partake in every event. And as he kissed Elizabeth and his children good-bye evening after evening, he had told himself that the strenuous demands on his time due to the perilous situations the colonies faced would soon pass. Now there were no evenings left to give her his attention, no time to spend in her sweet presence.

With a deep groan, Joseph sat on the edge of the bed and buried his face in his hands. No tears were left within him, and though he tried, he could not find the words even to pray. He sat there in silence as the night wore on, the silence broken occasionally by the dull groan of a soul in agony.

The sound of footsteps outside his window, followed by a light rap on the door below, roused him from his lamentation. He listened to the muffled voices as one of the apprentices spoke with the mysterious messenger who sought care for one of his own loved ones.

The front door closed, and Joseph went to the window, watching the dark, burly figure below as it disappeared into the shadows, heading in the direction of Boston's north square.

A soft knock on the bedchamber door shifted his attention from the scene below. Without waiting for a reply, Jack slowly opened the door and hesitantly poked his head inside. Fully expecting to find his brother in bed, he was startled to see Joseph standing by the window and, except for his frock coat, still fully dressed.

"Who was that?" Joseph asked as soon as Jack entered.

"Paul Revere." His reply was spoken softly as he closed the door behind him.

"Paul?" Joseph asked with concern. "Who is ill?"

"His wife." Jack was hesitant, and his concern for his brother was obvious. "Her condition has deteriorated this past week."

Sara Revere had been unable to regain her strength after the birth of her eighth child.

"Have you consulted Dr. Jeffries about it?" Joseph was aware and grateful that Jeffries had taken it upon himself to watch over Jack and William.

"Yes. Dr. Jeffries has been working with us. Mr. Revere sought him out first tonight, not wanting to disturb you. But Dr. Jeffries is already out on a house call."

"How bad is she?" Joseph asked.

"She is dying. From Mr. Revere's report, it appears she may not make it through the night."

Joseph turned his head toward the window and gazed in the direction Paul had disappeared. With a deep sigh, he empathized with his friend.

He was silent, his attention momentarily drawn to Elizabeth's wedding band on the small finger of his left hand. Then, turning toward his brother, he said, "Get dressed while I restock my bag." Joseph could not remember the last time he had used it.

The years of unrest and turmoil had united many men with shared convictions. Many of them carried their relationships far beyond the patriotic comradeship of meetings such as the Long Room Club or the North End Caucus. This was the case with Joseph Warren and Paul Revere.

Although it was a common practice for men of education and prominence to surround themselves with friends of their own social order, Joseph did not have a high regard for this practice. Quite simply, the son of a farmer had met and befriended the son of a French immigrant, and Joseph's rise to prominence did not alter his friendship with Paul Revere in any way.

The grief both men now experienced drew them closer still. Both had shared their most cherished dreams and memories of the women they had buried, their beloved helpmates. Now they found they could lean on one another for comfort and support. Many evenings during their period of mourning, Joseph and Paul could be found together. They would share their fears, plan for their futures, or just quietly discuss a topic of mutual interest. Such moments together reinforced the bonds of this unique friendship.

"Perhaps we should go over to the *Gazette*. They are meeting tonight," Paul said.

Joseph glanced at him without responding.

"We need to get involved again, Joseph."

"I know it," Joseph finally agreed though he found it very difficult to be motivated. "And I really do need to get out of this house. The silence here is maddening!" Joseph added as he somberly looked about the kitchen.

"Maddening?" Paul questioned, leaning forward in the chair and placing his mug on the table before him. He then joined Joseph in his study of the room about them, for what, he did not know. "I rather enjoy the quiet here," he said, continuing the search. "My home is in a state of total confusion in the evening. There are little ones running every which way! My mother, God bless her, is getting too old to deal with so many children."

Joseph stopped his mysterious search. The scene Paul had just described somehow seemed inviting. He smiled warmly at his friend. "I would gladly trade the chaos of your home for the quiet here." Then, standing and picking up the two mugs from the table, he added, "Jack will be leaving next month." The smile upon his wan face had vanished.

"Has it been two years already? My, but the time passed quickly!"

"Too quickly. But he is ready to be on his own. He needs to establish himself and plan for his own family. I will miss him. I will miss him a great deal. He will be moving to Salem."

"Salem? Why so far?" Paul asked. The town was twenty miles north of Boston.

"There is an over abundance of physicians in Boston right now," Joseph replied. "He would have a difficult time here. Salem is in need of good physicians. " Though he tried not to show it, his depression over the impending separation was obvious.

"I'm sorry to hear it," Paul said. "I know just how much his company means to you. Especially now."

"Is it ready yet, Papa?" Josey impatiently inquired.

"Is it ready?" little Dick echoed, straining to get a better view of the crudely carved wooden boat on the kitchen table.

"Almost," Joseph reassured them as he attached the tiny sail Betsey had made from a swatch of muslin around the masts with twine. "It is ready!" he finally announced, holding the boat up for all to see.

"It is a fine boat!" Betsey exclaimed from across the table.

"It certainly is," her grandmother agreed, moving behind the girl and resting her hands on Betsey's shoulders. "I have seen the many boats your father and uncles made as lads. This fine boat of yours is as seaworthy as any of theirs," Mary Warren praised the beaming Josey.

"Please, can we sail it now, Papa?" Josey asked.

"Please?" Dick echoed.

"How long before dinner, Mother?" Joseph inquired.

"At least an hour," she said, glancing toward the roaster and kettle in the fire-place.

"Shall I stay and help, Grandmother?" Betsey asked. As she twisted her body to look up at her grandmother, Mary detected the longing in the nine-year-old's eyes to be excused from the task. Her father's visits were not as frequent as any of them would hope for, due to his responsibilities in Boston, and Betsey wanted to be with him every possible moment.

Mary Warren bent down and kissed the girl's bonneted head. "I believe I can manage things here. Why don't you go with them to the pond."

As she glanced up from the girl, she met the appreciative smile on her son's face.

The boys ran ahead to the pond as Betsey walked alongside her father, her small hand safely clasped within his. Josey and Dick impatiently yanked off the shoes from their stockingless feet and waded into the water. They excitedly called to their father and sister to witness the miniature ship's ability.

Joseph positioned himself comfortably on the soft grass under the old maple tree, and Betsey kicked off her calfskin shoes and sat next to him. Her mid-calf, striped dress of lilac and maroon flowed gracefully about her feet, covering her gray stockings.

The little girl was delighted to have her father all to herself. During every visit, Betsey had question after question for him about how her baby sister was faring. Her curiosity would then turn to her Uncle Jack. Had her father heard from him since his last visit? Might he come down from Salem soon to see them?

With nothing left to ask on that subject, her focus would turn to William Eustis, whose genuine affection for the children had endeared him to them as though he was an uncle.

"Papa, it's a fine boat!" Josey exclaimed, running from the pond with Dick at his heels. They both plopped down on the grass next to their father and sister. "Some day I shall sail a fine ship," he exclaimed. "Perhaps I'll even be the captain!"

Joseph smiled as his son shared his dreams. "So you want to be a sailor, eh?"

"Yes, sir!"

"Me, too! Me, too!" Dick added, wanting to imitate his older brother whom he so admired.

Joseph laughed as he pulled the younger boy close to himself.

"Perhaps you will be a captain on one of Mr. Hancock's merchant ships."

"Oh, no, Papa! I shall be on a mighty warship like those we've seen in the harbor. Wouldn't it be all right to be in His Majesty's navy?"

Before Joseph had time to react to the question, Betsey responded. "Josey, I already told you that you couldn't become an officer like those born in Great Britain! Sailors steal American boys and force them to serve in the navy. And those warships that were in the harbor were not here for our good! The king hates us and sent the ships to do evil to us! Would you serve on a ship sent to do evil to us?" The young girl was out of breath by the time she finished.

Seven-year-old Josey seemed perplexed, unable to understand what his sister was saying. Joseph was aware of his distress and was surprised at how much Betsey had learned from conversations she had overheard.

"Perhaps when you are of age, after you have completed your education, you may be able to join His Majesty's Royal Navy. Perhaps by then you will be given the same respect as any other Englishmen wishing to become an officer," Joseph began, laying a hand on Josey's leg. "But for now, as your sister said, this is not so. Our young men are not given respect. For this reason and others, our men do not join. Because of this, there are those in the navy who feel justified in forcing some of our men into serving. As for the king hating us, I am not certain this is true, Betsey," Joseph said, smiling lovingly at his daughter. "Do you remember from Scripture the accounts given of the kings of Israel?"

The children nodded eagerly, anticipating a story.

"Then you remember King Rehoboam, the son of Solomon. He inherited from his father the mightiest and richest kingdom on the earth at the time, but there was turmoil in his kingdom. We are told that taxes were oppressive and that his subjects asked that they be reduced. We are not given detail on how long or by what means the people pleaded with the king.

"King Rehoboam sought much counsel in dealing with the situation. Some told him to listen to the people and respond favorably to their pleas. Others advised him to increase the already oppressive taxes and physically punish his subjects for complaining.

"Foolishly, the king followed the advice of the latter, thus causing a rebellion and division in his kingdom. From that time on, the mighty nation of Israel was divided into two separate and distinct kingdoms: Judah and Israel."

Joseph paused, giving the children a moment to think about what he had told them. "We, King George III's subjects, have repeatedly made our pleas to him to relieve our oppression. He, like Rehoboam, has followed the counsel of those who advise more oppression and punishment. I do not think Rehoboam hated his subjects, nor do I think our king hates us. He is just ill advised. We should pray that His Majesty reconsiders such counsel before his kingdom becomes divided as Rehoboam's was."

"If it becomes divided, Papa, I shall never be in the navy," Josey complained.

"If it should become divided, son, and my prayer is that it does not, then I am certain the new nation these colonies form shall have a navy of its own in time. Whether you serve in the Royal Navy of Great Britain, with the respect due a Colonial Englishmen, or in the navy of these united American colonies, you may serve proudly, my son!"

· 10 ·

Saltwater Tea

RESUMING AN ACTIVE role of leadership again among the Sons of Liberty proved difficult for Joseph. He sat through the meetings, but he was unusually quiet as his mind wandered to his personal problems. Josiah's safe return from the southern colonies provided Joseph the strength to go on.

With the disease once again in remission, Josiah appeared as healthy as Joseph had ever seen. As was hoped, the warmer climate of the South, as well as the wide variety of fresh fruits and vegetables available throughout the winter months, had proved beneficial to his health.

Not only did his restored health cause Joseph to rejoice, his attempt to persuade the colonies to unite through the Committees of Correspondence was met with great interest. The immediate task at hand was for the Boston Committee of Correspondence to lead the way in communicating with the new committees being established.

"I can repair it," Paul announced after examining the broken medical instrument. He placed the tongs safely upon a high shelf behind his order desk. The shelf was already lined with various items demanding his attention: cups accidentally melted, their handles in need of repair; bowls disfigured by the same means; old tankards waiting to be melted down and fashionably reformed.

Upon another shelf that dominated the wall opposite the entrance to the silver shop were Paul's finished works of art: flagons, cups, christening bowls, a sugar bowl and creamer, and magnificent pieces of church silver. Some were tastefully designed with cast shells, others with scrolls or pineapples. The rays from the late afternoon sun that poured through the open shop windows illuminated the beauty of the polished silver.

"I'll have this ready for you by tomorrow afternoon. It will be as good as new!" Paul said with a smile for his friend. "I'm delighted you stopped by. I was just getting ready to head home for supper. Why don't you join us? We can go to the meeting from there," he said.

"I appreciate the invitation, but my noon meal was eaten much later than noon," Joseph answered with a smile. "Perhaps another time?"

"Of course, anytime. You know that. But you'll miss the announcement—" Paul began and then stopped abruptly as the sharp beating of the steel hammer in the adjacent room stopped. He walked to the door and peeked in, offering brief instructions to the apprentices.

"I would have liked to have you present for the announcement," Paul said, redirecting his attention to his friend. He fastened the top button of his shirt snugly about his thick neck.

"What announcement?" Joseph asked.

Paul grinned. "Rachel Walker has agreed to marry me!"

"Marry you? I did not realize that your relationship with Miss Walker was that serious," Joseph said, stunned by the news and by the fact that Paul had not confided in him sooner.

"I know it's quick, and I'm not sure how folks will react—it—it—being only four months since Sara passed on, but the children need a mother. We can't continue as we are now! Rachel loves the children, and they have really taken to her. Being left with so many children, I wasn't sure that I'd find anyone who'd be willing to take on such responsibility. She's a good woman, Joseph. I'm certain she'll make a fine wife." Paul's face was aglow.

"I am sure she will, Paul, and I am very happy for all of you. Congratulations!" With as warm a smile as he could manage, Joseph offered Paul his hand. Though he sincerely wished the best for his friend, his own loneliness intensified with this sudden announcement.

Upon leaving the silver shop, Joseph decided to take a walk through the Boston Common.

The Common was pleasant and always full of activity on early autumn evenings. Families walked along the pathways, the children shrieking joyfully as they chased after one another. Lovers walked along hand in hand, completely oblivious to anyone but their companions.

Joseph smiled sadly as he remembered how he had once strolled these same paths with his family. It seemed that Elizabeth was always carrying a baby, while he held a little one by the hand with another propped upon his back.

He recognized many faces as he walked along. He could easily approach any one of them and strike up a conversation, but tonight he preferred to be alone.

Paul's news had triggered this sullen mood, and viewing the families contentedly strolling along added to his distress. He lamented that he had not seen his own children for almost two weeks.

Is it too late to stop by and see Polly? he wondered. The Stileses lived only a short distance from where he now stood. But he hesitated. He feared that expecting to visit without prior notice might be an intrusion. Polly needed a good home to stay in, and she had that now. Joseph was reluctant to jeopardize that in any way.

Then he remembered that payment for her care was due. Reaching into his pocket, Joseph quickly determined how many coins he was carrying. There was more than enough to pay the Stileses. Payment would be his excuse for the sudden and unannounced visit.

"Dr. Warren, come in, sir, please!" Mr. Stiles pleasantly greeted him upon answering the door.

"I hope I am not interrupting your supper."

"Not at all, sir. Mrs. Stiles was just preparing the baby for bed. I will tell her you are here."

To Joseph's delight, little Polly immediately recognized him as she entered the room upon Mrs. Stiles's hip. Her dark eyes twinkled as she laughed with glee, reaching out to her father.

"She's taken a few steps since you were last here, Doctor," Mrs. Stiles announced, handing the baby to her father.

Though the words pierced his heart, Joseph managed to smile in response. Elizabeth had always been the one to bring him such news. Together they would coax their babies into showing off their newly acquired skill, sharing the sense of pride and joy this milestone brought.

He held the baby close and tenderly kissed her curl-covered head. "So you are getting ready to walk, are you?" he said softly.

"If you would like, you can take Polly into the parlor. There is a rocker there," Mrs. Stiles suggested.

"Thank you, madam." Joseph was put at ease by her understanding smile. Turning to Mr. Stiles, he added, "I need to pay you for Polly's care." Securely holding the baby against him with one hand, he reached into his pocket with the other, pulling out two silver coins. He handed them to Mr. Stiles.

In the parlor Joseph seated himself in the rocking chair, cradling the tiny girl in his strong arms. He was always amazed at how much she resembled her mother. Polly was the living picture of Elizabeth.

Slowly rocking back and forth, Joseph tried to remember the words to the lullabies he had heard Elizabeth sing. So very often in the stillness of the night, he had listened to the rhythmic creaking of the rocking chair in their bedchamber that accompanied Elizabeth's soothing melody as she sang one of their little ones to sleep.

He held Polly closer to his chest and began to hum one of the tunes. The words quickly came to his mind. Softly, he sang them to his daughter.

Polly's dark eyes studied her father's face, taking in every detail. Her tiny hand reached up to touch his lips, his cheek, his chin. Relaxing in his strong arms, the baby struggled to stay awake and enjoy her papa's company. Though she fought hard to keep her eyes open, she lost the battle at last. As her body lapsed into a peaceful slumber, a distinct smile of total contentment appeared on her small face.

Oblivious to his surroundings or to the fact that he was due to attend a meeting, Joseph continued to rock his little girl.

"I cannot believe that they would even dare propose such an act, never mind carry it through!" John Hancock raved. "This Tea Act is Parliament's most foolish move yet! Have they gone mad? Do they truly expect we will just accept it?"

"Yes, they do," Joseph answered with no show of emotion. The eyes of every member of the Long Room Club were now focused on him as he calmly scanned a copy of the Tea Act, unaware that he commanded such attention.

"The English tea will be a great deal less expensive even with the hidden tax. They know that we are extremely fond of tea in the colonies. And they know that we are tired of the green tea from Holland. Such a price difference will cause many in the colonies to forget their opposition to the tax and buy the tea. Principle will be forgotten in favor of their purses."

"Certainly you do not condone this!" Hancock exclaimed.

"Of course not. I am just telling you what is bound to happen. We must be honest, John," Joseph said with a raised brow. "It is not the tax that has you so vehemently opposed. It is the fact that a monopoly is being forced on us."

Hancock scowled at him from across the table, knowing full well what Joseph's words implied.

"Great Britain is coming to the aid of the East India Company rather than see it go bankrupt. How much tea is reported to be stored in their warehouses?"

"Forty-million weight. A seven-year supply!" someone yelled out.

"Forty-million weight," Joseph repeated slowly. "And are all the merchants in America going to be able to profit by this overabundance of outrageously inexpensive tea? No, just a handpicked few are to be given the privilege. And that, Mr. Hancock, is why you and almost every other merchant in America are enraged. You are excluded—denied any profit from this forced sale!"

Hancock sat in silence, unable to defend himself.

"John, no one here blames you," Joseph continued. "We are all infuriated that Great Britain is attempting to monopolize the sale of tea. And if it can be done with tea, why not with other commodities? Private enterprise is seriously threatened with this act."

In the days that followed, the Committees of Correspondence quickly began communicating their opposition to this latest act. As the news spread throughout America, many of the merchants appointed to sell the tea now refused out of fear of retaliation from fellow colonists or because of their own convictions. But Boston was not able to report such good news.

Governor Hutchinson's sons were among the appointed consignees of the tea for the port town. They would not yield their privilege, no matter what the pressure.

On November 28, 1773, the first ship loaded with the detested cargo sailed into Boston's harbor. The captain was persuaded by the Sons of Liberty to postpone docking for two days. This postponement, they hoped, would provide enough time for the Sons to make an attempt to have the tea returned to England. They were mistaken.

When the ship finally docked, it was decided in an unofficial town meeting that an armed guard would be present on the wharf to prevent any of the tea from being unloaded. By law, the colonists could prevent the unloading of the cargo for up to twenty days during which time they could attempt to persuade the merchants to return it to England. After twenty days, if the ship remained unloaded, it was subject to governmental seizure. The cargo would then be sold at auction.

Shortly after the first ship's arrival, two more ships loaded with tea joined her at the wharf. All were placed under guard as the Sons worked frantically to legally rid themselves of the tea.

"If that tea is unloaded, it will be a major victory for Great Britain over us!" Sam said fretfully after listening to various reports from members of the Long Room Club. Meetings and demonstrations had proved effective in persuading the tax commissioners and ship owners to agree to have the tea returned. Yet, their reluctant decision was ineffective without the governor's approval. Without Hutchinson's signature, the ships would not leave the harbor, and Hutchinson emphatically refused to send the cargo back to England.

"We have fought a good fight, gentlemen. But with the governor's refusal, there is little else we can do," Dr. Benjamin Church announced.

"The fight is not over yet, Dr. Church," Joseph began, holding him under a steady gaze. "We will continue to meet with Hutchinson through the sixteenth of December, our final day before the cargo is seized."

"And if he continues to refuse? Perhaps the tea could be mysteriously destroyed prior to its unloading. Fires upon such cargo ships are not at all unusual, are they Mr. Hancock?" Dr. Church asked.

"No, not unusual, but not right if you are suggesting arson, Doctor! The tea is the responsibility of Great Britain. The ships are privately owned. I will have no part of destroying another man's property!"

"None of us would, I am certain!" Joseph agreed, glaring at Dr. Church. "But the tea cannot come ashore. If it does, I fear blood will be shed. The men of this town—of this entire colony—may be impossible to restrain if this should happen."

"I agree with you, Dr. Warren," Dr. Thomas Young remarked. "And every patriot throughout the colonies is anxiously awaiting our response. If the tea can be forced on us, it will be forced on them also."

Sam Adams stood and began pacing the floor. "Great Britain will have established her monopoly and collected her taxes. Soon more monopolies will be forced—more taxes collected against our will. Such a victory for Great Britain may very well be our total defeat!" He was obviously greatly disturbed that none of their actions thus far had been successful.

"We are in a desperate situation," Josiah declared. "We must somehow destroy the tea without damaging private property."

"Why not dump it into the harbor?"

Joseph looked around the room, unsure of who had made the suggestion.

"If disguises are worn and little is said, perhaps then we could safely manage it," Paul responded thoughtfully to the idea.

"Yes, Paul," Sam agreed, patting Paul's shoulder as he passed by. "If we plan well enough, perhaps we could! Be orderly in your conduct. No destruction of anything but the tea!"

"And all the tea must be destroyed," Parson Cooper added. "None of it shall be taken home by those involved. None whatsoever, no matter how tempting."

"Agreed, sir," Joseph responded. "That would be construed as thievery. Destruction of private property and thievery would make it a mob riot."

"Nor can it be seen as an act of the town or of any particular group of individuals," Sam added. "Those involved must be trusted to keep quiet. Few, very few of those in this room, should participate, and their identities must be kept secret. If anyone here is interested to make sure that all proceed in an orderly manner aboard the ships, speak to Dr. Warren or myself.

"Paul, can you get word out to those Sons of the highest reputation. We'll need about 150 strong men and boys—those who can keep their mouths shut!"

"I can."

After socializing a bit upon the adjournment of the meeting, everyone soon departed except Sam and Joseph.

"William Molineux and Thomas Young volunteered to be aboard the ships," Sam announced.

"Paul wants to be there," Joseph added.

"One to each ship. Good."

"I plan to be there, too," Joseph stated matter-of-factly.

"There is no need for you to take the risk since we already have three," Sam firmly protested.

"Ah, but someone has to keep an eye on Dr. Young!"

"You two make a fine team on the Committee of Correspondence. I was not aware that you still had animosity toward one another."

"We do not. I just want to be certain that nothing goes wrong. I want to take charge of the third ship."

"I thought it was Dr. Church that you didn't trust. Dr. Young also?" Sam asked smartly, his brows cocked.

"I cannot fathom how an atheist reasons, Sam. If he believes there is no God, then by what standard does he determine right from wrong? As far as Dr. Young is concerned, he has no one to answer to for any secret thoughts or deeds. I will feel better keeping an eye on him."

A final appeal to Governor Hutchinson was made on December 16. As 700 inhabitants of the Massachusetts Bay Colony awaited his reply at the Old South Meeting House, they were encouraged and inspired by the words of those who had led them in their stand for liberty.

To everyone's great surprise, Josiah Quincy rose from a seat in the east gallery. His father sat proudly at his side. Josiah's illness had hindered him from making lengthy orations and his great eloquence and remarkable delivery were sorely missed. As though equipped with strength from heaven itself, Josiah, with his typical, steady, clear, and commanding voice, boldly spoke out against the measures of Great Britain.

A Tory friend of Josiah's brother was present. The man stood and, pointing to Josiah, began to yell, "Such words will no longer be overlooked by the government, Mr. Quincy! Measures to punish such disloyalty will soon be taken!"

Josiah replied coolly, "If the gentleman who just spoke intended in friendship, as a father, to warn me, I thank him. If, on the other hand, his intent was to terrify or intimidate me, I despise him."

As Josiah spoke he saw the awaited messenger come through the doors. He pointed to the messenger and then raised his arms toward heaven, projecting his voice so that even those outside the meetinghouse could easily hear. "I see the clouds that now rise thick and fast upon our horizon, the thunders roll and the lightnings play, and to the God who rides on the whirlwind and directs the storm, I commit my country!"

Sam Adams stepped forward and received the governor's final message. Then he walked to the pulpit and solemnly declared, "This meeting can do nothing more to save the country."

A statement that was interpreted as defeat by most of the crowd was greeted with what sounded like Indian war whoops from the gallery. The crowd strained to see what the commotion was about.

Suddenly, from the shadows of the gallery, there appeared a large group of men in ragged clothes—their faces covered with grease and soot. Together they streamed out of the Old South Meeting House, crying, "To Griffin's wharf!" and "Let's make salt water tea!" A throng of people followed close behind, cheering them on.

Many notable figures lingered at the Old South. Sam Adams, Josiah Quincy, John Adams, and John Hancock were among them. Yet a few of their usual companions were nowhere to be found, including Joseph Warren.

"I understand you have something for me," Paul Revere said after the last patient left Joseph's surgery.

Joseph pulled out a thick letter from the inner pocket of his frock coat. "The Boston Committee of Correspondence's rendering of last night's occurrences. It is signed, sealed, and soon to be delivered to the Philadelphia Committee," he said with a smile as he handed the letter to Paul. "Are you absolutely certain that you are up to making this trip, my friend?" Joseph asked, aware that Paul had spent the entire previous night on one of the tea ships, dumping the tea and also cleaning up afterward.

"I'll catch some sleep this afternoon. I plan to leave shortly after sunset—" He stopped speaking as the door to the surgery opened and quickly placed the letter in the inner pocket of his greatcoat.

John Adams entered, his greatcoat and tricorn dusted with snow. "Mr. Revere, how convenient to find you and Dr. Warren together. I have heard something you both are certain to find of interest," John announced before Joseph or Paul even had a chance to greet him. "Gentlemen, it was my understanding that the identity of those involved in last night's affair was not to be revealed. Yet, there are some who are freely identifying two prominent figures in last night's events!"

"What are you talking about, John?" Joseph asked with alarm, concerned for the safety of those involved.

"I just passed by the Bunch of Grapes Tavern. The men inside are joyously singing a song about last night's events. It is a catchy little tune—now how did that verse go? Ah, yes, 'Our Warren's there and bold Revere, with hands to do, and words to cheer, for liberty and laws!'"

Paul and Joseph glanced at one another, obviously upset by the news.

"I'll stop by the tavern on my way home. Rest assured, I'll put an end to such songs!" Paul exclaimed. "Lord willing, I'll see you both upon my return from the city of Philadelphia."

"God's speed to you, Paul," Joseph said as his friend turned to leave.

"Apparently, you did not smear enough grease on your face last night, Doctor!" John teased.

"And what makes you think I was there? The men in the tavern must have mistaken someone else for me," Joseph replied, his eyes twinkling.

"Perhaps, but I saw no sign of you after the meeting."

"Come now, John. You know I get house calls at all hours."

"And no doubt, Dr. Young was on a house call also? Strange though, I heard a rumor that a few of last night's participants attempted to steal some of the tea. One of them was thought to have been Dr. Young."

Joseph was aware of it. He had ordered Young to be searched for concealed tea, but he did not respond to John's remark. He was disturbed that so much was already being said on the streets.

"Have you had time to prepare the ointment we discussed?" John asked.

"Yes, I have," Joseph replied. Reaching for a bottle on the shelf, he moaned softly as he lifted his arm.

"Dr. Warren, last night's activities were best left to the young apprentices of Boston and those Sons who are accustomed to hard physical labor," John said with a chuckle.

"I tell you, John, I am definitely not as fit as I once was! I realized last night just how spoiled I have become. I cannot remember the last time I swung an ax!" he said, finally admitting to what John already knew.

"Yes, I have noticed that you are putting on a few extra pounds!"

"Thanks to the kindhearted ladies of the Brattle Street congregation. Not a week passes of late that I do not receive three or four invitations to dinner."

"Why is it that I feel you are complaining, Doctor?" John asked.

"Because, sir, there is always an ulterior motive behind these invitations.

Always there is a young widow or marriageable maiden present. I tell you, John, it is embarrassing!" Joseph declared as John began to laugh. "How can I convince these gracious ladies that I am quite capable, with the help of the Almighty, of finding myself a wife?"

"And what is the problem with the women you have met?"

"I am sure they are all fine ladies. It is just that..." Joseph paused for a moment and considered what it was he wanted to say, "I am not ready to begin courting again. It is true that I'm lonely, but I am lonely for Elizabeth. I miss her and the relationship we had."

"You will always miss Elizabeth, just as I would Abigail if anything were to happen to her. But you are not trying to replace Elizabeth, just as none of your other children could replace the little one you lost."

Joseph seemed deep in thought, but he made no response to John's words.

"Well," John continued, "I suppose I had better tell Mrs. Adams that she need not concern herself with making arrangements to have you to dinner so you can meet her spinster cousin."

"Please, John, do!" Though Joseph wore a smile as he spoke, John saw the pleading in his eyes.

Reactions to the news of Boston's remedy to the Tea Act varied as it spread quickly from colony to colony. Some felt the act of destroying the tea to be a magnificent demonstration. Others were shocked by it. It would take time for the news of Boston's "Tea Party" to reach Great Britain. The winter seas would delay crossings, and by then any decision on the king's part in dealing with the tea's destruction would be further delayed.

For a few months' time, the patriots of Massachusetts Bay continued their daily routine, unhindered by parliamentary interference.

• 11 •

Mercy

THE SURGERY DOOR opened, bringing Joseph from the examination room to see who had entered. Instantly he recognized Thomas Cushing, a high Son of Liberty and occasional patient. At his side was a woman Joseph did not know. Though she held onto the arm of her escort, Joseph did not recognize her as a member of the Cushing family.

"Good afternoon, Dr. Warren. I fully expected, given the late hour, that you would not be here still," Thomas Cushing said, reaching up with his free hand and removing his tricorn.

"I am finishing up with a patient. If you will give me a minute, I will be ready to see to your needs, Mr. Cushing," Joseph said with a curious glance at the woman. Without offering Thomas Cushing the opportunity to respond, he disappeared back into the examination room.

When he again entered the waiting area, Mr. Cushing was gone, but the woman remained. After seeing his patient to the door, Joseph turned his full attention to her. She seemed lost in her thoughts, not even aware of his gaze. Gracefully pushing a misplaced lock of blonde hair back under her lace cap, she returned her hand to her lap. She was an attractive woman—with soft, delicate features and fair skin—probably about thirty years old, he determined. Her clothing was of the quality one would expect a member of the Cushing household to have purchased from England before the boycott. Homespun for a family of means would never be worn in public. And though her gown was silk—a shade of emerald that was quite unique—it bore the signs of wear with snags and tattered seams. What was once a white stomacher and fichu no longer appeared bright and new, but dull with age.

As if sensing him, the woman slowly looked in the direction where he stood. The expression on her face did not seem to reflect pain. Was it anger he detected in her soft blue eyes?

"May I be of assistance to you, Mrs.—?"

"Scollay, sir. Miss Mercy Scollay."

"Any relation to John Scollay?" Joseph asked, referring to the town selectman and high Son of Liberty.

"Yes, sir. His daughter."

Joseph nodded in silent acknowledgement. "Well, Miss Scollay, what seems to be the problem?"

"I have injured my ankle, Doctor," she said, lifting her skirt slightly as she looked down at her left ankle. "I foolishly slipped on the cobblestones."

"You would be surprised at how many people come through that door for the very same reason," he offered, sensing her embarrassment over the situation. "Sometimes I wonder if we would be better off without the roads being laid in stone. It certainly can be a hazard in wet weather. Shall we wait for Mr. Cushing to return?" he asked, ever aware of the extreme modesty of the Puritan woman and their need to have a family member or friend present before a physician could even examine a twisted ankle. "I did not realize the Cushings were related to the Scollays."

"Sir?" she replied, obviously confused by his statement.

"Mr. Cushing? Is he a relative?"

"Oh no, sir. Mr. Cushing witnessed my fall and was kind enough to escort me here," she replied as she attempted to stand. It immediately became clear that she could put no weight on the injured ankle.

"Please let me help you, Miss Scollay," Joseph said, offering his arm for support just as Thomas Cushing had done.

"I must confess, Doctor, that I did not lose my footing except through my own clumsiness," Mercy offered, limping into the examination room. "I stormed out of the seamstress shop in such a rage that I was just not paying attention!"

"The seamstress shop? What could possibly occur there that would upset you so?" he asked, certain that her answer would have something to do with a poor fitting or the wrong material used for a dress or some such complaint.

"The women of this town spend their time complaining about the stand their men have taken for our liberties. They complain that their husbands are giving money to the cause. They complain that they have to go without English tea and may have to go without imported fabric again. I tell you, Doctor, the women of this town are more concerned about their apparel than they are about their own liberty!" she exclaimed as Joseph helped her up on the examination table.

Joseph grinned, delighted by the enthusiasm of John Scollay's daughter.

"I am quite serious, sir!" she assured him, misinterpreting the reason for his smile. "I have even considered writing a satire on this very subject!" she added as she bent over and gently removed her satin-covered shoe and the hosiery from her injured foot. She carefully laid them upon her lap.

"Well, by all means, Miss Scollay, write it!" Joseph exclaimed. "I would be happy to review it for you. Then we can see about getting it printed." He took hold of her foot and pressed his fingers hard against her ankle, feeling for a possible fracture.

Mercy winced slightly, biting her lower lip as the pain intensified. "Printed?" she asked through gritted teeth, gripping the sides of the table in response to the discomfort his prodding accentuated.

"If it is good," he said as he began to gently rotate her foot. "We seldom hear from any Daughters of Liberty. Such a satire could have a great impact upon the women of Boston. That is what you want, is it not?" He completed his examination and looked up at her. "I could have it printed in either the *Massachusetts Spy* or the *Gazette.*"

Mercy sat in silence, visibly astonished that the satire she had only considered writing was ready to be put into print as far as Dr. Warren was concerned.

"You have not fractured any bones. A bad sprain is what you have," he announced as he walked to the shelf for a liniment. "Do you have a way to get home?" he asked, opening the bottle and pouring some of the liquid into his hands.

"I could hop," she answered with a ready smile.

Amused by her response, Joseph looked up and laughed. "I have a few things to take care of here, then I will be happy to escort you."

"Oh, no, Doctor! Please, I could not impose upon you!" Mercy insisted as he gently applied the liniment. "Perhaps if I could send a message to my father, he or one of the servants would come and get me. Do you have a servant here who could take the message for me, or perhaps a child? I intend to pay them for their trouble," she said, picking up the stocking.

"Both my servant and apprentice are out, and the children—" he paused for a moment. "The children aren't home, either." He handed her the bottle of liniment after she slipped on the stocking and shoe.

Mercy noted the sorrow in his tone, and she suddenly felt foolish as she remembered a conversation between her father and their own family physician, John Jeffries. He had told them about the death of Dr. Warren's wife and how he was forced to live apart from his children.

"Believe me, Miss Scollay, you are not imposing," he said, offering his hand to help her down from the table. "I have nothing planned for the remainder of the day, one of those rare, quiet evenings at home that I have come to detest," he heard himself say, but he could not take it back. Quite embarrassed for his behavior in front of a patient, especially one who he had only just met, he looked at Mercy, intending to apologize.

"You will be doing me a favor," he confessed, his eyes locked on hers. There was no need to apologize or explain his behavior. It was clear to him that somehow she understood.

"She needs to get off that ankle," Joseph informed John Scollay after Mercy briefly explained her mishap to her father. "The ankle should be elevated with cold packs applied to it. I will stop by Dr. Jeffries' surgery and tell him of your accident. He may want to look in on you in the morning," he said to Mercy.

"Well, my dear, you heard the doctor. I will call the servant to help you to your chamber," John Scollay began.

"My chamber? Now, Father, I can hardly retire to my chamber when we are having a guest for dinner.

"Dr. Warren, you will stay? We must insist that you do!" she said as she laid an impelling hand on her father's arm. "Tell him, Father. It is our way of showing how much we appreciate him seeing me home."

"Of course, Dr. Warren. We insist that you stay!" John joined in under his daughter's coaching.

"Miss Scollay, you are supposed to get off that ankle," Joseph said firmly.

"I will, Doctor, as soon as I get washed up for dinner. I will sit on that chair," she said pointing to a particular chair at the dining room table. "And I will prop my foot up on the one right next to it. I promise," she added with a sweet smile that revealed two dimples.

Joseph did not think she would be very comfortable at the dinner table in such a position, but he could see that she was determined to have her way. And, truth be told, he welcomed the opportunity to escape an evening alone.

"Please come in and make yourself comfortable," John Scollay offered after Mercy began to climb the staircase with their servant woman at her side. He led Joseph into the parlor. The elaborate, Venetian wallpaper instantly captured his attention with its scenes of life along the waterways of Italy.

"I hope you can pardon my daughter's exuberance, Doctor," John Scollay said apologetically as both men sat down.

"Pardon it?" Joseph exclaimed. "Sir, I find her exuberance to be quite refreshing!"

"Really?" the older man studied his guest in silence for a moment.

"Your daughter possesses a strong sense of patriotism," Joseph commented, not sure what to make of his host's awkward silence.

"Yes, yes, she does. And I can assure you, Doctor, she is quite sincere," John Scollay replied. After a brief pause, he added, "I feel I must warn you, though. She will, no doubt, take advantage of your being a guest in our home this evening."

A forced and very weak smile came to Joseph's lips upon hearing the warning. Ah, Joseph thought, another evening of the typical conversation I find myself so bored with at the numerous dinner tables I am invited to by the ladies of the Brattle Street congregation. I had hoped tonight's conversation would be different—not the usual attempt at trying to impress me with the domestic abilities and natural-born sense of mothering possessed by all the young widows and spinsters they have me meet. It is so obvious and humiliating—but I suppose even that is easier than enduring another lonely evening at home.

"My daughter," John Scollay continued, distracting Joseph from his gloomy thoughts, "is well informed of our position and our latest public dealings with Great Britain. At times she even seems to be able to sense what is going on behind closed doors," he remarked, referring to the secret dealings of groups like the Long Room Club.

Joseph raised his eyebrows in response to John's remark.

"She is a great admirer of yours, Dr. Warren—the stand you have taken, I mean. She has read all of your work. I am certain Mercy will have many questions for you. She is not shy!"

Joseph laughed, relieved that Miss Mercy Scollay was not interested in impressing him with her wifely abilities after all. "No, Mr. Scollay, she certainly is not shy!"

"And she can be quite bold," John's tone was grave.

"Are you implying that your daughter may be rude?"

"No!" John seemed disturbed that he had given this impression. "It is just that, if she should disagree with a point you make, she will tell you. She will be polite about it, but she will let you know. And she is likely to take it further than that. She may offer suggestions of her own on how to approach a certain problem!"

Joseph did not respond, and his blank expression gave no clue to his host of his thoughts.

"I do not want you to be offended by her. Others have not known what to make of Mercy, but perhaps you can understand. She has spent too much time in the company of her brothers and myself. With her mother dying at such a tender age, I am afraid that in many ways we had too great an influence in her life."

"Offended?" Joseph echoed with a pleasant smile. "I always enjoy intelligent conversation and would like to think of myself as being able to reevaluate any course of action in light of new insight."

"By a woman?" John Scollay was astounded.

"If it is done with proper respect, just as I would expect from any man. My mother, sir, possesses this same quality that you describe in your daughter. So did my wife. She had a similar upbringing to that of your daughter. She was my dearest friend. I came to depend on her insight. She was not always right, but there were times that, had I not given heed to her wise and prudent suggestions, I would have been in the wrong.

"I do not feel threatened by such behavior, Mr. Scollay. In fact, I welcome it! Often our women view things in a different light than we do, and therefore they can call our attention to things we may have overlooked."

John Scollay's face was aglow as a wide grin spread across his lips as he realized that Mercy was to meet her match. This unusual dinner guest was not only a man who could hold his own against her vivacious spirit, but one who would enjoy her company as well! The flame of hope, which John Scollay had believed to be completely extinguished, was suddenly rekindled. Perhaps Mercy was not destined to spinsterhood after all.

Mercy's entrance into the parlor upon the arm of her servant was graceful, despite her obvious limp. Joseph's attention was focused on her as he rose to his feet. He failed to see the twinkle in John Scollay's eyes, and that his grin had become wider still.

"Good evening, Doctor," Abigail Quincy greeted Joseph after answering his knock. Hidden behind his mother's flowing skirt was little Josiah, peeking his head around to get a glimpse of the visitor.

"Good evening, Mrs. Quincy," Joseph replied with a warm smile. With his medical bag in one hand, with the other he removed his hat and stepped inside. Looking down at the small boy, he asked, "Is that you, Master Josiah?"

"Yes, sir," the timid youngster responded as his head disappeared behind his mother's skirt again.

"Well, let me have a look at you, lad," Joseph said.

The four-year-old boy slowly stepped alongside his mother, holding tightly to her skirt with one hand. He was dressed in a cream-colored nightshirt and cap, his brown curls falling loosely about his small shoulders.

"How are you this evening, young sir?" Joseph asked.

"Fine, Dr. Warren," he replied, his eyes cast downward.

"I am delighted to hear it," Joseph responded with an affectionate pat on the boy's head. He directed his attention back to Abigail and said, "I am here to see your husband."

"He is in his study and has been expecting you."

"Then I will not keep him waiting any longer. Good night, young sir," Joseph said as he walked toward the closed door of Josiah's study.

"Good night, Doctor Warren," the little voice called back.

Josiah opened the door before Joseph had a chance to knock. "I thought I heard you. Come in." He threw a quick smile at his wife and son as he closed the door behind them.

Joseph removed his greatcoat and made himself comfortable in the seat facing Josiah's desk. "I am relieved to see I do not need this," he said, placing his medical bag on the floor beside the chair. "From the urgency of your note, I was not sure."

"To be honest, I wish it were a matter you could take care of with that bag," Josiah began as he sat down. "My brother extended to me an invitation to dine with him this afternoon. I had hoped the invitation was because he wanted to spend some time with me to catch up on family matters and such—" Josiah's grief over the separation between his brother and himself was evident.

"Samuel received a letter from a friend in Great Britain, a friend in high places. According to this letter, the Crown is demanding that those involved in the destruction of the tea be arrested and sent to England to stand trial."

"We expected as much," Joseph said with a shrug. "First they have to determine who was involved and prove their accusations."

"Samuel has a list of so-called perpetrators. He showed it to me. Your name heads the list."

"Really?" Joseph asked calmly. "Does he have any proof?"

"Not that I could determine."

"Then it is no more than a threat. We have been living with such threats for years now," Joseph calmly replied.

"It is different this time," Josiah was visibly upset.

"How so?"

"Those rumored warrants we have been hearing about for so long—well, at least three do exist. There is one for you, one for Sam Adams, and one for John Hancock. The governor has refused to use them thus far, fearing the reaction of the people. Samuel is putting pressure on him to issue them," Josiah informed him.

"Did you see the warrants?"

"I did. They are official."

"What is the charge?" Joseph braced himself for the answer.

Josiah hesitated. "Sedition," he uttered barely above a whisper.

Joseph took a deep breath and remained silent. He knew this was what the charge would be, but the expectation did not lessen the impact.

"I guess Samuel's purpose in telling me all of this was to frighten me into disassociating myself from the Long Room Club and the Sons. My brother does not understand that a man who is already under a death sentence is not easily frightened!" Josiah said in reference to his illness.

"Do you think Hutchinson will issue the warrants?" Joseph asked.

"He still has the people of this colony to contend with. The vast majority of them support you. He may very well have a riot on his hands if he does, and he knows it," Josiah pointed out.

"The solicitor general must be looking for a commendation of some sort. Why else would he be so persistent in this?" Joseph began as he leaned forward in the chair and rested his forehead in his hands. "I considered him a friend. He ate at my table and I at his. We knelt in prayer together. He stood with us in this fight. Now, to secure his prestigious title and win the praise of men some 3,000 miles away, will he actually betray us?" Joseph looked up at his friend and saw the agony in Josiah's face. "I am sorry," he said. "He is your brother, and I know you love him. I am sorry—"

"You have nothing to be sorry for," Josiah assured him. "I do love him, but what he is doing is treacherous."

"Have you told Sam and John?"

"Yes. They have decided to destroy any questionable material addressed to them or written by them. I strongly suggest you do the same. And keep in mind, Joseph, if they move against you, they will twist even the most innocent remark to support their charge of sedition."

John Jeffries flipped through the pages of his daybook as it lay on the rolltop desk, stopping periodically to copy down certain information. Patiently, Joseph waited, relaxing in the overstuffed, winged-back chair. His eyes drifted about the room. *It is just like Jeffries to have such elaborate decor in his surgery,* Joseph thought as he admired the scenic paintings upon the walls. *But, then again, what is one to do when paintings are passed down from generation to generation? A home can only accommodate so many—*

"That is it," John said, disrupting Joseph's thoughts. John closed the daybook and handed Joseph the information he had copied. "My apprentices can handle most of my cases. It is only these few that will need your attention. It disturbs me a great deal to leave now," John continued as Joseph scanned the papers. "Mr. Wright's condition is guarded. Mr. Collins' recovery from surgery is slower than it should be. Mrs. Phillips is threatening to go into premature labor. I have a strong suspicion she is carrying twins, so be prepared. Miss Brown—"

"We have been over all of this, John," Joseph interrupted with a compassionate smile. "You have told me everything I need to know. I will take good care of them in your absence."

"I know you will. It is just that—"

"It is just that you are overdue for a holiday," Joseph finished the sentence for his friend. "John, leave your patients to me. Go and enjoy yourself!"

"Enjoy myself?" John exclaimed. "I do not expect to enjoy myself! You do not understand. It is my wife's cousin's wedding." John lowered his voice and leaned forward in the chair as though he feared someone might overhear him. "I will be spending three days in Salem with my in-laws!"

"I did not realize you had a problem with your wife's family," Joseph responded, trying to conceal his amusement over John's distress.

"Do not get me wrong. They are fine people. We invite them to dinner often. We spend a few hours together. We talk, we laugh, they go home, and everyone is happy. But at this wedding, there will be brothers and sisters, aunts and uncles, nieces and nephews, not to mention cousins as many as three times removed—all of them together at once, and all of them expecting free medical care."

Joseph laughed.

"It is not the least bit amusing!" John insisted. "For three entire days I will have to listen to them tell me about their aches and pains."

"Well, you be sure to tell them that there is a brilliant young physician right in Salem who will be happy to see to their needs," Joseph suggested with a grin.

"Jack?" John asked.

Joseph nodded.

"Why would they pay him when they can hound me for free?" John rolled his eyes as he flopped back in the chair. "I will just have to endure it. I do plan to stop by and check on your brother while I am up there, though. I should have let you know sooner and you could have written—"

As John spoke, Joseph pulled a sealed letter from his pocket. "I took a chance that you might visit him." He handed the letter to John.

"Jack must be all settled in by now. Has he found himself a bride yet?" John asked, leaning forward again as though eager to hear Joseph's reply.

"No," Joseph said with a chuckle. "He has been busy with his work."

"Then he has established a practice of his own?" John asked. "I thought he was still with old Doc Holyoke."

"He is still with him, but Jack is treating most of Holyoke's patients."

"Good for him. When Holyoke decides to retire, Jack will take the practice over." John said, sinking back into the chair with a definite look of contentment.

"Why do I get the feeling that it is not really Jack's welfare you are concerned with?" Joseph asked in a suspicious tone.

John hesitated for a moment. "That brother of yours is talented, perhaps too talented. I understand he has already made a reputation for himself among the physicians in Salem. His ability to diagnose as accurately as he does is uncanny. And his surgical skill—Joseph, he is only twenty-two years old! He performs surgery as though he has been at it for ten years! I tell you, if he sets up a practice here in Boston, we both may very well lose some of our own patients to him!"

Joseph wore a proud smile.

"I am already losing patients to you. I do not need to worry about him, too!" John complained. Though his face appeared stern, there was a twinkle in his eyes.

"Losing patients to me? Who?"

"John and Mercy Scollay!" John exclaimed with a teasing smile.

"Miss Scollay twisted her ankle outside my surgery. Should I have refused to treat her and sent her to you instead?" Joseph asked with a laugh.

"I understand you have been making calls on the Scollay home. Are you denying these visits have been of a medical nature? Ah, then they must be social calls. Are you visiting John Scollay, or is it his daughter's company you seek?"

Joseph did not respond, but smiled in return to John's boyish grin.

"I knew it!" John exclaimed with the clap of his hands. "A perfect match, too! John Scollay must be delighted. Mercy will make a fine wife. She is a great cook, loves children, and is every bit as idealistic as you are! No doubt about it, you two were made for each other!"

"Wait just a minute, John!" Joseph objected, raising his hands in protest. "I have begun courting Miss Scollay, it is true, but there has been no talk of marriage."

John shrugged. "You would not have even considered courting her unless you were pretty sure she was the one. When are you going to tell her? I am certain she feels the same. Now, that will be a wedding I will enjoy myself at!"

Joseph shook his head slowly as he studied his friend in silence. There was a trace of a smile upon his lips. "Your arrogance is truly astounding."

"Arrogance?" John echoed with a chuckle. "A small child could see the sense in it. She possesses every quality you could want in a wife, and the fact that she is thirty-four is a positive factor. Being mature, she will not be overwhelmed by her responsibilities of motherhood and seeing to the needs of apprentices.

"And as for Mercy's outlook, well, every woman in Boston considers you the most eligible male. Mercy must be the envy of countless women!" John laughingly said, obviously quite pleased with himself.

"I always thought Hancock held that title," Joseph commented.

"Hancock likes to think he does, but quite honestly, Hancock loves himself a little too much. The dream of becoming Mrs. John Hancock has been long forgotten by many a maiden."

"Well, do me a favor and keep your opinion about my private life to yourself for the time being," Joseph said with a smile as he stood. "Mercy has certainly captured my attention, and to be truthful, it is my intention to ask her to be my wife, but—" Joseph paused, fixing his eyes on his friend's. "I have not yet made my intentions known to Mercy or her father, and I do not want you, your wife, or anyone else to make them known for me. Do you understand me, sir?"

"You know you can trust me!" John said, the perpetual mischievous twinkle in his dark eyes.

"Like a snake," Joseph replied.

"Now, Joseph, considering the fact that I am so graciously turning Mercy and her father over to your practice, you should give serious thought to naming your first son after me," John suggested with a grin.

Joseph simply smiled. Without a word, he turned and walked toward the door. "John Warren," he muttered, standing at the door with his hand on the knob. He turned his head to face John. He appeared thoughtful. "John Warren is a fine name, indeed. Yes, I can certainly promise that should we marry, our first son will be named John."

John's face brightened with the announcement.

"I will see you when you return, John. Try to enjoy yourself." Joseph opened the door and left the room.

As he walked back toward his surgery, Joseph could not help but laugh aloud at the thought of John Jeffries gloating over the belief that a son would actually be named for him. How long would it be, Joseph wondered, before his arrogant friend realized that the name of John would naturally be given in honor of Mercy's father.

It suddenly occurred to him that the sooner he made his intentions known to Mercy, the better. He changed direction and headed for Paul Revere's shop. He had seen the fine pieces of gold jewelry Paul had crafted. A delicate necklace or brooch would be the perfect gift to accompany his proposal.

· 12 ·

The Boston Port Bill

A PATRON BURSTING into a respectable tavern such as The Bunch of Grapes was enough cause for concern. The fact that the patron was John Hancock brought a true sense of alarm.

Instantly he spotted John Adams, Josiah Quincy, and Joseph Warren at their usual table in a darkened corner. "I was told I would find you here!" he exclaimed breathlessly. His face was unusually pale, even for Hancock. In his hand he clenched a folded document.

"Sit down. Sit down, Jay," John Adams instructed, trying to quiet the scene as others began to look on. Still sitting, he pulled a vacant chair out from under the table.

Hancock slumped into the chair, holding the document toward John Adams with a trembling hand. He then picked up his friend's mug and took a large gulp of its contents.

"What is it?" Josiah asked impatiently as John Adams unfolded the paper.

"The king has ordered the port of Boston closed to all shipping!" Hancock blurted, without waiting for John Adams to respond.

"What?" Joseph exclaimed as Hancock took another gulp of John Adams' drink.

"Punishment for destroying the tea . . . the ports are to remain closed until the tea is paid for in full."

"Is it so, John?" Josiah asked John Adams as he continued to read the crumbled document. John's face now appeared as pale as that of his childhood friend's.

John Adams simply nodded, his eyes fixed on the paper before him.

"June first—by June first!" Hancock added.

"That is only three weeks away!" Joseph exclaimed. "It will never happen. The people will not stand for it. The livelihood of too many colonists hangs in the balance. The governor will never allow it!" he rambled.

"Governor Hutchinson has been summoned to appear before the king to give an account of the situation," John Adams began in a mournful tone, his eyes still on the paper. "A military governor has been appointed: Major General Thomas Gage, along with 4,000 troops to see that the Boston Port Bill is enforced and the town brought into subjection. He is also to arrest all those in Boston suspected of sedition and transport them to Great Britain for trial."

"That means each one of us, gentlemen!" Hancock said, reaching up and subconsciously tugging at his cravat.

"How can the tea possibly be paid for if the ports are closed?" Josiah asked.

"A good portion of our food supply and firewood comes through the port as well," Joseph added. "Come winter—surely the king has a reasonable time limit on this punishment?"

"No. The ports are to remain closed until the tea is paid for in full, or until we starve," Hancock replied.

Joseph took a deep breath and said, "Then starve it will be. For even if the men of this town were to agree to pay for the tea, with the port closed we are hopeless to even make the attempt."

"I do not believe we will starve. The outrage of this act will bring the sister colonies to our aid. I am certain of it," Josiah said with confidence. "Through the Committees of Correspondence, we will obtain the help we need."

"Josiah, nothing can come by sea," Hancock stated. "How are we to get such large quantities of supplies from other colonies with the port closed? And how are we to pay for it?"

"The ports in Rhode Island are not closed, nor those just north of us in Marblehead, Gloucester, or Salem. Everything can be shipped to these ports and transported to Boston by land."

"And how do we pay for it?" Hancock asked again.

"We ask for donations. If the king can close the port in Boston, he can close it anywhere. Certainly, our sister colonies will realize this. We must unite—"

"There is more," John Adams interrupted, finally laying the paper on the table. "The second act of this bill orders the dissolution of the Massachusetts Charter."

"But it has been the outline of our civil government for well over a hundred years!" Joseph lamented, picking up the paper as if hoping to find that it was not so. "What do they propose to take its place?"

"Royal appointments. Not even a jury will be called except that it is handpicked by those with royal appointments." John Adams gazed vacantly at the wall before him. Then turning his attention to Joseph, he continued, "And if the outrage of these intolerable acts against Massachusetts Bay—Boston in particular—are not enough to send shock waves throughout the colonies, then the final act listed certainly will have that effect."

Joseph read the final portion, entitled The Quebec Act, and then looked at

Josiah and handed the paper to him. "Parliament, with the king's approval, has finally given their permission for the land beyond the Allegheny mountain range to be settled."

Josiah was obviously confused, for the colonists had desired this land for settlement for many years. "Why should that upset our sister colonies? It seems to be an appeasement, a means of causing them to overlook our suffering in light of what they may obtain. In fact, some may take this opportunity to head westward."

"No, Josiah. You do not understand. Read it," Joseph said, pointing to the paper.

"In truth, gentlemen, The Quebec Act may prove to be Parliament's greatest blunder," Hancock stated, looking from John Adams to Joseph.

"Indeed, you may be right, Jay. I believe the hand of Providence may be at work here. To close that rich farmland off to English colonists, who have petitioned Parliament to gain access to it for more than ten years now, and then offer it instead to the French colonists in Quebec, is an insult. One that our sister colonies will not lightly receive. They may differ in their opinions of whether our decision to destroy the tea was morally sound and therefore may shrug at the acts being brought against us. But they will not shrug at the fact that they, too, are being punished."

As the first of June approached, Boston prepared itself for the impoverishment to come. Ships loaded with food and fuel supplies pulled in to dock. Merchants prepared to close down their warehouses, leaving scores of men without any means to provide for their families.

British men-of-war invaded the harbor, their cannons once again threatening the town. British soldiers in their bright red coats, which the Bostonians had come to detest five years earlier, again crowded the streets.

Yet, in the face of impending hardship such as Boston had never witnessed, her inhabitants found strength and encouragement. The seafaring traffic normally destined for Boston was now to be rerouted to the smaller port of Marblehead, north of Boston. This small, struggling town now had the opportunity to prosper greatly. But the merchants of Marblehead, sympathetic to the cause of liberty, refused to gain financially at Boston's expense. In a gesture that genuinely touched the hearts of patriot and Tory alike, they opened their empty warehouses to the Boston merchants free of charge.

Desiring heaven's strength and protection, the Puritan colony appointed days of prayer and fasting. Such solemn occasions were not unusual for Massachusetts Bay, but as their trials intensified, such days became more commonplace.

The first of June was to be such a day. Word from other colonies informed the Bostonians that they, too, would spend this day in prayer and fasting for Boston's sake. This brought much encouragement.

But more than the dedication of one day was needed. The tea would not be paid for. Even in the face of certain starvation, Boston's Sons of Liberty would not cower and bow. A move of God's hand to provide aide to the destitute town was necessary for its citizens' survival.

When the dreaded day arrived, it was greeted by the dull mourning sound of muffled church bells echoing throughout Boston. The fast and supplications to heaven began with the tolling of the bells.

Now an eerie silence replaced the commotion of the wharves where men had once busied themselves from sunrise to sunset. One passing by this deserted area could almost hear the ghostlike sound of the giant masts blowing in the wind. Seagulls with their shrill cry circled in confusion, protesting the absence of fishing vessels, which had once crowded the wharves.

Warehouses stood empty. Men roamed the streets aimlessly, and women sat at home in tears, unsure of what would become of their families.

Then with growing faith, the people of Boston watched as, one by one, their prayers were answered.

Supplies began arriving, not from the sea, but by land. They first came from the neighboring communities. Then the contributions of sister colonies: rice from South Carolina, sheep from Connecticut, money from Virginia . . .

"It will take some time to print enough copies to circulate. We will begin first thing tomorrow," Benjamin Edes announced to the members of the Long Room Club as he flipped through the numerous pages in his hands. "It is a fine work, Josiah. I am astonished that you wrote it as quickly as you did."

"Not such a difficult task, Mr. Edes, when you consider that my physician had me confined to my bedchamber the past few days," Josiah stated, casting a sideways glance at Joseph. "But I fear that there may be many grammatical errors throughout the text."

"Few grammatical errors that I detected," the former schoolmaster, Joseph Warren, observed. He, too, was amazed at Josiah's accomplishment. His zeal never seemed to weaken even while deathly ill. Had he been a healthy man the past four years, Joseph wondered how much more he might have accomplished. "Is there any chance that we can circulate this in England as well as in the colonies?" Joseph asked.

"I have been considering the same thing myself, Doctor," Sam Adams replied. "I am sure our friends in England will be interested in the arguments put forth in Josiah's work."

Josiah Quincy's paper, entitled, "Observations of the Boston Port Bill," soundly confronted the numerous violations of English law that the Bostonians now faced. Such logic would hopefully sway those who remained uncertain as to whether Boston deserved such severe and illegal punishment.

"Any problems encountered by the Donations Committee?" Sam asked.

The Donations Committee, to which both Joseph and Josiah were elected, was created for a two-fold purpose. First, its members were to respond with letters of appreciation to the many towns throughout the colonies and abroad that had sent food, supplies, or money.

Secondly, they were to organize the things that were donated. Work forces were set up so that a man could work for the things he needed. This, it was agreed, was the best method of distributing the supplies. Different jobs were planned, such as repairing roads and wharves

"A very stirring letter was delivered today, along with supplies from a sister colony. I thought you might be inspired upon hearing it," Joseph announced.

Sam nodded his approval for Joseph to proceed.

"'This contribution is for suffering brethren who are standing in the gap between us and slavery. We are but few in number, and of small ability; and, as we earn our bread by the sweat of our brow, shall ever hold in utter detestation both men and measures that would rob us of the fruits of our toil; and are ready with our labor, with our lives, and with our estates, to stand or fall in the common cause of liberty. And, if we fall, we shall die like men and like Christians, and enjoy the glorious privileges of the sons of God.'"

Silence filled the room for a moment as each man contemplated the words.

"Such a short message. Yet, I feel greatly strengthened by it. What more needs to be said?" John Adams asked thoughtfully. "Gentlemen, we shall continue to pray that our efforts to unite and determine a peaceful settlement of differences with the mother country be blessed during the upcoming Continental Congress."

"And that an immediate means of relief be found for Boston," Josiah added.

"Sam, I have scheduled a fitting for you with my own tailor," John Hancock suddenly announced.

"What is this you are talking about, John?" Sam asked, aware of the smiles appearing on the face of each man present.

The members of the Long Room Club had determined that the man who was certain to have the greatest impact at the congress being called in Philadelphia to discuss the severity of the situation with Great Britain should make a good impression.

"We have decided that you should be fitted with a new suit for your important trip to Philadelphia. It is a gift from all of us," Joseph quickly responded, fearing that John's answer might be less tactful.

"A new suit? But the ones I have are quite comfortable. Brother John, are you being fitted also?" Sam asked John Adams, who was to attend congress with him.

"No, Sam. John is not being fitted. John does not need a new suit. You do!" John Hancock said curtly. "Sam, you shall be representing Massachusetts Bay. You should appear dignified and respectable."

Much was being done to alleviate the immediate crisis in Boston and throughout the colonies. The Committees of Correspondence continued their work of informing and gathering information. The Donations Committee kept busy with the needs of the Bostonians. All of Massachusetts anxiously awaited the scheduled meeting of the First Continental Congress.

It was felt that a representative from Boston should sail to Great Britain and relate the true situation. Not only was there an urgent need for reliable representation in Great Britain, it would be equally important to gather information to assist the distressed colony in making sound decisions.

Representatives from the colonies had been sent in the past, but now—at this crucial moment—Boston needed her own. Such an important mission could only be entrusted to a man well versed in the present situation, someone eloquent in speech and gifted in diplomacy.

Of the men who qualified for this mission, none was able to undertake it at the present. With warrants out for their arrest, Sam Adams, Joseph Warren, and John Hancock would certainly be arrested upon their arrival in England. John Adams was scheduled to be in Philadelphia. And although Josiah Quincy would prove an excellent representative, it was out of the question to ask him.

Josiah's health was rapidly deteriorating, his remissions growing shorter in duration. The warmer months of spring and summer no longer brought extended relief. Josiah's friends would not even consider asking him to attempt this mission.

"You can put your shirt back on," Joseph said, disturbed at what he had discovered during the examination. Josiah's lungs were filling with fluid. Even as Joseph looked at his friend, he saw death upon his face with its gaunt, sickly appearance, exaggerated by the slight bulging of his walleye.

"It has come to my attention that decisions were made in regard to me in which I had no say," Josiah casually remarked.

Joseph was puzzled.

"The mission to England," Josiah said as Joseph handed him the ruffled, cotton shirt. "Why was I not informed of the discussions concerning this?"

"You had just recovered from your last attack, my friend. You were not able to attend those meetings."

"I trusted you to keep me well-informed of the meetings when you came to visit me, Doctor. Apparently I was wrong!" he exclaimed, slipping his arms into the shirtsleeves.

"Calm yourself, Josiah," Joseph urged, wanting to avoid the possibility of triggering a painful, coughing spell. "It was a thought we considered. Nothing came of it. There is really nothing of importance to tell you."

"Nothing became of it because you all felt that there was no one qualified who could undertake the task. I disagree!"

"Oh? Who have we overlooked?" Joseph asked as he sat down at the secretary, preparing to enter Josiah's present condition in his daybook.

"You did not overlook anyone—you disqualified me, and I definitely object!" Josiah said sternly.

Joseph looked up from the daybook and studied his friend in silence for a moment as Josiah busied himself with the numerous shirt buttons. "You are right. We disqualified you, and with good reason," he said calmly, which aggravated the young attorney all the more.

"I am in remission!" Josiah exclaimed, looking up.

Joseph's only response to Josiah's exclamation was a regretful look, but the look spoke volumes.

"There is enough time for me to get to England. Then perhaps the climate there will prove beneficial," Josiah argued, standing up from the examination table and grabbing his waistcoat from a nearby side chair.

Joseph still did not respond.

"I have heard that it is possible for some in my condition."

"For some the response is quite remarkable, but others do not do well at all," Joseph said. "We cannot be certain that the climate there will help you."

"I am willing to take that chance. I can be of service there, Joseph! I know I can! I will go at my own expense, of course. I was planning another trip to South Carolina this fall anyway, Joseph." He spoke quietly, earnestly, his eyes now locked with those of his friend's. "I want to go. I want to be of service. Do you have any idea what it has been like to stand back watching while everyone else proceeded with the work to be done? Do you know how frustrating it is to decline invitations to give orations because my illness will not permit it? I watched helplessly as you all boarded the tea ships, after which I was forced to walk home alone in the darkness, not able to even stand on the wharf with the crowd because the damp, night air was harmful to me."

Joseph listened in absolute astonishment. Josiah had been one of the most trusted, outspoken, and fervent leaders among the Sons of Liberty. His name was well known throughout the colonies for his work on the Committee of Correspondence, as well as his trip to the South two years earlier. But his convictions were so strong—his love of liberty so true, he was not satisfied with his own accomplishments and wanted to do more.

"Even if your condition should improve in England," Joseph began reluctantly, "you run the risk of being arrested. If our attempts to circulate your paper were successful, then your name is well known by our enemies as well as our friends."

"Ah, yes, but my brother's name is known and respected by our enemies. Regard for his royal appointment may just give me the protection I need. And my defense of the king's soldiers after the Massacre is also in my favor."

Joseph considered his answer for a moment and then asked, "What about your family, Josiah?"

"My father and father-in-law will provide for them."

"That is not what I mean," Joseph replied quickly. He knew that the Sons of Liberty would undertake the support of Josiah's family should he go on this mission. "A trip to England will take more time than one to South Carolina—precious time, Josiah."

Josiah smiled. It was a sad smile, but genuine. "We seem to have a reversal of roles, Doctor. Do you remember the scene that was played out two years ago when you and Sam encouraged me to travel south?"

"I do." The words were spoken quietly, hesitantly, as Joseph kept his friend under a steady gaze. "That was different, Josiah."

"How so?"

"I had no doubt about that trip being beneficial to your health—."

"My prayer is that I return from this trip in better health than I have known of late. I feel I must do this, Joseph, and your approval is what I need to persuade the others."

"And what about Abigail and your father? How will they react to this trip?"

"If they can see that the trip may be mutually beneficial to my health and the state of our country, then they will accept it wholeheartedly."

Josiah walked over to the desk. Leaning upon it with his hands spread before him, he stared intently at Joseph. His eyes reflected his great distress, and in frustration he continued, "We are both aware that we desperately need a representative over there. What is wrong with you?"

"I do not want to be responsible for sending you to your death!" Joseph was becoming irritated with Josiah's persistence.

"You will not be responsible," Josiah's response was immediate.

"Then why do you need my support?"

Josiah did not reply.

"I know we need a representative there. I have spent many a sleepless night contemplating the trip to Britain myself. But I could do little good from a prison cell!" Joseph lamented.

"They will not arrest me."

"You cannot be certain of it!" Joseph exclaimed.

Josiah dropped his head for a moment, slowly shaking it in frustration. Then, fixing his gaze on Joseph again, he began to speak in a pleading tone. "Four years ago, when you first diagnosed my condition, you gave me your word that you would help me avoid self-pity."

"You cannot hold me to that vow under these circumstances!" Joseph protested.

Josiah lifted his arm and pointed at his friend. "I will hold you to that vow!" His voice was trembling. "I need your help desperately. Allow me to stay involved. Allow me to aid my country! Very soon I will not be here to offer protection of any sort to my family—allow me to at least attempt to protect their liberty—something my children and their children will benefit from long after I am gone. Please!"

Joseph closed his eyes and took a deep breath, releasing it slowly. He could not deny his friend's pleas. "I will do as you ask and recommend that you sail to England," he somberly responded. "I will speak to Sam about it this afternoon."

With the approval and support of the members of the Long Room Club, Josiah made secret preparations to set sail for Great Britain. Only his most trusted family members and intimate friends were informed of his plans.

As the first morning rays of the August sun glistened down on the still waters of Boston's harbor, Josiah Quincy began riding northward to Salem. From there he quietly boarded a ship destined for England.

Last minute instructions had been given and good-byes exchanged. Joseph and John Hancock watched in silence as the coach and four horses carrying Sam and John Adams to Philadelphia pulled away.

With feelings of excitement and apprehension, they considered the job before the Massachusetts delegates to the Continental Congress. Somehow they must convince the delegates from the sister colonies that the inhabitants of Massachusetts Bay were not wide-eyed ruffians bent on initiating hostilities with the mother country. It seemed inevitable that hostilities would break out soon, but not because the inhabitants of Massachusetts wanted this.

Boston was a powder keg about to explode. Military support from the sister colonies was vital. Without it, any attempt by the inhabitants of Massachusetts to stand up to Great Britain would be suicidal.

As Joseph lost sight of the coach, he turned his attention to the affairs before him. John Hancock and he had been elected to the Massachusetts General Assembly, which was scheduled to meet in Salem. There men from all parts of the colony would discuss the problems at hand and seek a way to find answers to the immediate crises while waiting upon the decisions of the Continental Congress.

• 13 •

Mounting Frustration

THE CHAISE GLIDED effortlessly across the snow-packed road. *If it weren't for the biting cold wind, it would be an extremely pleasant ride,* Mercy thought as she pulled the heavy wool blanket over her shoulder. She considered the ride to be a fair exchange—the jolts and bangs of travel when the wheels were used were more uncomfortable than the cold air when traveling on runners was so much smoother and faster.

Mercy took hold of Joseph's arm and snuggled close to him. She gazed up at his face, studying it in the dimness of twilight. Apart from his nose and cheeks being red, he did not show any discomfort in the cold.

Joseph's thoughts were elsewhere as he guided the horse on the familiar route from Roxbury to Boston. He usually was quiet after visiting the children, and Mercy respected his need to be alone with his thoughts.

She listened to the sleigh bells jingle in sync with the chattering of her teeth, grateful that Joseph's preoccupation prevented him from hearing them chatter.

"Polly has adapted quite well to the move," Joseph suddenly offered, taking Mercy by surprise.

"Yes, she seems very happy to be with her sister and brothers," Mercy agreed.

"I am glad they are together again," he said, though he did not display any emotion. There was a brief silence. "Do you realize it has been almost two years since I had them with me? Two years—" he repeated, obviously upset at how long it had been.

Mercy squeezed his arm. "Perhaps it is time to bring them back to Boston."

"Mercy, you know I wish we could marry now, but things are so uncertain. Hutchinson did not dare issue the warrant, but Gage is a military man accustomed to carrying out orders. He may very well act on it. I cannot—"

"I cannot marry you until things settle down some," Mercy interrupted, mimicking Joseph's tone as well as his words. She continued, "and think of the hardships that would befall you should we marry now and I be arrested."

"That is exactly right!" Joseph exclaimed with a smile, slightly amused by her rather good imitation.

"When I accepted your marriage proposal, it was with full knowledge that there was a warrant out for your arrest. But I will not try to convince you against your better judgment—" her voice trailed off.

"No? Well, that would be a first." Joseph's eyebrows were cocked as he looked at her, pretending to be dumbfounded.

"No," she echoed with a light laugh in response. "And when I suggested the children return to Boston, it was not in reference to our getting married. I simply do not see why they cannot live with me!"

"What are you scheming?" he asked with an affectionate smile.

"There is plenty of room in my father's house. I have been entertaining the thought for a long while. This way you could see them every day, and I will be able to adapt to the responsibilities of motherhood before we are married. It will make the transition much easier when we do wed. Don't you agree?"

"It does not matter whether or not I agree," Joseph replied with a chuckle. "What about your father? He certainly should have some say in this matter. After all, it is his house!"

"Well, of course! I will speak to him about it this evening. But I know he will think it is a wonderful idea!" Mercy said with a confident smile.

"Will he?" Joseph seemed doubtful. "It's been a long time since John Scollay had little ones underfoot."

"My brothers bring their children by often," Mercy was quick to point out.

"It is not the same. Your nieces and nephews stay for a few hours and then go home. To have children there twenty-four hours a day—well, Mercy, it is quite different," Joseph assured her with a smile.

"Your children are very well behaved," she offered in their defense.

"I am not saying they are not, but children will be children. They are full of energy and need constant instruction."

"I certainly do not expect them to behave perfectly. Neither will Father!" Mercy exclaimed and laughed. "But you paint such a gloomy picture, Joseph!"

"I do not mean to. I just want to make sure you are seeing this realistically. The thought of having them close by is—well—I cannot fully express my joy, nor the gratitude I feel toward you for even considering it," he said, looking at Mercy with deep affection. "Mercy, they are a part of me. Their lives are forever intertwined with mine. They are ever in my thoughts and prayers. Sometimes sacrifices are necessary. My needs or wants often become secondary to their needs and wants. Do you understand what I'm trying to say?"

"Could it be that parenthood requires not only an investment of one's heart but one's soul as well?"

Mercy's reply touched Joseph deeper than she realized.

"I am eager to make the investment," she added with all sincerity.

"To be sure, talk to your father. But after you present this plan of yours to him, let me speak to him," Joseph said. "In private," he added with emphasis and a smile. "Before you go preparing the spare bedchambers, I need to be certain that your father is not being coerced into taking the children."

Mercy appeared perturbed.

"It is not that I mistrust you, Mercy," he offered with a smile. "But I have observed that your father has a difficult time denying you anything you ask of him."

John Scollay was willing—in fact, eager—to provide a home for the Warren children. Though they were not living with their father, the close proximity provided them with a more normal family setting. Joseph was able to see them daily and able once again to act as their father in providing for them as well as in instructing and disciplining them.

Whenever possible, he would dine at the Scollay's—falling into the old family routine of reading from Holy Writ with the children and spending some carefree moments together before tucking them into bed. Then, as the joyous laughter of contented children was hushed, the house grew quiet and still.

As the children drifted off into peaceful slumber, Joseph was often forced to leave the domestic tranquility of the Scollay house to attend one meeting or another. Leisurely evenings were a luxury in which Joseph Warren could not indulge. Time was precious, and living in such turbulent conditions demanded that he spend it wisely.

When those rare evenings did occur, with no pressing engagements calling him out and no emergencies to attend to, then plans would quickly be made to invite guests to the Scollay home. Usually the guests included a mixture of Whig, Tory, and British officers alike. Paul Revere was often present, as was Dr. John Jeffries.

With Jeffries usually came three British officers whose kindness had earned them the friendship of many a Bostonian. Colonel Hugh Percy, the highest-ranking officer among them, was also the youngest, though by his gaunt, sickly appearance one would not think so. He was an English nobleman, an earl with the distinguished title of lord, and his gentle manners and magnetic personality had quickly won him the friendship of John Hancock. He dined each evening with the Hancocks, which caused rumors to abound among Whigs and Tories alike.

The second of the three officers was Major John Pitcairn, a proud Scotsman.

Despite his strict discipline, his genuine concern and affection for his marines earned him their devotion. Although his habit of shouting profanities at his troops during drilling sessions caused great distress among the Puritan inhabitants of Boston, they patiently endured, noting his sincere attempt at piety on the Sabbath.

Pitcairn was a family man at heart. The separation of 3,000 miles of ocean from his wife and ten of his children was difficult, and he found much comfort in having his eldest son serving under him in Boston. Being quartered close by the Revere's home was comforting as well. The constant activity of Paul's many children warmed his heart.

The third officer, Major Small, like Pitcairn, was greatly experienced. He had spent much time in the colonies during the French and Indian War. It was then that he had come to understand and admire the independent spirit of the colonists and formed true and lasting friendships with colonial militia officers.

Most evenings during the Scollay home gatherings, an effort was made to avoid discussing the political situation between Great Britain and the American colonies. This was very difficult at times. On occasion one side or the other gave into temptation, throwing out a stinging remark and then pulling back to wait for a heated reaction. Words would often be exchanged, but tempers never flared.

Mercy watched as friendships developed among these men. She had been aware of the mutual respect her fiancée and Dr. John Jeffries shared. It was a respect that went beyond their shared profession. They had affection for one another that somehow overlooked their obvious ideological differences, but to witness friendships develop between Joseph and these British soldiers—this fact she found absolutely amazing.

The scriptural mandate to love one's enemy was a teaching with which Mercy was well acquainted. Joseph, it seemed, had no difficulty putting it into practice. When she questioned him on his ability to overlook the threat these men posed to all that he stood for, he replied sincerely and without hesitation, "I bear no personal animosity toward them because of our disagreements. I despise the institutions, not the individuals!"

As circumstances became more trying between the Sons of Liberty and the unwelcome British troops, it proved difficult for Joseph and the others to put their differences aside. Even then, their remarks usually were guarded out of respect for the other and only spoken while Mercy was out of the room aiding in the preparation of refreshments for her father's guests or tending to the children. Whenever she returned, all appearance of friction would cease.

"It has come to my attention, Dr. Warren, that some of my men have been harassing you. Tell me, is there any truth to the tune they have written about your having once sold milk in the streets of Boston?" Colonel Percy asked with a teasing grin, exaggerated by his hollow cheeks and long, bony nose.

"Yes, as a child, sir," Joseph replied.

"It is an amusing song, I must say—"

"Is that the best your lads can come up with, Colonel?" asked Major Pitcairn. Although he was stocky in build and stern in manner, his features were surprisingly delicate. "My marines have come up with some splendid nicknames for the good doctor, most of which I shall avoid repeating in the company of our Puritan friends." Grinning and expecting a reaction, he glanced over at Joseph, who offered only a polite smile in response. "I must say, Dr. Warren, my favorite of all is their reference to you as the 'rascally apothecary!' Quite suitable!"

"Now Major, that remark could apply to any number of physicians in Boston. In fact, I thought they were mistaking me for Dr. Jeffries!" Joseph replied, still smiling as he glanced at John Jeffries.

"No, no sir, they most certainly were referring to you. They tell me that you are becoming annoyed by their terms of endearment."

"I will admit, Major, that constantly being harassed by your soldiers as I am is somewhat irritating. It amazes me that supposedly courageous military men are too cowardly to face me directly with their remarks but must call out from buildings or the darkness of alleys."

"We understand, Doctor, that your Committee of Safety has ordered the routine exercising of town militia and the storing of military supplies," Major Small changed the subject so suddenly that he almost caught Joseph off guard.

Joseph tried not to let his surprise show. Out of the corner of his eye he could see that Paul, too, was forcing himself not to react. The fact that Major Small knew of these plans, which had only been agreed on the night before, verified a suspicion both he and Paul had had for some time. There was a spy among the most trusted patriot leaders, and although they had their own suspicions as to who it was, they had no proof and absolutely nothing tangible upon which to base their feelings.

"British law requires that our militia be trained and prepared to defend the colonies," Joseph answered calmly.

"Yes, Doctor, but only to defend the colonies against the enemies of Great Britain. Who is it that the Committee of Safety fears that they are so strictly drilling the militia?" Colonel Percy asked in a friendly tone.

"The militia companies have lost all form of discipline. They have not been drilled on any regular basis for years," Joseph replied quickly. Then adding with an impish grin, "The great military discipline of the king's troops has inspired us!"

"Oh, yes, Doctor, I am sure it has," Major Pitcairn responded with a chuckle.

"So, with regard to the order that military supplies be stored, it would not have anything to do with the king's cutting off all military supplies to the colonists, would it, Doctor Warren?" Major Small asked.

Joseph hesitated before answering. The barrage of questions from all angles was obviously preplanned. He glanced over at Paul, who appeared to be at ease. Joseph knew better.

"Major Small, one never knows when such supplies may be needed. Indian attacks are always a threat. If there were an Indian uprising on the frontier, we would need to aid our fellow colonists. And to be quite honest, sir, his majesty's refusal to export military supplies to the colonies is very distressing indeed!"

"Tell me, Mr. Revere, how do you fit into the seditious activity here in Boston?" Colonel Percy asked with a grin, perhaps thinking he might have better luck in catching the silversmith off guard.

"Seditious activity? Colonel, I'm not sure I know what you're referring to!" Paul replied, never thinking that his participation in standing up for his inalienable rights was in any way seditious.

"It truly does have us baffled, sir, how you became involved with what appears to be the inner circle of rebels, all of which are, by our reports, men of higher education and means," Colonel Percy remarked. "Could it be that you are the medium of communicating the plans of this elite group to those of lesser education who will carry out their plans?"

"You are mistakenly comparing the social practices of Great Britain with those of Massachusetts Bay," Paul responded without any sign of being insulted by Percy's remarks. "Friendships are not based on social stature here."

"I will wager, Mr. Revere, that if the mischievous schemers in this rebellious town call for their fellow provincials to take up arms, you shall not find those of higher learning among them. They will feel that they have too much to lose: substance, prestige, and power. They will not endanger themselves or their wealth when the commoner can be manipulated to perform for them," Major Small commented with his gaze fixed on Joseph.

Joseph found the comment both irritating and amusing. The insinuation that he would expect another man to face a danger that he himself would avoid angered him. Yet, to think that he was a man of any wealth was comical. True, he had just a short time before been very comfortable financially, but since Elizabeth's death he had begun devoting more time to this fight for liberty than to his practice of medicine. Much of his money had been put toward the purchase of military supplies. His bills were mounting, forcing him to seek the financial assistance of his brother Jack.

"Surely, Dr. Warren, you will not be among them if the order is given to take up arms?" Major Small asked.

Paul, John Scollay, and Dr. Jeffries nervously fidgeted as they awaited his response. Mercy's heart pounded as she listened to the conversation from the kitchen. Could this be a way of trapping him in his words? A possible snare set by men whose feelings of friendship were now outweighed by their frustration at being stationed so far from home with no hope of returning in the near future?

All eyes were on Joseph. Carefully he chose his words. "Depend on it, my friend," he said, his blue eyes intently on Major Small. "Whenever a hostile trigger is pulled against my countrymen, you will find me among them."

"Joseph, you cannot be serious!" John Jeffries exclaimed. "Would you actually do harm to another man? You have been trained to heal, not maim and kill! How could you, a physician, justify this?"

Joseph rose from his chair and walked over to the fireplace. He remained quiet, staring at the dancing gold and orange flames. Then, turning toward the men in the room, he spotted Mercy standing in the doorway with a tray full of refreshments. She hoped her presence would provide a means of ending the present direction of the conversation.

"Here before you, gentlemen, is the reason I can justify any defensive action I may be forced to take," he said, pointing toward Mercy. "If I must fight to defend my family from the horrors of slavery, then I will do so without hesitation. We shall fight, if need be, with the God of armies at our side—for our families, for posterity— that they may enjoy the freedoms granted us by the Almighty!"

"Warren, have you given serious consideration to your fate—or you, Mr. Revere?" Lord Percy asked, his eyes darting from one man to the other in anticipation of a response. None came. "If you take up arms against the Crown, you should hope for the gallows, gentlemen. But I sincerely doubt your end will come so easily! Great Britain has been indulging in a more dramatic form of execution for those guilty of treason these days. Have you not heard?" he paused, again looking for a response.

Joseph's eyes met Paul's. Both were keenly aware of Great Britain's recent barbaric form of execution. Now in their gaze they offered one another strength and encouragement as the nightmarish scene was about to be presented to them. Joseph wished that Mercy had not come into the room so that she might be spared the gruesome details.

"Surely you have heard, gentlemen, but perhaps I should refresh your memory,"

Percy said as he walked over and stood in front of Joseph. "Forgive my ungentle-manly behavior, Miss Scollay, but maybe upon hearing this, you can talk some sense into Dr. Warren." He had directed this comment to Mercy, but his eyes had remained locked with Joseph's. "They will hang you, all right," his barbs now directed to Joseph, "but not long enough to kill you. You will be taken down to have your innards cut out and burnt while you scream in agony."

Mercy gasped.

Joseph looked at her but was unable to bring any comfort as Colonel Percy continued, now fixing his fiery gaze upon Paul.

"You will beg for them to kill you. Then—only then—will they grant your request by cutting off your head and quartering what remains of your body. That is the sentence for treason, gentlemen! And I can assure you that it is a repulsive scene, even for one accustomed to the horrors of war as I."

"We are aware of it," Joseph calmly responded to the colonel while still looking at Mercy. "But regardless of Great Britain's form of punishment," he continued, directing his full attention to Colonel Percy, "I will stand to defend my family in the face of hostile oppression. If death is the price I must pay to ensure their freedom, then I shall gladly pay it. It would be a far better thing to die gaining their liberty than to live out my life in the shackles of thralldom. When liberty is the prize, who would shun the warfare, who would stoop to waste a cowardly thought on life?"

Walking to the tray, which Mercy had set down, Joseph gestured to the men to take a mug for themselves. Then he raised his mug, toasting, "To his Majesty, King George the Third!"

Without hesitation, Paul and John Scollay repeated the pledge in unison, "To his Majesty, King George the Third!" All three officers were startled by the apparent sincerity of their "rebellious" companions and hesitated more than a moment before joining in with their chorus.

John Jeffries was certain Joseph had offered this toast in an attempt to throw the officers off guard, thus subduing them and taking control of the rest of the evening.

Joseph's expression gave no hint of any such scheming. On the contrary, he had made the pledge with what seemed to be genuine sincerity.

Jeffries was baffled. He did not understand what appeared to him a blatant contradiction in the desire of these friends. They wanted freedom but not independence. He viewed them as idealists, not willing to face reality. Because of his affection for them, he wished they would give up their idealistic dream before it was too late.

Dinner at the home of Sam and Betsy Adams was always an event. Though Joseph found his mind wandering, he attempted to follow the conversation at the table.

Sam was exuberant. Having returned from Philadelphia earlier in the day, he had much to share. The conversation was of food, people, and the architectural differences between the buildings in Boston and Philadelphia. The Long Room Club was scheduled to meet later that night, and it was then that Sam would discuss the details of the Continental Congress.

There was no doubt that Betsy Adams delighted in having Sam home. Her countenance radiated her love for him. Though she continued to dress in her plain style and the house remained in need of numerous repairs, the table she set was always magnificent. The china and silver sparkled before the backdrop of the dingy, peeling paper and paint. The overabundance of food—veal, ham, potatoes, carrots, breads, and pies—was truly a feast fit for a king.

Joseph had determined at his first visit to the Adams's home with Elizabeth many years earlier that Betsy Adams was the finest cook in Boston, and Elizabeth had wholeheartedly agreed! He remembered now how disturbed Elizabeth had been by that first meeting with Sam Adams. Oh, how much had occurred in those few short years!

As his thoughts lingered upon Elizabeth, he caught a glimpse of Mercy out of the corner of his eye. How vastly different they were in some ways. Elizabeth's features were dark, and Mercy's fair. Elizabeth was reserved in social settings, and Mercy was bold at such gatherings.

He looked across the table at Dr. Samuel Adams Jr., who was laughing at a remark Mercy had made. Joseph smiled in response to young Samuel's vibrancy. He enjoyed spending time with his former apprentices, having determined many years before that he would make every effort to keep them within his family circle.

"It was an extremely interesting delegation that had assembled in Philadelphia," Sam said. "Some of Virginia's delegates—Washington and Henry—were most impressive. That Henry is a firebrand for liberty."

Joseph heard Sam's words and immediately recognized the names of these delegates. He was fully aware of their fiery reputations as Sons of Liberty.

"Both Cousin John and I agree that John Rutledge of South Carolina has a great likeness to you. 'The Joseph Warren of South Carolina,' we called him. You would get along remarkably well with him, that is, if you could overlook that southern drawl," Sam said with a grin, looking straight at his distracted friend.

Suddenly serious, Sam continued. "I was beginning to lose hope that the Continental Congress would come to an agreement on anything. The bickering was almost constant; the distrust of one colony for another was evident. The only thing the delegates seemed to unite on was questioning the motives and virtue of Massachusetts Bay. It was true that many of them believed that we have become defiant and are attempting to overthrow the king to take control of America ourselves!" Sam chuckled as he spoke, more it seemed as a release of tension rather than because he found the idea humorous.

"I am certain the other delegates did not know what to make of us. The five delegates from Massachusetts Bay were expected to be loudmouthed rabble-rousers, but it was we who sat as quiet as mice through many of the sessions. They were not ready to hear what we had to say.

"We left our colony in a desperate state but did not know how to tell about our situation without driving the other delegates farther away.

"Then Paul Revere arrived with an express from Boston. You can imagine how my heart sank, expecting as I did an announcement that hostilities had begun at home. But when Paul sat beside me and assured me that all was well, I relaxed as the moderator read The Suffolk Resolves from the paper before him."

Sam stopped speaking. Staring intently at Joseph, he then continued with a twinkle in his eyes, "It was your work, was it not?"

Joseph considered the question put to him. Although he had drafted The Suffolk Resolves, the newly formed Massachusetts Provincial Congress, an assembly that was considered illegal by the present governing authority in the colony, had unanimously voted on it. Joseph felt uneasy about taking full credit for the resolves.

"You wrote it," Sam stated, not waiting for Joseph's admission. "I am too familiar with your work not to readily recognize it. Your Suffolk Resolves are the boldest statement made yet! They accomplished what we could not. Within a few minutes, these same men who had been battling among themselves were totally silenced. I do not think there was a dry eye in the room as they applauded your resolves."

Sam's own eyes appeared moist as he recalled the scene. "They were unanimously voted on. They opened up constructive communication among all the delegates."

Mercy lifted her hand from her lap and placed it on Joseph's limp hand, which lay upon the table.

"Did he share this work with you?" Sam asked her.

"He mentioned it to me—never in great detail, though," she replied, a proud smile upon her lips.

"He painted a fine picture of our military 'guests.' How did you put it? 'The streets of Boston thronged with military executioners. Our enemies have flattered

themselves that they shall make an easy prey of this numerous, brave, and hardy
people, from the apprehension that they are unacquainted with military discipline.
We therefore advise—'" Sam paused, again staring intently at the younger man.

Joseph was expressionless as he listened to Sam quote the words he had struggled over only a few weeks before.

"What was advised?" Mercy asked, looking from Sam to Joseph.

Joseph did not seem to hear the question.

"That strong militias be formed from each town throughout all the colonies,
and that they be drilled regularly," Sam answered for him, studying Joseph as he
spoke. "That the late acts of Parliament be disobeyed and independent provincial
governments be established, as we now have here in Massachusetts. That Crown-
appointed judges be disregarded. That all trade with Great Britain be cut off—" Sam
stopped suddenly. "Here I am praising your accomplishments, my friend, yet you
remain troubled."

"I am sorry, Sam," Joseph replied. He had intended to joyously welcome his
friend back from Philadelphia. A carefree social evening had been planned, but he
had too much on his mind. He turned to Mercy and offered a weak smile as he gently squeezed her hand. Then standing, he walked behind the chair and leaned upon
it as he spoke. "'We cheerfully acknowledge George III to be our rightful sover-
eign,'" he began quoting a portion of The Suffolk Resolves with pretended enthusiasm. "'And heartily recommend to all persons of this community not to engage in
any routs, riots, or licentious attacks upon the properties of any persons whatsoever, but by a stead, manly, uniform, and persevering opposition, to convince our
enemies that in a course so solemn, our conduct shall be such as to merit the
approbation of the wise and the admiration of the brave and free of every age and
of every country.'"

With his eyes cast downward he slowly shook his head, obviously upset by his
own words. "I am not sure how much longer we can hold things together here, Sam.
Since we received word from the Continental Congress that in the event of hostilities, support from the sister colonies would come only if Great Britain were the
offender, we have become the most restrained people in America. But how long
must we continue in this manner?"

Sam did not reply. He was aware that his friend needed to vent his mounting
frustration.

Joseph looked at Sam, his eyes aflame. "I have met with General Gage so often
in an attempt to avoid any conflicts between his soldiers and our people that I have
lost track! The troops and Tories mock us for our cowardice. Our endurance of their
persecution is seen as submission to their strength!

"The majority of our men can hold up under the constant taunting and even walk away from a direct confrontation." He suddenly paused as he considered the ladies present and continued in a calmer tone, although his eyes became moist with tears. "But no man can be expected to remain complacent while his family is abused. I am being called upon to care for such cases more and more, as is Dr. Adams," he said glancing at young Samuel, who nodded in agreement. "Soldiers who are trying to prove their superiority are bullying the boys. The girls are being defiled. Dear God! A fair number of them are with child. Do you know what it is like to face an enraged father and a weeping mother, having to persuade them not to react to such abuses? 'Patience,' I tell them, 'patience'—" His voice drifted off in disgust.

"Joseph, you know I sympathize with the plight of this town. There was no one more upset than I when the Congress voted support for us only in the case of defensive action. But I am confident that, if we continue to endure the hardship upon us, we shall then convince our sister colonies that we are not so aggressive and troublesome as they have imagined us to be. We shall, in time, gain their trust and unconditional support."

"In time!" Joseph remonstrated. "How much time? I fear we may have another massacre on our hands before they are convinced! It is inevitable that hostilities will begin. The questions still remaining are, 'When?' And, more paramount, 'Shall we face Great Britain alone?'"

The winter months of 1774–75 passed slowly for the patriots of Boston. Each day offered new problems for them.

Preparation for the long, cold, winter months had become a frightful task. The means to buy the wood necessary to keep the homes fairly warm were nonexistent. No jobs meant no money. Even barter became a difficult form of trade as too many sought to obtain their needs through it. Yet as the winter months closed in upon them, the bitter cold, which had always gripped the New England colonies by mid-December, did not arrive. January and February did not produce the dreaded nor'easters, with their blinding snow and drifts as tall as a man, but instead remained mild and unseasonably warm. Food supplies continued to arrive from the other colonies.

Muskets, ammunition, gunpowder, cannon balls, shovels, tents, medical supplies, food staples, and the like continued to be gathered secretly. Women gave their pewter to be melted for musket balls. Men sacrificially provided the necessary finances to obtain supplies. The Committee of Safety ordered these supplies to be hidden in different areas outside of Boston. Wagonloads of this cargo were moved from town to town, hidden under bales of hay, piles of manure, or in other ordinary disguises.

The British already had confiscated a depot of concealed supplies in Cambridge. This action caused a general alarm throughout the countryside. However, the leading Sons of Liberty quickly brought the situation under control, and bloodshed was prevented.

Another attempt to confiscate supplies in Salem was thwarted by the alert, bold people of that town. Their unyielding refusal to allow the soldiers to enter the town center was enough to turn the troops around without their much-sought-after booty.

Despite the great sacrifices of the people to provide them, supplies were scarce. When hostilities eventually broke out, as the patriots of Massachusetts knew they would, these stored supplies would quickly dwindle away. The loss of the Cambridge depot was detrimental. Another loss would prove devastating.

The approach of March brought the fifth anniversary of the Boston Massacre. Though the townspeople felt it important to commemorate this infamous day, none were willing to take on the responsibility of delivering the oration, for with it came the threat of personal danger from British soldiers or Tory sympathizers. Joseph Warren, convinced of the importance of this commemoration, volunteered for the task.

Crowds began to flock into the Old South more than an hour before the time scheduled for Joseph's speech. Sam Adams, John Hancock, and Benjamin Church watched from the pulpit, astonished that, except for the front pews, the meeting house was filled. The atmosphere grew tense as the designated hour approached. Men and women nervously conversed about the rumor circulating that General Gage had devised a plan for the patriot leaders to be assassinated during the commencement. Part of the rumor was that a soldier would bring an egg, throwing it at Dr. Warren as he spoke. This would be the cue for the others involved in the plan to make their attack.

That warrants for the arrest of Adams, Hancock, and Warren existed was common knowledge. Why Gage had neglected to act on them was a mystery. It was assumed that, like Hutchinson, he feared a general insurrection from the people. If Gage now ordered their assassination, few in Great Britain would object.

A commotion was heard at the entrance of the meetinghouse as about forty British officers paraded into the building. A sudden, terrified hush fell upon the crowd.

Showing no apprehension over the threat of danger, Sam Adams politely invited the newly arrived spectators to occupy the front pews, which were still vacant. As the soldiers advanced up the aisle, one of them tripped, falling into a pew. As he regained his balance, those near him witnessed a slimy, butterlike substance that looked like crushed, raw egg ooze out between the brass buttons of his bright red coat.

Undaunted by their stumbling comrade, the other officers proceeded to occupy the indicated pews, as well as the steps leading to the podium.

Unable to find a seat, people stood in the aisles, completely blocking the doorway. Men and women crowded outside, hoping that the speaker's voice would carry far enough that they, too, might hear.

All was in readiness to begin, but there was no sign of Dr. Warren. The patriot leaders assembled on the podium began to address the crowd as they waited for the appointed speaker. As the time passed, Sam Adams became concerned. Had Joseph decided the danger was too great? Sam knew him too well and could not believe this to be true. Perhaps he was being forcibly detained!

An hour after the scheduled start, Joseph's chaise pulled up across from the meetinghouse. Those gathered around the doors quickly recognized him, and word that the doctor had finally arrived spread through the assembly.

As Joseph climbed from the chaise, the people gathered outside were surprised by his attire. He was not clad in the usual knee breeches and frock coat, but was adorned instead in a white, draping, ankle-length robe styled after a Roman toga.

Such an act was subtle, yet its effect dramatic. Throughout the years of turmoil with Great Britain, the Sons of Liberty had often drawn on the example of the ancient Roman Empire. She once stood as the mightiest empire on earth, but she steadily drew away from the constitution that had made her great, which eventually brought her to her knees.

"Dr. Warren!" a man's voice called from the side of the meetinghouse. "Sir, you'll never get in through the door. The aisles are impassable. You'll have to enter through a window!" The man directed Joseph along the side of the building to a ladder propped up to one of the huge, paned windows.

"This window is directly behind the pulpit," the man assured him.

Joseph lifted the robe to avoid tripping and began to climb the ladder.

"Dr. Warren," the man began and then hesitated as if uncertain about continuing. "There are about forty British officers inside."

Joseph nodded in acknowledgement and continued up. Sam helped him through the open window.

"I was growing concerned. What detained you?" Sam asked.

"One of my patients took a turn for the worse."

"I am sorry to hear it," he said, placing his hand on Joseph's back as he escorted him to the podium, which was draped in black. "As you can see, we have a few of the king's finest among us," he commented, referring to the British officers that lined the front of the meeting house.

"I expected as much," Joseph calmly responded as he stepped up to the podium. He scanned the audience, including the officers who cluttered the steps to his side. All was silent. Nervous excitement filled the air as the crowd waited. The faces of the multitude plainly revealed their apprehension.

With a reassuring smile, Joseph began. "My ever-honored fellow citizens, it is not without the most humiliating conviction of my want of ability that I now appear before you. You will not now expect the elegance, the learning, the fire, the enraptured strains of eloquence that charmed you when a Lovell, a Church, or a Hancock spoke, but you will permit me to say that with a sincerity equal to theirs, I mourn over my bleeding country. With them I weep at her distress and with them deeply resent the many injuries she has received from the hands of cruel and unreasonable men."

As he spoke, he was ever aware of the power an able orator had over his audience. One moment he could have them weeping in remembrance of those killed five years earlier and enraged to the point of revenge the next. He took full advantage of his ability, while still firmly holding to the directive of the Continental Congress.

To kindle the flames of revolution was one thing—for the people must be emotionally prepared for the inevitable—but to set them ablaze so they might lose control was to be avoided.

Occasional hisses from the British officers were countered by the applause of the audience. His oration was so emotionally charged in its attack against the colonies' enemies in Great Britain—even discreetly mentioning the king himself—that one of the British officers rose from the steps leading to the pulpit. As Joseph spoke, this officer held up his tightly clenched fist. Slowly opening his hand, he exposed the musket balls he held.

Those close enough to witness the scene gasped at the silent threat. Without pausing in his words, Joseph glanced at the handful of musket balls and smiled. Infuriated and embarrassed that his threat did not upset the speaker, the officer quickly sat down.

"The man who meanly will submit to wear a shackle condemns the noblest gift of heaven and impiously affronts the God that made him free," Joseph continued. "Our country is in danger, but not to be despaired of. Our enemies are numerous and powerful, but we have many friends. Determine to be free and heaven, and earth will aid the resolution. On you depend the fortunes of America. You are to decide the important question, on which rest the happiness and liberty of millions yet unborn. Act worthy of yourselves."

The people began to stir uncomfortably as the sound of passing troops was heard outside the meetinghouse. Rhythmically they marched to the beat of drums and the shrill cry of the fife. Suddenly the music and the marching stopped. As terror began to grip his audience, Joseph stretched out his arm and motioned for their attention once more. He continued, ignoring the presence of the troops outside.

"But, pardon me, my fellow citizens, I know you want not zeal or fortitude. You will maintain your rights or perish in the generous struggle. However difficult the combat, you never will decline it when freedom is the prize. An independence of Great Britain is not our aim. No, our wish is that Britain and the colonies may like the oak and ivy grow and increase in strength together. But whilst the infatuated plan of making one part of the empire slaves to the other is persisted in, and it appears that the only way to safety is through fields of blood, I know you will not turn your faces from your foes. I know you will undauntedly press forward, until tyranny is trodden under foot."

He heard the troops outside move on. As his audience relaxed, he secretly breathed a sigh of relief himself and concluded his oration.

Certain that all the idle threats hinted at by the British soldiers were now behind them, Sam came forward to the pulpit. There he offered his appreciation to Joseph on behalf of the people. Suddenly the British officers began pounding their canes on the floor, and their cry of "Fie! Fie!" Many in the crowd mistook their cries for "Fire! Fire!"

In a panic the people struggled for the door, certain that a mass slaughter was about to take place. Unable to get through the throng of people, men and women alike began jumping out the windows!

Shouting to regain the attention of the crowd, Joseph, Sam, John Hancock, and Dr. Church were able to calm the crowd once more. To their great relief, no one was seriously injured.

"What's this? Still lingering over the breakfast table at this hour?" John Jeffries asked as he entered the kitchen of the Warren home unannounced. Joseph was slumped over the table holding a hot, wet towel against his left cheek. He looked up at John, his facial expression reflecting the pain he felt.

"Are those teeth still bothering you?" Joseph's moan answered John's question. "You look terrible, Joseph," he continued as he sat down at the table and helped himself to one of the biscuits Joseph could not eat.

"You were up all night, weren't you?"

There was no response.

"Did you take some laudanum? Obviously not, for it surely would have deadened the pain enough to allow you a few hours of sleep. Why you did not let me pull them the last time they acted up is beyond my comprehension!" he said shaking his head as he rose to his feet. "Well, you said you would ride out to Dedham with me to check on a patient. Come on, and let me pull them so we can be on our way!"

"Mr. Eustis will be pulling them," Joseph mumbled as he tried to move his mouth as little as possible when he spoke.

"Eustis? You are going to let an apprentice pull them?"

"Better him than you, Jeffries. Gage has probably instructed you to cut out my tongue while you are at it," Joseph came back smartly, though muffled.

Dr. Jeffries grinned at him. "I do not take orders from Gage, but I am certain he would be delighted if it were to happen!"

"To be certain," Joseph replied with all seriousness as he removed another steaming towel from the pot on the table.

"You had better take advantage of my generous mood, my friend. Consider this a professional courtesy."

"Thank you, but no. Mr. Eustis can perform a simple tooth extraction."

"Now, Joseph, it is one thing to have an apprentice extract a tooth directly under your supervision, but quite another—"

"But nothing! My apprentice is capable even though yours may not be!" Joseph knew full well that John's students were trained as well as his own, but he was in too much pain to patiently overlook the insults of this friend. His discomfort and exhaustion at the moment caused him to question why he even considered John Jeffries a friend.

"I am ready, sir," William Eustis announced from the doorway.

"Enjoy my breakfast, Doctor. I'll only be a moment," Joseph said as he tossed the towel back into the pot.

"Oh, no, Warren, I would not think of denying you my loyal support at a time like this," John Jeffries replied, grabbing another biscuit to take with him.

As Joseph sat in the chair, preparing himself for the extractions, he spotted the bottle of rum on the shelf. Great was the temptation to take a few swigs before William began. After all, every other patient undergoing such a procedure was encouraged to indulge, in an attempt to relax them and help deaden the pain. But he knew he could not. He needed to remain alert and clear-headed.

Joseph opened his mouth wide and tightly grasped the arms of the chair as William leaned over him with the extractor. He was prepared for the pain as he felt the instrument grab hold of one of the offending teeth.

"Eustis!" Dr. Jeffries called out suddenly as he jumped to his feet. "Are you certain you have the right tooth?"

William jumped back, startled by the outburst. Joseph sat straight up in the chair, glaring at John.

"Sit down and be quiet!" he shouted with such authority that John knew he had gone too far in his antics.

"Ignore him, William," Joseph said calmly to the confused apprentice. Then bracing himself once again, he had his teeth quickly extracted and the wounds packed with absorbent cloth.

"Does Revere know you will be by for a fitting?" John asked. Both physicians always recommended that their patients have Paul Revere carve artificial teeth for them to replace the ones that were pulled. Paul's talent in fashioning the finest silver pieces in the colony had aided him in carving to precision the small ivory teeth.

Joseph nodded, unable to speak with the cloth in his mouth.

"When Revere is done, no one will know you have lost those teeth," John offered. Then, smiling mischievously, he added, "You will be silent for the entire ride to Dedham. Imagine that! Do you have any idea how many men in Boston would take undue advantage of such a situation? Unable to debate, unable to comment at all—" Then placing his arm around Joseph's shoulders, he walked toward the door with his friend.

"Now, Joseph, about the oration you delivered last week—quite stirring indeed, but certainly you do not actually believe most of what you said! Why, let us consider some of your more absurd remarks—"

Joseph smiled as John rambled on. The relief from the excruciating pain he had been suffering felt so good that even John Jeffries could not aggravate him now. Moreover, he had other things on his mind. These matters would occupy his thoughts all the way to Dedham, and he could ignore John's ramblings entirely.

• 14 •

Those Who Sow in Tears

VERBAL ABUSE FROM soldiers and Tories had intensified, and it had become a constant, nagging irritant to Joseph, who was growing weary of it all. The name-calling and cussing every time he set foot outside were difficult to patiently endure, but when the abuses were spoken behind his back from darkened alleys, they were maddening because he never had the opportunity to confront the rude offenders. He was not certain what he would do if he came face to face with any of them, but he longed for the opportunity to find out.

Their intent was to wear him down, of that he had no doubt. But it was a strange kind of torture. By now the British were well aware that the Continental Congress had instructed the Bostonians to remain passive and refrain from conflict. What better way to destroy any hope of support from the other colonies than to provoke Boston's leading "rebel" to violence?

As Joseph faced the insults day after day, he began to fear that their plan might prove effective. William Eustis was aware of his teacher's frustrations, and he nervously watched for Joseph's response every time an insult was hurled.

On an especially trying day, the two men rode out of Boston together. Problem after problem had arisen all morning, and Joseph was in an unusually tense state. Now he was needed in Braintree.

They rode past the British guard on the narrow strip of land leading out of Boston. Joseph and William politely exchanged greetings with the soldiers on duty, but as soon as they had passed, one of the soldiers yelled out, "It won't be long before you're hanging from the gallows, Warren!"

To William's horror, Joseph pulled sharply on the reins, jerking his horse around. Then at a full gallop he rode back to the guard post. William quickly followed, hoping he could bring his teacher's rage back under control.

"Who said it?" Joseph shouted at the soldiers, who were taken by surprise at this reaction. None of them dared confess. He glared at each man, still not sure what he would do should one of them admit to the remark. One by one, their eyes dropped as they tried to avoid his searching glare. Then, turning his horse around, he rode away. William was at his side.

"These fellows say we will not fight! By heavens, I hope I shall die up to my knees in blood!" Joseph exclaimed.

Mercy, her father, and William feared for Joseph's safety. The verbal abuse he received during the day was reason enough for concern, but what might occur in the dark of night worried them even more. What would prevent a few of the soldiers from ambushing him under the cover of darkness as he responded to the summons of a patient?

Late one evening as Joseph and William were preparing to leave the Scollay's and head for home, a messenger came to the door. Joseph's services were needed at the home of Mrs. Smith, an elderly widow who lived alone. Mrs. Smith often called on him. Rarely was she ill—just lonely. He never let on that he knew she only wanted his company, but he would listen patiently as she told him her troubles. Then he would prescribe a simple, harmless remedy. He would then sit and visit with her for a while.

As far as Mercy, John Scollay, and William were concerned, such visits were no longer safe. They all felt he should only answer the night calls of those in dire need.

Joseph disagreed. He was responsible to come to the aid of his patients, whether their illness was real or imagined.

"The Widow Smith needs me," he said in response to their protest, "and I intend to go to her! Your concern for my safety is appreciated. John, may I borrow a brace of pistols?"

Mercy gasped as her father nodded.

Joseph walked over to the cabinet where John stored his firearms. Taking two pistols from within, he carefully loaded them and placed them under his frock coat. "If they attempt an ambush, I will be prepared to at least put up a fight," he remarked calmly, gestured for William to come as he walked out into the darkness.

The British troops could hardly make a move before the people of Boston were abuzz with talk. Thus, when the transport barges used by the men-of-war were taken ashore for repairs, every soul in Boston was aware of the activity in the harbor.

It was not unusual to pull such barges up for repair with the arrival of spring. This alone was little cause for concern to the patriot leaders, but when coupled with the news that 1,000 more troops, accompanied by three British generals, were now en route to Boston's shore, it was cause for great alarm.

The arrival of the reinforcements would force General Gage into some sort of action. Of this there was little doubt among the Sons of Liberty. Perhaps he would move even before the reinforcements arrived in order to save face before his fellow generals for his tolerance of the "rebellious" attitudes so far.

The Sons of Liberty kept a sharp eye on the activities of both British soldiers and Tories through a spy system, which came to be known as "Warren's Watchers." Joseph's home became the patriot headquarters.

As additional British troops sailed closer to the New England shores, Boston's more outspoken patriots sensed danger in remaining there any longer. Many began to make preparations to move themselves and their families to the safety of the countryside.

A soft drizzle fell outside as dinner was served at the Scollay home. The small fire in the hearth was enough to chase away the slight chill of this damp, April evening.

The children were entranced by the story John Scollay was telling them of his boyhood. Periodically they would lift the spoons to their mouths without losing their concentration. The exaggerated story and the effect it had on the children amused Joseph, Mercy, and William.

A knock on the door did not disturb the storyteller or his attentive young audience, but the others heard it. A social call at the dinner hour was unlikely. No doubt someone was in need of medical attention. Mercy sighed softly, not yet accustomed to having Joseph called out at all hours. Hearing her sigh, he threw her a quick smile. She would adapt soon enough.

"Excuse me, Dr. Warren, but the solicitor general is here to see you, sir," the servant woman announced.

"Samuel Quincy? Is he alone?" Joseph's surprise was obvious.

"Yes, sir. He's quite alone."

Joseph glanced at Mercy, whose face had suddenly grown pale. John Scollay did not continue his story but sat staring silently at his future son-in-law. The adults did not dare to verbalize their fear that Samuel Quincy may very well be there to arrest Joseph.

Casually, Joseph wiped his mouth with his napkin, placing it beside the plate when he was finished. Pushing his chair deliberately from the table, he stood up. Then walking behind Mercy, he gently laid his hand on her shoulder. She quickly grasped it in an attempt to hold him back.

"He is alone, Mercy. Surely he would not come alone to serve a warrant on me," he said softly.

Samuel Quincy stood in the foyer, nervously fidgeting with his hat.

"How can I help you, Samuel?" Joseph asked, with a forced smile for this one-time friend who was now such a threat.

"I am sorry to disturb your dinner, Dr. Warren, but my sister-in-law asked me to come for you."

"Abigail? Is she ill?"

"No, sir. It is the baby. She has come down with another fever. Abigail is quite frightened that the seizures may begin again."

"I will get my bag."

"What does he want?" Mercy asked anxiously as Joseph came back.

"Josiah's daughter is ill again. That poor child has been sick more often than not since her birth," he said, obviously distraught over the situation. "William, you had better come with me."

"Can I do anything to help?" Mercy asked.

"I will send word if Abigail needs you," he replied, suspecting that Samuel's wife was already there.

Throughout the night, Joseph and William tried to bring the baby's fever down, but to no avail. Abigail watched in horror as her baby's tiny body was overtaken by seizures, and by dawn the small child was too weak to continue her tenuous hold on life.

In despair Joseph, William, and Parson Cooper, together with the mother and other family members, mourned the loss of the precious child. Even now, her father was somewhere upon the frigid waters of the Atlantic Ocean returning home from his mission.

The tragic death of the Quincy baby ushered in an epidemic. As the fever quickly picked its victims, mostly children, the red quarantine flags began to appear upon many doorposts as a warning those who passed that the fever had invaded those homes.

Once more Dr. Joseph Warren endured the lengthy hours an epidemic demanded of him. Weary from lack of sleep, he went on his rounds from house to house every day.

Upon arising from a typical all-too-short rest, Joseph once again began to gather his supplies in preparation for the house calls he had to make. The sudden arrival of a messenger boy delayed his preparations.

"A message from Miss Scollay, sir," a lanky, young lad announced as he handed Joseph a sealed letter.

A pleased smile came over his face as he opened it. No doubt Mercy's pen would implore him to take care of himself. She had been very understanding during this, her first epidemic as his fiancée. His visits to her of late had been few and brief.

To his surprise, he found a brief, hastily written message: "Betsey and Polly have taken ill. Come as soon as possible."

Deeply troubled, Joseph instructed William to finish collecting supplies and then meet him at the Scollay's. With haste, he departed.

Josey and Dick greeted their father upon his arrival. To his relief, both boys appeared in good health.

"Where is Miss Mercy?" he asked. Before the boys could answer, Mercy appeared on the stairway. Her face was drawn from lack of sleep. In her arms she carried a bundle of soiled bed linen.

"They came down with the fever during the night," she explained. Her deep concern was revealed in her voice. In an attempt to comfort her, Joseph gently squeezed her arm as he passed her on the staircase and continued up them in silence.

"Perhaps we could take them to Roxbury this very afternoon," John Scollay suggested to Mercy and William as Joseph busied himself with the girls. "No one would suspect a thing. The children often visit their grandmother."

"Are they strong enough?" William asked, trying to evaluate the situation. Just then Joseph appeared on the staircase.

"This house is under quarantine," he announced as he descended the stairs. Then, turning to a servant, he instructed her to find the materials needed for the quarantine flag.

"Before we hang the flag, we should consider the situation," John suggested.

Joseph sank into an easy chair, gratefully accepting the cup of tea Mercy offered. He made no attempt to respond to John's suggestion. Both curiosity and the temptation to find a way to remove his children from Boston kept Joseph silent, ready to listen to any suggestions offered.

"We can move the children before anyone knows they are ill," John proposed. Mercy quickly ushered the boys into another room as her father spoke in an attempt to spare them from becoming upset by the conversation.

"Perhaps Father is right, Joseph," Mercy offered after the boys were gone. "If we wait and the British move while they are under quarantine, it may be impossible to get them out of Boston."

"But are they strong enough to travel?" William asked again.

Joseph looked at his student but did not answer. He was struggling with his own conscience, battling within himself over what he knew to be right and his instinct as a father to protect his children at all costs.

He continued to gaze at William as thought after thought poured through his mind. The responsibility he felt as a physician vehemently opposed his feelings as a father.

As he studied young Eustis, who was obviously uneasy by now—wondering if his question had somehow upset his teacher—Joseph realized he had a responsibility to fulfill to him.

"Dr. Eustis," he finally said, addressing his beloved apprentice with the title he was so close to officially obtaining. "Can one justify breaking a quarantine on the basis of fear that a situation may or may not occur?"

William hesitated in his reply as he considered the question put to him.

Joseph did not wait for his reply. "I love my children dearly and want nothing more than to have them safely outside of Boston when Gage makes his move. I am to blame for not moving all of you sooner. I put it off for too long. How could I have been so neglectful?" he muttered in despair as the servant entered with a small red flag.

He arose from the chair and walked across the room, taking the flag from her. "Dr. Eustis and I have treated many children stricken with this fever. We have lost some. So far, it has been confined to Boston. The countryside is still free of it, thank God. Can I risk introducing this fever to the children in Roxbury? Shall another man's children die because I am afraid that the British might move before mine are out of quarantine?"

Turning to Mercy, he added, "I will speak with the Reveres. Perhaps we can move the children over there. I placed a quarantine sign on their doorpost only last night."

"Why would we move them to the Revere's, Joseph?" Mercy asked, apparently confused.

"So that you and your father can leave Boston."

"Leave Boston? But my place is here with the children!" she responded immediately and without reservation.

"I cannot ask you to stay, Mercy."

Mercy walked over to him, stood in front of him, and placed her hands on his arms. "Joseph, when I accepted your proposal of marriage, I also accepted the responsibilities of being a mother to your children. I shall remain with them."

"Thank you." His words were barely audible, but his gratitude and love shone forth from his eyes.

With the red flag in hand, Joseph walked to the door. As he placed the signal of the quarantine on the doorpost of the Scollay home, he silently pleaded with heaven to forestall the trouble to come.

The next meeting of the Massachusetts Provincial Congress was quickly approaching. Joseph was expected to attend.

The fever had about run its course. William assured his teacher that he could care for those who were in the process of recovery, as well as any other situations that may arise during his absence. Joseph knew full well that William was capable of this. His term of indenture had ended, and William was in reality a full-fledged physician. Joseph intended to send him out on his own as soon as the epidemic had passed. He wanted the young man out of Boston before any trouble began.

With Polly and Betsey out of danger, even Mercy encouraged Joseph to attend the meeting. Together with Sam Adams and John Hancock, he rode to Concord, where the Congress was scheduled to convene.

The sessions of congress were lengthy, the atmosphere tense as delegates from throughout the colony discussed their troubles with Great Britain. The warning of approaching conflict had been sounded for years, and some of the delegates had grown weary of the constant alarm. Others were frightened that talk of such conflict was certain to bring it upon them, as if ignoring the facts would delay the inevitable.

The delegates from Boston fully comprehended the severity of the situation. Joseph Warren became spokesman for the Boston delegates, and he was determined to make the others understand how serious conditions were. He took the floor frequently, imploring the Massachusetts Bay delegates to keep their militias in readiness for an imminent move by Gage. Yet, in spite of the information that indicated something was afoot, his words seemed to fall on deaf ears.

The result of the sessions was not what Joseph had hoped for. When the Congress's president, John Hancock, finally called for an adjournment, Joseph flung himself back in the hard, wooden chair, muttering to himself in frustration.

"The Marblehead militia will be instructed to stand ready at all times," a familiar voice spoke from behind the chair as a long, thin hand was placed upon his back. Joseph turned in his seat to find Marblehead delegate Elbridge Gerry standing there. With a weak smile, Joseph communicated his appreciation to his long-time friend.

"You have the support of the town militias and minutemen even if their delegates are hesitant," Elbridge continued. "The minutemen take great pride in their claim of being prepared on short notice. None even go to the field to plow without bringing their musket, lead, and powder. You give the word from Boston, and you shall have immediate support!"

"I have no doubt of this myself," the voice of John Adams joined him from behind. "Braintree's militia will fall out when the word is given. Cousin Sam tells me that you intend to return to Boston despite his wife's letter warning you not to come home."

"Betsy Adams' letter stated that Gage was prepared to arrest Sam and John Hancock. My name was not mentioned," Joseph retorted as he gathered the papers on the table before him.

"When Gage realizes that Sam and Jay have outmaneuvered him, he may just turn on you," John warned.

"I am aware that it is a possibility, but I intend to chance it. My family is still under quarantine, and my patients are in need of me. I will continue to watch and report on any goings on as long as possible."

"How much longer can your Masonic position protect you?" John asked, the concern evident in his expression.

"Long enough to keep me one step ahead of Gage, I hope." Joseph's position as Provincial Grand Master commanded the respect of fellow Masons, which included many British soldiers, officers, and enlisted men.

"Be sure that you get out at the first sign of trouble. Oh that we could return to our carefree days at Harvard," John said mournfully.

"Carefree? We certainly did not think so at the time!" Elbridge exclaimed.

"Harvard—it seems so long ago," Joseph said softly as he stood up. "Little did we realize then—" But he did not finish his thought. Each man silently contemplated his own ending to this unfinished sentence.

"John, when will you be leaving for Philadelphia?" Elbridge inquired.

"Lord willing, in a week. How I wish that Sam could bring himself to ride a horse. We could make much better time. I have tried time and again to help him overcome this ridiculous fear he has," John complained, shaking his head. "Can you imagine being confined to a coach with Sam and Jay bickering for most of the trip?"

Joseph and Elbridge groaned with sympathy at the thought.

"I have a week left with my family, then what? How long shall we be gone? A month? Two? Six? And what shall we return to? The uncertainty of it all, gentlemen, is absolutely unnerving."

Each man was keenly aware of his unsettled future. With kinds words of encouragement for one another, they said their good-byes.

After a vain attempt to conceal his yawn, Parson Jonas Clarke pushed his chair away from the table and stood up. "I should like to remain, gentlemen, but I cannot seem to stay awake any longer. Please make yourselves at home."

The country parson had kindly offered his home as a place of refuge to his cousin John Hancock and Sam Adams upon hearing they were unable to return to Boston. They planned to stay in the Lexington parsonage until their departure for Philadelphia. The small parsonage was full, even without these distinguished guests, for Parson Clarke had eight children. But a comfortable room was made ready for company, including Joseph, who was spending the night before his return to Boston in the morning.

"I will be retiring myself, Cousin Jonas," John Hancock announced in a weary tone. "When do you plan to head out, Joseph?"

"At first light."

"Then I will say my good-byes now, my friend." John extended his hand to shake Joseph's. "Be careful. And please do keep us informed of any moves the British may make."

"You can depend on it, John. And may God grant the Massachusetts delegates wisdom as you represent us in Philadelphia."

"I will be up before you leave, Doctor. Good night, gentlemen," the parson said.

"Good night, Parson," Joseph and Sam responded in unison.

"What are you grinning about, Doctor?" Sam asked as Joseph returned to his seat, plainly amused by something.

"How you and Hancock shall survive the next week living in such cramped quarters—even sharing a bed. Then having to travel all the way to Philadelphia together! Actually, I should probably be pitying the Clarkes even more—poor things."

"Very funny, Joseph," Sam began, "but I expect the parson will keep us in line while we're here. And Cousin John, with great exasperation, will attempt to keep us in line all the way to Philadelphia!" he finished with a chuckle.

"Poor John!" Joseph said, still grinning.

"Yes, Cousin John does get quite frustrated."

"Oh, I am not referring to John Adams. It is Hancock I feel sorry for!"

"Hancock? Hancock!" Sam exclaimed in feigned disbelief.

"Sam, you purposely vex him," Joseph accused.

Sam smiled mischievously. "Yes, I suppose I do. But it is just my way of keeping him humble, reminding him of his modest beginnings! I do have a great deal of affection for the man. Surely you know that?" Sam's tone had suddenly become serious and concerned.

"I know it. I have never questioned it," Joseph assured him.

"Well, the Provincial Congress shall have the nomination of a new president as its first order of business upon returning," Sam stated.

"Hmm, yes. Hancock has served us well in that position," Joseph said.

"You shall serve as well, if not better," Sam offered with a smile.

Joseph appeared surprised by Sam's words.

"Surely you must be aware that they plan to nominate you?"

"No, I was under the impression from the last few sessions that most of the delegates do not agree with me on some vital issues. In fact, Sam, I have the distinct impression that this Congress adjourned early in an attempt to shut me up!"

Sam suddenly realized how upset Joseph actually was.

"You are preparing them for war. They do not want to face that reality. Many are deluded into thinking that if they can get you to stop talking about it, the problem will go away."

Joseph stood up and began to pace the floor in frustration as Sam continued.

"Influential and respected men like Elbridge Gerry are behind you. You will be nominated. You possess the needed qualities to preside over the Provincial Congress and guide it in the right direction."

"I do not want the nomination, Sam," Joseph stated matter-of-factly.

Over the years, he had accepted, even volunteered for, many important and often dangerous positions. Sam had witnessed him perform tasks no one else would. He put his heart into everything he undertook, always ready to do what was necessary for the cause of freedom. Yet he never sought praise, nor did he ever seek an elected position. He was not trying to make a name for himself or seek the approval of men. He simply did what he believed had to be done. This quality, among others, had earned him the respect and admiration of both those who agreed with and those who disagreed with his convictions.

Sam had never known Joseph to let his pride interfere with responsibilities in the past. "Do you mean to decline the nomination?" he asked.

"I do," the answer came without hesitation.

"I wish you would reconsider—"

"I have committed myself to the Committees of Correspondence and Safety. This work requires much of my time. Just keeping an eye on things in Boston demands a great deal of concentration, and I must have time to spend with my patients and my family—"

"I suppose it does not really matter anyway," Sam interrupted, disregarding Joseph's objection.

Joseph was surprised by the interruption and a bit perplexed by Sam's statement.

"Whether or not you accept the title of president, you shall be the president,"

Sam replied to Joseph's unspoken question. "They will seek your guidance. You have been committed to this cause from the start, and there will not be a man left in Massachusetts Bay after we leave who has devoted more of himself to our cry for liberty than you. Decline the nomination if you feel you must, but be ready to take on the responsibilities just the same."

"They respect my opinions? How can they when they mistrust my judgments? Why else would they draw up a list of do's and do not's for me to follow in calling out the militia?" he asked in an aggravated tone.

"They are only being cautious, trying to keep you from making a mistake that any one of us could make under extreme pressure," Sam offered.

"Come on, Sam!" Joseph exclaimed in disbelief. "You do not believe that any more than I do! If the truth were known, it is because they want to prevent me from making any move! They say I cannot call the militia out if the troops march out of Boston without their backpacks."

"Hardly a cause for alarm, Joseph. When have you ever seen them march without them? Even while drilling, they are required to carry provisions," Sam responded, sincerely wanting to ease his young friend's anxiety.

"True. But what if Gage is informed of this order from the Provincial Congress? He shall be—and if I were Gage, I would simply have them march without the packs. Then my hands are tied, and the British are free to plunder our supplies without a contest."

Sam remained quiet, thoughtfully studying Joseph for a moment.

Joseph's pacing stopped when he stood across the table from Sam. He leaned on the table, looking intently into the older man's gray eyes. "You know there is an informer among us, Sam, and Gage will certainly be wise to all our activities these past few days."

Silence filled the room as the men stared at one another. Joseph anxiously awaited a response.

"I trust your judgment," Sam's words finally broke the silence. "Do what you must to protect our supplies. If at all possible, confer with members of Congress. If this is not possible, then—" He did not finish the sentence, and Joseph understood that he did not intend to. "I have kept you up longer than I intended. The sun will be rising soon."

"Sam," Joseph said with a sense of urgency, still leaning on the table. "Something is going to happen soon, very soon!"

"I know!"

"Somehow, someway, you have to make those men in Philadelphia understand.

If we must face the British Empire alone, we shall. But would to God our sister colonies come to our aid!"

"I understand," Sam replied somberly. "I am worried about your returning to Boston, Joseph. If Gage is determined to have John Hancock and me, it will not be long before he comes after you as well. Who else of consequence remains there?"

"Paul. But he will not leave until the last possible moment. His family is still under quarantine."

"Has Dr. Church left yet?" Sam asked, surprised that Joseph had not mentioned him in his list of club members.

"No, but I doubt that he is in any real danger," Joseph replied, trying to avoid Sam's eyes.

"At the first sign of trouble, you and Paul get out of there!" Sam instructed, ignoring Joseph's last remark. "When did Josiah leave England?"

"About eight weeks ago."

"Then he should be here soon. What is it, Joseph? You look troubled."

"It is a long, damp sea voyage."

"All his correspondence assured us of his good health."

"I realize that, and I believe the climate there was beneficial to him. But the trip home? Forgive me, Sam. I cannot help but worry about him."

"If Josiah's report proves vital to the course we must take, have it brought to Philadelphia immediately. If Josiah cannot personally deliver it, send it by Revere or a courier as trusted as he," Sam carefully instructed. Suddenly Sam became strangely silent.

To leave, with the future of Massachusetts Bay in such uncertainty, was difficult for Sam. He rose from the chair and walked to where Joseph stood. A handshake was not an appropriate good-bye for these good friends whose mutual convictions had held with them the threat of arrest and death for the past ten years. They had never failed one another. Thinking similar thoughts, their hearts beat in unison for the very life of their country.

In the stillness of this early April morning, Samuel Adams and Joseph Warren warmly embraced, uncertain of when or if they would meet again.

As the first rays of the rising sun stole through the cracks in the old barn, Joseph busied himself with saddling his horse. He could hear footsteps approaching the barn, and as the creaking door was slowly pulled open, he looked up, expecting to greet one of the Clarke children coming to milk the cow.

"Dr. Warren, I was afraid I had missed seeing you off!" Parson Clarke exclaimed, moving to the opposite side of the horse.

"You should not have concerned yourself with it, Parson," Joseph replied with a smile as he gave a final tug on the cinch.

"I wanted to offer you some words of encouragement before you headed back to Boston. I realize how emotionally draining the past few days have been."

A weak though appreciative smile was all Joseph could muster.

"As I lay on my bed last night, I prayerfully considered what words I might offer you. Psalm 126 came to mind. I preached on that text recently. Are you familiar with it?"

Joseph's eyes brightened as he considered the Psalm mentioned. "Israel's freedom from her captivity," he stated.

"Then you probably are aware of the promise there, Joseph? 'They that sow in tears shall reap in joy.' I have no doubt that God has felt your sorrow and taken notice of the tears you have shed for your oppressed country in the privacy of your prayer closet. He has heard the supplication and seen the tears when you have come to Him on your knees alongside the two men who are still at rest within my home. Those who 'sow in tears shall reap in joy'—we must believe it!"

"If it comes to war, Parson, some of us will die. We will not be doing any reaping in this life, but perhaps our children will reap what we have sown," Joseph replied, a glimmer of hope in his eyes.

"Our children will, and I trust the joy awaiting those who shed their blood will be greater than our finite minds can imagine!" Jonas Clarke offered.

"I believe you are right, Parson. I do believe you are right. Can you tell me, sir, will the men of Lexington come if I should be forced to call out the militia? Will they fight if fired upon?" Joseph asked, desperate to know he had support.

Parson Clarke's response was immediate. "I have prepared them for this very hour."

• 15 •

Lexington & Concord

SOMETHING IS MOST certainly afoot!" Paul Revere exclaimed to Joseph as his friend came riding up to his door. Paul had been anxiously awaiting his return from Lexington for many hours.

Joseph listened intently. "About midnight the transport boats were launched. They now rest under the protection of the men-of-war. The light infantry and grenadier have been mysteriously detached from their regiments. Rumor has it that they are on undesignated duty."

"Undesignated duty? No one has word of what this might be?"

Paul shook his head.

"Something surely is afoot!" Joseph repeated Paul's words. "It is curious that Gage would detach those particular troops . . ."

The grenadiers were Gage's heavy-duty troops made up of his largest soldiers. The light infantry companies were the fast, active troops.

"I wonder what he is up to?" Joseph thought aloud as he pulled out a map of Massachusetts Bay. "He must have been alerted to all our depots by now."

"Worcester? Concord?" Paul began naming off the towns where the supplies were being stored.

"Worcester is more than forty miles—too long a march," Joseph remarked as he studied the map. "Gage is aware that we would get wind of such a long march and have plenty of time to prepare. Concord has to be his destination. If they march at night, they could reach Concord by daybreak."

"Surprising everyone," Paul added.

"That would be Gage's intention, but the surprise may well be on him," Joseph replied. "We cannot risk losing the supplies in Concord. It would prove to be our undoing. Secrecy is of the utmost importance. Gage must not suspect that we may be on to him. If the troops are called out to march on Concord, we must be prepared to warn the countryside. Two riders will be needed—you, of course, and—" Joseph paused as he considered who else could be trusted with this highly delicate information.

"What about Billy Dawes? He's actually very good at play-acting," Paul suggested. "I believe he could talk himself out of any situation that may arise in getting past the British."

"An excellent choice," Joseph agreed. "He will ride out to Concord by this route," Joseph instructed as he ran his finger over the map through Boston and then down over the Neck into the countryside.

"You will have to cross the Charles River to Charlestown. Have a rowboat hidden on the shore. This is perhaps the more dangerous route, Paul. You will be passing right under the guns of the Somerset," Joseph paused, looking up from the map to see if Paul had any objection.

Both were keenly aware that the Boston Port Bill prohibited even rowboats to be upon the water. If the watch on the British warship *HMS Somerset* was to spot Paul, it was very likely he would be shot on sight.

"If it must be done, it will be under the cover of darkness with muffled oars. I think I can make it safely across, Joseph."

Joseph nodded. "Let us pray you will not need to make this trip. But in the event you do, with both you and Billy Dawes riding, the chances are good that one of you will reach the destination unhindered by British patrols. See to it that arrangements are made for a horse to stand ready for you in Charlestown."

"I fear Gage may have a two-fold purpose in marching to Concord." Paul's statement captured Joseph's full attention. "We've had reports that he knows Sam and John are hiding out in Lexington. Are you aware that he's determined to take them into custody?"

"Dr. Church's handiwork, no doubt—" Joseph muttered with disgust.

"Church was there?"

"He was there, spouting off his patriotic slogans, playing his part to the utmost—" Joseph's words drifted off as if he sought to detach himself from them. "God forgive me—forgive us both, Paul, if we are wrong about that man. But there is an informant, and I just cannot shake the feeling that it is Church."

Paul fully understood the quandary Joseph felt.

"Any word of my arrest?" Joseph asked.

Paul chuckled. "Do you think I'd risk being close by if I knew they were after you, Joseph?"

"Why not?" Joseph returned with a smile to match Paul's. "That way they can kill two birds with one stone. No doubt they intend to get you as soon as they get me. What good is a Warren without a Revere?"

"I think we're both safe for the moment!" Paul replied, again laughing.

"Glad to hear it! But we must inform Sam and John of matters here. Can you ride out to Lexington today?"

Paul nodded.

"Then head over to Concord and see that the militia company moves all of the supplies to safety immediately."

"As good as done," Paul replied. Then standing, he headed for the door.

"Paul," Joseph called after him.

Paul turned around.

"There is a chance we may become trapped in Boston. Just in case, we need to arrange a signal, a way of informing the countryside of Gage's move."

"Christ's Church has the highest steeple in Boston. It can be seen for miles," Paul began. "If their move is by night, perhaps we can devise a signal with lanterns in the steeple."

"Good idea! Be certain the people in Charlestown keep a strict vigil in watching the steeple each night. One lantern will indicate that the British are marching by land, over the Neck. Two will indicate that they are crossing by the river. Then, if you and Billy are trapped here, the Charlestown militia will be responsible for alerting the countryside."

"And what about our families?" Paul asked, more as a thought than a question, for he already knew the answer. As his eyes met Joseph's, he realized that there was nothing to say in response, for he could not do anything to remove them while they still were under quarantine. Their shared grief lingered.

The attitude of various British officers seemed strangely altered on the afternoon of April 18. Preoccupied and somewhat aloof, they moved about the streets of Boston without even a greeting for those who had befriended them.

Uncertain of the significance, Joseph took note of it. Perhaps something was about to happen, and they were mentally preparing themselves. Or maybe it was just the negative effect of the depressing weather. A chilling rain continued to fall as the April winds whipped through the streets and alleyways.

A summons early that evening to attend a patient in need of his care proved to clarify Gage's intentions beyond a shadow of a doubt.

"Dr. Warren, thank you for responding on such short notice." Margaret Gage stated, quickly instructing her servant to leave the sitting room and close the door behind her.

Mrs. Gage's flowing dark hair, soft brown eyes, and delicate, fair features were designed in such a fashion as to make her strikingly beautiful. Combined with her stunning figure, elegant dress, and poised carriage, she had the ability to draw the attention of most any man. It was commonly known that she was unhappy with her military husband, many years her senior, and this made Joseph uncomfortable.

"Dr. Lloyd is your physician. Why have you not summoned him?" Joseph asked, fully aware of the danger of the situation and wanting to avoid any unnecessary trouble with General Gage.

"Dr. Lloyd is on an emergency call. And I am told that you are as fine a physician as he, if not better—." Normally self-confident, Margaret Gage appeared anxious as she nervously twisted a laced handkerchief in her hands. She stepped to the window overlooking the busy street below.

"Are you ill, madam?"

"Yes," she said, gazing out the window as though fearing the imminent arrival of someone. The lingering rays of the setting sun glistened against the rose-colored silk of her gown.

"What is the nature of your illness, Mrs. Gage?" He was growing impatient with her odd behavior.

"It is my heart, Doctor. My heart is torn in two." Finally she turned her head to look directly at him.

"To be honest, Mrs. Gage, I am not comfortable being here alone with you. I recommend that you wait for Dr. Lloyd."

"Dr. Lloyd cannot help me," she said with a sob as she quickly turned back to the window in an attempt to compose herself.

"Please, Mrs. Gage, then have the servant return, or open the door."

"I cannot. Nor would you want that, I'm certain!"

"Madam! I do not believe I can help you." Joseph quickly made his way to the door, prepared to flee this dangerous situation.

"No, Dr. Warren! Indeed you cannot help me, nor did I expect you to. For the truth is, I must help you!"

He placed his hand on the doorknob. "Madam, I must go."

"My husband intends to march his troops to Concord this very night. They are under orders to destroy any military supplies found there and to arrest Mr. Samuel Adams and Mr. John Hancock, who are residing at the home of Parson Jonas Clarke in Lexington."

Joseph's head spun around with the sudden realization that his worst fears were about to be realized. Her attention remained fixed on the street below as she continued to twist the handkerchief.

"How do you know this?" he asked.

"My husband, of course. His orders have been made known only to myself and to Lord Percy."

"Why have you chosen to tell me?"

She turned her head to face him, tears streaming from her dark eyes. "Because America is my home, Dr. Warren. And I believe that what you are attempting to do is good and right. I cannot idly watch as the colonies are forced into subjection to the raw might and power of Great Britain. I love my husband dearly, but I love my country and my countrymen as much, so alas, my heart is rent in two."

"It is a very courageous thing you have done," Joseph assured her.

"Courage? Madness? I know not which!" Her attention went back to the street. "When my husband discovers my treachery, he will be crushed. And I fear my marriage will be in jeopardy."

"Certainly not, madam! I will never reveal how I came to this knowledge! I will take it to my grave, madam," Joseph promised, hoping she would somehow find comfort in his words.

"I thank you, Doctor, but in truth it does not matter. My husband knows that Lord Percy would never speak of the secret orders to another soul. And he suspects my loyalties are not with the Crown, therefore—"

"Then why did he tell you?"

Margaret Gage only looked at him, but offered no response.

"Mrs. Gage, what can I do to help you?"

"You must leave me a remedy of sorts to help me explain the reason for your visit. And you must keep your promise to tell no one that I was your informant. And lastly, Doctor, I would implore you to pray for me. For no matter what my decision had been—whether to share this information with you or to keep it secret—the results for me would have been the same. The guilt will follow me the rest of my days."

By eight o'clock that evening, the transport barges stood in readiness to move men across the Charles River. The troops gathered on the Common in full battle gear, wearing all but the customary backpacks. There was no doubt in Joseph's mind that the absence of the backpacks was a direct result of Gage's being informed of the recent orders of the Provincial Congress.

Joseph considered the tremendous responsibility upon him as he paced back and forth across the parlor floor. He longed for the counsel of those he had worked alongside through the years of turmoil, yet none could help him now. He would be forced to make this decision alone.

Should he call out the militia and possibly bring about a bloody conflict with the mother country? Should he oppose the military strength of England, which boasted the mightiest army on the face of the earth? Or should he ignore the marching of the British troops, thus putting the needed military supplies at risk, knowing that such a loss would very likely bring the Massachusetts Bay Colony to its knees.

The decision before him was one of death and destruction or slavery and shame. The happiness, the security, and lives of his fellow colonists hung in the balance, and the burden of this responsibility seemed too great for him to bear alone.

Dropping to his knees in the middle of the large, dark room, he pled for divine guidance. He remained on his knees until he was certain that the decision he was about to make was the right one.

Messages were delivered to the homes of Billy Dawes and Paul Revere that they should pay a visit to Dr. Warren immediately.

Paul Revere briskly walked the darkened road and alleys. The rain had stopped, but the howling wind continued, sending a chill up his spine. When he came to the Warren house, he knocked as quietly as possible.

Joseph responded quickly, opening the door only enough to assure himself that the visitor was a trusted friend before gesturing for Paul to enter.

"I received a message that you wanted to see me," Paul said. His dark eyes, which had been shut tight in deep slumber just a short while earlier, were now wide with excitement.

"Gage has ordered the troops out. They are headed for Concord. It is time to call out the militia! Be sure to warn Sam and John to seek different shelter. Billy Dawes just left. He has been instructed to warn them also."

"Are they moving out over the Neck or by the river?" Paul asked.

"The barges stand ready for loading."

"Two lanterns—," Paul said softly.

"Two lanterns," Joseph echoed. "I will send word to have them hung in the steeple immediately."

"Are you ready to leave?" Paul asked with concern.

"I have some things to take care of here—papers to burn. Dr. Townsend and Dr. Adams have agreed to care for my patients. I must meet with them still. I hope to be out before sunrise." He paused, then continued in a most somber tone. "Paul, you have delivered many important messages for the Committee of Correspondence, but none thus far has equaled the importance of the message you bear tonight."

Paul fully understood how vital it was that the message be delivered. "Well, then

I had better get started, my friend," he said awkwardly, uncertain of how to say good-bye. So much could happen within the next few hours. "Gage will be after you as soon as he learns that the militia is out. Please don't remain here too long."

"I will be out before word reaches Gage. Be careful crossing the river, and watch out for any British that may be patrolling the countryside."

"I will."

Aware that the time had come to proceed, Paul embraced his friend, said good-bye, and then departed.

The town crier's voice carried across the darkened streets as Joseph made his way from Dr. Townsend's house to the Scollay's. "Three o'clock and all is well!" His words echoed through Joseph's mind again and again. If only it was so!

He slowed his pace, purposefully becoming more alert to his surroundings. Boston was so poorly planned, with her crooked streets and alleyways. In the stillness, he could hear the waves gently slapping against the wharves that jutted into the harbor. Once a bustling metropolis, Boston was now brought near to ruin by an unrighteous government. Boston—the home he had come to love! An eerie foreboding engulfed him as he viewed the darkened streets, illuminated only by the oil street lamps. How things had changed in the past year. How much would they change in the year ahead?

In spite of the late hour, Mercy and her father sat up awaiting his visit. They knew he would be forced to leave tonight.

"Is it safe for you to be out on the streets?" a concerned John Scollay inquired.

"Gage will think I am making house calls and will not suspect that we are on to him," Joseph replied, lifting his medical bag.

"Will you be leaving soon?" Mercy asked nervously.

"With the first light," he replied somberly, aware she was upset. She wept silently as he pulled her close. "You be sure to keep working on that wedding gown," he whispered softly into her ear.

Mercy tilted her head back to look at him, surprised by his words.

"The thought of a spring wedding appeals to me. What about you?" he asked. His countenance expressed his deep love. "I do not know what tomorrow holds for us, but if the Eternal shall see fit to keep me from harm, then rest assured I will work diligently to unite us all once again." Mercy wanted so to believe this. He could see a glimmer of hope in her soft, blue eyes even as he spoke.

"Do you think Gage will—" Mercy's voice trembled. "Do you think he will seek to harm us?"

Joseph had not realized her fear that this could happen. He held her closer, blaming himself for not sensing her fear earlier.

"No, Gage will not harm any of you," he said tenderly. "He may summon you and your father for questioning. He may even order a search of the house, but he will not harm you."

"And if he questions us, should we remain silent?" John asked, not wanting to say anything that might be used against his fellow countrymen, against his future son-in-law in particular.

Joseph looked at the older man and briefly considered his question. "If a battle is fought tomorrow, any answers you may give will not make a bit of difference." Then turning back to Mercy, he said, "Come, I must say good-bye to the children." Hand in hand, they walked up the stairs.

Betsey and Polly slept peacefully side by side. Joseph lovingly looked upon the younger girl, her dark curls pouring out of her nightcap. As he pulled the blankets up around the three-year-old's shoulders, he again realized how very much she resembled Elizabeth. Bending over her sleeping form, he tenderly kissed his youngest child.

When he turned to Betsey, his nudge caused her to awaken. Then taking her up into his strong arms, he carried the drowsy child to the next room where her brothers slept. Dick slept on as Joseph awakened only Josey.

"I will be going away for a while," he began. The sleepy children struggled to become alert. "You remember that we discussed the possibility of my having to leave Boston for a while? I want you to be on your best behavior. Help with the younger children. Show proper respect to Miss Mercy and Mr. Scollay."

Both children nodded in agreement to their father's instructions.

"How long will you be gone, Papa?" Josey asked.

"I have no way of knowing, son," he replied hesitantly, wanting to offer some hope of a short separation to the boy. But unsure if his son would understand if the separation proved lengthy, Joseph decided to leave his answer at that.

"Here, Betsey, I think you are old enough to keep this," he said as he twisted Elizabeth's wedding band off his smallest finger. Betsey watched in silence as her father placed the ring on her finger. She understood that the ring was eventually to become hers—yet, her father had treasured it, having worn it himself since her mother's death. Betsey suddenly realized the grave dangers he faced.

"Papa, I'm afraid!" she cried.

Joseph pulled both children close, quietly reassuring them of his love and offering hope of a joyous reunion. After kissing the sleeping Dick, Joseph spent a few tender moments with Mercy before departing.

Anxiously pulling his watch from the pocket of his waistcoat, Joseph checked the time once again—almost seven o'clock. Daylight had broken more than an hour earlier, yet still there was no word from Paul, Billy Dawes, or anyone.

He continued gathering the few items that were to be carried out of Boston with him. Many of his personal belongings had gradually been sent to the farm in Roxbury, anticipating his eventual need to flee. Gathered on the kitchen table were his fully-stocked medical bag, daybooks, an antique book of the Psalms, his tricorn, and his cane. He picked up the small book and safely tucked it into the inner pocket of his wool frock coat.

A loud rap on the kitchen door caused him to jump. Cautiously, he opened it.

"Dr. Warren. I have a message for you, sir." James Lovell stated in a low, grave tone. Joseph gestured for the trusted member of the Sons of Liberty to enter.

"Have you news from Concord?" Joseph asked apprehensively.

"News from Lexington, sir!" the lanky young man exclaimed, though his expression remained somber. "Seventy members of the Lexington militia unit waited upon the green as the British approached en route to Concord. Shots were fired, sir. Eighteen of the militia were hit."

A chill ran through Joseph's body. "And British casualties?"

"None to my knowledge, sir."

"Then the British opened fire?"

"My understanding is that the Lexington militia was only observing the passing British troops. I do not know for certain who fired first, Doctor."

"Have you any news of Sam Adams and John Hancock's whereabouts?"

"No, sir, only that they are safe. The concern at present is for you, Dr. Warren. You must get out of town before General Gage receives word. Please come with me, sir!" James declared.

Joseph gathered his belongings and followed the messenger into the streets of Boston, heading toward the Charles River. They came to a secluded spot on the river's bank where a man in a rowboat awaited their arrival.

"Doc Warren, I've heard rumors that shots have been fired! Is it true?" the oarsman asked as Joseph stepped into the boat and sat down.

Joseph looked at the frightened man. "Yes, it is true," he said with a comforting smile. "But keep up a brave heart! They have begun it. That either party can do. But we will end it! That only one can do."

When they reached the town of Charlestown on the opposite shore, a horse was standing in readiness. With the possibility of British patrols about, Joseph knew it was not safe to ride on the main roads. He kept to the wooded paths as much as possible as he headed toward Menotomy where the Committee of Safety was ordered to assemble.

At one point he was forced out onto the open road. He proceeded at a gallop, while keeping an eye open for another path in the safety of the woods.

Suddenly spotting a regiment of British soldiers ahead, he quickly yanked on the reins, coming to a dead stop. It was too late. They had already seen him. Joseph thought he recognized some of the faces. He considered turning the horse about but realized that might seem too suspicious. Hoping to appear timid, he lowered his head in an attempt to hide his face.

Two soldiers began to walk toward him. Silently he prayed that they did not know him by sight.

"State your business," one of the soldiers ordered.

"I am making house calls to my patients." He tried to alter his voice a bit. The soldier looked at the medical bag attached to the saddle.

"What's your name?" he asked, straining to see his face.

"Stevens. Dr. Samuel Stevens," Joseph quickly replied, using his grandfather's name.

"Stevens, eh?" the soldier repeated with a look of uncertainty.

"Have ya seen the others about, Doc?" the second soldier asked.

"Others?" Joseph queried, not sure if he meant soldiers or colonists. "I have not seen anyone."

"Come on, let's tell the captain," the second soldier called out as he walked away.

The first soldier hesitated, his eyes continuously fixed on Joseph's face. "Doc Stevens..." he began. Joseph turned his eyes toward him, "you'd best get off the road. It's not safe out here." Joseph responded with only a nod of his head.

Slowly he turned the horse about, not wanting to appear overly anxious. With a sigh of relief and a prayer of thanks, Joseph diligently searched out a wooded path and continued on to Menotomy.

Although no one could yet anticipate the outcome of the day's events, plans had to be made to avoid mass confusion. Such plans were the responsibility of the Committee of Safety.

Military headquarters were to be established in Cambridge. The means of housing and feeding those who fled Boston, as well as those who might come from neighboring towns and colonies in response to the call to arms, had to be dealt with. Houses had to be prepared to serve as hospitals for any casualties, and supplies had to be delivered to them without delay.

As members of the Committee busied themselves with their assignments, Joseph felt it his duty as chairman of the Committee to find out firsthand what was happening on the battlefield.

It was nearly two o'clock in the afternoon when he set off, musket in hand, together with French and Indian War veteran General William Heath. By way of back roads and wooded paths, they headed in the direction where musket fire had last been reported.

The cold, penetrating dampness that enveloped the militia on the Lexington Green at sunrise had given way to pleasant sunshine. The earliest blossoms of spring had shown themselves as the men hurried on unaware.

Dread and fear gripped Joseph's heart as they made the two-mile trek to the scene of the battle. They made only occasional comments as they anticipated the possibilities of what lay ahead.

They heard the sound of musket fire in the distance, but it became louder as they continued on, assuring them they were headed in the right direction. Reports had indicated that the militia had harassed the British troops throughout the morning as the British struggled to make their way back to the safety of Boston. From behind trees, stone walls, and houses, the hard-fighting colonials took their aim. With their bright red coats and white cross belts, the British proved to be easy targets as they hurriedly retreated down the dirt roads. They clearly were unaccustomed to and unprepared for this unorthodox means of waging war.

Houses that were now engulfed in flames along the roadside gave evidenced of British retaliation. As the men drew closer to the sound of the battle, they spotted the bodies of British soldiers sprawled across the stone walls or lying abandoned in the dust of the road.

"Chest wounds mainly," General Heath commented as he strained to observe each body they passed. "They're aimin' for those cross belts."

General Heath stopped. "Look here," he said, pointing to some newly budded underbrush along the path they were following.

Joseph's eyes immediately focused in the direction indicated, stunned at the sight of three sets of shoes protruding beneath the pile of small tree limbs and dried leaves.

General Heath carefully pulled back the tree limbs, exposing the bodies of three colonial militiamen.

After taking a deep breath, Joseph momentarily diverted his eyes, wanting desperately to run from the gruesome scene.

"They must have been put here by those in their militia unit. Probably afraid some of the British might be looting the bodies. I'm sure they intend to return and bury them later," General Heath said.

Joseph nodded in reply.

"Look at the wounds, Doctor. There's no careful aim on the part of the British. They're aimin' too high."

Joseph did not respond as he viewed the three men—or what appeared to be men. The faces of two were disfigured beyond recognition. The third had no face left at all.

"Are you all right, Doctor?" General Heath asked.

"No, General, I'm not," Joseph replied with a shiver as he turned away from the corpses. His body was soaked with perspiration as he struggled to fight back the overwhelming sense of nausea.

General Heath replaced the branches, tossing leaves on top. Then coming from behind, he laid a comforting hand on the younger man's shoulder. "Your response is to be expected," he said.

"To be expected?" Joseph cried out in shame. "I am a physician. I have viewed wounds every bit as gruesome. I have cut into human flesh time and time again."

"To view a body mutilated as a result of an accident is quite different," General Heath offered, his hand still resting upon Joseph's shoulder.

Joseph turned his head to face the general. "I viewed the aftermath of the Boston Massacre."

"Yes, but you were not responsible for ordering those men to be in the line of fire."

"Oh, God!" Joseph cried out, choking back a sob. "Dear God, what have I done?"

General Heath stepped in front of Joseph, his hands, strengthened by years of farming, clutching Joseph's upper arms. "You did what you had to do! You did the only thing you could do. And these men—" he said, gesturing to the corpses, "these men willingly turned out because they knew it was so. And there will be more, Doctor—today, tomorrow, perhaps for years to come—and you must not blame yourself!"

With a deep breath, Joseph ran his hand across his face. Looking beyond General Heath to the dirt road, he pulled into focus the sight of the bodies of British soldiers littering their path and the sound of musketry further down the road.

Joseph looked at his friend, grateful for his empathy but unable to express his feelings. "We had better be moving on, General," he said.

The two men crouched low, carefully moving among the trees and shrubs as they approached the line. A brief counsel with the officers of the militia units indicated that no uniform plan of strategy existed. No one individual was in command of the many units assembled. Quickly sizing up the situation, William Heath and Joseph Warren took command, bringing a new confidence and sense of determination to the men.

The British were attempting a seventeen-mile retreat on a road that would eventually take them back to Boston. The colonials' tactics, which had been masterfully carried out throughout the day, were ordered to continue. The men were to get ahead of the enemy troops, hiding behind the stone walls and trees. Others were sent into houses within firing range. In deathlike silence these inexperienced, though well-trained, soldiers awaited the enemies' arrival.

As the British came within sight, Joseph's heart pounded as loud, so it seemed to him, as the rhythmic beating of the drums. With the butt of his musket propped against his right shoulder, he prepared to take aim on the approaching men. On which man would he fire? Which man would he attempt to kill? His hand trembled as he chose his target. Could he pull the trigger? Perhaps Jeffries was right. Perhaps one trained to heal should not partake in such destruction of human life!

The men around him began to discharge their muskets, yet Joseph hesitated. Enemy fire was quickly returned, but Joseph's musket still remained silent. A terrified cry from the woods shifted his attention.

"I've been hit!" a fellow colonist called out.

Between the trees and shrubbery Joseph could see the injured man. The front of his breeches were already soaked with blood. "The femoral artery!" he spoke the words aloud, aware that he must get to the man or he would bleed to death in a matter of minutes. Yet the distance was too great between them, and the British were taking aim at anything that moved.

"Someone apply pressure to the wound!" Joseph yelled above the popping of the muskets and the terrified cries of the man.

A colonist, crawling upon his belly, came alongside the fallen man. "What do I do, Doc?" he cried.

"Push against the wound with every ounce of strength you have! Use both hands! Push hard!"

The injured man offered little resistance as the severe blood loss had its effect.

"How long, Doc? How long?" the colonist cried out again.

"Until I can get there! Do not let up!"

With a keen sense of urgency, Joseph raised the musket to his shoulder, the battle still raging within. Could he deliberately kill a man? "No, not a man," he whispered to himself. "A target—only a target." He quickly glanced at the two men in the woods, one hanging on to life by a thread, and the other soon to be in agony him-self as every muscle in his upper body worked to save the life of his fallen comrade.

Joseph took careful aim at the white cross belts atop the bright red background. He squeezed the trigger, ignoring the kick of the musket against his shoulder and the fact that the white-and-red target fell from view. Quickly reloading, he sought another such target. Again and again and again until the enemy moved out of range.

He grabbed hold of the medical bag at his feet and ran toward the two men. "Do not let up, not yet!" Joseph ordered as he opened the bag. Immediately he removed a strip of leather about two inches wide. He searched about his feet and grabbed hold of a thin branch, quickly breaking a small piece off. He worked quickly, maneuvering the leather strip under the injured thigh above the bullet wound and twisting it, holding the tourniquet snugly around the thigh with the use of the small piece of wood.

"You can let up now," Joseph said, placing his hand on the back of the man who continued pressing on the wound.

The man only nodded in response. His expression clearly revealed the energy he had exerted. Backing away, he grabbed dried leaves to wipe off the blood drip-ping from his hands.

Joseph tore open the pant leg, exposing the wound to make certain that the tourniquet was working. Aware that he was unable to do anything more for this man under these circumstances, he still felt for a pulse and checked the pupils in each eye to determine the degree of shock. "Does anyone know this area?" he asked the few men that remained.

"I do," a man clad in a farmer's frock stated.

"Good. You will need the help of another. Get this man to a physician. Do not, under any circumstances, loosen that tourniquet. Do you understand?"

"Yes, Doc," the farmer replied.

Joseph and the others scurried through the woods to rejoin those who were again engaged in battle. Musket balls flew in a fearful exchange of fire. Men fell on both sides.

Positioned behind a stone wall, Joseph took careful aim. As soon as he squeezed the trigger, he felt the force of a British musket ball as it whizzed past his left ear. Stunned, he dropped to the ground behind the wall, and blood began to drizzle down the side of his head and neck. Suddenly aware that the lead ball had grazed him, Joseph lifted his hand to his head, only to discover that a clump of hair and small piece of flesh were gone. The nerves finally responded, and a burning, throb-bing pain set in.

He sat still for a moment, trying to recover from the shock of a near-fatal shot. Then, as he opened his powder horn to reload the musket, the appearance of a woman off in the woods captured his attention. Still in her nightclothes, she had a blanket draped about her shoulders. Like a frightened animal, she moved through the woods, bending low as she searched out a place of shelter.

In the distance, the shouts of fellow patriots could be heard as they confronted a stray band of British soldiers.

Joseph carefully made his way toward the area where he had last seen the woman. He heard her sobs as she crouched behind the trunk of a large oak surrounded by thick, thorn-filled underbrush. Terrified, she gasped as he approached, tightly clutching the blanket around her.

"I will not hurt you," Joseph said softly, reaching out to her. "I am a physician." As he spoke, the muffled cry of an infant could be heard from beneath the blanket. The woman carefully uncovered the small child.

"My children! My children!" she exclaimed as she grabbed hold of Joseph's arm.

"Where are they?" he asked.

"In the house! They're burning the house!" she cried frantically, pointing to a house set back behind the trees. "The soldiers—they forced me from my birthing bed—threatened to kill me and the baby both! I was able to hide the children in the cellar. They said they were going to burn the house!" At the point of hysteria, she stopped speaking, gasping for breath. Then hearing others approach, she clutched him tighter still.

Joseph turned and was relieved to see two colonists coming from the direction of the houses.

"Dr. Warren, is that you?" one of the men called out as he recognized the patriot leader. "We've just encountered a handful of redcoats bent on terrifying women, children, and old men. They've been burning our neighbor's homes."

"Did you see my young ones?"

"No...no, we didn't see any children about." Terror again gripped her heart upon hearing his answer.

"They are safe in the cellar," Joseph assured her.

"Mrs. Clayton, let me take you and your children to my house. We're back from the road. No redcoats will bother you there," one of the men suggested. "My womenfolk will be happy to tend to your needs."

Her neighbor placed his arm around her waist, partially supporting her weight. Walking back into the woods, he escorted the mother and her child to safety.

As Joseph bent down to pick up his musket, blood drizzled into his eye, and his head began to throb. In all of the excitement, he had forgotten about the wound. He had no time to concern himself with it now.

The battle raged on for many more hours as the patriots shadowed the pathetic British troops. As they approached Charlestown, the battle-worn British soldiers drew upon all of their strength to hasten their pace. Beyond Charlestown lay the river, where transport boats were waiting to take them to the safety of Boston.

Even though darkness had long fallen over the battle-torn colony, the patriots insisted upon pursuing their enemies to the very borders of Charlestown. Only then did they silence their muskets and consider the cold dampness that had set in. Their bellies ached from lack of food during the day.

Scattered campfires began to appear here and there, encircling the boundaries of Boston. Men began to relax around the fires' warmth as they recalled the day's events. Though physically exhausted, the excitement of the day kept them from sleeping.

Joseph traveled the few miles to Cambridge on horseback. He was aware that the members of the Provincial Congress and the Committee of Safety, as well as militia officers, would be awaiting his arrival at headquarters. There was much to plan for and discuss, but they would have to wait. His first concern was that the physicians had ample amounts of supplies and help.

A deserted Tory mansion in Cambridge had become a military hospital. Joseph's arrival went unnoticed as fellow physicians and their assistants bustled about as they cared for their many patients.

The house was filled with agonizing moans, which were momentarily silenced by occasional screams from an adjoining room. Joseph surmised that surgeries were being performed there.

He recognized many of the physicians about him, including his former apprentices. William Townsend and Sam Adams Jr. had chosen to remain in Boston to see to their patients and his. All were accounted for, except Jack.

Another scream from the next room echoed throughout the house as surgeons worked frantically to save a life, often at the expense of a limb. With a shudder, Joseph regarded the screaming man who had been whole and unmaimed that morning.

"Joseph?" the sound of Jack's voice saved him from the encroaching torment of the guilt he felt because of the sounds of pain and suffering all about him. "I have

been worried about you. It was rumored that you were in the heat of battle throughout the day," Jack said, removing a blood-soaked apron. An older woman gave him
a clean cloth to wipe off the blood covering his hands and spattered upon his face.
"You have been injured!" he exclaimed after catching a glimpse of his brother's
head.

"It is nothing—only a flesh wound," Joseph responded. Unconsciously, he
reached up and touched the wound.

"Let me have a look at it," Jack insisted, guiding his brother to an empty chair.
"I cannot tell how deep it is through this caked-on blood and dirt. I need to clean a
wound here!" Jack yelled out, sending one of the women scurrying for a bowl of
water and cloth for bandaging. "It came frightfully close, Joseph," Jack murmured,
gently wiping away the dirt and dried blood.

"How long have you been here?" Joseph asked, seemingly unconcerned at his
close call with death.

"We received word in Salem by midmorning. I came down with the militia. I
was busy on the battlefield for a short while. I guess I have been here for maybe
three hours now."

"How are things faring?"

"We are swamped with casualties, as you can plainly see. Some are not going to
make it no matter what we do. We are trying to keep them as comfortable as possible. Those in greatest need, with a chance for survival, are being treated first. Most
of our patients are British soldiers," Jack paused, expecting Joseph to react, but
Joseph was not surprised by the news. The British did not have the means or the
time to concern themselves with their wounded. They had been forced to leave
them on the roads. "Many of our wounded were taken to their own physicians.
Thanks be given!" Jack said with all sincerity.

"Are supplies holding out?"

"So far, no problem."

"Good." Joseph rose from the chair as soon as Jack had finished bandaging his
head. "Be sure the British receive the same care as our own men."

"Of course," Jack responded, not at all surprised by his brother's instructions.

"I will check on things here in the morning. You can find me at headquarters if
you need me."

"Joseph, did you see Eben?" Jack asked as an afterthought.

"Eben? No, did you?"

"A few hours ago. He's fine," Jack assured him noting his brother's worried
expression. "He has set up camp with the Foxboro militia."

Their conversation came to an abrupt halt as two ragged, tired colonists came through the front door carrying an elderly man upon an old, moth-eaten blanket.

"Help us! Somebody help us!" one of the men cried.

Jack and Joseph immediately responded, guiding the men to the nearest available makeshift bed. They carefully lowered the blanket with the old man on it onto the straw mattress.

"Joseph, do you see this!" Jack exclaimed getting his first good look at the elderly man. A bullet had mutilated his face, and as Jack tore open the man's frock, multiple bayonet wounds were exposed in his abdominal and chest cavities as well as in his arms and legs. "What evil would possess a man to such an act?" Jack exclaimed.

"We need help!" Joseph yelled, bringing Drs. Benjamin Church and William Eustis to their side.

"Get him into the other room!" Benjamin Church said, gesturing toward the operating area.

"No room in there! No time!" Jack replied, frantically trying to control the bleeding from a gaping abdominal wound. "I smell perforated bowel," he said, looking up at his brother.

"Set up right here!" Joseph ordered the others, equally frantic with a gushing chest wound.

"It is a hopeless situation," Benjamin Church stated, having been forced during the day to make numerous similar decisions. "Did you hear your brother, Dr. Warren? This man has a perforated bowel. Even if he does not die from blood loss or shock, peritonitis will surely kill him."

Joseph continued to work. Jack followed his lead with William Eustis coming to his aid.

"Use some common sense, Warren! This man has at least thirteen bayonet wounds and half his face is gone! He has to be close to seventy years old!" Church prattled on.

"Is there anyone else available to help us?" Joseph called out, ignoring Benjamin Church's objections. Three women quickly set up the needed supplies. Reluctantly Benjamin Church rolled up his sleeves and offered his assistance.

Joseph turned his head in an attempt to locate the men who had carried in the old man. He spotted them huddled in a corner of the bustling room. "Do you know this man?" he called.

Timidly, the two men walked to the foot of the bed, diverting their eyes from the scene before them. "We know him. His name is Sam Whittemore. He's from out Medford way."

"How old is he?" Jack asked, even though his eyes were focused on the sutures he was making in the intestinal wall.

"Eighty. Sam is eighty years old."

All four of the surgeons glanced up quickly at the man who spoke, surprised by his response.

"Eighty years old," Benjamin Church mumbled.

"How did this happen to him? Why would this helpless, old man be treated so brutally?" Joseph asked.

"Old Sam ain't helpless, Doc. No sir, he ain't helpless. When he got word that the redcoats were marchin' back toward Charlestown, he gathered every weapon he owned and borrowed a few from his neighbors. With a brace of pistols, a musket, and a saber he came down near Cooper's Tavern where our militia unit was waitin'. He hid himself behind a stone wall, just where the road branches off toward Charlestown. Old Sam actually managed to bring down three British regulars before he was hit in the face. We were driven back and figured he was dead. The regulars came over the wall after Sam and began to bayonet him. When they finally moved on, we came back to take his body home, but he was still alive—still conscious at the time."

"He was still conscious at the time?" Jack echoed the words, glancing at his brother from across the bed.

"Yes, Doc, he was. Old Sam ain't helpless, and I'll tell ya somethin' else. Old Sam ain't gonna die, neither!"

Activity abounded at the Cambridge headquarters as men tried to piece together the day's events and plan for the immediate future. Reports continued to arrive from the many militia units that had answered the day's alarm. The reports aided the men in their plans, but none of them answered the question Joseph was most concerned with at the moment: who had fired the first shot?

In all probability, the Continental Congress would base their support of the Massachusetts colonists upon the answer to this pivotal question. Those in England would ask as well. All of Europe would want to know who had begun the aggression.

Pens continued to scratch their figures on paper as the men added up casualty reports, how many prisoners were taken, and the number of men volunteering their services. Such was the atmosphere when Paul Revere entered the room. Filthy and exhausted, the usually robust Frenchman quietly sat down at the long, rectangular table in the first unoccupied chair he came upon. At the head of the table,

Joseph stopped writing and leaned back in his own chair, turning his full attention on his friend.

"Are you all right?" Paul asked Joseph, visibly alarmed by the bandage around his head.

Joseph simply nodded. "I heard you ran into a British scouting party last night," he answered, anxious to hear Paul's account of what occurred.

"Yes. Dawes and a young physician named Prescott were with me. Both managed to make their escape. I was questioned for a short time. They even threatened to blow my head off at one point," he said with a nervous laugh. "But when they discovered that the militia was already out, they lost interest in me."

"Sam and John are safe?" Joseph inquired.

"Comfortably tucked away in Woburn awaiting their departure to Philadelphia. They spent the day in the swamps. Can you imagine John Hancock up to his knees in swamp water?" Paul asked with a tired chuckle, amused by the thought. "He had me racing to the tavern in Lexington to rescue some papers he left there. I just made it to the edge of the Green when the shooting began—"

"You were on the Green when the first shot was fired?" Joseph leaned forward, suddenly more alert.

"Yes, Joseph, I was there. Why?"

"Who fired the first shot? Did they fire first?" Joseph asked excitedly. Silence filled the room as all eyes focused on Paul.

Paul looked around, feeling uneasy with the sudden attention. "Well, I don't know," he replied with the shrug of his shoulders.

"You were there! What do you mean, you do not know?" Joseph's frustration was evident.

"My back was to the Green. I was concerned with getting Hancock's papers back to him—"

"Hancock's papers?" Joseph shouted as he flopped back in the chair. "Today may turn out to be the beginning of a long and bitter war, and you did not think it important to watch what was occurring on the Green?" he paused, shaking his head in disbelief. Then, leaning again forward, he continued. "You must have seen something. Smoke from a musket? Perhaps you heard someone identify where the shot came from? Think, Paul, think!"

"No, Joseph, I don't know who fired first," Paul responded, his voice strained and defensive. "My back was to the Green, and I turned to look after the first shot was fired. By the time I turned my head, the British had opened fire."

Joseph pounded his fist on the table and rose from the chair. He walked to the window, gazing out into the darkness. Silence filled the room until a knock on the door was heard.

A boy, no more than sixteen years old, entered. His face was covered with dust, his hair askew, his filthy clothing torn and tattered.

"Dr. Warren?" he asked softly, searching the faces in the room for a response.

"Here," Joseph said, not budging from his position at the window. The boy walked over and handed him the papers he carried.

"This is a report of the Lexington militia, sir. Captain Parker sends his apologies for the delay. We had our dead to bury this afternoon."

Joseph fixed his gaze upon the lad. "Are you a member of the Lexington militia, son?"

"Yes, sir."

"Were you on the Green this morning?"

"Yes, sir."

"Tell us what happened, lad," Joseph said calmly.

Nervously, the boy looked about the room. "About—about eighty men waited on the Green as the sun came up. The British marched quietly, no fife or drum sounding. When they came into view, we could see that we were badly outnumbered. Captain Parker told us not to fire unless fired upon, but that we should stand our ground. We weren't on the road. We weren't blockin' their passage, sir. But they didn't stay on the road. They came onto the Green toward us. Their officers began shoutin' out orders, all different. No one seemed to have command. We were told to disperse, so Captain Parker had us slowly backin' off. Then one of the British officers yelled out for us to lay down our weapons, but before anyone could respond a shot was fired!"

"By whom?" Joseph quickly asked.

"Sounded like it came from the direction of the British, but no one was sure. Everything happened so fast after that. They fired a volley at us. We were all so stunned, and we hesitated a bit before returnin' the fire." The boy's face grew pale. Elbridge Gerry guided the young soldier to an empty chair.

"Eight of our men were killed," the boy continued, his voice trembling. "I've known 'em all my life. I grew up with their families, sir. Jonathan Harrington dragged himself across the Green to his house with a bullet lodged in his chest. He managed to reach the house, fallin' dead at his wife's feet. Jonas Parker was wounded in the first volley. He was determined to stand and fight though. As he was reloadin' his musket, a lobsterback charged, drivin' his bayonet through poor Mr. Parker—"

Joseph took a deep breath, his own eyes watering as he watched the boy struggling to control his quiet sobs.

"I joined myself to a militia unit from Action, and we followed the British to Concord," the boy went on after regaining the capacity to speak. "Many more now joined us as militias from other towns answered the alarm. We spotted some British soldiers on the bridge leadin' to Concord. They were tearin' the planks up, hopin' it would keep us from followin'. None of our officers seemed certain of what to do. Then we saw smoke. It appeared that Concord was aflame! Most of the men had answered the mornin's alarm, leavin' the women and children alone.

"Captain Isaac Davis of Acton led his militia company down toward the bridge. He said his men were not afraid to confront the redcoats even though the others hesitated. Soon others followed, inspired by his courage. When they neared the bridge, the redcoats opened fire. Dr. Warren," the boy looked at Joseph in disbelief, "our men didn't have their muskets aimed, and still they fired on us. Captain Davis was killed instantly. Seein' this brave man fall, the others opened fire, chasin' the British off. Poor Captain Davis," the boy said mournfully. "They say he left a widow and five young ones, sir."

Joseph and Paul shared an anxious gaze, each suddenly aware that the other had come very close to death within the past twenty-four hours. Joseph realized that tension and exhaustion had brought on his outburst a few moments before. Now it somehow seemed utterly foolish.

"Son, when did you last eat?" Joseph asked, redirecting his attention to the boy.

"I—I don't remember, sir."

"Step into the kitchen before you leave. Tell the servant to make a plate up for you," Joseph said with a comforting smile.

"Lad!" Joseph called out just as the boy was about to leave the room. "Parson Clarke—is he all right? Did he fight today?"

"Yes sir, he was on the Green with us, his musket in hand. No harm came to him." Seeing that the doctor was satisfied with his answer, the boy left.

"We may never learn who fired first at Lexington, but we know who did at Concord!" Joseph said as he walked from the window back to the table. "Gentlemen, the British were the aggressors, opening fire on our men. We shall prepare two statements. One shall be for the Continental Congress, the other to be sent to England. It is vital that our statement reaches England before Gage's twisted account of today's events. So let us begin!"

• 16 •

The Aftermath

IT IS FINE weather for a ride to Philadelphia, Paul. I trust it will hold up through tomorrow," Elbridge Gerry commented as the three men stepped out of the house that served as headquarters for the Massachusetts Provincial Congress. Remarkably thin, Elbridge's appearance was like that of a scarecrow. His clothes hung limply from his tall form.

The day was indeed beautiful. With barely a cloud in the pale blue sky, the soft, warm breeze carried with it the sweet scent of lilac and the melodious chirp of the chickadee. Joseph removed his tricorn, closed his eyes, and took a moment to bask in the pleasant sunshine. The warm rays of the sun rejuvenated him as they poured down upon his head and face.

"I wonder, Dr. Warren, if you might like to make this trip in my stead?" Paul asked with a grin for his friend.

Joseph opened his eyes and looked at Paul. "What a delightful thought!" he said, smiling. "To escape Watertown for two or three days, to spend time in personal counsel with Sam again."

"I do believe experiencing a few short hours of Philadelphia's bustle would help you appreciate Watertown a bit more," Paul agreed with a chuckle, referring to the small farming community seven miles west of Boston that had become the temporary capital of the Massachusetts Bay Colony.

Many of the colonists who had fled Boston were now crammed together in the houses that had been abandoned by Tories who had fled to Boston as a safe refuge.

"How is your family adjusting to their new home?" Elbridge asked Paul.

"Quite well. But we are accustomed to being somewhat crowded. My house in Boston isn't large. Here in Watertown we are sharing the house we live in with the Knoxes as well as Benjamin Edes."

"How is Benjamin holding up with the Revere brood scampering about him all day?" Joseph asked with a weak smile.

"Tolerably well, I would say, considering."

"Is it Henry Knox you speak of? The Boston bookseller?" Elbridge asked.

"The very same." Paul replied. "That man has acquired a keen knowledge of artillery, Joseph."

"Artillery? A bookseller?"

"Indeed. Many a British officer has ordered books through Henry's shop. Henry often read the military books before the customer came by to get them. He has become fascinated with artillery."

"Such knowledge may come in handy one day," Joseph commented. "That is, if we are ever to obtain enough artillery to concern ourselves with the use of it. The few field pieces we have will do us little good."

"And what of your family, Joseph. Is there any possibility of their being released?" Elbridge asked.

The question took Joseph by surprise. As he redirected his frustration over the lack of cannon to Elbridge's words, he took a deep breath. "Only by an act of God," he replied.

Paul reached out and placed a comforting hand on his friend's shoulder.

"How is it that your family was released, Paul?" Elbridge asked, aware that British Admiral Samuel Graves had ordered that Boston be surrounded with a ring of boats to stop any woman or child who attempted to leave the town. The Admiral knew that the presence of the women and children would be protection against the town coming under direct attack.

"I paid a British soldier to get them out," Paul replied.

"Could this same man be persuaded to escort your family out as well, Joseph?" Elbridge asked.

"No. My family is kept under careful surveillance, as is Sam Adams's son."

"What of an exchange? Is there no hope left?" Elbridge asked. As chairman of the Committee of Safety and president of the Provincial Congress, Joseph was in frequent communication with General Gage about such matters.

"At the present, no. Gage has not respected the terms of exchange. It was to be that if we sent a Tory family seeking refuge in, then they would send one of our families out. We continue to allow the Tories to pass peaceably through our lines into Boston. Gage does not reciprocate."

"Then perhaps we should stop allowing the Tories safe passage into Boston," Paul suggested.

"We could not do that. I would not force these people to remain in the countryside against their will," Joseph answered.

"In the long run, Gage will have the greater problem," Elbridge began. "How is he to feed so many with us laying siege to Boston? How are they to keep warm come winter? He will be hard pressed to get enough wood and supplies shipped to him from any of the sister colonies—not now." Being a bachelor, Elbridge did not understand the full impact his words would have on Joseph. For along with the British and Tories caught in Boston, his children, Mercy, and her father, as well as Samuel Adams Jr., would face the forced hunger and cold of the approaching winter.

Paul sought for a way to quickly change the subject. "What news beyond this official message from the Provincial Congress can I relate to Sam and the others?" Paul asked, patting the sealed letter in his coat pocket.

"Have you read that letter yet?" Joseph asked.

"No, not yet."

"Please, be certain that you do, then reseal it. That way you can relate much of the information even if you are forced to destroy the letter. In it we have informed the Continental Congress of the state of this siege. We have but 16,000 men, and these are ill equipped. We have put a call out for help to our sister colonies for well-supplied men. Few have responded."

"Have you received word from Quebec?" Paul asked. He remembered that it had been mentioned at one of the congressional sessions that Joseph had sent word to the northernmost colony, entreating them to join the others in their struggle with Great Britain.

"Yes. They wish to remain neutral."

"And the local Indian tribes?"

"The same," Elbridge answered the question with a sigh. "We must pray that the British do not bribe them into fighting against us as the French did. When did you say the Committee of Safety is scheduled to meet?" he asked Joseph.

"Eleven."

"Then I had best be on my way," Elbridge replied, checking his pocket watch. "I have a few matters to attend to before that meeting commences." After bidding each man good-bye, Elbridge departed.

"How are you holding up?" Paul asked his friend, concerned by the grueling schedule Joseph was forced to keep.

Joseph took a deep breath. "Would that I could divide myself in two—nay, three. For the hospitals are in dire need of a chief surgeon, yet no one who is qualified is willing to take on the responsibility."

"Somehow you must be sure to take care of yourself. You cannot do everything!"

"Indeed I cannot," he acknowledged with a weary sigh as he pulled a folded letter out from within his frock coat. "The very reason for this. It is a personal letter for Sam, but I want you to know its contents. Destroy it if you must."

Paul looked at him questioningly as he took the letter.

"I have implored Sam to persuade the members of Congress to appoint a commander in chief for this army."

"I understand our own John Hancock has such aspirations," Paul said with a weary chuckle.

Joseph rolled his eyes and smiled.

"Did you suggest Artemas Ward for the position since he already has command?" Paul asked.

"Artemas Ward has command in name only. He has so many ailments we can expect no more than minimal attention to the needs of this army," Joseph said, referring to the French and Indian War veteran who was commissioned general of the Massachusetts forces. "I did not suggest General Ward. However, I did make a suggestion to Sam."

"Who?"

"Colonel George Washington from Virginia. Have you met him?" Joseph asked.

Paul nodded. "Yes. He strikes a rather commanding appearance. Well thought of, but very reserved. Perhaps too reserved for such a position."

"I do not think so," Joseph responded. "The accounts given of him helping to save the remnant of General Braddock's troops at The Battle of the Monongahela are impressive. Sam and John Adams speak highly of him as a humble man, a man of deep conviction."

"But will New Englanders take to a southern commander?"

Joseph laughed. "Paul! Will New Englanders take to a New England commander?"

"You have a point there," Paul conceded with a chuckle. He was all too familiar with the stubbornness and independence of the people who lived in the northernmost colonies.

"There is something else in that letter you must be made aware of," Joseph indicated, pointing to the letter that remained in Paul's hand. "The very reason I beg you to destroy it if you should be intercepted by the British. In response to Gage's refusal to release Sam's son, my family, and the others from Boston, I have asked Sam to implore the delegates of the Continental Congress to take into custody all Crown-appointed officials throughout the colonies until the hostages in Boston are set free."

Paul empathized with his friend's pain. "Do you think Congress may actually act on it, Joseph?"

"No, but I have to try anyway, Paul."

With the immediate crises of battle wounds behind them, the physicians of the provincial army now faced lingering infections as well as symptoms of the diseases occurring in men who were encamped so closely. They needed a chief surgeon. Those with the necessary years of experience refused the position, except for Dr. Benjamin Church. But Joseph could not bring himself to give Church the appointment even if the extra burden fell upon his own shoulders, which already carried a heavy load.

"My greatest fear at the moment is an outbreak of smallpox," Joseph said to the physicians congregated about the table. "Dysentery, fevers, coughing—this I expect. This will be ongoing. But an outbreak of smallpox would prove disastrous."

"Is it true that someone has already contracted it in Roxbury?" Dr. Benjamin Church asked.

"Yes. General Gage has released two individuals from Boston under the guise that they desired to be returned to live with their families as per the conditions of exchange. These situations were immediately brought to my attention. From what we can gather, neither individual has family members among us. Both were already extremely ill at the time of exchange."

"He is trying to rid himself of the pox," Dr. Lemuel Haywood stated.

"Indeed he is. All who come out of Boston from now on will be quarantined. No exceptions. Now, is there any other business that we must contend with, gentlemen?" Joseph asked, searching the faces about him.

"Only that Mr. Whittemore has requested to speak with you when you have a moment," William Eustis stated.

A broad smile came to Joseph's lips. "It would be an honor to speak with him. How is he doing?" he asked. The feisty old man had defied all odds by not only surviving his numerous battle wounds, but the severe infections that followed.

"That man has such a will to live. I promise you he will out live us all!" William exclaimed as the men gathered their papers, commenting among themselves about Sam Whittemore's endurance.

"I was informed that I might find Dr. Warren here," an unfamiliar voice inquired of the women in the adjoining room. A strange man stepped into the open doorway, obviously unaccustomed to the sights, sounds, and mingled odors of festering wounds, fevered bodies, and intestinal disorders he had experienced in his journey through the hospital ward.

"Dr. Warren?" he asked, searching the faces around the table.

"Are you seeking John or Joseph Warren?" Joseph asked.

"Joseph Warren," the reply came.

"I am he."

"I have a verbal message from the Gloucester Committee of Correspondence, sir," the man stated and then hesitated.

"Is this a private message?" Joseph inquired, wondering about his hesitancy.

"No sir."

"Then feel free to relay it."

"A merchant ship arrived in Gloucester's port this morning. Mr. Josiah Quincy was a passenger aboard."

Joseph's spirits were instantly lifted upon hearing that Josiah had finally arrived home. But when the messenger paused again, Joseph braced himself to receive the news that his friend was in dire need of medical attention.

"Doctor Warren, I am sorry to inform you, sir, but Mr. Quincy did not survive the voyage. The Gloucester Committee extends their deepest sympathy to Mr. Quincy's family and to the Boston Committee of Correspondence. It seems that Mr. Quincy was feeling ill when he set sail. The voyage weakened him all the more. He passed away three days ago." The messenger stopped speaking as he anticipated a response.

Joseph was motionless, stunned by the announcement.

"One of the sailors stayed with Mr. Quincy throughout his last days. This sailor delivered letters to us, which Mr. Quincy had dictated to him," he said handing Joseph the two letters in his hand. "One is for Colonel Josiah Quincy. The other is for Mrs. Abigail Quincy. The sailor also mentioned that Mr. Quincy's last wish was that he would relay important information to Mr. Samuel Adams or to you, Dr. Warren."

"Is there not a letter for Mr. Adams or myself?" Joseph asked, his clouded thoughts alarmed by this last statement.

"No sir. Mr. Quincy refused to verbalize what the message was or entrust it to writing for fear it might fall into the wrong hands. Mr. Quincy repeatedly stated that he had been deceived. Whether this had anything to do with the message for you or was brought on by the fever, the sailor didn't know."

Joseph was too shocked to respond.

"Transferring the body to Braintree will be a long ordeal at this time of year, with the muddy roads to contend with. Sea travel to Braintree past Boston is out of the question with the British patrolling the harbor. We are willing to provide a proper burial for Mr. Quincy's remains in Gloucester." The messenger waited for a response, but still there was none. Joseph appeared not to even hear his words. "If you would prefer, Doctor, I will travel to Braintree and inform Mr. Quincy's family.

Perhaps someone might give me directions from here," he said, looking at the grief-stricken faces of the men assembled.

"No, there is no need. I will inform his family," Joseph finally replied.

"Then, sir, will you please tell them that we shall need word about Mr. Quincy's burial. Assure them that he will be buried with the honor and respect due him."

"Of course." Without saying another word, Joseph slowly rose from the table. Firmly grasping the two letters, he slouched toward the door.

"Joseph," Jack called out, breaking the mournful silence of those seated at the table. "Shall I go with you?"

"No. It is not necessary. You are needed here," he answered. "But could you please see that a horse is made ready? And also deliver word of Mr. Quincy's death to the members of the Provincial Congress. Inform them of my whereabouts, if you would, please."

Outside, Joseph was alone with his emotions—alone to grieve. Weakened by the shock of the news, he searched out a bench in the garden to sit upon. Intense feelings of loneliness and fear threatened to overtake him. With deep, uncontrollable sobs he mourned for this dear friend, this young and zealous Son of Liberty. Oh, how he would miss his company and his counsel, the very counsel he had been so anticipating.

[ital this graph]What was his message? Could it have brought a peaceful solution to this violent outbreak, or would it have only intensified our determination to be rid of these British oppressors from America's shores? And was he truly deceived? If so, in what manner? By whom?

Joseph leaned forward with his head buried in his hands and continued to torture himself with questions to which no answers could be found.

"Could more bloodshed be avoided by this information?" he cried out loud to heaven. "Why is it you choose to keep this from us?"

The announcement that the horse was ready prompted Joseph to leave the bleak solitude of the garden. As darkness spread over the countryside and the coolness of evening fell upon the land, he made the lonely trip to Braintree.

How would he break this news to the dear colonel? Josiah had died with no loved ones to hold him, no minister to comfort him, and no physician to bring him relief from the excruciating pain. The colonel's eldest son was long dead from consumption, and now his youngest had joined him. The only remaining son stood in opposition to everything his father held dear.

And what of Abigail? Poor Abigail! Having just buried her infant daughter, she now had to bury her husband. How much sorrow could one woman bear?

And yet, Josiah's family had understood and agreed with the reasons he had been willing to risk the time he had to live for the sake of his country. Only three days from the shore, heaven had prohibited him to set foot upon his native land again. Unaware that the first shots had been fired, unaware that his fellow country-men had already laid down their lives for the liberty they held so dear, just as he was about to do. Perhaps not in so violent a manner, but sacrificed for his country all the same. Those who were blessed to know him would always remember Josiah Quincy as "The Patriot."

From Bunker Hill one had a clear view of Boston. The area was safely separated from the town by a wide stretch of river, but the hill had become the subject of many debates for the Committee of Safety. Some of the higher-ranking officers insisted that it should become a strategic post at once. Others opposed this view, fearing that such a move would bring on a certain British attack that the colonial army could not presently handle.

The most outspoken officer in favor of occupying the hill was Connecticut's General Israel Putnam. A veteran fighter of the French and Indian War, he was well known for his courage throughout the New England colonies. "Old Put," as he was affectionately called, was a bold and daring man. He strongly opined that the hill could be easily occupied and defended, and he claimed he could accomplish this feat with only 2,000 men.

General Armetas Ward of the Massachusetts militia was in direct opposition to Old Put. Also a veteran of the French and Indian War, this old soldier was as cautious as Putnam was daring.

Time and time again the Committee of Safety heard both arguments. Joseph found himself frustrated by the drastic differences of opinion between these two highly respected officers.

As General Putnam once again presented his argument in his usual loud and aggressive manner, Joseph paced the floor as he listened, quite certain that the final decision would fall on him this day. With the officers unable to agree and the Committee itself confused, Joseph felt it necessary to use his position as chairman to put an end to the argument. When General Putnam finally finished speaking, Joseph stopped pacing. He leaned on the back of his chair and looked straight at the general.

"General Putnam, thou almost persuadest me!" Though his expression was serious, Old Put detected a twinkle in his eyes. "I fear that such a move would be rash at this time. We need more men, ammunition, and certainly heavy artillery. But, General, if you should be forced to take the hill, do not be surprised to find me there by your side."

"I hope not, Doctor," General Putnam returned. "Let we who are old and can be spared begin the fight. You're young and needed in council. There'll be plenty of time for you to join in the fightin'. It won't be over soon, I'm afraid."

The decision was made, and Bunker Hill remained unoccupied, even by the cattle that had once grazed along its slopes. Abandoned by the livestock, the grass grew waist high, hiding the rail fences. Alongside it sat Breed's Hill, smaller in size and closer to the river. It, too, stood abandoned.

When he was desperate to be alone, Joseph sought the serenity of Bunker Hill. Here he would steal a few moments to collect his thoughts. Often he found himself longingly gazing at Boston across the water's expanse, as he had done so many years before when treating the sick on Castle Island. The time he had spent there caring for those stricken with the pox seemed so long ago now. The desire to return home that had gripped his heart then did so now, but with a different intensity, a different urgency. However, he knew this was utterly impossible.

Shortly after daybreak, Joseph sat upon the hill as a gentle drizzle fell from the May sky. His mind was preoccupied and his thoughts far off.

"Excuse me, Doctor. I am sorry to disturb you, but I have been wanting to speak privately with you."

Joseph was startled by the unexpected intrusion.

"You are a captain with one of the Connecticut militia companies?" Joseph recognized the odd-looking man from drilling sessions. His moon-shaped face, bulging eyes, and undersized mouth struck a peculiar image—one not easily forgotten—and seemed somewhat exaggerated against the militia unit's red coat and buff facings.

"Yes, sir, New Haven's Second Company, Governor's Foot Guards. My name is Arnold, sir. Benedict Arnold."

"Well, Captain Arnold, if you do not mind sitting on a damp rock, then please do make yourself comfortable and tell me what is on your mind."

"Sir, I am sorry. Perhaps I am intruding on your time."

"No need to apologize, Captain. To tell you the truth, a distraction is welcome. My mind is on my family," he said, staring across the river toward Boston. "They are just a few minutes walk from the dock over there," he pointed to the area. "I know those streets and alleys so well I could find my way in the blackest night."

"A wife and children?" Captain Arnold asked.

"Four of the most beautiful children in Massachusetts Bay," Joseph said with a proud smile. "And a fiancée both gracious and beautiful. I miss them greatly. Do you have a family, Captain?" he asked as he turned to look at Captain Arnold.

"Yes, sir, I do."

"Then you understand. Before we left Boston, I remember from time to time seeing British soldiers standing upon a wharf staring out over the harbor. They were lost in thought with most somber expressions on their faces. I know now what had them so transfixed. Across that vast ocean were their homes—their families. That is what they were thinking about. Three thousand miles of ocean separated them from their loved ones. Less than one mile of river separates me, yet I have about as much hope of seeing my family right now as they do of seeing theirs..." His voice trailed off in pensive tones.

Shaking his head to clear the troublesome thoughts, he declared, "Enough of my homesickness. Please forgive me, Captain! Please, tell me why you sought me out," Joseph inquired, trying to quell the depression that sought to overtake him.

"Well, Doctor, it is common knowledge that we lack military supplies, especially heavy artillery. I know where we can attain some."

"Tell me about it, sir!"

"By trade I am an apothecary, but other business ventures have caused me to make trips north through the northern regions of the New York colony. There is a British fort up there—"

"Ticonderoga?" Joseph inquired.

"Yes, a fort that sees little action and therefore has few soldiers stationed in it." Joseph listened attentively. "Are you certain of this?" he asked.

"Yes. I have been there. I have seen the layout and the number of cannon. I feel confident that it can be taken with only 400 men, and I am willing to try."

"Since it is in New York territory, Captain, our Provincial Congress will need to notify the Congress of New York first."

"Is there time for this, Doctor? Can we afford any delays?"

"Frankly, no. Gage may come up against us any time now," Joseph replied thoughtfully, "and we are not equipped to face him."

"What would it take to get such a mission underway?" Captain Arnold persisted. His confidence worked to convince Joseph that it might be worth an attempt.

"The support of both the Provincial Congress and the Committee of Safety."

"Can you attain their support?"

"If a proposal is presented properly," Joseph said thoughtfully. "You make a report of what you have seen at Ticonderoga. List what you will need in supplies and how long you estimate such a mission will take. I will present your proposal myself."

"Then you personally support it?" Captain Arnold asked.

"Sir, as you said, we need the material. At the moment, I have no other options for acquiring such material," Joseph replied as he rose from the rock upon which he had been sitting. "I am about due to attend a meeting now. Will you walk back to headquarters with me?"

Captain Arnold stood. He was ready to walk with him.

"You say that you are an apothecary?" Joseph questioned.

"Yes, sir, I am."

"Since the Port Bill went into effect, I have not seen much information out of Europe on new medicinals, Captain." As the men walked, they discussed this matter that was of interest to both their professions.

Both the Provincial Congress and the Committee of Safety not only approved Captain Benedict Arnold's proposal to capture Fort Ticonderoga, but they were so impressed with the soundness of his plan, that they promoted him to the rank of colonel. He set out with 400 men in the hope of taking possession of the needed artillery.

The adjournment of yet another lengthy meeting of the Committee of Safety marked the end of the long and exhausting day. There were only a few hours left until the beginning of the next, which promised to have its own share of problems.

A number of resolutions, requests, and personal letters awaited delivery to the delegates in Philadelphia. Though the hour was late, an express rider for the Provincial Congress—Paul Revere—had been summoned to pick up the dispatches so he might get away at first light. Upon arriving at headquarters, he was surprised to find that only Joseph and Connecticut's militia general, Israel Putnam, remained. Both men were still seated at the table.

"I am sorry to have inconvenienced you, Paul." Joseph said upon seeing him enter the room. "You will not be riding express this week after all."

Paul was confused. "What has happened?" he asked, certain that Joseph must have a good reason for this sudden change of plans.

"I have decided to have our old friend, Dr. Benjamin Church, make the trip in your stead."

Israel Putnam detected the sarcasm in Joseph's voice. Carefully he watched the interaction between the two men. Paul did not verbally respond to Joseph's announcement. A very observant man, General Putnam noted that words were not necessary. Paul had communicated quite well without them. By the expression on his face, Israel knew that Paul clearly understood Joseph's reason for the sudden change in plans, and no more discussion was necessary. This intimate, wordless interaction caused the general's curiosity to get the better of him.

"Why on earth would you be sendin' Dr. Church to ride express? It would seem to me that his bein' a member of both this committee and the congress, as well as a skilled doctor, would require that he remain present. Surely, Dr. Warren, you jest."

"John Adams has been plagued by an eye ailment since he arrived in Philadelphia. Dr. Church shall serve the dual purpose of delivering our communications and treating Mr. Adams," Joseph explained, trying to sound convincing. It was true that John was ailing, but sly Old Put did not believe that it was necessary to send Dr. Church to him.

"Bein' a New Englander myself, I am keenly aware of the prejudices some of our own have toward outsiders. Are you tellin' me that John Adams is one of these and therefore will not trust a Philadelphia doctor?" General Putnam returned with a grin.

Joseph tried to gaze at him without expression. Old Put was indeed a sly one. Of course, Dr. Church was not sent out for this reason, and Joseph could not let his friend John Adams be depicted as prejudiced against outsiders. Trusting General Putnam, he decided to share the concern he and Paul felt about Dr. Church.

"What I am about to tell you is not to be discussed with anyone else, General. Do you understand?" Joseph's words were spoken with the authority his position of leadership granted him.

"I understand," the disciplined officer answered.

"I intercepted this," Joseph said gravely as he pulled a neatly folded paper from his waistcoat. "It was intended for Colonel Thomas. As you can plainly see, it is clearly signed by Dr. Church." As Joseph handed the paper to General Putnam, Paul moved closer so he could look on as well.

The message itself was simple, but if it had reached its destination, the consequences would have been devastating to the colonials. Contrary to General Armetas Ward's orders, Benjamin Church had instructed Colonel Thomas to remove his men from the Roxbury guard post and relocate to another point. Had the Colonel done this, the British would have had easy access into the countryside and would have taken them by surprise.

General Putnam's face blanched as he read the instructions. "Has the man gone mad?" he shouted in horror.

"Does Church's position as a member of the Committee of Safety grant him the authority to give such orders?" Paul asked with alarm.

"No! Certainly not without General Ward's approval, and that of the Committee!" Joseph exclaimed.

"Surely he must have considered the results of this move had Gage gotten wind of it!" General Putnam's unbelief was evident.

"He knew exactly what he was doing," Joseph returned while staring at Paul. Paul shared the deep sorrow he detected in his friend's voice. They had been betrayed. It was no longer merely speculation or intuition. Doubt no longer remained. Such treachery, although suspected for so long, left both men feeling as though they had been pierced with a knife.

"Treason?" General Putnam asked.

Joseph and Paul looked at him, stunned by his choice of words. The general himself was surprised at the word he had uttered. Treason was the charge Britain had leveled against each one of them. It seemed strange indeed to make the accusation against one of their own, especially since they did not even have their own established country.

"I perceive that you have suspected him before this incident," General Putnam remarked.

"He's a crafty fellow—" Paul began and then stopped suddenly. He was not certain of how much Joseph intended to tell the General.

Joseph looked thoughtfully from Paul to General Putnam and then began to speak. "Dr. Church always seemed to be easily befriended by the governors of Massachusetts Bay—Bernard, Hutchinson, then Gage. It all appeared innocent enough. After all, we all had friends among the Tories and British soldiers. Then suddenly Church was able to acquire property well beyond his means."

"But I understand he was quite a prominent physician in Boston," General Putnam commented.

"Yes, but I am aware of the size of his practice, and, although he was doing well financially, it was not enough to purchase and maintain the two homes he had."

"An inheritance perhaps?" the general asked.

"It would have been recorded with the General Court. We checked. There was no such inheritance," Paul replied.

"News of our plans, discussed in utmost secrecy, began to reach Gage and his officers within hours of our meetings. Such peculiarities raised our suspicions," Joseph added.

"His seemingly fearless desire to return to Boston recently to obtain medical supplies further aroused our uncertainty," Paul continued. "I asked him to stop by my home to deliver a letter to my wife. He claimed that Gage confiscated the reply she intended to send back with him. I believed his story, but now I wonder."

"I tried to persuade him not to make that trip. I feared for his safety," Joseph paused, looking at the note in the general's hand. "There was never any reason to fear. He returned unmolested just as he had predicted. And to keep us from further suspecting shady dealings, he brought us the promised supplies. Who knows what vital information he may have given to Gage? No doubt he informed him of all our weaknesses, and heaven knows we have an abundance of them! He provided us with inspiring orations, poems, and letters. He even stood with us at Lexington and Concord. Whenever we thought we had him, he would pour on the patriotism, causing us to think ourselves vile for having doubted his sincerity."

"But now you truly have him!" exclaimed Israel Putnam.

"No. No, we do not have him. Not yet." Joseph leaned back in the chair with a far-off expression. Paul and General Putnam were both confused by Joseph's response. "I no longer have any doubt that Benjamin Church is an informer. But if I were to bring him before the Committee of Safety right now, I fear he would find some way to elude the charges. He will say the signature was forged or some such thing. He has already covered his tracks. I attempted to trace that note back to Church. It went through a number of carriers, and all of them deny that Church gave it to them directly. Obviously one of them is lying, too.

"Dr. Church is a highly respected man. He even has Sam Adams fooled. There are those who will believe whatever he tells them. Bringing him to trial without better evidence will cause division among us, and we cannot afford this. In order to bring charges against the man, we need to catch him in the act or discover a frightened crony who will reveal to us his treacherous deeds.

"Right now I cannot risk having him around. I am sending him to Philadelphia in order to protect us."

"But aren't you concerned that he might inform Gage of the dealings in Philadelphia?" Paul asked.

"What he might learn there will take too long to relay to Gage for it to do us any harm. I want him far away from us as soon as possible. With the arrival of three more generals and 1,000 more troops, Gage is bound to attempt a move against us. We cannot risk having Church informing him of our present weaknesses or creating new ones as he attempted to do today!"

"I have concluded that you have missed your calling, Dr. Warren!" Parson Samuel Cooper's odd greeting came as a surprise to Joseph.

Joseph rose to greet the parson. After shaking his hand, he offered the parson a seat at the empty table.

"Do you have a minute to visit, Joseph?"

"The committee has just adjourned, and by my calculations I have a good thirty minutes before I have to head over to Watertown to meet with the congress. I am delighted to be able to spend that time with you, Parson!" Joseph answered with a warm smile. "I have missed your company and your counsel."

"I am sorry I do not get to see you more often, but with so many out there in want of spiritual guidance, I stay very busy," the parson replied.

"Influence such as yours is vital to our success, sir. Now what is this about me missing my calling?" Joseph asked.

"It has been reported to me that the ceremony to commission officers into this army is a very moving spiritual experience and that you are the reason for this!" Parson Cooper said with a grin.

Joseph was uncertain as to whether the parson approved of his method of commissioning officers or not.

"You should have made theology your major study at Harvard, although it would appear the theological studies you had there were enough!" he added, still grinning. "Certainly you are aware that not too long ago the parsons of this colony were also the physicians, much like the Levitical priesthood. To care for the individual's spiritual needs as well as his medical needs were the responsibility of our early parsons."

"So you think I should be a minister of the Gospel, do you?" Joseph asked, amused by Samuel Cooper's suggestion.

"Judging from the charge you give the newly commissioned officers, I should say so! I understand you not only have the soldiers shuddering as they contemplate their moral obligations before the throne of the Almighty, but every other person in attendance as well!"

Joseph took a deep breath as he leaned back into a more comfortable position. "Excuse me for saying it, Parson, but I in no way desire the task before you. I can readily deal with physical pain and suffering. This became a continuous reality in my profession. But I simply cannot patiently tolerate the selfishness of man, a reality I suspect you face as often as I face suffering."

Joseph paused and shook his head in disgust. "You cannot imagine how often men come to me seeking commissions for which they are not even qualified. Some are so bold as to demand them! I never had any idea of the selfishness of people until I came to this leadership position."

"It would seem that you are handling the situation quite adequately," Parson Cooper responded.

"I choose those who seem most sincere to serve, but even then, sometimes I am uncertain. To charge them before God is the only reassurance I have of their sincerity to serve and not simply to bear an officer's title."

"I will have to attend the next ceremony." The parson's countenance suddenly changed, and his relaxed smile disappeared. "Have you heard that the British turned the Brattle Street Meetinghouse into a barracks?" he asked.

Joseph detected tears in the beloved parson's eyes as he nodded in reply.

"No doubt you have known for some time but have tried to spare me the news." Although it was true, Joseph chose not to respond.

"It grieves me to think of how much destruction they have probably caused to that building."

"Much of your life has been spent there," Joseph sympathized. "Many memories."

"Yes, many memories. My father was parson there for fifty years, and I have been for more than thirty now."

Joseph was aware of this but sat in silence, sensing the parson's need to talk.

"I remember a certain skinny, young physician's apprentice when he first attended services there," he said with a twinkle in his eye. "How many memories I have of your family—when you and Elizabeth stood before me to exchange your wedding vows. She was little more than a girl then."

Joseph smiled, fondly remembering that evening himself.

"Then came the children to be baptized. Ah, those are happy memories!" Dr. Cooper added, purposely failing to mention the tragic ones.

"I trust I shall stand before you again at that very same altar with my second bride and bring more babies for you to baptize!" Joseph offered, smiling contentedly at the thought of it. The parson returned the smile, hoping for Joseph's sake it would be so.

"Do you remember when you requested that I seek to exchange your family box for that of the Lewis family?" Parson Cooper began to chuckle. "Old Mr. Lewis was stunned. He could not believe that you would want to trade your choice box for his. Being right next to the door, it was the coldest seat in the building as well as the one with the most distractions."

"The very reason I requested it. The vast majority of the time anyone entered during the service, it was to call me out to attend a patient. Such distractions were hardly fair to the rest of the congregation. By sitting near the door, only you and my family were aware of my being summoned. It is true that we had to bundle up more in the winter—add a few extra coals to the foot warmers. But we all felt better about being there." Joseph had always thought that it was Mr. Lewis who had done him a great favor in the trade.

"How many hours did we meet in my study? You, Sam Adams, John Hancock, Josiah Quincy? How many hours did we struggle with the moral dilemma we faced, seeking divine guidance for this distressed land?" the parson asked.

"Too many to give account of, sir."

"Yes, hours of fearfully seeking heaven's approval before continuing. Well, they can take the building, but they cannot take the memories," he said as he rose from his seat at the table.

"Will I see you at the service on the Sabbath?" Parson Cooper asked as he mounted his horse.

"As always, sir," Joseph replied. He watched as the parson rode off.

· 17 ·

Last Goodbyes

JACK REINED HIS horse in as he scanned the group of men assembled in the field to his left. He had been told that his brother intended to participate in the drilling exercise of Rhode Island's Kentish Guards, but—try as he might—Jack could not spot Joseph among the colorful uniforms of the militia unit: red coats faced with green, white waistcoats and breeches, and black half-gaiters.

Off in the distance at the edge of the wood, he observed two men conversing. The hatless figure wore the smart uniform of the Kentish Guards, and even from a distance his tall and well-formed appearance commanded respect. The other man, equal in height though more slender, wore the attire of a civilian. The tailored, black wool-challis frock coat and breeches were not easily recognized from across the field as belonging to Joseph, but his brilliant blond hair clearly revealed his identity.

Jack dismounted and hitched his horse to a sapling before he began to walk along the edge of the field, keeping clear of the movement of the marching troops. As he drew closer to Joseph, he detected the telltale signs of his brother's weariness. His finely tailored clothing hung loose about his thighs and shoulders, and his normally erect posture seemed slouched. Even his hair reflected the pressures upon him, for Jack had never before seen Joseph appear in public without properly powdering his head. Even as Jack drew close enough to be identified, Joseph failed to notice his brother even though he seemed to be looking straight at him. Dark circles below Joseph's bloodshot eyes came into plain view as he drew closer.

The lively conversation between the men stopped as Jack approached, and Jack quickly moved alongside Joseph and placed his hand on his shoulder.

"You are a very difficult man to track down these days, Dr. Warren!" Jack said with an affectionate smile.

"Jack!" Joseph exclaimed, placing his arm around his brother's shoulders. "What are you doing here?"

"I am ready to head back to Salem, but I wanted to be certain to see you and say good-bye."

"Of course, of course. But first—" Joseph looked at the militia officer, "General, this is my brother, Dr. John Warren." Then turning to Jack he added, "This is General Nathanael Greene."

General Greene reached out a muscular hand toward Jack's.

"General Greene is commander of the Rhode Island forces." Joseph interjected.

"I am aware of that," Jack replied, holding the handsome Rhode Islander under a steady gaze. He calculated the general to be Joseph's age. His hair and eyes were similar in color to his brother's as well. "General Greene, you have already established a fine reputation for yourself. The discipline of your units is the envy of many an officer from the other colonies."

"Thank you, Doctor," the general replied with a boylike grin that expressed the pride he took in his men. His massive form somehow became less threatening as he relaxed. "I have good men to work with. But the true test will come under fire."

"That man could break my hand with no effort at all!" Jack commented after Joseph and he bid farewell to General Greene.

"He is an iron master. He forges anchors," Joseph informed him. "He is also a Quaker," he added, fully expecting a response.

Jack's expression revealed his surprise. "A Quaker? He seemed to be a military man through and through!"

"Indeed. My understanding is that he rose from private to the rank of brigadier general within a matter of days!"

"How is that possible?"

"I do not know. But Rhode Island truly has the most disciplined and well-equipped troops, and most credit for this goes to Nathanael Greene. Speaking of Quakers, have you met Miss Abigail Collins?" Joseph asked.

"We have not been formerly introduced," Jack replied with a smile.

"What is so amusing?"

"Every time that girl opens her mouth, I find myself distracted. It sounds as though she is reading from the Holy Writ with all her thees and thous. Out of respect for the reading of Scripture, I stop whatever I am doing only to discover Miss—Collins, is it?"

Joseph nodded.

"Only to discover Miss Collins carrying on what is a normal conversation for her."

Joseph laughed. "You will adjust to it."

"I suppose. Why are you so concerned about her? And what is a Quaker doing here in the first place? What an odd time for a Quaker to pay a visit on this colony!"

"She is the daughter of a prestigious member of the Rhode Island Assembly. Her father is concerned that the British might invade Providence. He thought his daughter would be safer with us for the time being," Joseph explained.

"Safer with us?" Jack exclaimed.

Joseph shrugged in reply. "I am sure she must be homesick and must feel out of place. Perhaps you could show her friendliness, maybe even give her personal instruction in patient care."

"By the time I get back, Miss Collins will probably be the best-trained nurse in the hospital. She is a pretty girl, and there are many bachelors among the physicians who will be only too happy to be of assistance to her," Jack pointed out.

"Did you go by the farm to say good-bye to Mother?" Joseph asked.

"Yes."

"I have not been able to get by in some time myself. Is she well?"

"It is difficult to say," Jack began, causing Joseph to become alarmed. "She did not give me much opportunity to ask about her welfare. She was too concerned with yours."

"Mine?" Joseph exclaimed.

"Yes. It seems she has been gathering bits of information about your exploits from the men stationed in Roxbury."

Joseph detected the hint of a smile on his brother's face. "Exploits? What have they been telling her?" he asked, amused by Jack's choice of words.

"She heard all about your participation in moving the livestock from the harbor islands—under enemy fire. She also knows about the recent prisoner exchange you took part in."

"Is that all? Certainly she has no reason to worry about that!" he said.

"It would seem that she is of the opinion that a physician should be concerned with caring for the injured and not with risking his life to relocate livestock or with meeting enemy officers to discuss the terms of prisoner exchange," Jack expressed their mother's views. "Most of all, she is worried about your general health," he added.

"I trust you relieved her concerns by telling her that I am well."

"No. I could not lie to her," Jack replied. "You are not well, and it does not take a physician to make that observation. You have lost weight—"

"I needed to lose some weight!" Joseph protested with a smile as he patted his midsection with both hands.

"Not that much," Jack commented as he quickly scanned his brother's body. "You have not looked this scrawny since your Harvard days!"

"My Harvard days?" Joseph chuckled. "You were no more than a babe then. How could you remember?"

"You would be amazed at how much I remember from my earliest years," Jack responded somberly.

Joseph felt certain that he was referring to their father's death, but he did not dare question him about it. Occasional bouts with depression and nightmares still plagued Jack, something he chose not to discuss with even Joseph.

"You are obviously not eating," Jack continued. "And being aware of the long meetings you attend—well into the night, only to begin again early in the morning—I know you are not getting enough sleep, either. You have made frequent mention of headaches to me, no doubt from tension and sheer exhaustion."

"And you told Mother all of this only to cause her more worry?" Joseph asked.

"No. I just said that I did not lie to her. I managed to change the subject without saying much at all about you. But the fact is, she has reason to worry, and so do I. I recommend a three-day stay at the farm to recuperate from the pressures you are under," Jack said matter-of-factly.

"Three days!" Joseph exclaimed. "I could not even consider leaving these responsibilities for one day!"

"If you drive yourself much longer, you may be forced to your sickbed."

Joseph was surprised at his brother's tone. He could not recall him ever having used it before.

"I love you, Joseph," Jack said, as if ashamed of being so stern. "I do not want to see you become ill."

Smiling, Joseph placed his hands on Jack's shoulders. "I promise you, Dr. Warren, I will eat more regularly and try to sleep more. But at this point, that is the best I can do!"

Jack did not return his brother's smile. His only response was a deep sigh before he asked, "What is this I hear of you being elected major general of the Massachusetts forces?"

"There is talk of it. Nothing more than that."

"And if they should proceed with it?" Jack asked, holding his brother under a steady, anxious gaze.

When Joseph failed to respond, Jack surmised his answer. "You intend to accept the position, don't you?"

"Jack, what would you have me do under the circumstances?" Joseph protested.

In frustration, Jack pushed his brother's arms away. "Artemas Ward holds the post. Let him deal with it!" he shouted.

"You do not understand, Jack." Joseph said calmly. "We are losing what little discipline we have within the militia units. The Rhode Island forces respect

General Greene, but they do not respect General Ward. New Hampshire is shaky, yielding to the authority of our Provincial Congress for only the time being. Connecticut does not respect any commander, not even their own! We have no firm command. Men are leaving daily, and there is nothing we can do to keep them here."

"And somehow you are going to be able to stop this?"

"Yes. For some reason, I continue to hold the respect of the men. For a period of time, they will submit to my authority, hopefully long enough for the Continental Congress to appoint a commander in chief."

"Dear God, Joseph!" Jack uttered in frustration. He momentarily turned his back on his brother, then faced him once again while he pled. "You cannot do it all. Promise me you will resign as president of the Congress and chairman of the Committee of Safety if this commission should come through. Promise me!"

"Indeed, I will resign. You have my promise."

"And is Gage about to move against us?" Jack searched his brother's eyes for the truth.

"He must move soon. Generals Howe, Burgoyne, and Clinton have arrived with 1,000 more troops. He is under orders to bring us into submission by whatever means necessary. He must move soon."

"But you have no definite word?"

"Nothing yet, though we suspect he will attempt to occupy one of the hills. Most likely it will be Bunker Hill. It is strategically positioned close enough to the river that the British may have easy access to it while overlooking us."

"Any word yet from Colonel Arnold?"

"No. We have heard nothing, but we continue to be hopeful that he will return with the cannon before we are forced into another engagement." Again Joseph placed his hands on Jack's shoulders. "I have told you everything I know. I appreciate your concern. And as much as I hate to see you go, you had better be on your way if you want to get to Salem before nightfall," Joseph added. The brothers slowly walked to Jack's horse.

"It should not take more than a couple of weeks to get my patients situated with other physicians in the area. If any trouble breaks out, you can be sure I will head back immediately."

Joseph nodded. There was an awkward silence.

"Well then, I had best be on my way," Jack finally said, taking a firm hold of his brother in a warm embrace.

"I will miss having you close by, Jack." Joseph held him tight. "Be sure to come back as soon as you can. I need you here."

"I will. Rest assured that you are in my thoughts and prayers," Jack replied.

Joseph did not release his hold.

"Are you all right, Joseph?" Jack asked.

Although Joseph released his embrace, he kept his hands on Jack's upper arms. Jack noted the tears in his brother's eyes. "Joseph, what is wrong?"

"Nothing. I'm fine. I just hate to see you leave, even if it is only for a short time. Now, get going!" he said, motioning that Jack should mount the horse.

After Jack was in the saddle, Joseph looked up at him. "God bless you, Jack," he said, "and always remember that I love you."

With a light slap on the horse's rump, Joseph sent his little brother on his way.

The men stopped what they were doing. A few began to boldly make their way to the tether post as others, less brash, followed somewhat timidly behind. Most of the soldier-farmers simply watched from a distance. At silent attention they paid their respects to the approaching rider.

Joseph reined the horse in at the tether post amid the enthusiastic greetings and outstretched hands of those already gathered there. Some, aware of his recent election to the rank of major general, offered a formal salute.

After dismounting, Joseph returned the handshakes and took a few minutes to converse with the men, encouraging them with his words.

"Good afternoon, General Warren."

He turned in the direction of the familiar voice to find Colonel David Brewer, a longtime friend of the Warren family, offering a formal salute.

"Good afternoon, Colonel," Joseph said. "My commission is not yet official," he reminded his friend.

"We are aware of that, sir, but wish to display the proper honor deserved."

"Thank you."

"The old farm looks a bit different, sir, wouldn't you say?" Colonel Brewer asked with a chuckle. His militia regiment presently made their encampment on the Warren property.

"Indeed it does, Colonel," Joseph answered as he viewed the scene about him. The grazing pasture, enclosed on three sides by a three-foot, stone wall, was covered with makeshift tents constructed of old blankets and canvas tarps. The tents extended beyond the pasture onto the side yard of the old, saltbox farmhouse. "These tents are adequate against the weather?" Joseph asked, concerned that the men be dry and warm.

"We have had few complaints thus far, sir."

"Good. I must pay a visit to my mother. I will speak to you before I leave." Joseph patted his friend on the shoulder and headed toward the house.

"Well, look who we have here," Sam said with a smile for his brother. "General Warren, please have a seat!"

"Joseph!" Mary Warren exclaimed, jumping from her chair to greet him.

Joseph greeted her with a kiss on her cheek.

"Are you hungry? Let me get you a plate, son," she said. Without waiting for a response, she found a clean plate on a nearby shelf and brought it to him.

"How are you doing, Sam?" Joseph asked, occupying a chair across from his brother and helping himself to the roasted chicken, peas, and Indian meal pudding that his mother set before him.

"Can't complain. And yourself?"

"I am fine. I expect quite a good crop this year and an early harvest if this warm weather continues."

"It is unseasonably warm. The army will be interested in purchasing much of your produce," Joseph assured him.

"I plan to sell it to you at a low price. It's the least I can do. Sort of my way of serving," Sam said. His extreme shyness prevented him from doing any more than this.

Joseph sympathized with his brother, never ridiculing him for this problem. "Such a deed will be greatly appreciated, Sam. We desperately need men like you who are able to supply us with provisions."

"Jack came by to visit a few days ago, the day he headed back to Salem. Where you able to say good-bye to him?" his mother asked.

"Yes. He told me he had been by."

"Have you had any news about Mercy and the children?" she asked.

"No," Joseph replied sadly.

"Samuel found Josey and Dick's boat," she said pointing to the mantle where the small, wooden boat sat. "Won't they be happy to learn it's been found? They were so pleased when you sailed it with them and so very disappointed when they lost it."

Joseph's eyes remained fixed on the small toy, fondly remembering the delightful afternoon when the boys had first sailed it.

"I found it in the tall grass along the edge of the pond," Sam informed him.

"Be sure to tell them in your next letter that it's been found," Mary instructed. Her words distracted Joseph's attention from the toy.

"I have not been able to get letters through to them."

Mary did not respond. She finished her meal in silence as her sons conversed. Though Joseph attempted to draw her into the conversation, she remained unusually distant. When everyone had finished, she began to clear the table.

"Mother," he said, reaching up and gently taking hold of her arm as she continued to silently clear the table. "Please sit down."

She hesitated, then put the plates back onto the table and sat next to him. He positioned himself so that he was facing her. Joseph took her hands in his and said softly, "From Sam's greeting when I arrived, I know you've heard about my commission."

"Yes, and I suppose congratulations are in order. It certainly is an honor," she replied, avoiding his eyes.

"I am not looking for your praise. I need to know what you are feeling."

She did not respond.

"Mother, you are obviously upset about this."

"Yes, I am, Joseph!" she finally admitted. Her voice was controlled but strained. "I am upset! I struggled to see that your education was completed. You were educated as a physician, not as a soldier! Does this army have so many physicians that they can spare you? What of your training, Joseph?"

"I have had many opportunities to put my medical skills to use in the past few weeks, and I have no doubt but that I will use them in the weeks to come." He paused and smiled softly at her. "Mother, from your struggles to educate me, many more physicians have been trained. My former apprentices have all offered their services. They are the result of your sacrifice. Jack—he will be the acclaimed physician of the family! Already he is showing remarkable skill and receiving much praise! And he is so young yet.

"Now my services are in greater demand as a military leader. With so many different militia companies, the men are confused. It is difficult for them to know who is in charge. The Continental Congress delays in sending us a commanding general. Someone must take that position here until such a commander arrives. I have been chosen to fill that role until then."

"And when shall this commander arrive?" Mary demanded.

"I have not even received word that one has been decided upon."

"And if a battle is fought before he arrives?"

"Then, I fear, I shall be in the midst of it," Joseph said tenderly.

Mary pulled her hands from his and stood. She needed to put distance between herself and her son as she attempted to control her emotions. She was not one to give in to emotional outbursts, but fear for the safety of her eldest son consumed her now.

"Why do you have to fight?" she cried. "I was told the position of head surgeon has not been filled. This is a position you are well qualified for!" she sighed in despair. "Please, do not continue to risk your life in battle!"

"There are other men who can fill that position, Mother."

"Oh, Joseph!"

Rising, he went to his mother and enfolded her in his arms. "Mother, now is no time for one of America's sons to shirk from the most hazardous duty. I will see my country free, even if I must shed my last drop of blood to make her so."

"Are you expecting a confrontation with the British?" Sam asked.

"Yes," Joseph answered, wanting to prepare them both.

"Soon?"

"Yes, but I can say no more now."

Mary wiped the tears from her cheeks and looked up at her son. "If you should be forced into battle, please send me word of your safety as soon as possible."

He could not deny her this request. "As soon as I am able, a messenger will deliver a note in my own hand to tell you of my well-being."

After warm embraces for both his mother and brother, Joseph made his way to the door.

"Please do give Eben and his family my love when you next see them." And without another word, he departed.

After leaving the farm, Joseph contemplated the visit scheduled with John Jeffries that night. He had taken the risk of sending a short message to John by secret courier to ask John to meet him at midnight on Clark's Wharf in Boston.

Such a meeting was dangerous. Of that there was no doubt. If Joseph were discovered, he would be taken into custody immediately. But knowing that the docks were deserted at such a late hour and trusting John to come alone, as instructed, Joseph was willing to take the risk. This was his only way to deliver a letter to Mercy and the children, his only hope of communicating to them his love and concern.

He also felt he must attempt one last time to win John Jeffries over to the cause of liberty. This longtime friend whose opinions differed so greatly from his own convictions was desperately needed to head the medical department. His gifted surgical skills were equal to Joseph's—the finest in the colony.

As midnight approached, Joseph quietly made his way down to the banks of the Charles River. A rowboat carefully hidden beneath the thick underbrush along the banks awaited him. He pulled it into the shallow water before taking strips of cloth that had been stuffed into the pocket of his frock coat and wrapped the oars with them to muffle any noise his rowing might cause. Unbeknown to his companions in Cambridge, he secretly made his way across the river's expanse.

The moon and stars that reflected softly off the dark waters guided him as he glided to the opposite shore. The silence of Charlestown behind him and Boston ahead sent a chill up his spine. He had never felt so completely alone.

What if John does not come? Or, worse still, what if John betrays me by inform-ing one of his many friends among the British officers of this meeting? With thoughts such as these, Joseph reconsidered the hazardous meeting and was tempted to turn the boat around and return to the safety of Charlestown. And yet he continued on, gently lifting the oars out of the water and placing them back in. Each stroke was conscious. Each stroke deathly silent.

He cautiously approached the dock, and after securing the boat, he turned and slowly climbed the ladder up onto the structure. Then, standing in the shadows, he anxiously waited. The town crier could be heard in the distance declaring his report at midnight. Joseph knew that he was on time, and yet there was no sign of John. He waited patiently as the night wore on. Any attempt to view his pocket watch proved futile, with the consuming darkness about him. Frustrated by his foolishness in believing John would come, Joseph decided to leave.

As he stepped from the shadows, the sound of an approaching horse was heard. Quickly he moved back and listened. His heart pounded in his own ears as the horse and rider drew near. It took a few moments to recognize the figure upon the horse, but as he drew close enough, Joseph knew it was John.

"John, I am here," he announced in a barely audible whisper. "Thank you so much for coming."

John dismounted and nervously looked about the dock. "I would have been here sooner but was detained by a patient," he offered in a similar whisper. As if fright-ened, he kept an awkward distance from Joseph. "Have you gone mad, Warren? What on earth possessed you to come here like this? Do you realize how dangerous this is?"

"Yes, I do," Joseph softly replied, moving closer. "Please, tell me, how are Mercy and the children?"

"Mercy and the children?" John asked in astonishment. "Is that why you have risked being captured—to ask of their welfare?"

"That is part of my reason for being here, yes."

"Well, then, let me tell you just how they are! They miss you terribly. Dick and Polly question why it is you do not come home. Betsey and Josey pretend to be brave. Mercy—Mercy just takes each day as it comes, careful not to let the children see her cry. Beyond that, they are well, Dr. Warren!"

Stunned by the bitter, cruel words, Joseph remained silent—motionless.

"What else brings you here?" John asked, fully aware of the reaction his words had caused.

"I came to offer you a prominent position as a surgeon in the colonial army."

John chuckled, more for the dramatic effect than because he was amused. "Warren, I thought you knew me better! I would not take an office under anybody, including you!"

Joseph was not certain whether or not he was joking.

"I have the authority to appoint you as the head of the medical service. I shall not be serving there."

"Then the reports are true. You have been commissioned a major general." His statement was more of a question. He seemed startled by the realization and momentarily perplexed by his friend's offer.

"It is true. And I wish for you to take this position, for there is not a man in this colony more qualified for it."

"I cannot, Joseph. You know I cannot!" His words were spoken so quietly Joseph could barely make them out.

"Please, John," Joseph sighed in response, reaching out to touch his friend's arm.

"No."

There was an awkward silence.

"Would you do me a favor, John?" Joseph asked, pulling a letter from his frock coat. "Please give this to Mercy for me. I did not seal it. This way you do not have to worry that you might be passing on a secret message," he said with a forced smile. "Feel free to read it."

"I have no intention whatsoever of reading it. I will seal it myself to avoid caus-ing Mercy any embarrassment, Joseph." John's attention was momentarily drawn to the letter in his hand.

"Thank you." Joseph was relieved that his friend trusted him and grateful that he respected his privacy in communicating with Mercy.

Suddenly looking up at Joseph, John declared, "Come with me and deliver this letter yourself! Please, Joseph, come back with me and forget this insane notion of fighting the entire British Empire!"

"Oh, yes, John," Joseph assented, laughing nervously as he spoke. "To be sure, Gage will welcome me with open arms!"

"You will be pardoned. I have been told that Gage offered a pardon. Surely you are aware of it!" John exclaimed.

"Yes. I received word of Gage's offer of amnesty," Joseph's tone made clear the disgust he felt. "This offer is made to all political offenders, save Sam Adams and John Hancock. Do you really believe Gage has the authority to make such an offer? Just a few minutes ago, you questioned my sanity for risking this meeting. Why should you have been worried if Gage is prepared to forgive me?" The last two words were said with more than a touch of sarcasm.

"It is one thing to sneak over here with the intention of returning to your rebel army, and quite another to admit to being misled and throwing yourself at the mercy of those in authority!"

Though Joseph's initial reaction was to lash out verbally at his friend, he wisely restrained himself. Finally realizing that John simply did not understand. Try as he might—time and again—to explain his convictions, for reasons unknown to Joseph, John was somehow incapable of grasping what he said.

"Our stand is not wrong, John. I have not been misled. We are not in rebellion. We are hoping to bring about a revolution."

John sighed in frustration. "A revolution, Joseph! Consider what you are saying!"

"We long to return to the form of civil government our English Constitution guarantees. We long to be the free subjects of our King. We do not want anything new or different. The 'rebels,' if any are to be labeled as such, are those who have deviated from our Constitution and our adherence to the Common Law."

"I fear that you are destined to die upon the gallows!" John responded with great emotion. "You will leave your orphaned children with nothing but a legacy of shame and humiliation!"

"No, John! If Providence has destined me to die for this cause, then it will be on the field of battle, for this is far nobler! And my children already know that what I am doing is in the hope of making them free that they might live with dignity!" Turning, Joseph prepared to descend to the water below.

"Joseph!" John called after him. He moved behind Joseph and placed a hand on his friend's shoulder. "Please, do not let us part like this. I will deliver your letter to Mercy first thing in the morning. I will assure her that you are well."

Joseph turned to face him. "I cannot adequately express how grateful I am, John, how grateful I am for all that you have done for them in my absence." He reached out his hand to John, then descended into the boat and returned to Charlestown.

Once again, he was alone.

· 18 ·

The Final Day

EVERY DAY WAS a gift from God to be enjoyed to its fullest! Betsy Palmer had held to this belief throughout her life. As she gazed out the open bedchamber window, delighting in the beauty of the summer morning, she whispered, "But it is only mid-June! It is not even summer yet!" An unseasonably warm breeze flowed through the window, gently caressing her cheek.

The streets below were already bustling with activity. She had been born and reared in this very house—her father's house. Never had she witnessed the streets of Watertown so alive. As a child she had longed to live in Boston with its constant ebb and flow. In a very real sense, now Boston had come to her. And though she grieved the tragic circumstances that made it so, she could not help but take delight in the new friendships and exciting opportunities it brought.

As a new bride and with her mother dead, Betsy longed for the companionship of other women. With so many families having fled Boston to find safe refuge in Watertown, she found more than ample opportunities to meet new friends.

As she contemplated her pleasure in her new relationships, she thought of Mercy Scollay. Dr. Warren, who had been physician to her father's family since Betsy was a small girl, had taken up residence with them. With childlike faith, she frequently prayed that the Warren family would by some miraculous means be released from Boston.

Betsy eagerly anticipated developing a friendship with Dr. Warren's fiancée, and she occasionally spoke to him about it as a way of encouraging him. She felt it was her duty to encourage him so he did not lose heart. He would always smile in response, and once or twice she was sure she detected a smile in his eyes, an uncommon occurrence since he had come to Watertown, she noted sadly.

The sound of the grandfather clock downstairs drew Betsy's attention away from the window. It was seven o'clock, and breakfast would be on the table. Quickly she slipped her stocking feet into delicate satin slippers and made one last attempt to direct the spiraling, brown curls falling around her face back under a lace cap.

As usual, the men had gathered at the breakfast table ahead of her. There they would discuss the day's activities as they politely awaited her arrival. Normally, the conversation was loud and lively enough that Betsy could follow it as she approached the room. This morning, however, such was not the case. The men conversed in low, grave tones. The atmosphere in the room was unusually solemn, so much so that even Betsy's radiant smile went unnoticed.

As she observed those around her, she surmised that something important was about to occur. Both her husband and father appeared tense—lost in their own thoughts. Dr. Warren was restless. He ate his breakfast quickly, giving the impression that he was already late for the meeting scheduled for more than an hour later. Finishing his meal before any of the others were half done, Joseph excused himself and rose from the table. Then, as if he had forgotten something, he turned to Betsy.

"Mrs. Palmer," he said, surprising her with such formality. "It would be greatly appreciated if you and the household servants would gather linens and prepare bandages with them. I'm afraid we may be in need of them soon." And with that he left the house.

Betsy was as dumbfounded by his instructions as by his formal address to her. He rarely referred to her as "Mrs. Palmer," and he never did he do so when only in the company of her family.

He had spent many a tense vigil at her bedside during her sickly childhood. They had developed a rather unique bond during those life-threatening illnesses.

She recalled how often she would watch him from her sickbed as he sat in the chair by her side. Thinking she was asleep, Joseph would bury his face in his hands and in heartfelt prayer begged for wisdom in further treating her, not that he was unsure of himself but that he knew he had done all he could do and humbly acknowledged his need for divine intervention.

She loved him, and as a child she had dreamed of marrying him. As an adult, she found it difficult to define her affection for him. It was not the same as her feelings for her husband, but rather a love for one who had been with her to the edge of life and then pulled her back from the grip of death.

She would always love him, and he her. He had affectionately referred to her as "little girl" for as long as she could remember. How she enjoyed this pet name! But today she was "Mrs. Palmer." She didn't understand it at all.

Joseph came back to the house twice during the day to retrieve papers. He was restless and, though very talkative, gave no hint as to why the bandages would be needed. But he repeated the instructions again, greatly increasing Betsy's level of anxiety.

"Good day, Doctor—er, excuse me, General Warren," William Eustis greeted Joseph with a welcoming smile. "I am afraid it will take some time for me to become accustomed to your new title, sir," he apologized.

"Between you and me, William, it will take some time for me to become accustomed to it," Joseph replied cheerfully as he warmly patted the younger man on the back. "How are we situated here?" he asked as he walked through the hospital, observantly studying the conditions about him.

"It is relatively quiet, as you can see, sir. The only patients are those with varying forms of camp fever. We are well stocked, as per your order. One of your patients is here, sir. John Adams' son, young John Quincy," William announced, gesturing toward the operating room.

"Is something wrong with the lad?" Joseph asked. Before William had a chance to reply, Abigail Adams bustled from the operating room. She was clothed in a plain, country dress and cap one would expect to see her in while on the farm, not at all the fitting attire for a trip to Cambridge. She spotted Joseph immediately and moved toward him quickly and with desperate determination.

"Please, Dr. Warren, you must look in on my son!" she stated, dark eyes ablaze.

"What has happened, Mrs. Adams?" he asked.

"He took a bad fall. His finger is broken. They insist that it must be amputated! I told them no, but they will not listen to me," she replied. She anxiously searched his face for a favorable response.

Quickly, Joseph turned from her and headed in the direction from which she had just come. Without taking time to knock on the door, he entered the operating room. Abigail followed closely behind. The physicians in the room appeared rather startled by the unannounced entrance.

"Excuse me, gentlemen, but I have just learned that a friend of mine is paying a visit," Joseph stated, not wanting to further alarm the young boy. Joseph quickly spotted the tear-stained face of John Quincy straining to catch a glimpse of him between the group of doctors standing in front of the table. Joseph was relieved that none of his former students were among them.

"What is this I hear of you injuring a finger?" The physicians stepped aside as Joseph moved in front of the operating table. He extended his hand to the boy. Slowly John Quincy placed his small, injured hand into Joseph's large one.

"It hurts really bad, sir," the young boy's voice trembled noticeably.

"You are a brave lad," Joseph said as he studied the mangled finger. "But I must ask you, John Quincy, to be braver still while I examine it."

The boy promised that he would try, knowing full well how painful this examination would be as the other physicians had already examined it.

"Dr. Miller," Joseph said, addressing the man standing beside him, "Mrs. Adams has informed me that you feel amputation is necessary."

"For such a fracture, yes. We have all agreed that it is the proper treatment," he replied, his tone slightly defensive.

"The proper treatment? I concur that it is a complicated fracture, but we can attempt to set it. We have nothing to lose, gentlemen," he said looking at each of the men.

"Are you not concerned that infection will set in? Take note of the lacerations he has sustained. The circulation of the finger will be sluggish," Dr. Miller pointed out, defending his position.

"If the finger becomes infected, we can promptly treat the infection. Perhaps we can improve the circulation with the use of leeches. If it does not respond favorably, then, and only then, we will be forced to take it."

"With such a fracture, the finger will never be strong again," one of the other physicians interjected.

"It is my belief, Doctor, that a weak finger is better than no finger!" Joseph replied, somewhat annoyed by the remark. Then, looking at John Quincy, he said with a smile, "Young Mr. Adams here is a very strong lad. If we are patient, I believe we will see this finger heal and regain much of its capacity as well."

Then, directing his attention to the young boy, he smiled tenderly. "John Quincy, what is your age? Are you nine?"

"Yes, sir," the trembling voice replied.

"I know of a lad who was the same age as you are now, in a similar predicament. Many a physician would have amputated that lad's finger, but the family physician refused to do so. By waiting, the pain that boy felt was prolonged, but his finger was saved."

"Were you his doctor?" John Quincy asked, his large, tear-filled eyes staring up into Joseph's.

"No, I was the lad," Joseph replied, holding up his hand for John Quincy to see the partially amputated thumb.

The boy was amazed. "I never noticed that before!" he gasped, timidly reaching out to touch the thumb. "Does it hurt, sir?"

"Not at all. Nor will your finger once it begins to heal. Because of that physician's patience, I lost only the tip of this thumb. I have always had full use of my hand. We are going to try to save your entire finger, but I will not lie to you, John Quincy. It will be very difficult to set. You will be in great pain while I work on it," Joseph warned, laying a comforting hand on the boy's small shoulder and squeezing it gently.

"I know you wouldn't hurt me except to do what's best, sir—" John Quincy replied as a tear slowly rolled down his cheek.

"Mrs. Adams, please come here and let the boy hold on to your hand while I set this finger," he suggested, remembering what a comfort it was for him to have had his mother do the very same so many years ago. As the other physician's observed, Joseph proceeded.

The temperature throughout the day had proved stifling. Even now as the night wore on, the heat continued relentlessly. Contrary to the rules of etiquette, the men had abandoned their frock coats and waistcoats, sitting about the dinner table in their shirtsleeves, their cravats comfortably loosened.

Betsy envied their ability to alleviate their discomfort so easily as she drooped beneath her bulky gown and layers of undergarments. She was grateful for the slight breeze from the silk fan in her hand.

There was little conversation about the table as the men, seemingly having gone all day without a bite to eat, devoured the food before them. On the other hand, Betsy had little appetite and merely toyed with the broiled fish and rice upon her plate.

"They will fortify which hill? Breed's or Bunker?" Betsy's father, Thomas Hunt, asked after wiping his mouth with the linen napkin and settling back in the chair, his enormous hunger now appeased.

"Bunker—it sits adjacent to Breed's but is further from the water. The distance will provide added safety from the ship's cannons and offer the British troops a more difficult approach."

"And though further inland, it will prevent Gage from occupying any of the other hills he had intended upon," Betsy's husband, Joseph Palmer, added.

Joseph nodded as he continued to eat.

"When are the militia units to march?" Thomas Hunt asked.

Joseph gazed across the room beyond Betsy, who sat opposite him at the table. She twisted her upper body to view the grandfather clock behind her.

"The march is getting under way even as we speak," Joseph replied.

A sudden chill ran up Betsy's spine as she observed the time and heard his words. It was nine o'clock. Silence reigned as the chimes struck one by one.

"Then do you expect a battle tonight?" she asked, aware that the fear she had experienced throughout the day was apparently warranted.

"Not tonight. But come sunrise, when the report reaches Gage that we have fortified the hill, he will attempt to drive us back," Joseph said matter-of-factly.

"We?" Betsy cried in alarm.

"You do not intend to be among those occupying the hill?" Thomas exclaimed.

"Indeed, I must. I cannot order men to such a hazardous duty and not expect to partake of it myself!"

"Please do not expose yourself!" Thomas pleaded. "Joseph, you are needed in council. Do not put yourself at risk!"

"I have accepted the responsibility and danger of the rank of Major general. I must be with the men," he responded calmly.

"Please, Dr. Warren, listen to my father. Please do not go!" Betsy begged, reaching out across the table to touch his hand.

He looked at her with tenderness in his eyes, preparing to respond.

"Any news on the cannon at Fort Ticonderoga?" Joseph Palmer asked, preventing Joseph from giving Betsy an answer.

"No."

Betsy's thoughts became a blur as she fought the overwhelming urge to disrupt the conversation about which militia units would be involved, how many rounds of ammunition each unit would carry, who was to be in command of the troops, how the fortification was to be constructed—

She wanted to scream at them all, "Stop!" She wanted to make her father and her husband understand that their focus should not be on the details of this horrid battle, but on convincing their friend—her friend—to remain in a place of safety.

Certain that she would be unable to contain herself much longer, Betsy rose from her seat, laying her fan on the table, and walked toward the door.

The conversation behind her continued, the words torturously resounding in her head. She remained frozen for a moment, her body trembling as her hand held tightly to the knob.

"Betsy, where are you going?" her husband's voice asked above the clamor of her mind. Then Dr. Warren's.

"Gentlemen, let us drink to our glorious victory on Bunker Hill!"

Suddenly he stood at the buffet table to her side, pouring wine into goblets for each of them.

"Come, my little girl, drink a glass of wine with me!" His voice was full of excitement and emotion.

Betsy turned her head to face him. He was already staring at her. In the space of time it took for their eyes to meet, Betsy witnessed a change in his entire countenance. Within his blue eyes she saw reflected the same desperation and fear she had witnessed as a child when she clung to life as if by a thread. A violent shiver engulfed her body as she recalled that scene. Then, ever so softly, too softly for any-one else to hear, he spoke to her again.

"For I am going on the hill tomorrow, and I shall never come off."

Though his body longed for sleep, it would not come. Joseph tossed and turned as the unrelenting chime of the grandfather clock announced each passing hour.

The night was hot, the air heavy and still. To add to Joseph's discomfort, his head ached. Nothing he attempted alleviated the intense pain.

The house was quiet. Everyone else had lapsed into peaceful slumber hours ear-lier. He alone could not experience its soothing comfort. His mind refused to stop working as thought after thought poured through it.

Construction of the redoubt was well underway, and there was no turning back. With the morning light would come enemy fire. In his mind Joseph reviewed the plans that would unfold the next day if everything went according to plans. He had spent many hours preparing for the events that would soon occur—listening to sug-gestions, thinking and rethinking strategies, informing officers, and preparing supplies. He had questioned opinions and had had his own opinions questioned. When everything had been said, he had given approval to it all.

He had given his approval, but he was not at peace with it. The victory should belong to the colonials if the redoubt could be adequately constructed by sunrise. If the men could hold up under enemy fire— If the ammunition was sufficient— If colonial reinforcements could be sent in— If— The small word began to haunt him. The men were still green, and few had ever experienced fighting under fire. Would the shaky discipline of the ranks hold up? If only Colonel Arnold had returned with the heavy artillery he went for. If only the sister colonies had provided more men, more ammunition—If only— If only—

With the familiar sound of the cock's crow through the open window, he real-ized that dawn was at hand, and there was no sense in trying to sleep any longer. He sat on the edge of the rumpled bed vigorously massaging his forehead in the vain hope of easing the pain.

Although he was not due at headquarters for five more hours, Joseph decided he would ride to Cambridge early. There he could receive any news that might come from the hill.

His clothes lay draped over a chair. Great care had been given in choosing what he would wear. Before putting on his waistcoat, Joseph took time to admire it.

Mercy had made the garment for him. Both the material and the tailoring were as fine as any John Hancock could boast. It was pale blue in color. "To match your eyes," Mercy had told him. The buttons were covered in silk with a matching silk fringe to border the hem. Such a garment was for special occasions only: balls, weddings, and baptisms. It was the type of suit one would be buried in.

The thought lingered for a few seconds. Was that why he had laid this particular suit out? "No!" he whispered, as if saying it out loud would help convince him. This is the outfit one would choose to wear to a victory celebration! he managed to tell himself. A victory that will force the mother country to reconsider her stand.

After he had finished dressing, Joseph picked up his medical bag, tricorn, and the small book of the Psalms from the desk, which he carefully placed in his pocket. By the light of a small lantern, he then made his way to the stable.

Dawn's first rays were just beginning to burst forth as the horse trotted down the well-traveled road to Cambridge. No other travelers had ventured out yet. Farmers within the houses he passed were preparing for the tasks of their day, and housewives kindled the kitchen fire as they called for their sleepy children to climb out of bed. No one was aware of the men who anxiously waited within the redoubt on Bunker Hill. None of them realized that brave men on both sides would die this day.

At headquarters in Cambridge, Joseph quietly stepped inside and removed his hat. He gently closed the door behind him, careful not to disturb those who still slept.

The jostling ride on the horse had worsened his headache. The constant, pounding pain brought on waves of dizziness and nausea, and Joseph leaned against the door, his head buried in his arm as he attempted to shake the feeling.

"Joseph? Is something wrong?" came the voice of Elbridge Gerry.

Joseph did not respond, only adding to Elbridge's concern.

"Were our men discovered on the hill during the night, Joseph?" Elbridge asked with alarm.

"No," Joseph replied softly as he turned toward him. As soon as Elbridge saw his face, he realized that Joseph was ill. The color was drained from his cheeks, and his face dripped with perspiration.

"Sit here!" Elbridge said, motioning to a nearby chair.

Joseph declined the offer but found it difficult to stand without holding on to the back of the chair.

"You are feverish," Elbridge assumed, noting his perspiration. "You should be in bed!" Taking a clean handkerchief from his frock coat, he wiped his friend's forehead.

"I intend to lie down until the meeting. A few hours of sleep should cure this oppressive headache."

"Use my room. I will see that you are not disturbed. Can I do anything for you?" Elbridge asked with concern.

"If you could steep a pot of this, I would greatly appreciate it," Joseph replied, fumbling through the medical bag. Normally he was able to find a sought-after item in no time at all, but the pounding intensified as he lowered his head to look into the bag. "Here," he said, holding his forehead with one hand as he handed Elbridge a small package of chamomile root with the other.

"Can I get you something to eat?" Elbridge asked, wanting to be helpful.

"No—no, thank you!" he answered quickly. Though he appreciated the offer, the thought of food was totally repulsive. As it was, he would have to force the tea down in the hope of relieving the headache.

"This letter arrived last evening from Boston." Elbridge pulled a piece of paper from the pocket of his frock coat and handed it to Joseph. "It was addressed to you and the Committee of Safety. Thinking it might demand immediate attention, I took the liberty of opening it. It is from one of our men in Boston, James Lovell. If you will remember, his brother Benjamin was appointed clerk in the office of the British artillery. It seems that Benjamin Lovell managed to create a mix-up in the cannon balls. Many of the cannon balls will be oversized for the cannons being used today, thanks to Mr. Lovell's quick thinking."

Joseph unfolded the paper but was unable to read it, for the words seemed all a blur to him.

Elbridge could see his difficulty. "Shall I read it to you?" he asked.

This news should have caused great excitement, but at the moment Joseph could not seem to muster any. "No, I will just wait and read it to the Committee members," he said as he slowly folded the letter again and placed it in his own pocket. "I intend to preside over the meeting before I go up to the hill," he casually announced.

Elbridge studied his friend, not sure he had heard him right. "What? Joseph, you cannot be serious!" he exclaimed.

Joseph appeared dumbfounded. "Elbridge, the Provincial Congress elected me major general. It is my duty to be there."

"The commission is not yet official. It is your duty, at present, to preside over both the Provincial Congress and the Committee of Safety. And that duty, sir, should prevent you from even entertaining the thought of participating in this engagement!"

"No! I cannot help it! I must share the fate of my countrymen. I could not bear to listen as the cannons fire, yet remain inactive. I should die if I were in comfort and safety while my fellow citizens are shedding their blood for me!" Joseph's heartfelt reply came.

"It would be madness for you to expose yourself! As surely as you go there, you will be slain!"

Joseph's weak smile met the grave expression of his college chum. *"Dulce et decorum est pro patris mori,"* he replied, patting Elbridge on the shoulder as he moved toward the staircase.

As those words, "It is sweet and fitting to die for one's country," rolled over and over again in his head, Elbridge tried but could find no reply to argue Joseph's statement. He watched in silence as his friend ascended the stairs.

Suddenly Joseph paused. Elbridge waited, hoping that he had changed his mind. He should have known better.

Though he did not turn to face his friend, Joseph began to speak. His voice was filled with emotion. "I fear for the future of Great Britain. Prolonged military conflict with us shall weaken her, opening her to the attack of her enemies in Europe. I do not want this to happen."

"I am certain that none of us do," Elbridge agreed.

"Why must it be this way? Why?"

Elbridge did not reply.

"Be sure to awaken me for the meeting or if any news arrives from the hill that demands my attention," Joseph instructed, forgetting about the chamomile tea.

Again Elbridge did not reply.

Joseph made his way to the hot, stuffy bedchamber. In a daze he removed his shoes and pulled off his frock coat and waistcoat, tossing them in a heap on a side chair. With a firm grasp on his skull, he slowly lowered himself upon the bed.

The pain was unbearable. The room seemed to spin as the nausea gripped him. With his eyes shut tight against the sun's rays and the whirling scenery, he prayed fervently for sleep to come.

Despite the thoughts and questions that continued to torture him, despite the heat and humidity, despite the rumble of cannon fire that began to echo in the distance, his mind finally yielded to the sleep his body demanded.

As Joseph slept, the hours passed. The Committee of Safety met.

General Israel Putnam brought news from the redoubt that the militia companies were under fire from the British men-of-war. British troops were preparing to cross the river and form for an attack. He informed the Committee that the plans to build the redoubt on Bunker Hill had been changed. Military engineers thought it best to put the redoubt on Breed's Hill, a move they regretted with morning's light. For now it was apparent that being closer to the river, Breed's Hill was subject to damaging cannon fire. The march for the British troops would be shorter and easier than if the colonials had occupied Bunker Hill as planned.

Elbridge Gerry had never agreed to awaken his friend as instructed. Relieved that Joseph had slept through the meeting, he hoped that sleep would continue to keep him captive until the threatened battle was well underway, thus preventing him safe passage to the fort.

Upon the adjournment of the meeting, the news of the engineer's change of plans, as well as the minutes, were placed in a neat pile on the table. When the Committee Chairman finally did awaken, he could easily review what had transpired in his absence. Each member then departed from headquarters to attend to their various duties, and Joseph continued to sleep.

A mournful silence had settled over Cambridge. The streets were deserted as young Dr. Townsend rode into town.

He had been visiting patients on the outskirts of Boston when he learned the colonials had attempted to occupy Breed's Hill. Certain that his services would be needed Townsend made his way to military headquarters in search of his former teacher.

He was alarmed to find no members of the committee in the lower level of the house that served as headquarters as he searched for someone who might be able to direct him to General Warren.

Disturbed by the eerie atmosphere, the young man shivered as he listened to his footsteps echo throughout the house, joined only by the dull rumble of occasional cannon. Upstairs he discovered one door tightly shut. Standing motionless before it, David finally gave it a light tap.

On the opposite side, Joseph lay sprawled upon the bed. As a physician, he had developed the uncanny ability to sleep through disturbances. His sleep was often sporadic, and his subconscious mind had been trained to ignore much. The voices of men conferring downstairs had not disturbed him; the sound of cannon fire had gone unheard; even the intense heat had finally been ignored. Yet his subconscious mind was trained to react immediately to the softest nudge on the shoulder, a whispered call in the dark, or a light tap on the door.

"Come in," Joseph called out drowsily as he sat up on the edge of the bed.

Cautiously, David opened the door, poking his head through before entering.

"David?" Joseph was surprised to see him, fully expecting Elbridge.

"I am sorry to have disturbed you, sir. When I learned of today's confrontation, I thought I could better serve you here."

"What time is it?" Joseph asked, noticing that the shadows in the room seemed more in line with an afternoon sun.

"It is close to two o'clock by now," the younger man replied.

"Two o'clock? Is the Committee of Safety still in conference?" he asked rising to his feet.

"No sir. We are alone here."

Joseph could not help but reveal his confusion upon hearing the reply. He walked to the open window and listened to the distant cannon fire.

"Do you know if the British are preparing to attack?" he asked. The younger man shook his head from side to side.

Joseph picked up his rumpled waistcoat and put it on. "I fear that your services will be needed, Doctor. If you can wait long enough for me to have a cup of chamomile tea, I will walk to the hill with you." After slipping on his shoes, he reached over and grabbed his frock coat. The letter Elbridge had given to him was still in the pocket. While in a state of near-physical collapse, he had placed it there. Now he could remember only bits and pieces of his conversation with Elbridge, and he did not remember the letter at all.

"Chamomile? Are you ill, sir?" David asked as he followed Joseph downstairs.

"A lingering headache. Sleep relieved it a great deal. It is much better now. The tea should help. Have you paid a visit to my family recently?"

"Yes sir, I have. A few days ago, in fact."

"Are they well?" Joseph had believed John Jeffries' report, but he needed to hear it again.

"They are fine, sir, and in good health. Polly came down with a cold a few weeks back, but she has recovered nicely. That little girl certainly has the ability to melt my heart! She so resembles her mother," David said with an affectionate smile.

"To be sure." Joseph's spirits were lifted by David's words, and the thought of little Polly and Elizabeth brought a smile to his own lips.

When they reached the kitchen, Joseph placed the chamomile root in a teapot, pouring hot water into it from the kettle that hung over the smoldering embers. "And how is Samuel holding up?" he asked, referring to Sam Adams's son.

"He stays busy," David began. "Gage will not allow him passage out of Boston, so he has taken on the bulk of all our patients within the town while I visit those around Boston."

"That makes for a lot of traveling on your part," Joseph commented.

"I do not mind."

Joseph smiled at the younger man, proud of his dedication. "Has Gage harassed Samuel or the Scollays?" he asked.

"No. He questioned them at first, but he does not seem to bother with them now," David assured him.

Joseph poured a cup of the steeped tea for himself and offered some to David.

"Thank you, sir," David said. He picked up the teacup and followed Joseph into the dining room.

"Does my family have enough to eat?" Joseph asked as he placed his cup and saucer on the dining room table next to the papers that were left for him by the Committee of Safety. He ignored the documents, instead focusing his full attention upon David and awaiting his honest reply.

"Yes, sir. In a sense, Samuel and I have felt ourselves to be a part of your family since our apprenticeship. You can be sure that we are watching out for them in your absence. Dr. Jeffries has been checking in on them as well."

Joseph placed his hand on the younger man's shoulder. "Thank you, David," he said with heartfelt appreciation.

"It is the least we can do, sir."

Joseph sat down at the table and began to read through the minutes of the committee meeting. David sat down opposite him.

The fact that the redoubt had been constructed on Breed's Hill rather than on Bunker Hill as planned visibly alarmed Joseph.

"Is something wrong, sir?" David asked.

Joseph looked up at him, the possible consequences of the news consuming his thoughts. "We—we have had a major setback, and I do not know if we can recover from it." Without another word, he went back to reading the minutes as he finished drinking the tea. Then standing, he said to the younger man, "Let us be on our way." Both men retrieved their medical bags and hats from the foyer table. As they prepared to leave, the door opened.

"I was told that you were ill," Paul Revere stated, surprised to find Joseph and David in the foyer.

"I am feeling much better."

"Are you going?" Paul began, struggling with his words. "Are you still planning on going to the hill?"

Joseph nodded. "You are the only one who has not tried to dissuade me."

"I wouldn't do that. If you feel you must be there, then that is where you must be," he said with a weak smile. "No doubt there will be a dispatch for Philadelphia by day's end."

"Indeed there will, with news of victory, I pray. Get some sleep, Paul. You'll have a long ride ahead."

"I intend to do just that." Paul reached out his hand to receive that of his friend. "I will pray that God's blessing be upon you this day, General."

"Thank you, and I will see you this evening, Paul."

Just outside of Cambridge, Joseph and David encountered 2,000 colonial soldiers preparing to march to the redoubt. Concerned about the men who had spent the night entrenching the hill, Joseph instructed the officers to see that a wagonload of provisions be sent forward to them.

On the west side of Bunker Hill, they came upon the first casualties of the day as fellow physicians were treating them. Injured by the ships' cannon, the men lay on the hard earth as physicians prepared to have them moved to the military hospital in Cambridge.

David offered his assistance as Joseph knelt beside William Eustis and quickly began handing the young physician bandages. The injured soldier seemingly ignored the pain as William worked on his leg.

"There are a fair number of men waiting on the summit of this hill, General," the soldier said as he lifted his upper body, supporting his weight on his elbows. "If they go on to join those in the redoubt, we can face them redcoats with confidence!" Lying down flat, he took a deep breath as he fought the pain. "They're about ready to attack, sir. I regret havin' had to leave so soon."

"You are to be commended for your service throughout the night, my friend," Joseph replied with a warm smile, placing his hand on the injured man's shoulder. "Is the redoubt complete?"

"Enough to provide protection for those fightin' within it."

"Good," Joseph said, looking off in the direction of the redoubt, although he was unable to see it from where he stood. Turning his attention back to the soldier, he asked, "May I borrow your musket?"

Upon hearing Joseph's request, William stopped working and apprehensively stared at him. He said nothing.

"I guess I won't have need of it today," the soldier replied as he struggled to lift the musket that lay by his side.

Joseph reached over and took the musket and cartridge box from him, smiling in response. "I expect Jack will probably be on his way down from Salem soon," he said to William as he stood and draped the box around his neck.

"I am sure he will," William answered.

"I will stop by the hospital as soon as I am able. Tell Jack—" Joseph stopped as if unsure of how to finish.

"Sir?"

Joseph stared back toward Cambridge, apparently deep in thought. "Never mind," he finally said, finding it difficult to express his deepest emotions through another. "Just tell Jack I expect to see him in the morning. And William," he paused again, tenderly gazing at the young man, "I know this has been difficult for you— just coming out of your apprenticeship. You are handling yourself extremely well. I want you to know how proud I am of you."

"Thank you, Dr. Warren."

Joseph smiled affectionately at his former students and their patients. Then, turning away, he continued up the hill, musket in hand.

· 19 ·

The Battle of Bunker Hill

UPON THE SUMMIT of Bunker Hill, Joseph spotted General Israel Putnam taking command of the troops that had gathered. As Joseph approached, Israel ceremoniously saluted him.

"General Warren, I'm surprised to see you, sir. When I was at headquarters this morning, I was informed that you were ill."

"I am feeling much better now, General Putnam."

"I'm sorry to hear it, sir."

Israel's strange response caught Joseph by surprise. "Excuse me?" he replied, certain he must have misunderstood.

"This battle can be fought without you, sir," Israel replied. "Your commission is not yet official. You're not duty bound to be here. We'll need you in council when this is finished." Israel realized by the determination reflected in Joseph's eyes that his words were spoken in vain. "Do you mean to stay, sir?"

"I do."

"Then, General Warren, I shall take your orders."

"Because my commission is not official, I have none to give but have come as a volunteer." He turned his attention toward the redoubt on Breed's Hill. It was almost square in shape, roughly fifty yards to a side. The walls were close to six feet high and about a foot thick. A breastwork made of stone and dirt extended to the left of the redoubt for about one hundred yards. Behind this, men were working on a second breastwork that consisted of rail fences covered with bushes, hay, and grass extending eastward to the edge of the Charles River.

"That's Colonel Stark's Connecticut regiment on the east side of the redoubt," Israel informed Joseph, pointing to the breastwork. "Stark's men will take cover behind that fence."

Joseph became alarmed upon hearing this and made no attempt to hide it. "They will be cut down! That fence will give them little protection from bullets!"

"If all goes as planned, General Warren, the enemy will have no time to fire on them. The fence is well camouflaged. By the time the British realize our men are there, it will be too late. A volley of fire from our line at that close range will do great damage."

Although still concerned for the safety of the men, Joseph had no choice but to trust the judgment of the more experienced officers.

"Where can I be most useful?" he asked.

"Go to the redoubt. You'll be covered there," Israel instructed.

"Do not think I came here to seek a place of safety," Joseph replied, annoyed by what he perceived as an attempt to protect him. "But tell me where the onset will be the most furious."

Still pointing to the redoubt Israel said, "That is the object of the enemy. If it can be defended, the day is ours."

"Why are these men not going forward, General Putnam?" Joseph asked, referring to the troops that stood with them on the hill.

"I intend to organize them and bring them over myself, sir. That's why I'm here."

"Then see to it, General," Joseph said and set out toward the redoubt, undaunted by the British men-of-war that fired steadily in their direction in an attempt to keep any reinforcements back.

Upon Joseph's arrival, a cheer resounded from the men within the earthen fort. Exhausted from a night of labor, they were becoming uneasy as they witnessed the arrival of the British troops on the shores below. The presence of one so important as Joseph Warren somehow rekindled their courage and offered them the hope of victory.

"Your orders, General Warren?" the officer in charge, Colonel William Prescott, inquired with a salute as Joseph approached. Standing over six feet tall, this strong veteran of the French and Indian War remained cool and self-possessed in the face of imminent danger. He was neatly attired in a uniform that consisted of a light blue coat and a three-cornered blue hat.

"I have no orders to give, Colonel, but have come as a volunteer to encourage a good cause. I desire to learn from a soldier of your experience," Joseph said. Then, looking about the redoubt, he became confused. "Colonel, your orders were to bring a thousand men with you. Have you sent some to aid Colonel Stark at the rail fence?" He estimated only about 500 men were in the fort.

"No sir, the rail fence is well manned. I sent some to the breastwork, and a detail of snipers are stationed in the empty buildings of Charlestown." Colonel Prescott paused, his gray eyes fixed upon Joseph's. "Many of them, sir, have simply deserted."

Joseph knew the men were green, but he had thought they would hold out longer than this.

"Two of our men were killed by cannon fire earlier. One had his head blown clean off, and the other suffered a similar fate," the colonel said as he looked down at his long coat, which was splattered with blood.

"My orders to have them buried immediately were countered by the clergy present. As I feared, the graveside service they insisted on gave our troops too much time to dwell on their own possible fate. The weaker ones couldn't handle it. I've been informed that an entire regiment left, led by their commander!"

"Charges will be brought against that officer when this is over," Joseph assured him, furious at the thought that he had probably commissioned the man himself.

"General," Prescott began, "the troops we have consist of many who have never been under fire. We have retired soldiers, farmers, mechanics—physicians," he said, gesturing toward Joseph. "Some are barely old enough to shave, others so old they are nearly feeble, and there is at least one who is half mad."

Joseph was disturbed by the colonel's last description. "Half mad?" he echoed, expecting more detail.

"James Otis is here, General. I spoke to him myself. When he learned of our plans, he borrowed a musket and managed to make his way over. From what I understand, his family is unaware of his whereabouts."

"They will be worried sick!" Joseph exclaimed. He gazed about the redoubt, hoping to locate Mr. Otis. "You should have ordered him off the hill, Colonel."

"I did, sir, but he would have none of it! He claimed it was his argument against Parliament that stirred us, and now he feels responsible to stand with us."

Though still troubled over Mr. Otis's safety and present state of mind, Joseph was forced to shift his attention to the British troops.

"Well, well, it looks like they have finally finished their picnic," Colonel Prescott announced, pointing to the swarming red figures on the shore. "They took time to have a picnic, General. I don't think they take us seriously at all. Our men— the snipers in Charlestown—have been instructed to shoot down officers as they ascend the hill."

Joseph looked down at the old town to the right of the redoubt. All was still, seemingly deserted.

"I passed reinforcements on the way. They should arrive soon with provisions for the men," Joseph announced.

"That's good to hear!" the colonel replied. His concern for the well being of his command was evident. Without another word, he jumped up onto the wall of the redoubt.

Joseph watched in astonishment as the colonel walked fearlessly along the wall, exposing himself to enemy fire. Enthusiastic cheers arose as he made the announcement of reinforcements and provisions. But this enthusiasm was short-lived as the sound of fife and drum echoed from the shore.

After jumping down into the safety of the redoubt, Colonel Prescott viewed the flurry of activity through a spyglass and then handed it to Joseph.

"I'm afraid the reinforcements won't make it in time, General!" he declared.

A morbid silence settled over the redoubt. Many of the colonials' hearts sank in momentary terror as they viewed the assembled British lines, more than 2,000 strong. In precise military formations, the troops began their ascent of the hill. Their bright red coats were clearly visible, their bayonets glistening under the blazing June sun.

"They will have a rough time climbing this hill with those backpacks on," Joseph remarked as he took another look through the spyglass. "Each must weigh more than fifty pounds. This intense heat will make them feel heavier still."

"And the hillside is riddled with broken fence rails, an obstacle course that will do much to slow them down," Colonel Prescott added. Jumping upon the wall again, he shouted his orders.

"The enemy will be upon us soon, men. The reinforcements may not arrive, but I am confident that we are strong enough to face the redcoats alone. Hold your fire until the order is given. We shall let them get close, very close, before opening fire. We do not have lead or powder to waste. Every shot must count! Aim low, my men. Remember you are shooting downhill. Remember, the musket will naturally pull up upon firing. Pick off the officers. If enough officers fall, the confusion will lead to their retreat."

He jumped down from the wall and positioned himself next to Joseph. Both men prepared their muskets.

Joseph chanced a look around the redoubt as he awaited the enemy's arrival. The men appeared transfixed by the steadily advancing red lines. He recognized many of those near him, even spotting Parson Cooper speaking words of encouragement among the men.

"They think our left side is weak. Thank God, Stark got that rail fence up in time!" Prescott said in earnest.

All eyes were fixed upon the approaching troops as they marched up the hill in a long column, one regiment behind the other. Then, as they drew nearer to the redoubt, the columns spread out into a long line.

As they encountered the rail fences beneath the tall grass, the march was halted only long enough for the troops to smash the fences down with the butts of their muskets. Soon the fifes and drums began to play again, and the sergeants shouted curses and swore to keep the men in line. Despite the obstacles they encountered, the enemy continued to advance. Loaded muskets were positioned on the redoubt wall, nervous fingers held ready against the triggers.

The familiar popping of occasional musket fire was suddenly heard from the direction of the deserted Charlestown buildings. A few British officers fell, the result of the sharp eyes and perfect aim of the colonials stationed in the deserted buildings.

Momentary confusion halted the British lines closest to Charlestown as they concerned themselves with the sniper attack, but all too soon they reformed and continued their march.

Out of the corner of his eye, Joseph caught a glimpse of Colonel Prescott raising a sword above his head, preparing to give the order everyone breathlessly awaited. Each man's heart pounded violently. Perspiration rolled off their foreheads, as much from nervousness as from the blistering sun.

The enemy was within 150 yards—130 yards—110 yards. Still Colonel Prescott held back the order to fire. The men became restless, even daring to turn their attention from the targets before them to look at their commanding officer who still held the sword high. Joseph remained confident, understanding the wisdom in the colonel's strategy. A musket's accuracy was unreliable beyond a hundred yards.

William Prescott did not, even for a moment, shift his attention from the approaching troops. Yet he sensed the waning confidence of the men about him.

"Hold your fire, my men!" he calmly shouted, as if giving simple instructions to his own sons.

The British field pieces fired upon the redoubt to cover the advance. Then silenced, they were pushed forward to keep abreast of the infantry's march and fired once again. This routine continued until the cannons became bogged down in the high grass and broken rail fences.

"Hold your fire, men—Hold—Hold!" Colonel Prescott yelled.

The British continued on. Eighty yards—seventy yards—"Hold—Hold!"

When they came as close as sixty yards, the colonel brought the sword down. "FIRE!" he shouted. The long-awaited order set off a volley of musket fire, each ball doing great damage at such close range.

British soldiers fell, screaming in pain as those near them began tripping over the bodies. Quickly regaining their footing, they marched on. Blindly obeying their orders, they marched, stopping briefly to fire another volley at the earthen wall. This was answered by still another discharge of musket fire from the redoubt.

British casualties were numerous, many of them officers. As Colonel Prescott had predicted, the enlisted men became confused as their officers fell. Retreating, the British left their dead and seriously wounded sprawled along the hillside.

A triumphant shout of victory echoed within the redoubt and along the rail fence and breastwork. Newfound energy had been discovered after the long hours of labor.

"They'll be back," Colonel Prescott shouted to Joseph, as the men continued to cheer what they thought was a final victory. "They'll be back!" he shouted to the men, bringing an immediate halt to the premature celebration. Their energy was quickly redirected into preparation for a second wave of attack.

Joseph busied himself with the few who were injured, dressing their wounds and speedily sending them off to the hospital in Cambridge. Again he collaborated with Parson Cooper, one of them working quickly to save a life and the other attempting to bring comfort to a soul. The sound of fife and drum from the shore brought Joseph back to Prescott's side.

"Stark's regiment fared as well as we," the colonel reported to Joseph. "Colonel Stark is familiar with British infantry tactics and thus kept the Light Infantry from racing along the beach and outflanking the redoubt. Had he not kept them from getting behind the redoubt and rail fence, we would have been defeated. Stark estimates the Light Infantry had 300 casualties on that first attack."

"Few of Howe's Light Infantry remain then," Joseph commented.

"Indeed. This means Howe will be forced to make a frontal attack. Putnam has men on the hill behind us. He's attempting to rally them to come forward."

"It would seem to me that he has had ample opportunity to do so!" Joseph responded gravely.

"It would seem so," Prescott agreed, exchanging a concerned, knowing glance. "It is possible to hold this fort without reinforcement. It has always been my belief that the men responsible for building a fortification are the best suited to defend it. If we inflict as much damage to the British as in the first attack, then they will not return," Colonel Prescott said as he gazed out upon the sprawled bodies before them.

"Unless Gage sends in his own reinforcements," Joseph offered, making certain that the colonel was prepared for such a possibility.

"If that should happen and General Putnam is unable to rally his own men forward, then we shall be forced to retreat."

"Though we may be forced to retreat, Colonel, we shall do them infinite mischief. And our men shall be assured that the British army is not invincible!" As

Joseph spoke, a volley of heavy artillery sounded, followed by a shout from the redoubt.

"Charlestown! Those devilish redcoats are firing on Charlestown!"

Within a few minutes, the wooden structures of the old town were engulfed in flames.

"They're destroying the town to prevent more sniper fire," Colonel Prescott lamented. All watched in disbelief as the flames rapidly spread, engulfing hundreds of homes. The ascending smoke hovered, forming a thick, dark cloud.

"Boys, we shall be under attack again shortly!" Colonel Prescott shouted above the clamor, directing the attention of the men away from the sobering scene in Charlestown.

"We'll use the same strategy. Fire low! Aim at the gaiter buttons. Remember the officers. Look for the gorgets!" he said, referring to the throat plates worn by the British officers. "Men, don't fire on the enemy until you see the whites of their eyes!"

Disturbed by this last order, many murmured among themselves that their commander intended to draw the enemy even closer this time.

The noise of the burning town intensified as crackling timbers crashed to the ground. The constant barrage of cannon fire from the men-of-war and British field pieces was joined by the shouts of spectators crowded onto the housetops of Boston and the moans of the fatally wounded British soldiers that littered the hillside.

The sound of fifes and drums from the shore below pulled the attention of the spellbound provincial soldiers from the tormenting scene about them. The advancing line of British warriors was obviously intent on finishing the matter, and every mind within the earthen fort found relief in focusing its attention on standing ready for their commander's orders.

The British lines advanced, smashing down the hidden fences and dodging the bodies of fallen comrades. Fearlessly they pressed on under the orders of their officers, ignoring the heavy weight on their backs, the blistering sun, and the thundering sound of Charlestown's destruction.

Obviously troubled, Joseph handed Colonel Prescott the spyglass after examining the enemy's advance.

"Is something wrong, General?" the colonel asked as Joseph carefully positioned his musket on the wall.

"Major Pitcairn is bringing his marines up," the reply came.

"Pitcairn is a fine soldier," Colonel Prescott commented, remembering his great military ability during the French and Indian War.

"Pitcairn is a fine man," Joseph added, acknowledging their friendship. Colonel Prescott threw a glance at Joseph but offered no words, for he found none suitable.

As the enemy closed in, they began to open fire upon the redoubt. Again Colonel Prescott lifted his sword and repeated his words of restraint. "Hold your fire! Hold! Hold!"

The swarming red line continued to advance, discharging the muskets once more. Pitcairn was in plain view now. Desperate—aware of the order to fire at the officers—Joseph struggled, wanting to call out to him, to urge him to take cover. But even if Pitcairn heard his pleading over the din, the attempt to save him would be in vain. For Major Pitcairn was a soldier first and foremost, and he would carry out his orders or die in the attempt. All Joseph could do was keep himself from firing in the direction of his friend.

Closer, closer still, the British line advanced, their faces coming into plain view. Perspiration could be seen dripping from their chins and noses, and the agony of the brutal climb could be seen in their trudging steps and harrowed countenances.

"Hold! Hold!" Colonel Prescott continued to yell. Hundreds of trembling fingers began to ache as they held ready against the trigger. A few went off. In a fury, Colonel Prescott ran along the wall of the breastwork, kicking the leveled muskets that had been fired prematurely.

Upon hearing the muskets discharge and then seeing Prescott's form on the wall, the advancing British wildly fired at the redoubt. British officers began hitting the leveled muskets with their swords. Their shouts could be heard above the clamor of the fife and drum.

"Hold your fire!"

"We are out of range!"

"We will take the redoubt with only the bayonet!"

Unscathed, Colonel Prescott jumped down from the wall, again raising the sword above his head.

"Hold! Hold!"

The whites of their eyes! The whites of their eyes! He actually meant it! Many a man screamed within his mind. The waiting—waiting. Forever waiting!

"Fire!" A thunderous volley of musket fire immediately followed Colonel Prescott's shout. The screams of British soldiers torn through with lead filled the air.

After discharging his own weapon, Joseph found himself unable to divert his eyes from witnessing the fate of his friend. In horror he watched, knowing that numerous guns had taken aim on the marine commander. Major Pitcairn's body was riddled with lead, the force of the impact jerking him backward into the arms of his son. The younger Pitcairn gently lowered his father to the ground, barricading the mortally wounded body with his own.

Joseph quickly reloaded his musket, his heart pounding violently, not in fear but from his inability to respond to the war scene before him.

"Take a deep breath! Take a deep breath!" Joseph found himself whispering as he fought back the emotions that threatened to consume him in response to the heartrending scene. He forced his mind to focus on the next target as he scanned the approaching line. Epaulet or gorget—look for an epaulet or gorget. Not many left. Found one! Aim low. Aim at the gaiter button. Squeeze trigger. The musket's kick against his shoulder was the only indication that the gun had fired as the sound blended with those of a hundred others.

Volley after volley pushed the staggering, broken British line back. Some crawled. Some ran, slipping on the blood that covered the tall grass. Once again, countless bodies were left behind, many within a few yards of the redoubt.

"Do they dare face us again?" a voice called out to Joseph and Colonel Prescott. The two men fixed their gaze on one another as they considered the question.

"We'll have to wait and see," the colonel finally called back. Then, turning to Joseph, he said, "It will take longer for them to regroup this time, if they even do. I can't imagine that they would attack a third time unless Gage sends reinforcements. Surely, he'll consider the price too steep already."

Joseph propped his musket against the earthen wall and picked up the medical bag that lay by his feet. As he tended to the wounded within the redoubt, those whose courage was waning hovered about, begging to be chosen to transport the injured soldiers to the hospital.

Everyone displayed extreme signs of fatigue, having gone without sleep for more than twenty-four hours and without food or drink since early that morning. The sun continued to beat down relentlessly, and the earthen fort offered little escape from its blistering rays. A few men were beginning to suffer from dehydration and sunstroke. Others pretended to be suffering in the hope of being sent to safety. And when all else failed, little by little the fainthearted began to sneak away.

Joseph moved about the fort offering words of encouragement to the men, trying to lift their spirits. As he made his rounds, he spotted James Otis sitting by himself in a small spot of shade against the dirt wall.

"Mr. Otis," Joseph addressed him softly. "How are you, sir?"

"Dr. Warren! Dear, dear, Dr. Warren!" James responded warmly, holding his hand out. "You look surprised to find me here!"

"Yes, I was surprised when I learned of it," Joseph replied with a weak smile. Desperate to escape the sun, he chose not to face his friend but instead sat on the ground alongside James.

"I do not see why you were surprised! Well, I suppose when one considers my madness."

As his words drifted off, Joseph lifted his weary arm and placed a hand on James' shoulder in a gesture of friendship and comfort.

"My thoughts are very clear right now, Doctor," he continued. "I am here for the very reason you are here. Because it was our words, our convictions, our deep desire for liberty that helped open the eyes and hearts of these," he said, gesturing toward the men in the redoubt.

For a brief moment, Joseph's mind wandered as he reflected on the arguments of this man who had roused him to action ten years earlier. Though it was his intention to insist that James Otis leave the redoubt and be escorted to the safety of Cambridge, he found he could not do so. James needed to be there every bit as much as he did.

Joseph removed his tricorn and tilted his head back, resting it against the earthen wall. Vacantly staring at the activity in the redoubt he said, "So often after our meetings in the Long Room, I would lie upon my bed in the stillness of the night and reflect on the words that had been spoken and put down on paper. I would shudder to consider the path we were taking. How will future generations view this bleak period in the history of Great Britain? How will history paint us? I wonder still," he paused for a moment. "If we are victorious in our bloody struggle for the return of our freedom, then we will be praised for generations to come. But if we fail, we shall be a reproach throughout the world. We will be looked upon with scorn. Few remember for long the reasons why men rise up against tyranny if in the end they are defeated."

"Then we cannot allow them to defeat us, my friend!" James said as he patted Joseph's leg. A youthful glow suddenly illuminated the older man's face.

Joseph turned his head to look at James Otis.

"No, Mr. Otis, we cannot allow them to defeat us. And your presence is an inspiration, sir. The British once tried to crush you. Yet, here you are, willing to risk your life for the truths you made us aware of so long ago. They are trying to stop us here today, but they will not succeed. Our cause is just!"

"General Warren!" a man called out. "An old man has collapsed over here!"

Joseph reached for his medical bag and said, "I will talk to you later, Mr. Otis. In Cambridge."

"I shall look forward to that meeting, Doctor." James stated, patting Joseph on the back as he leaned forward to stand.

After treating the elderly man for heat exhaustion as best he could, Joseph had him escorted off the hill.

Exhausted, he returned to where he had left his borrowed musket and sat his weary body on the ground, hoping to rest for a few minutes. Again removing his hat, he placed it on the dirt floor next to him and wiped the perspiration from his brow with the sleeve of his coat. He rested his arms upon his bent knees and slowly lowered his forehead to his arms, closing his eyes.

The sounds around him seemed to intensify. The cannonballs continued to whistle through the air, plummeting with a loud thud against the outer walls of the redoubt. The charred timber crashed as flames leveled the old town below. The chants and mocking from those assembled on the rooftops of Boston carried across the river's surface and up the bloodied hillside.

The moans from the dying British soldiers grew louder and louder still. Joseph longed to go to them and provide relief from their suffering, but such an attempt would be suicidal. He was forced to abandon them to a slow, agonizing death under the blazing sun. Their desperate cries for help began to haunt him.

The odor of death hung in the air. The putrid smell of torn flesh, perforated bowel, and copious amounts of blood exposed to the summer heat mingled with that of gunpowder, charred timber, and the smoke from Charlestown drifted over Breed's Hill upon the faint sea breeze.

The back of his throat ached from the dry, sooty air. His mouth tasted of dirt. I want a drink, he thought. A cup of cool water, and there's not a drop in the fort!

The fort. His mind hung on the word as it drifted off to another time. He was suddenly transported to a wintry scene in which the brisk, fresh air felt good against his hot, red cheeks. All three of his brother's were there—Eben, Samuel, and little Jack. And Elizabeth. Oh, Elizabeth, you are covered with snow, darling! The fort—the fort—Jack, Elizabeth. I must defend the fort against Eben and Samuel's frigid attack!

"It isn't fair that they should aim the snowballs at a woman!" little Jack exclaimed in Elizabeth's defense.

"Samuel! Eben! Stop hitting my wife!" Joseph called out.

"All is fair in war!" Eben hollered back, throwing yet another snowball in Elizabeth's direction.

Joseph looked at his wife, her cloak bespattered with snow and her countenance aglow with the excitement of the game. "He is right, you know!" Joseph said to her with a playful smile.

Suddenly Elizabeth was gone, and the delightfully cold winter fort with her. Scenes of Major Pitcairn took their place. The lead balls tearing into his flesh. His son's pathetic attempt to protect his father from further harm, then when the shooting had ceased, taking his father's wounded body into his arms and stumbling down the hill to find help. All is fair in war—.

Would to God I could die up to my knees in their blood! The words resounded in his mind again and again and again. He had meant it. With his entire being he had meant it, but his words were followed by those of Another, "Death and life are in the power of the tongue."

Jolted back to his present circumstance, Joseph considered the nightmarish reality around him. He wanted to cry for the brave Major Pitcairn, his grieving son, and for the wounded that had been left to die. The wounded—some of whom he himself had shot. Was he prepared to shoot again if another attack were to be made? Of course, he must. He must defend their liberty! The conflicting emotions were difficult to deal with, and his exhausted mind too weary to sort it out.

"I thank thee, O Lord, for sparing me to fight this day!" a feeble voice prayed aloud through a parched throat. A few yards from Joseph sat an elderly man dressed in a gray farmer's frock. He was quiet now, gazing intently into the heavens. His countenance was peaceful amidst his surroundings.

Inspired by the old man's prayer, Joseph took the small book of Psalms from his pocket and began to read, finding comfort in the words before him.

Colonel Prescott returned from conferring with both General Putnam and Colonel Stark.

"Putnam came face to face with Major Small in the last attack," Colonel Prescott related to Joseph. "Were you aware that Putnam and Small had served together against the French?"

"Yes," Joseph replied, bracing himself for the news that Major Small was dead. He was troubled by the thought that General Putnam was faced with the situation of having to act against a friend on the battlefield.

"Putnam couldn't bring himself to let the men fire upon the major," the colonel said. After a brief pause, he added, "There can be nothing more confusing or heartbreaking than civil war. Friends—even kin—stand opposed, sometimes to the very death."

Joseph appreciated the colonel's words as he tried to assure the younger man that his bewilderment under these circumstances was normal.

"I discovered what the delay is with our reinforcements," Colonel Prescott announced, obviously troubled.

Joseph looked at him questioningly.

"They're held up on Bunker Hill. At least 3,000 men armed and fresh for battle! The provisions you spoke of are there as well—fresh water for the men."

"What is holding them back, Colonel?"

"They're confused, or just plain scared. Many of our officers have failed us today, General. The men don't have enough confidence to follow them into battle, or perhaps the officers aren't even trying to lead! Putnam's gone over to urge them forward again."

Disgusted by the report, Joseph took a deep breath, coughing on the smoke that was quickly accumulating over the hill.

"Gage is determined to have us, I'm afraid," Colonel Prescott said looking through the spyglass. "He's sending reinforcements. May God have mercy on us."

"Colonel, we do not have more than 200 men left in the fort," Joseph said. "And we are low on both powder and lead."

"And if the smoke continues to drift in this direction our visibility will be great-ly reduced. If only Putnam would get those men over here," the colonel replied as he lowered the spyglass, rubbing his eyes, which were beginning to sting from the smoke. Both men gazed at one another in silence for a brief moment, aware that they must be prepared in case Putnam was not successful.

"The powder will last longer than the lead," the colonel said, handing Joseph the spyglass. After wiping the sweat off his forehead with the back of his hand, he removed his cocked hat and wig and tossed them to the ground. He then picked up a large, floppy, brown hat that sat upon the redoubt wall and placed it on his bald-ing head. "We can load the muskets with stones and nails if necessary."

"If we can manage to fire two or three volleys at close range, we may send them back again," Joseph suggested. "They do not know how undermanned we are, or that our ammunition is running out."

"There's definitely not enough ball for three volleys, maybe not even two. We'll be able to fill them with one round of lead, though. If they're not driven back by that, then they'll be over the wall fast. We're not equipped for hand-to-hand com-bat. Few have bayonets or swords. Should they get over the wall, most of the men will have only the butts of their muskets to fight with. General, I'll be forced to order a retreat."

"After the first round is spent, have those with swords and bayonets come to the front of the redoubt," Joseph suggested. "The others can position themselves in the back of the redoubt. They can load their muskets with whatever nails or stones they find and shoot the British down as they scale the wall. This should give us time for a more orderly retreat."

The colonel nodded his head in agreement.

"I will need a sword, Colonel," Joseph added.

Colonel Prescott took a firm hold of Joseph's arm. "Begging the general's pardon, sir. I would request that you go to the back of the redoubt. You'll have a better chance of a safe retreat from there."

"I will not set an example of looking out for my own safety, Colonel," Joseph calmly responded.

"It was not my intention to insinuate that you would, sir. On the contrary, the courage you've displayed today has inspired the men. But you'll be needed in council, sir."

"I appreciate your concern, Colonel, but I mean to provide the men with enough time to retreat, just as you do," Joseph replied with a ready smile and a pat on Colonel Prescott's upper arm.

"Then you mean to stay, sir?"

"To be certain."

"Mr. Curtis, find a sword for General Warren!" Colonel Prescott called out to a nearby soldier. Then, redirecting his attention to Joseph, he said, "Please, General Warren. Would you consider taking charge of the men stationed in the rear? I will command up front."

Joseph nodded. "I will take charge of the rear, Colonel."

Curtis returned with the sword and handed it to Joseph.

"They're preparing to march, General," Colonel Prescott informed Joseph as he fastened the waist belt with the scabbard upon it. "And they're leaving their backpacks behind this time, sir."

A brief council of war was held to instruct the officers within the redoubt of the shortage of ammunition and the plan for the attack should the reinforcements not arrive in time. The officers returned to their men and relayed the information carefully so each man fully understood what was expected of him. Nothing more could be done. The American colonists waited, many offering up silent prayers.

Fresh and ready to avenge their fallen comrades, the British line marched forward. Ignoring the breastwork, the sole focus of their attack appeared to be the redoubt.

With no sign of Putnam and the additional troops, Colonel Prescott ordered his men into position for the attack. The click of 200 cocking hammers resounded. In one sweeping motion the muskets were leveled upon the wall. The colonel drew his sword above his head as he waited for the perfect moment to expend the last of their lead.

No fingers trembled against the triggers now. The men within the redoubt had passed though their baptism of fire. They had driven the enemy back twice, and each was willing to oppose them again. They were ready to defend this fort until forcibly driven from the field of battle.

Sixty feet. Fifty feet. The colonel's sword remained in the air, his eyes riveted on the marching swarm of red.

Forty feet. Thirty-five feet. Still no order to fire, though the whites of their eyes were clearly visible.

Thirty feet. Twenty-five feet. The men waited, undaunted by their commander's delay—knowing—trusting his wisdom.

Twenty feet.

"Fire!" The word resounded though the redoubt as the powder from 200 muskets exploded at once, sending a mutilating volley of lead into the bodies of nearly as many men. The volley was followed by the sickening sound of screaming men—screams so loud that even the sound of the cannon was momentarily drowned out.

The British line disintegrated as the soldiers were knocked to the ground.

"Reload!" the officers within the redoubt shouted to their men. Stones and nails replaced lead balls. Quickly the barrels of the muskets rested once again upon the earthen wall.

Joseph watched as British officers struggled to bring order back to the ranks as soldiers hurriedly staggered down the hillside. Commands were given and ignored. Officers began hitting the soldiers, threatening to shoot the men themselves if they did not obey orders. Pitifully, the line was reformed, and the drum's rhythmic beat began their fateful but relentless procession up the hill.

Nineteen feet. One could see clearly the face of another.

Eighteen feet. Fear, panic, desperation! The faces along the British line all reflected the same expression.

Seventeen feet. Young faces, some mere boys.

Sixteen feet. One could almost reach out and touch them.

Fifteen feet. At this range anyone struck with a musket ball would be blown to pieces!

"Fire!"

The screaming—the horrid screaming that always followed as the nails and stones tore through flesh and shattered bone. Then breathless silence filled the redoubt as the British disappeared from sight as they fell wounded to the ground or ran, slipping on the slick, red grass. Too frightened to stand, they positioned them-selves on their hands and knees, pathetically crawling over and around corpses and wounded bodies and through puddles of blood, their uniforms quickly drenched. But would they regroup?

After observing the British through the spyglass, Colonel Prescott threw a nerv-ous glance in Joseph's direction. Joseph saw the first hint of fear in him throughout the day. He came close beside the younger man and spoke softly in his ear. "If they discover we shot nails and stones, they will regroup. And they'll be over the wall this time."

"They will not discover that until the surgeons begin removing them from the wounded," Joseph offered.

"We have slaughtered them today, General. At least a thousand casualties. A startling number of officers have been shot, the king's finest. I just saw General Howe himself being escorted to safety," the colonel said, glancing at the spyglass in his hand. "Looks like he took a ball in the leg or foot. Major Small was escorting him. He must have taken a ball himself—his arm was covered with blood. It's too steep a price for this piece of ground! A ghastly price for this foolish piece of ground!"

He took a deep breath and gazed at what remained of the confused British troops. "If they come again, and my guess is that they will. When they realize they can scale this wall, all fear will be replaced by absolute hatred."

"Colonel, it is time to bring the men forward who are armed with swords and bayonets," Joseph said.

Colonel Prescott sent two soldiers off to inform the officers of the situation and implement the plans that were discussed earlier. Turning back to Joseph, he said, "General, it is time for you to take command in the rear of the redoubt." There was uneasiness in his gray eyes. Suddenly he came to full attention and saluted Joseph. His salute was instantly returned.

The very last of the powder and a few remaining nails filled the muskets of the men who had been assigned the task of shooting the first few British soldiers that dared to scale the wall. Those with swords or bayonets were quick to come forward, each pensively contemplating the scene that was about to unfold.

The sound of the drums announced the British advance.

Silence filled the redoubt as the brave soldiers within awaited the inevitable. Not a thought was given to those things that had proved so terrifying before: the cannon's boom or the fire's devastation with its suffocating smoke, the burning sun and tormenting thirst, the aching, parched throats and stinging, bloodshot eyes, the chants from the rooftops across the river and the groans of the dying beyond the redoubt walls.

The focus now was the sound of marching feet and the sharp beat of the drum. All eyes scanned the walls—right, left, and center.

"Here they come!" Joseph shouted, spotting the black hats of the grenadiers and the tips of their bayonets glistening against the sunlight beyond the right rampart. The fifty men under his command immediately pointed their loaded muskets in the direction he indicated.

"Make this shot count!" Joseph yelled as uniformed legs in their white breeches and stockings with black gaiters and boots swung over the rampart.

Joseph's eyes remained fixed on the wall. All about him he heard the nervous muttering of the men as they waited. It seemed like an eternity of waiting.

"Extend to us your mercy, O great Jehovah!" one man uttered.

"Get over the wall! Get over the wall!" another mumbled helplessly.

"Lord Jesus, receive me into Thy Kingdom," a third prayed, preparing for what seemed inevitable.

Each man pulled the butt of his musket hard against his shoulder, ready to sight the barrel against the British cross belts the moment they came into clear view.

The first was over. A clear shot to the cross belt instantly took the soldier down. A second soldier scaled the wall, then a third. Each one met the same fate as the first. Undaunted, the British began to pour over the right wall, the American muskets rising to the challenge. Suddenly the stream of red began to flow over the left wall as well, and the Americans' powder was quickly depleted.

Right, left, and center the British poured into the redoubt. The agitated movement on the dry, dirt floor formed a thick cloud of dust that added to the density of the fire's smoke, making it difficult to identify friend from foe except in close proximity. As those in William Prescott's command took to the sword and bayonet, those in Joseph Warren's command began to use their muskets as clubs and to throw rocks, kick, and punch. Some even managed to yank guns from the enemy, turning and beating them with the weapons. They were too squeamish, even in the face of their own death, to plunge the fixed bayonets into their stunned opponents. Only Joseph held a sword, and he used it ferociously.

With a bloodcurdling cry, the British came against the colonials. The intense frustration that had built within them throughout the day now found its release. With a violent hatred and an insatiable desire for revenge of their wounded and dead, they sought their opponents.

Trampling over the corpses of fallen comrades, they sought out the colonials in a state of near madness.

"Surrender, rebels!" a British officer hollered through the clamor of steel against steel.

"No rebels here!" a colonist screamed back.

Musket stocks, rocks, sticks, and bare hands could not for long hold back the deadly skill of men expertly trained in the use of the bayonet. The seventeen-inch, three-edged blades soon found their mark as American bodies were penetrated and sliced with the merciless steel.

"Give way, men! Save yourselves!" Joseph somehow heard William Prescott's command through shouting and ghastly screams of his own men as the bayonets were skillfully thrust into abdomens and pulled downward causing intestines to spill out.

"Form a line! Shoulder to shoulder! Shoulder to shoulder before the opening!" Joseph shouted to his men. Instantly they obeyed, standing side to side in a solid line before the exit to the redoubt.

William Prescott's men emerged from the haze, darting behind the solid wall of colonists that protected their escape with no more than clubs, sticks, rocks, and fists. Prescott himself finally came through, the last to retreat.

"Pull back!" Joseph ordered the men on his left and right.

"Warren says pull back!" each man related to the men along side them.

Stunned by the ferocity and courage of this human wall, the British regulars did not realize that Prescott and his men had safely retreated and the only remaining Americans in the redoubt were slowly making their way to the exit, fighting for their lives with each backward step.

In the center of the line Joseph ordered the man to the right of him to retreat. As he obeyed, the space vacated was immediately filled as the line moved over, instinctively closing the gap as they had been doing whenever one of their own was wounded.

Joseph turned to the man on his left and gave the same order. One by one the strength of the wall was diminished; all the while they stepped backward, knowing that those few who remained in the end would have little chance, if any, to escape unharmed.

Certain that their backs would soon be against the rampart, Joseph turned to estimate its distance. Through the murky air he saw the dirt and clay, estimating it to be less than twelve feet.

"Break! Run!" Joseph yelled.

Without hesitation, the men bolted into the haze, some dropping to their hands and knees to avoid the certainty of British steel. Unable to see the exit through the smoke and dust, many frantically ran their hands along the earthen wall to find the opening, while others thought they had a better chance to escape by jumping over the wall.

With his sword flying, Joseph attempted to hold the onslaught of the enemy back, allowing his men precious seconds to make it to safety. The hardness of the redoubt wall took him by surprise as he felt himself back into it. For that split second his sword was dormant, just enough time enough a bayonet to find its mark.

As he felt the pressure of the blade's thrust into his left side, he slashed his opponent with his sword.

"O God!" Joseph screamed in agony as his attacker fell to the ground, pulling the three-edged blade with him, raggedly tearing through intestine and flesh though leaving the abdominal wall intact.

He pressed his left arm hard against the gaping wound as he ran his right hand along the wall, desperate to find the passage out. Finally happening upon it, he stumbled through, choking on the heavy dust and smoke. The consuming cough intensified his agony, forcing blood and excrement to flow from the perforated bowel. Still he forced himself to move forward away from the dust, though there was no escape from the smoke as it settled upon the hillside like a thick fog. He staggered to a rail fence, struggling to breathe. His chest ached as the smoke filled his lungs.

"He's been wounded! He's been wounded!" one provincial soldier shouted to another close by.

Joseph struggled to push himself away from the fence as he dazedly watched the two men approach, their words jumbled in his mind.

"General Warren, we'll help you off the hill, sir. Just put your arms about our shoulders, General!"

As the man went to lift Joseph's arm into the position, Joseph looked down at his abdomen.

Instinctively he placed his right hand on top of the wound, feeling for damage. Through the ribcage, through the rib cage, he thought with a groan as he made the afflictive examination. Chief viscera, left side—pancreas, stomach, intestine, internal bleeding—

"Come, General, let us help you!" the man insisted, pulling Joseph's hand away from his side.

"No!" he said firmly, aware that this wound was fatal and their attempt to save him would jeopardize their own retreat. Joseph forced himself to straighten up, despite the excruciating pain.

"Please, General, let us help you!" the plea came again.

"I am a dead man. Fight on, my brave fellows, for the salvation of your country!" The two men hesitated.

"Go now!" He shouted the command with such authority that they reluctantly started downward.

With one hand he pressed hard against the wound, and with the other he tightly grasped the sword as he stumbled down the hill.

"Warren!" the familiar voice of Major Small called from the dark cloud. The man Colonel Putnam had saved earlier now stood behind him, his own arm shattered by a musket ball. Four soldiers stood attentively at his side.

The soldiers lifted their muskets, taking careful aim at the "infamous rebel" before them. Surely, whoever killed this man would win the praise of the entire British force. A rumor was circulating that Gage himself had stated that Warren's life was equivalent to 500 ordinary colonials.

Joseph slowly turned his head to look at Major Small and his band of four. The blood continued to spill from his side, weakening him. The pain had become unbearable, and he almost welcomed the sight of the raised muskets, knowing that they would soon bring an end to his agony.

"For God's sake, Warren, surrender!" Major Small pleaded.

Joseph smiled weakly at him, faintly whispering, *"Dulce et decorum est pro patris mori—."* Turning away, he braced himself for the impact of the lead.

The pointed muskets of his men suddenly caught the major's eye. "Do not fire on him!" he yelled as he reached out with his sword to knock the muskets upward. But one went off.

As the blast of the musket sounded, Joseph's smile only broadened.

· 20 ·

Lest We Forget

JEFFRIES! JEFFRIES!"

Dr. John Jeffries heard the call but refused to leave his patient's side, even though it was the summons of a general. John had been on the battlefield throughout the night treating the wounds of the British soldiers and American prisoners who had fought the previous afternoon. It was estimated that the British suffered more than 1,000 casualties. Many of them had been killed instantly. Of those that survived, most would die of their wounds.

"Too precious a price for a blasted hill!" John murmured to the waiting attendants as he finished bandaging a soldier's leg. "Take him back to Boston," he instructed those assigned to help. Only then did he acknowledge General Howe's summons.

"How can I help you, General?" the exhausted surgeon asked.

"I have been told that you were well acquainted with Dr. Joseph Warren."

"Yes, I know him," he began cautiously, uncertain as to why his relationship with Joseph should concern Howe at this moment.

"Are you aware of any identifying marks on his body? Scars? Perhaps a birthmark? Anything like that?"

John did not answer. The general's questions confused his weary mind, and he feared what the next words might be.

"I have been told that Warren's body was buried in the trenches. I have ordered it pulled out. Never having seen the man, I have no way of knowing if it is really he. His face is said to be disfigured. I do not see how my men can be so certain!" the general exclaimed. "Well, Doctor, can you identify him?" he asked impatiently as John struggled with the impact of his words.

"Yes. I—I can," he stammered.

"Come along then," Howe ordered. He turned and headed toward the redoubt. John followed as if in a trance. As they walked, General Howe realized the doctor appeared stupefied. Howe stopped abruptly.

"How, Doctor? Tell me how you can identify the corpse?" he asked, suspecting that John's emotional state might have hindered his ability to comprehend the request he had made. Howe had many tasks before him, and he had no time to waste on this Tory surgeon's emotions over the relationship he may have had with the rebel leader.

"A portion of his left thumb is missing, and he has two ivory teeth," John heard himself speak the words.

Satisfied with the response, Howe continued on in silence.

The stench of death hung over the hill. John's stomach ached as he watched the soldiers callously dragging bodies of his fellow colonists to the shallow trenches that were to become their graves. His knees began to shake when General Howe pointed to a lifeless form lying face down on the ground before them. It was obvious to John that this body had been buried and exhumed, just as General Howe had indicated. A thick film of soil clung to the corpse. Dirt was accumulated in the folds of the clothing, and it stuck, with a poultice-like appearance, to the areas where blood had escaped: the back of the head and the left abdominal region.

"That is the one, Doctor." General Howe stated, still pointing to the corpse. John moved timorously toward the figure.

"Turn it over!" Howe shouted the order to the soldiers who stood close by.

Two uniformed men stepped alongside the body, roughly grabbing hold and violently tossing it about.

"O God, please, let it not be him!" John whispered the prayer as he dropped to his knees. Unable to bring himself to view the face, his eyes fell upon the upper torso.

"No! No!" he cried softly, realizing that the dingy, coarse, gray waistcoat was really made of a pale blue shade of fine silk with matching fringe along the hemline. John had seen it before. He had teased Mercy Scollay about it.

"Such fine fabric and tailorship for the likes of Warren?" he had said to her with a chuckle. Her beaming smile had gone undaunted. How proud she had been of this waistcoat and of Joseph's love for her.

John ran his fingers lightly along a small section of the soiled cloth. The treasured fabric. The endless hours of stitching. A bit of Mercy's heart put into each stitch of her skilled hands.

"Is it Warren?" Howe asked impatiently, forcing John to do that which he found completely impossible.

His eyes moved cautiously toward the head as he heard the sound of his own deep and sporadic breathing and felt the putrid air filling his lungs. A seizurelike tremor had taken control of his body.

He gasped when Joseph's face finally came into view. Suddenly on the verge of being sick, he turned his head away.

"Is it Warren? Is it really him?" Howe asked again, a note of excitement in his tone.

"Yes," John replied softly. The soldiers who had gathered, eagerly awaiting the doctor's verdict like a flock of circling buzzards, let out a perverted cheer. John grasped the cold, bloody hand lying next to his knees as if to comfort his lifeless friend. Overwhelmed with guilt for having refused to stand with Joseph and feeling his betrayal in giving the British cause to celebrate, he began to sob.

"You are quite certain of if?" Howe asked mercilessly.

John's face reflected the hatred he now felt. "I am certain of it. This is *General Warren!*" he exclaimed, emphasizing the title that the British had mocked up until yesterday's carnage. Then turning his attention back to his fallen friend, John tenderly pushed some misplaced hair back from the disfigured face.

"Well, what do you know? I did not believe it to be him. The president of their outlaw congress fighting in battle! Gage will be pleased to hear of it! Bury the scoundrel's body!" Howe commanded, then turned and walked away.

The two soldiers eagerly came forward, taking hold of the body so suddenly that John lost his balance and toppled to the ground. He watched in horror as they dragged the body back to the trenches. Struggling to his feet, John could feel his legs threatening to buckle beneath his weight. Completely drained, he stumbled to a nearby rock and dropped down upon it.

The soldiers pulled the frock coat and silk waistcoat off Joseph's body and began to rummage through the pockets like common grave robbers. John watched in disgust but could neither move nor speak to protest their crime. It was as though he were paralyzed. All he could do was watch.

"You can have the clothin'. I claim the prayer book with his signature in it. It should bring me a good amount at auction, eh?" one soldier crowed as he pulled Joseph's book of the Psalms out of his own pocket.

"What would ya have done if Howe discovered ya had that book? You'd be in a bad way holdin' back his identity like that," the other soldier remarked as he rolled the frock coat and waistcoat up, laying them at his feet.

The first soldier began to chuckle. "I told him it was Warren. He just didn't believe me. If I had told Howe about this book, why, he might have taken it himself as a memento!"

"I don't think Howe wants to remember this battle," the second soldier replied, referring to the tremendous losses the British suffered.

"Ah, but he got Warren! Did you see the way his eyes lit up when he was sure it was him?" As the soldier flipped through the pages of the small book, the note from

James Lovell informing the Committee of Safety of the oversized cannonballs fell out.

"What's this?" the second soldier asked, picking up the note. "Would ya look at this! A bloody rebel traitor left to do his dirty work in Boston! Do ya recognize the name? Lovell? It sure sounds familiar, doesn't it?"

The other soldier grabbed the note. "This rebel will be gettin' his just reward when Gage gets a hold of this!"

"And how will ya explain it to Howe when he discovers that ya found it on Warren? Ya told him the pockets were empty!"

"I'll say we overlooked it somehow. He'll be too caught up with discoverin' a spy to pay much care to it," he replied confidently. Then pulling his saber from its sheath, he said, "I have an idea. Howe said to bury the body. He made no mention of his head!"

John opened his mouth to scream. He formed the words on his lips, but no sound came. Suddenly another shouted the words he struggled for.

"No! Stop!"

The soldier froze, his saber still in mid-air. John turned to see Captain Mills, who was counted among Joseph's many British friends. He was quite obviously distraught by what the soldiers had intended.

"Bury that man with Christian decency as is due any Englishman!" the captain ordered. Then John saw him tip his hat while looking upon Joseph's body. So subtle was this gesture of respect that the other soldiers failed to see it. When the captain moved on, the soldiers lifted the body and tossed it on top of another, dressed in a gray farmer's frock. The grave was no more than three feet deep.

"What was it Captain Laurie said over the scoundrel's body the first time we buried him?" one soldier asked, a grin upon his face.

"That Warren and his seditious principles will remain in that hole!" the other soldier chuckled.

John had watched their barbaric deeds thus far. He continued to watch as the soldiers threw dirt upon his friend's body, each shovelful of soil accompanied with crude, insulting jokes.

John realized he had failed Joseph in life, but he was determined that he would not fail him in death. The rock upon which he sat would be the landmark to identify this unmarked grave. He would see to it that Joseph's family was made aware of the location. One day he would receive a decent burial attended by those who loved and respected him.

After the soldiers had filled in the grave, they moved on. John stayed, sitting on the rock and staring blankly at the mound of dirt that contained his friend's remains. Now he was free to weep and grieve. Finally.

John Jeffries wanted to be gentle in breaking the news of Joseph's death to Mercy and the children, but it was not to be. Stories of the battle reached the streets of Boston long before John was able to return.

At first Mercy refused to believe what she heard. But when she saw Joseph's book of the Psalms being auctioned off and the fine, blue waistcoat—stained with the blood of her dearest friend—she could no longer escape the dreadful truth.

Sitting down with his journal before him, Jack Warren made an entry dated June 17, 1775: This day, a day ever to be remembered by the United American Colonies, at about four o'clock in the afternoon, I was alarmed with the incessant report of cannon, which appeared to be at or near Boston. Toward sun-setting a very great fire was discovered, nearly in a direction from Salem to Boston; at the beginning of the evening, news arrived that a smart engagement had happened in the afternoon on Bunker Hill, in Charlestown, between the King's regular troops and the provincials; and, soon after, we received intelligence our own troops were repulsed with great loss, and the enemy had taken possession of the ground, which we had broke the night before. I was very anxious, as I was informed that great numbers had fallen on both sides, and that my brother was in all probability in the engagement. I, however, went home, with determination to take a few hours sleep, and then to go immediately to Cambridge with my arms. Accordingly, in the morning, at about two o'clock, I prepared myself, and went on horseback; and when I arrived at Medford, received the melancholy and distressing tidings that my brother was missing. Upon the dreadful intelligence, I went immediately to Cambridge, and inquired of almost every person I saw whether they could give me any information of him. Some told me that he was undoubtedly alive and well, others that he was wounded, and others that he fell on the field. Thus perplexed almost to distraction, I went on, inquiring with a solicitude which was such a mixture of hope and fear as none but such as have felt it can form any conception. In this manner I passed several days, every day's information diminishing the probability of his safety.

After three days of searching with no progress, in an act of desperation Jack set off on foot toward Boston. As he approached the guard post set up on the road leading into Boston, he tightened his grasp on the handle of his medical bag. He hoped to gain entrance under the guise of needing to treat a patient.

A number of sentries stood guard. All but one were occupied with civilians, some wanting to pass into the countryside on business and others, like Jack, wanting access to the town.

Jack walked up to the sentry who was unoccupied at the moment. He was a big man, intimidating both in his size and his hard, cold expression.

"State your business!" was the icy command.

"I am a physician," Jack replied timidly, holding up his bag in plain view. "My services are needed."

"Your name!" he barked.

"Warren, Dr. John Warren." As soon as he uttered the words, Jack realized his mistake. Had he not been so exhausted he would have used the name of William Eustis or David Townsend. Any name but Warren!

The sentry held Jack under a steely gaze. He began to cackle, thoroughly amused by Jack's revelation.

"Warren?" His tone made the name sound vulgar. "You're not wanted in Boston, rebel. And if you insist, I'll escort ya away in shackles!"

For a moment Jack was speechless. He could not leave without any information on Joseph, but did he dare to question this man?

"I am trying to locate my brother," he began softly, his voice filled with great emotion. "Please, do you know if he was taken prisoner?"

The soldier briefly considered the question put to him. As he saw it, he had two choices of how to answer. He could cruelly describe in intricate detail the fate of his brother, or he could refuse to answer altogether and intensify his agony of not knowing his brother's fate. He chose the latter. In reply to Jack's question, he offered only a vicious laugh.

Stunned by this callous reaction and quite certain the soldier knew where Joseph was, Jack began to plead. "Please, please tell me what has become of my brother!" Then grabbing the soldier's arm, he cried out, "For mercy's sake, please help me find him!"

Mistaking the physical contact for an act of violence, the soldier drew his saber from its sheath and brought it down hard along the left side of Jack's face.

The force of the blow caused him to stumble back. In a state of shock, he remained motionless for a moment, not yet aware of the gash upon his face. Slowly turning, Jack staggered in the direction he had come.

"Dr. Warren!" a young man called from the other side of the guard post.

Jack did not hear him.

The man walked past the guard and followed Jack. "Dr. Warren!" he shouted.

Still there was no response from the injured physician as the blood ran freely upon his frock coat and between the layers of clothing around his neck.

The younger man ran alongside him, placing his hand on Jack's shoulder. "John, are you all right? Please let me have a look at that laceration."

In a daze Jack turned toward the man. He recognized him: Adam Hill, a second-year apprentice of John Jeffries.

Adam guided Jack to a shaded area under a large maple tree on the side of the road and urged him to sit down. Suddenly Jack felt the burning sensation along his jawline as Adam pressed against it firmly with his own clean handkerchief.

"It will need suturing. You had better have it tended to as soon as possible," Adam suggested once he got the bleeding to stop.

Jack attempted to stand but found the task quite difficult. His legs were too weak to support his weight.

"You should rest for a few minutes, Doctor. I will sit with you."

Jack nodded and tried to smile to show his appreciation as he continued to hold the handkerchief against the gaping wound.

Aware that he possessed the information Jack sought, the apprentice considered how he should relate the devastating news. He wondered if Jack could handle any more emotional strain. Yet he could not in good conscience send the man off to continue this mournful search.

"I overheard you questioning the sentry," Adam began cautiously.

Jack made no response.

"I know what has become of your brother, John."

Jack looked at Adam, his countenance seeming to come to life again with a flicker of hope in his dark eyes.

"I am sorry, Doctor. I wish I could tell you he was in Boston," he paused.

Jack drew a deep breath and held it, preparing himself for the blow that he knew would be far more damaging than that of the sentry's saber.

"Your brother was killed on Breed's Hill. Dr. Jeffries identified his body for General Howe."

"Did he suffer?" Jack asked quietly, his eyes fixed on the ground.

"Dr. Jeffries thinks his death came quickly," the younger man responded, praying that Jack would not ask for any details.

With his face buried in his hands, Jack remained silent as he fought off the pent up grief that desperately needed to find its release.

When he finally lifted his head, his eyes were moist with tears. "What have they done with my brother's body?"

"They buried him on the hill."

The rapid increase in Jack's breathing revealed to the struggle within. That the enemy had buried Joseph in an unmarked grave—no doubt with great mockery—was more than Jack could endure.

"Dr. Jeffries witnessed the burial," Adam quickly offered, hoping to ease Jack's anguish. "He intends to show me the site before he leaves."

"Leaves?" Jack was confused.

"He is sailing to England within the week. He is troubled by what happened the other day, and he is deeply grieved by your brother's death. He wants to go before more blood is shed. I will bring you to the grave when the time is right."

"Why wait?" Jack asked with a sense of urgency. "You must bring John Scollay there! Mr. Scollay will see to it that Joseph receives a decent burial."

"No. Not yet!" Adam's firm response took Jack by surprise. "Let him rest in the unmarked grave for now. Give the British time to recover from the battle. They are greatly embittered toward the colonial forces, your brother in particular! They will desecrate his grave if you bring him into Boston."

Forced to trust that Adam would hold true to his word, Jack went back to Roxbury, insisting that he could make the trip alone. He needed time to grieve before facing his mother and brothers.

Within two weeks of the Battle of Bunker Hill, the commanding general whose appointment Joseph had strongly suggested arrived in Cambridge. The man chosen by the Continental Congress for this difficult position had also been Joseph's choice: Virginia's renowned hero, George Washington.

The summer and autumn passed with little event. The winter months wore on in the traditional stage of military dormancy. But the anticipation of spring activity sent General Washington and his newly named Continental Army into motion.

Purposely choosing the sixth anniversary of the Boston Massacre to make his move, General Washington strategically placed the cannon acquired from Fort Ticonderoga on a hilly section south of Boston known as Dorchester Heights. By morning's light, the barrels of the acquired British cannon looked down upon the occupied town of Boston.

Attempts by the British ships to engage the colonists in battle attempts failed as a fierce storm blew in over the ocean. What they had hoped to accomplish with the occupation of Breed's Hill had occurred on Dorchester Heights. The Continental Army now occupied a strong, strategic position. Twelve days later, the British troops and many Tory sympathizers loaded onto the British men-of-war and set sail from Boston's harbor.

Within a few hours of the British evacuation, those who had been forbidden to enter Boston for almost a year were able to return to their homes. They found the damage to standing buildings to be substantial. Many old houses had been torn down and used as firewood after the supply of trees and abandoned furniture had been depleted. Military supplies left behind had been destroyed and the medicinals poisoned.

Jack Warren went directly to the home of the Scollays to be reunited with his brother's orphaned children. From there he went to Breed's Hill, as he recorded in his journal.

> March 21, 1776: The hill which was the theater upon which the bloody tragedy of the 17th of June was acted commands the most affecting view I ever saw in my life. The walls of magnificent buildings, tottering to the earth, below; above, a great number of rude hillocks, under which are deposited the remains of clusters of those deathless heroes who fell in the field of battle. The scene was inexpressibly solemn. When I considered myself as walking over the bones of many of my worthy fellow-countrymen, who jeopardized and sacrificed their lives in those high places—when I considered that perhaps, whilst I was musing over the objects around me, I might be standing over the remains of my dear brother, whose blood has stained these hallowed walks—with veneration did this inspire me. How many endearing scenes of fraternal friendship, now past and gone forever, presented themselves to my view! But it is enough; the blood of the innocent calls for vengeance on the guilty heads of the assassins. O, may our arms be strengthened to fight the battles of our God!

With the evacuation of the British, the Continental Army prepared to relocate to the colony of New York. Mary Warren knew that many more changes were about to occur within her family. Both Eben and Jack served under General Washington. The thought of their leaving only added to her grief over Joseph's death.

Upon entering the old farmhouse, Jack was pleased to find not only his mother and Samuel, but Eben as well. "Good day, Mother," Jack said with all the cheerfulness he could muster. A solemn dreariness seemed to hang over the house, reflecting the innermost feelings of those who stood within its walls. He went straight to where his mother sat at the kitchen table and bent to kiss her cheek.

"Sam, Eben," he acknowledged the presence of his older brothers who sat at the table with their mother. "Eben, we will not be traveling with the main army to New York. After I explained to General Washington our need to see that Joseph has a decent burial, he has given permission for us to remain two weeks longer." He pulled out an empty chair next to Sam and sat down.

"I have spoken to Adam Hill. He has agreed to take me to the burial site next week. Paul Revere has also offered to help. Will either of you be able to come with us?" Jack asked hesitantly. It would be a gruesome task to dig up the remains of one's dear brother. In no way did he want to make Sam or Eben feel that they must be present, although he truly desired their support. Both men were silent, horrified by the thought of this undertaking. Jack fixed his gaze upon Sam.

"I can't, Jack! I'm sorry, but I just don't think I could be there!" Sam cried, burying his head in his hands. He saw his fear as shameful, and with deep sobs he lamented his shame.

"It is all right, Sam. I understand." Jack said tenderly as he reached over and gently stroked his brother's back.

"I'll go with you," Eben offered with a trembling voice.

Mary Warren wept silently as she watched her three remaining sons.

"I heard that Josiah Quincy's family brought his remains down from Gloucester yesterday. We will bring Joseph home, too!" Jack said with a forced smile.

"But what about a grave site? We don't have enough money to purchase one!" his mother pointed out.

"Judge Minot of Boston has offered the temporary use of his tomb. I thought it better to move Joseph to a temporary resting place than to leave him on Breed's Hill." Jack knew they would agree.

"Mother, did I tell you about General Washington's reaction when he visited the sight of the battle?" Jack asked. Mary only shook her head, completely unable to respond verbally.

"Some of the officers who had fought with Joseph that day told of his courage. The general was deeply touched by their accounts. With tears in his eyes, he stated to those about him that we lost our commander in chief that day. I think Joseph would have been honored to know that General Washington considered him thus."

The April wind drove the cold, drizzly rain hard against the Warren brothers and Dr. Adam Hill as they stood a short distance from the open trench.

"Last night's storm has made a mess of things," Adam Hill commented, pulling up the collar of his greatcoat against the brisk wind. He watched the three men within the trench struggle with the heavy-laden shovels as they lifted the mud out.

The Warren brothers failed to respond. Eben paced nervously, refusing to look in the direction of the shallow grave while Jack kept a constant vigil on the activity, inching his way closer and closer despite his brother's gentle protests.

"It should not be much longer. I am quite positive that this is the spot Dr. Jeffries said to search," Adam stated, gesturing to the rock that was to serve as the landmark.

"How many did Jeffries say were buried here?" Paul Revere shouted from the trench, pausing only long enough to wipe some mud from his brow with an equally muddy coat sleeve.

"Dr. Jeffries said that there is at least one other, a farmer in a gray frock. But there may be more. He was not certain," Adam called back.

"Will we recognize him?" Eben asked, agonizing over the thought.

"Surely his body is decayed beyond all recognition," Adam stated.

One of the men in the trench turned to Paul Revere, quietly asking the ominous question. "How are we to identify the corpse, then?"

With a deep sigh Paul began to dig faster, seeming to ignore his words.

"Mr. Revere," the man spoke again. "How are we to identify the corpse?"

Paul stopped digging and fixed his gaze on the man, his dark eyes clearly reflecting the anguish within. "I set two ivory teeth in his mouth only a year—only a year ago," he paused, his face somewhat contorted as he fought to regain his composure. "I can identify my friend. I will identify my friend."

As Paul returned to the gruesome task, he caught a glimpse of the upward movement of the shovel beside him. A piece of tattered, gray material lay entwined on the shovel's blade. Its appearance caused all activity within the pit to cease.

"Have you found something?"

"What have you found?" the brothers asked in unison.

"Jack," Paul called out tenderly, as he detected the odor of decaying flesh exposed by the last shovelful of dirt. "Maybe you and Eben should wait for us beside the boat. We can manage. There's no need for you to stay."

"No, Mr. Revere. I cannot go. I have to be certain it is Joseph," Jack protested.

"I'll make certain. You know I won't stop until he's found," Paul assured him.

Jack did not respond.

"Perhaps we should do as Mr. Revere suggested, Jack," Eben said. Stepping close beside his brother, he placed his hand on Jack's shoulder. "Please, Jack. Joseph would want us to remember him as he was!"

Still Jack offered no response. In a trancelike state, he kept his eyes upon the open grave.

"Jack! I can't bear to see him like this, and neither can you!"

Startled from the trance by his brother's outburst, Jack finally turned his gaze toward him. Without a word, he placed his arm about Eben's shoulders and walked toward the shore. Yet even as they walked, Jack could not help but look back. Halfway down the hill he stopped abruptly and turned.

"Have you found him?" he called back to the men.

"No!" Paul replied, his voice shaking. "No, it's not Joseph."

Jack remained in that spot, nervously rubbing the scar along the jawbone on the left side of his face. He apparently had forgotten that they were headed for the shore, as his attention was again drawn to the activity of the men. Eben took hold of his brother's coat sleeve.

"Mr. Revere, might this be him?"

Paul looked at the form that was surfacing beneath the shovel of the man standing beside him. "Could be. Keep digging," he said, noting what appeared to be blond hair. He felt his body tremble as he watched the others work to uncover the mass of corruption. The odor was almost unbearable, and the three men found themselves taking short, quick breaths in an attempt to avoid the gagging stench.

Carefully lifting the corpse from the shallow grave, the men gently laid it upon the muddy ground.

"Mr. Revere?" Jack called, anxious for his report. "Mr. Revere, is it Joseph?"

Paul heard Jack's question, but he did not want to answer until he was certain. He squatted next to the decaying form, gagging. His chest and neck muscles were tight as he placed his gloved hands on the decomposed jaw to make his examination. The ivory teeth were there, still fastened in place by Paul's own silver wire.

He closed his eyes, forcing himself to remember the clean, fresh face of his dear friend, his warm and ready smile. "We're here to take you home, Joseph," Paul whispered, his hands still grasping the skull.

"Mr. Revere," the pathetic cry came again. "Please, sir. Is it my brother?"

"Yes, Doctor," Paul shouted back with a sob, his eyes still closed. "Yes, we have found General Warren."

Eben tightened his grip on Jack's coat sleeve as he felt him lurch forward. Forcefully pushing his brother's hand away, Jack ran toward the men, oblivious to the pleas from both Eben and Adam Hill for him to stop.

As the men gently lowered the corpse into the awaiting coffin, Paul saw Jack approaching. He started to call out to him, to urge him to turn back, but it was too late. Jack fell to his knees beside the open coffin.

"No—No! What have they done to him?" he cried out, horrified by the mass of corruption within. So excruciating was his grief that Jack toppled to the ground in a state of unconsciousness.

The thick clouds and cold air threatened New England with the first snowfall of the season.

"Much too early for snow," Jack complained to himself as he pulled up the collar of his greatcoat.

He ascended the granite stairs that led into the Granary Cemetery. It was a well-worn path that led to Joseph's tomb.

Jack's visits here were regular. Somehow it helped him to come to this place. When others were present, his stay was short. On those occasions, he would simply clear the tomb and surrounding area of fallen leaves or weeds. And when flowers were in bloom, he would tend to them.

When he was alone, he would linger, freely sharing any news that would have been of interest to his brother. It seemed natural to Jack to do this. Though he believed that Joseph—in his eternal home—was already aware of all that was occurring, he felt a need to continue the fraternal bond they once shared.

Jack placed his medical bag on the ground next to him and pushed the leaves off the granite tomb.

"I know it is not my usual time to come by, but we just received the news from Yorktown!" he said, trying to sound enthusiastic. "The British have surrendered to General Washington! The war is all but over. General Washington will return with his troops to New York, and General Greene will remain with his troops in the Deep South until the last of the enemy has evacuated."

Jack paused, looking into the cloud-filled sky. "I should be ecstatic! All of Boston—all of America is rejoicing!"

He turned his gaze back toward the tomb. "John Hancock is planning a gala event to celebrate—in the usual Hancock style," he said with a rather somber chuckle. "There certainly is cause for celebration. By the grace of God, we have won our liberty and with it our independence, but I lost you!" Jack took a deep breath as he fought back his tears. "The price—oh, Joseph, the price was so high!"

Jack became silent as he sought to regain his composure.

"'Greater love hath no man than this, that a man lay down his life for his friends.' But will future generations realize that you willingly laid down your life for them? Those who are to reap what you have sacrificially sown, will they even care?

"There will be great celebration over our glorious victory, but I will not let them forget the steep price that was paid. The stately tree of liberty has flourished, for its roots have been watered with the blood of America's noblest sons.

"Dear God!" he cried out, lifting his eyes to heaven. His tears ran freely. "Do not let them forget. Please, please do not let them forget! And, my Lord," he bowed his head and closed his eyes, "let Joseph know how very proud I am to be his brother, and—and would you tell him that I love him?"

Afterword

Mercy Scollay insisted on caring for the children of her "dear friend." It was a daily struggle to make ends meet during this turbulent time. The estate of General Warren was completely depleted. He had put his heart and soul—his very life—into the fight for liberty and his money as well.

Mercy gratefully accepted the generous contributions of family members and friends such as John Hancock, Benedict Arnold, and the men at St. Andrew's Masonic Lodge. Sam Adams, aware of this financial burden, attempted on numerous occasions to persuade the Continental Congress to provide financially for the children of his martyred friend.

Mercy never married.

Jack Warren remained with the Continental Army. At first he insisted upon being allowed to fight in the ranks to avenge his brother, but he was later persuaded to remain in the medical corps. He proved to be a remarkable young surgeon, well ahead of his time. This seemed to have been something of a threat to his older colleagues, causing some friction between them. Therefore, when word arrived that a chief surgeon was needed at the army hospital that remained in Boston, Jack applied for the position. This would give him the opportunity to continue serving in the army, to still be with his family, and to be able to oversee the care of his nieces and nephews.

Jack's return to Boston also gave him the opportunity to pursue a more serious relationship with the Quaker girl he had met prior to leaving. Abigail Collins, whose father would be elected governor of Rhode Island, had come to Boston shortly after the outbreak of the war. Before long, she and Jack were preparing for marriage.

Shortly after Jack's marriage to Abigail, a small package was delivered to him from a minister in England. In it was the antique book of the Psalms that Joseph had taken with him into the battle. The page that had born his signature had been torn out. This minister had somehow come into possession of the treasured book and understood the meaning it would have to the family of its rightful owner.

By 1780 Jack and Abigail had Joseph's children living with them. Perhaps Mercy took ill, or perhaps Jack insisted on rearing the children now that he was in a position to do so. Whatever the reason, the young couple took this responsibility upon themselves, rearing their own children, which began to arrive annually, along with those of Joseph and Elizabeth. News from the Continental Congress in 1780 that it would aid in the support of the orphaned children was no doubt received with a grateful heart. Sam Adams's diligence had finally been rewarded!

Jack served at the army hospital for the duration of the war, returning to private practice thereafter. His fascination with human anatomy, which brought him some fame when he became the first known American surgeon to successfully amputate a man's arm at the shoulder, coupled with the fact that he loved to teach, led him to become one of the founders of Harvard Medical School. Dr. John Warren was the school's first professor of anatomy and surgery. He was also the founder of the Massachusetts Medical Society.

Dr. Edward Warren, the son of Jack, related in the biography of his father that he suffered from many bouts with depression throughout his life due to the tragic circumstances surrounding the deaths of his father and brother Joseph. As the eighteenth century passed into history and the nineteenth began, Edward Warren tells that his father was "almost out of love with life."

Dr. John and Abigail Warren not only reared the four children of his beloved brother, but they had nineteen of their own. Two of their sons became physicians. The eldest, Dr. John Collins Warren, became the founder of the Massachusetts General Hospital. His son, Jack's grandson, became the first physician in the United States to use anesthesia.

The tradition of physicians in the Warren line is said to have continued from generation to generation. Dr. Carolyn Matthews, sixth generation descendant of Joseph and Elizabeth, practices oncology today in the state of Texas. Her father, the late Church Matthews, was a brigadier general in the United States Army.

Betsey and **Polly Warren** matured into beautiful, accomplished young ladies. Having many suitors, under the watchful eye of their uncle Jack, the girls carefully picked their lifetime partners from among their admirers. Betsey married an army officer who would, in time, become a general. Polly married a physician.

Josey and **Dick Warren** attended Harvard College, but they did not follow in the profession of their father and uncle. Neither of the boys married. Falling victim to a sudden illness—first Josey, then Dick—the young men died despite their uncle's desperate attempts to save them.

Mary and **Samuel Warren** remained on the farm. Mary enjoyed the company of her sons and their families. She had thirty-three grandchildren, and her reputation for Christian virtue and charity was well known throughout the community. Annually she devoted herself to prayer and fasting on the anniversary of her eldest son's death. Her son Samuel, with whom she lived, enjoyed a quiet life on the farm and never married. So severe was Samuel's shyness that he could not even bring himself to eat at the homes of his brothers but insisted on taking his meals outside while the other dined inside.

Eben Warren and his wife, Betsy, raised a family of ten children on their farm in Foxborough, Massachusetts. He served as a selectman for that town, as well as a member of the General Court and of the State convention that ratified the United States Constitution. He eventually became a judge in Norfolk County.

During the winter of 1815, Eben had an accident that caused him to dislocate his shoulder. Because Jack was recovering from being ill, Eben called in a local physician.

Though many attempts were made to repair the shoulder, it could not be accomplished. When Jack learned of his brother's distress, he immediately went to him. Jack worked on Eben's shoulder throughout the night, finally successfully replacing it by morning light. After returning home, he became ill again. Two days later, thirty-four years to the day that he removed his brother's body from Breed's Hill, Jack Warren passed away.

Paul Revere's intimate friendship with Joseph Warren was further revealed upon the birth of Paul's eleventh child, Joseph Warren Revere, in 1777.

Paul lived a long and productive life. His desire to learn new things and seemingly fearless attempts to explore new job opportunities should be a source of inspiration to all. His service to his country went beyond his "midnight ride"—well into the eighth decade of his life.

Samuel Adams's relationship with Joseph Warren was described by Sam's biographer and great-grandson, William Wells, in *The Life and Public Services of Samuel Adams*: "The dearest friend he ever had was Dr. Warren, and the void created in his heart by the death of that brilliant young patriot was probably at no time completely filled. He did not forget the very great services rendered by this partner and special confidant. In all his plans prior to 1775, and, in his reminiscences of the Revolution in his old age, he recurred oftenest and the most affectionately to the name of Joseph Warren.

"From 1768, they had sustained each other through all the great movements in Boston, always in consultation, and acting in such harmony that the suggestions of one were often but the counterpart of the other's mind. The bond of friendship and unreserved confidence was perfect between them, despite the difference in age."

Sam's concern for the orphans of his friend was evident not only in his persistence with Congress to aid in their support, but also by the personal attention he gave to the children when in Boston. In a letter to Elbridge Gerry, Sam shared his concern for their health, education, and future.

Samuel Adams—Father of Independence—remained a delegate to the Continental Congress. His fiery spirit and genuine concern for the people made him a highly respected statesman.

Upon returning to Boston after the British evacuation, Sam and Betsy Adams discovered that the British had destroyed their newly furbished home. Destitute, Sam was forced to seek financial assistance.

Once the war had ended, unfortunately, so did the "usefulness" of this great patriot as far as many fellow citizens were concerned. Content in their newfound security, many men refused to heed the warnings of the once illustrious patriot leader. Though he was not elected to represent Massachusetts at the Constitutional Convention, he spoke out boldly against the proceedings.

He opposed the drafting of the original constitution vehemently from an antifederalist position. He refused to support any constitution without the rights of the people clearly laid out.

As a result of his public opposition to the original constitution and that of other prominent patriot leaders such as Elbridge Gerry and Patrick Henry, the Bill of Rights was drafted and added to the Constitution.

Though Sam Adams and John Hancock continued in their ambivalence, as witnessed again in their opposing views on the Constitution, they managed to serve together again as lieutenant governor and governor respectively. Upon the death of Governor Hancock, Sam greatly lamented the loss of this old and dear friend. He then replaced Hancock as governor of Massachusetts.

Upon Sam's death, he was buried in the Granary Cemetery with his friends: Warren, Otis, and Hancock. Humorously enough, his gravesite is almost as far as possible from that of John Hancock's, almost as if to tell us that even in death they were more comfortable with some distance between them.

John Hancock's name is widely recognized due to the courage he displayed in putting his bold signature upon the Declaration of Independence.

Mr. Hancock did a great service to the newly forming United States of America as president of the Continental Congress. He continued in this position until poor health forced him to resign. Returning to Boston to recuperate, he soon became personally involved in the affairs of his home state and was elected as the first governor to the state of Massachusetts.

He supported the drafting of the original constitution from a federalist position and as governor worked toward its ratification.

James Otis, who is referred to as "The Father of the Revolution," came off Breed's Hill unharmed. He never fully recovered from his mental breakdown. The remainder of his years was spent in the care of family members, including his sister, Mercy Otis Warren, who left us a detailed written account of this period of America's history. Her husband was the active patriot leader James Warren, no relation to Joseph Warren.

The death of James Otis was dramatic and somehow fitting: while leaning against a wooden post within a house, the aging patriot was hit by a bolt of lightning. He was buried in the Granary Cemetery in Boston alongside many fellow Sons of Liberty. Strangely enough, the roots of a large tree disrupted his grave some years later. When the remains were removed for reburial, it was discovered that the roots of this tree had twined around the skull of Mr. Otis.

Elbridge Gerry became a delegate to the Continental Congress and thus one of the signers of the Declaration of Independence. He was also chosen to attend the Congress in Philadelphia that became the Constitutional Convention. While there, he frequently verbalized his opposition to the proceedings of the convention. He was determined, as was his friend Sam Adams, that the rights of the people be clearly protected.

Mr. Gerry was appointed as the United States Minister to France under the administration of President John Adams. He also served as governor of Massachusetts and, finally, as vice president of the United States under President James Madison.

Dr. William Eustis served as a surgeon in the Continental Army until the close of the war. Returning to Boston, he was finally able to establish a private practice and became a prominent physician.

In 1785 Dr. Eustis decided to devote his life to public service. He served as United States minister to the Netherlands, governor of Massachusetts, and Secretary of War.

John Adams's record as a statesman is well documented. His reluctance to become involved during the early years of turmoil prior to the war can be viewed with a small sense of amusement now.

He served as a delegate to the Continental Congress and drafted the Massachusetts State Constitution. Thereafter, he became the United States minister to France and the first United States minister to Great Britain. In this office he stood before King George III, no longer as his subject but as the representative of a free nation by its own right.

John Adams became the first vice president of the United States under President Washington and the second president of the United States.

John Quincy Adams never forgot his last encounter with Dr. Warren, for he had saved the boy's finger. But John Quincy's gratitude could not be expressed to this man who was to die the following day. Throughout his life, John Quincy Adams reminisced on this, expressing his great respect for the beloved family physician, Dr. Joseph Warren. To this day, Dr. Warren's portrait hangs in the parlor of the Old House, also known as Peacefield, which is part of the Adams Historical National Park in Quincy, Massachusetts.

John Quincy Adams's life was devoted to public service. He was a United States ambassador to Holland, Prussia, and Russia; United States senator; member of the United States delegation to negotiate the Treaty of Ghent; secretary of state; sixth president of the United States; and, finally, a member of the United States House of Representatives. He remained in this office for seventeen years, considering them to be the best years of his public service.

Abigail Quincy, wife of Josiah Quincy, went to live with her parents shortly after her husband's death. Abigail never remarried. Family tradition tells us that upon receiving news of Josiah's death and only recently having buried her infant daughter, Abigail understandably feared for the life of her young son, Josiah III. She immediately began the daily ritual of dunking the boy in cold water early each morning, a treatment believed to preserve one's health.

Josiah Quincy III was only three years old at the time of his father's death, yet he esteemed the elder Josiah's memory throughout his life. He treasured the stories related of his father's patriotic fervor and his father's personal letters, journals, and various documents, editing his father's journals for publication. Though only thirty-one at the time of his death, Josiah Quincy Jr. left an indelible mark in Massachusetts law. Even today his skill as an attorney is highly regarded in the legal profession, which is reflected in the recent publication of his works, *Portrait of a Patriot: The Major Political and Legal Papers of Josiah Quincy Junior* (edited by Daniel R. CoQuillette and Neil Longley York, The Colonial Society of Massachusetts).

Young Josiah became the concern not only of his mother, but of both sets of grandparents and that of John Adams as well. The Adams's took a personal interest in the boy's welfare and education. Josiah Quincy III and John Quincy Adams, who were second cousins through Abigail Adams' grandfather, John Quincy, would remain intimate friends throughout their extremely long and productive lives and were often seen together during their closing years. Josiah III was elected to the Massachusetts state legislature and the U.S. House of Representatives. He served as mayor of Boston and accepted the presidency of Harvard College at a time when Harvard's future was questionable. His leadership saved Harvard from closing its doors forever.

Samuel Quincy boarded a British war ship upon the evacuation of Boston. He left his native country to return no more. His wife and children remained behind for a period of time, for she was sympathetic to the plight of her countrymen. Samuel held a prominent position in the British government throughout his life.

Dr. John Jeffries remained in England for the duration of the war, continuing his medical studies. In 1785, he and French aeronaut Jean Pierre Blanchard made the first hot air balloon crossing of the English Channel. Dr. Jeffries conducted various experiments during this flight in study of upper-air composition. Dr. Jeffries returned to Boston in 1790, reestablishing a successful medical practice.

Margaret Kemble Gage was born and reared in New Brunswick, New Jersey. After marrying British General Thomas Gage, she found her loyalties to be divided. Though no evidence exists that she informed Joseph Warren of her husband's plans the night of April 18, 1775, circumstantial evidence points to her indiscretion. Joseph shared the identity of his informant with no one; and he took his secret with him to his grave. Following the Battles of Lexington and Concord, Margaret Gage was sent to Britain aboard the *Charming Nancy*. She and General Gage remained estranged, and their relationship was never reconciled.

Dr. Benjamin Church was appointed chief surgeon of the medical department upon the arrival of General Washington to Massachusetts. Church served in this capacity until he was caught attempting to pass a coded message to the enemy. He was tried for treason and found guilty. History has since revealed that he had been an informant for many years prior to the outbreak of the war.

Samuel Whittemore, at the age of eighty, went out to meet the militia on Medford Road on April 19, 1775, equipped with his own private arsenal. After bringing down three British soldiers, he suffered thirteen bayonet wounds to his body and a gunshot wound to his face. Sam lived to be almost one hundred years old, and he insisted throughout his life that had he that day to live again, he would not hesitate to do exactly what he had done.

James Lovell was a young schoolmaster in Boston and a spy for the Committee of Safety. A colonel in the British artillery took an interest in James's sister and began to court her. This relationship provided the opportunity for James's brother, Benjamin, to serve as a clerk in the artillery office. Most likely James persuaded Benjamin to sabotage the British artillery by substituting the oversized cannon balls for the battle that was to be fought on Breed's Hill.

Upon finding the letter in Joseph Warren's pocket, the British arrested James Lovell as a spy. Benjamin was dismissed as clerk but not arrested. After spending much time in prison, his health severely taxed, James had great difficulty forgiving Joseph Warren for carrying the letter to the hill.

Though in time many of his old friends were to join him in the Granary Cemetery, Joseph Warren was not to remain there long. Since his body had been placed in a borrowed tomb and apparently was not properly marked to indicate its exact location, the spot of General Warren was forgotten for a while. However, his remains were eventually found and identified by his nephew, who then had them moved to a nearby church cemetery where his father, Jack, had also been buried. And so the brothers were together again.

This was the fifth burial of General Warren's remains, for it is said that he was buried as many as three times within hours of the battle. After his initial interment by the burial detail, he was removed for General Howe's viewing. Later, British General Burgoyne ordered the body exhumed to satisfy his own curiosity.

The remains were left undisturbed in the cemetery of St. Paul's Episcopal Church for thirty years. Then, as Boston expanded, a cry for more land to build upon was heard. The cemetery was to be used for this purpose.

When the remains of the Warren deceased were moved from the family plot for burial in a cemetery in Roxbury, the town of their birth, Joseph's remains were retained for examination.

Some were determined to see for themselves that the corpse that had been removed from Breed's Hill almost eighty years earlier was indeed that of General Joseph Warren.

The ivory teeth still remained, with the silver wire of Paul Revere holding them in place. A gaping hole through the skull further confirmed the identity of the skeletal remains.

Returning the relics to the grave would seem to have been the decent thing to do. Instead, the skull reportedly was put on display for a period of time. What the British soldiers failed to accomplish in their attempt to decapitate the fallen hero, his own countrymen did instead.

Joseph Warren was again laid to rest in 1855 in the peaceful surroundings of the Forest Hill Cemetery in Roxbury, Massachusetts (now part of Boston). He remains there to this day.

> *Among the dead was Major-General Joseph Warren;*
> *Whose memory will be endeared to his countrymen,*
> *And to the worthy in every part and age of the world,*
> *As long as virtue and valor shall be esteemed among Mankind.*
> *Massachusetts Provincial Congress*
> *June 20, 1775*

Harvard life 1759 - attitude to Fr war
WARREN - Hunter Properties
Research Hunters
Hanover Street - Green Dragon. Masons 99
Brattle Street congregation. 113
Mercy + John Scollay 184

LaVergne, TN USA
09 May 2010

182005LV00001B/134/P